DOS 4.3

File Management System

Walland Philip Vrbancic, Jr.

 lulu

ISBN 978-0-578-71547-6

I am ever so proud to dedicate this Book on the
DOS 4.3 File Management System
and all my previous achievements
to my Parents Wally and Melba
who continuously nourished my intellectual curiosity.

I am ever so grateful to my partner
Carlton D. Wong
who delightfully pretends to understand
what the Hell I am talking about!

If I have seen further than others it is because I have stood on the shoulders of giants.
~~~ Isaac Newton ~~~

Disclaimer of All Liability

Do not use the DOS 4.3 File Management System or this Book for any mission-critical applications or for any purpose in which a software error or a software failure could cause you financial or material loss. The DOS 4.3 File Management System and this Book are designed to enhance your Apple][computing experience, but they may contain design flaws that could inhibit the proper operation of your computer or result in the loss of recorded data on any storage device connected to your computer. When using the DOS 4.3 File Management System or this Book, you assume all risks associated with the operation of your computer and the potential loss of your data. If these terms are not acceptable to you, please do not use the DOS 4.3 File Management System or this Book.

Walland Philip Vrbancic, Jr., the administrator of applecored.net, makes no warranties either expressed or implied with respect to the DOS 4.3 File Management System or with respect to this Book, its quality, performance, or fitness for any particular purpose. Any risk of incidental or consequential damages resulting from the use of the DOS 4.3 File Management System or the use of information contained in this Book shall be assumed by you, the User. In no event will Walland Philip Vrbancic, Jr., or applecored.net be liable for any direct, indirect, incidental, or consequential damages resulting from any defect or deficiency in the DOS 4.3 File Management System or in this Book.

While all possible attempts have been made to ensure that the information contained within this publication is complete and accurate, the author shall have no liability or responsibility for any errors or omissions, or for any damages or data loss resulting from the use of the information, circuit diagrams, and example software programs contained herein. The author reserves the right to make any changes and/or any improvements to the DOS 4.3 File Management System or to the contents of this publication at any time and without any prior notice.

Preface

When Brian Wiser and Bill Martens discovered my DOS 4.1 documentation and software at applecored.net, they immediately contacted me and wanted Apple Pugetsound Program Library Exchange (A.P.P.L.E.) to publish my DOS 4.1 Manual. Ha! If only this would have happened back in 1982. That's when my co-worker, Randy at Rockwell, and I were actively reading many publications on Apple software and hardware, and Call-A.P.P.L.E. was one of our favorite publications. Needless to say, to be published by any of those computer journals at that time would have been crazy exciting, and certainly a cherished memory for a lifetime. I actually was very close to finishing DOS 4.1 when I agreed to have Call-A.P.P.L.E. publish the DOS 4.1 Manual, Build 45, and provide demo diskette images for DOS 4.1L and DOS 4.1H.

I wanted both versions of DOS 4.1 to provide the user with virtually the same computing experience, albeit the HELP command is found only in DOS 4.1H. This desire proved to be somewhat troublesome in that I was limited in memory for DOS 4.1L and I had ample memory for DOS 4.1H. It was the unused memory in DOS 4.1H that was the impetus to introduce the HELP command in the first place. At the onset I warned both Wiser and Martens that I could not stop creating more functionality in DOS 4.1, but they were rather insistent on printing the DOS 4.1 Manual for the Apple][community as it was. I finished DOS 4.1 with Build 46. Only Build 46 can now be found at applecored.net as well as its respective PDF.

My next area of exploration for Apple DOS was an attempt to port DOS 4.1H to Auxiliary memory. I was absolutely successful, I might add, but I could not successfully design an interface between *Lisa* (my most favorite 65C02 assembler) and this DOS residing in Auxiliary memory. Over the course of several months in effort, I could not realize a viable solution that would be elegant, save memory, and provide the roadmap for interfacing other utilities and tools to this DOS. But this effort was certainly not wasted! I documented what I had learned about Main and Auxiliary memory management and moved forward to other areas of exploration.

I decided that I would use DOS 4.1H as my initial model for DOS 4.3. Yes, DOS 4.3 does retain the "H" designation for High memory. However, there is no DOS 4.3L. So, I simply refer to my new DOS as DOS 4.3. The question then became, can *Lisa* be ported and function in Auxiliary memory? The answer to that question turns out to be a resounding "Yes!" With DOS 4.3 in Main Language Card memory and *Lisa* in Auxiliary Language Card memory, the user has access to virtually all of Main memory below 0xBE00 for source code, object code, and the symbol list. I saw this configuration simply as an exercise of many potential and new possibilities.

Now, if I can relocate *Lisa* to Auxiliary memory, what about doing the same thing for *Big Mac*? I have to say that this challenge was a bit uneventful because relocating *Big Mac* to Auxiliary Language Card memory was even easier to accomplish. My main focus in *Big Mac* was to align *Sourceror* and *Big Mac* in terms of their *SWEET16* sourcing and assembling abilities, though I do not believe *Big Mac* has ever been able to assemble all of its own *SWEET16* opcodes. This task turned out to be an extraordinary undertaking: I wanted *Sourceror* and *Big Mac* to disassemble/assemble MY version of the *SWEET16* opcodes. I discovered that *Big Mac* could not even assemble its own unique *SWEET16* EVAL opcode. This tells me that Bredon probably did not even use *Big Mac* to assemble his own *Big Mac* source code. I have to confess that there still remain two *SWEET16* branches in my disassembled *Big Mac* source code that are wrong, and I do not know their solution to this day. They occur at memory addresses 0xD2C1 and 0xD2DF. Furthermore, I have yet to discover how to force their execution in order to analyze the resulting behavior in *Big Mac*. I suspect these particular instructions may be part of MACRO handling, something I have had no reason to use. *Big Mac* and DOS 4.3 now complement each other beautifully.

During my journey in developing the DOS 4.3 File Management System, I discovered many more layers of File Manager functionality that were almost coded correctly. It beleaguered me no end when I would issue a CLOSE statement on the Apple command line in DOS 3.3 or in DOS 4.1, and something would be flushed to the volume in focus. What was it? Why? I found even more examples of questionable logic, wrong logic, and desperate logic. I literally tore apart many of those "weird" routines used by the CLOSE statement so that now DOS commands will finish completely and data will be properly flushed. All these issues and many, many more have been resolved in DOS 4.3. The final frontier I tore apart was the RWTS manager and format algorithm. Using a utility of my own design to scan a track for its raw data and display the structure of that raw data allowed me to develop my own algorithm for a complete and revolutionary RWTS manager.

I know the user will discover many fascinating developments in the DOS 4.3 File Management System: he will be left wondering how he accomplished anything in a timely fashion without having had those developments in any other version of a previous Apple Disk Operating System. I would take that as my greatest compliment.

Enjoy the ride!

Table of Contents

IV. DOS 4.3 Assembly Language Routines 159

V. DOS 4.3 Operational Environment 177

List of Figures

List of Tables

I. Designing Another New DOS

This publication describes the process and products I created when I decided to design and program an enhanced Disk Operating System (DOS) for my Apple //e. Wherever I am able, I have included schematic diagrams, code samples, equations, figures, tables, and representative screen shots to help explain what I have created and the reasons why I did so. As in my previous design of an Apple][DOS, i.e. DOS 4.1L and DOS 4.1H, this has been an incredible journey for me. With DOS 4.3 I have again re-imagined that time when I mostly lived, breathed, and worked on Apple][computers, hardware, and software development continuously for a good period of my life many, many years ago.

1. Introduction

I have been an avid Apple][computer enthusiast, hobbyist, and professional software programmer since 1983 when I became the proud owner of an Apple][+ computer. Besides the Apple][+, my initial system included an Apple][Language Card, a Disk][with an Apple][Disk Controller slot card, an Amdek color monitor, and an Epson MX100 printer with a Grappler+ Printer Interface slot card. During those early years I designed and built my own Apple][peripheral slot cards, made electrical and hardware modifications to my Apple][+ motherboard and keyboard, and wrote a substantial number of software programs using Applesoft BASIC (Applesoft hereafter) and 6502 assembly language. I soon acquired a Videx UltraTerm video display slot card and a Microsoft Z80 slot card. With the Z80 card I began writing Fortran programs that analyzed tomographic reconstructions of the human spinal column. A year or so later I added the Southern California Research Group quikLoader and PROmGRAMER slot cards, a Johnathon Freeman Designs (JFD) Parallel Printer Buffer, and an Axlon RAM Disk 320 and its interface slot card to my system.

I used C language in my professional programming career for the software development of ultra-high-speed data collection systems for tactical radar and sensor development. Now that I am retired from the aerospace industry I have always wanted to dig into, tear apart, and learn the intricacies of the last available DOS for the Apple][+. That DOS, DOS 3.3, was published on August 25, 1980. Then I recently came across another version of DOS 3.3 published years later on January 1, 1983. That DOS contains even more patches for the DOS APPEND command and a patch for Apple //e initialization. What I learned from the 1980 publication flabbergasted me: the software is exciting in its originality and concept vis-à-vis it was released just after the publication of Integer BASIC. However, I found the software to be somewhat juvenile in structure and implementation. Apparently, very little attention was given to software design and review. It appeared to me Apple made a strong push to release "something or anything" to consumers and vendors in order to begin marketing software products on diskettes. And history does reveal that Apple Computer did outsource DOS and contracted for it to be delivered within 35 days for $13,000 in April, 1978. Paul Laughton at Shepardson Microsystems wrote Apple's initial disk operating system using Hollerith cards, a card reader, and a minicomputer.

Now that I have the time and the continuing curiosity to delve into Apple][DOS, I have the unique opportunity to create my own version of DOS that contains the power and the flexibility I always thought DOS ought to and could have. I call this version of Apple][DOS, DOS 4.3 File Management System, and it requires an Apple][that contains Language Card memory. This document describes my eighth build of DOS 4.3. What a ride I have been on! Why? To see what I could do with this brilliant machine and its magnificent architecture!

2. Brief Overview of DOS 4.3

I know there are a great many ProDOS users in the Apple][community, but I never became interested in ProDOS. The work I did at Hughes Aircraft in the mid 1980's consisted of using assembly language for programming an operating system executive and interface driver routines on Gould SEL 2780, 6780, and 9780 mainframe computers. These computers hosted a proprietary operating system that allowed our team to simulate a radar processor traveling above the earth's surface in virtually real time. In order to accomplish that goal and simulate real time navigation, the computer's file system was essentially flat: each user had their own directory, and these user directories contained no subdirectories. I was very comfortable with the idea of a flat file system and it was very much like Apple's DOS 3.3. I was simply not comfortable with a slew of subdirectories exemplified by Apple's ProDOS. My thought was always "How does one remember the path to follow in order to find anything?" With the advent of the Macintosh computer and later when I became familiar with the UNIX file system, my subdirectory fears vanished and I cannot imagine a modern computer file system without subdirectories. However, I still remain passionate about Apple][DOS and I leave ProDOS to those who are comfortable with that operating system architecture. Though what I have seen of ProDOS recently, I believe it could definitely use a facelift, seriously. I also believe that ProDOS is better suited on a machine with a 16-bit processor much like that found in the Apple //gs.

I am sure many are curious and want to know what is new and different in DOS 4.3, and what makes this version of the DOS File Management System so special. Looking back over my previous build manuals for DOS 4.1, I realized that I should have included this vital build enhancement information with every build, if only for historical reasons. Like, which build did I solve the Track 0x00 utilization quest? Which build did I start labeling volumes? Which build did I solve the Disk Full logic error? Taken all together, I have done an incredible amount of research, writing, and software development to reach DOS 4.3, Build 8. And, to say the least, I have done an incredible amount of testing for every function under normal and abnormal (i.e. error) conditions. However small the list of items unique to DOS 4.3 may appear, I have spent countless hours developing and testing those items alone and in concert with the entire DOS 4.3 command repertoire.

DOS 4.3 is specifically designed to reside in Main Language Card memory. Language Card memory begins at address 0xD000, and it includes two banks of memory from 0xD000 to 0xDFFF and one bank of memory from 0xE000 to 0xFFFF. The user has complete freedom to use all memory below 0xBE00 where HIMEM is set. The foundation for DOS 4.3 was DOS 4.1H which introduced the HELP command. However, I have completely redesigned HELP in how it looks and how it works in DOS 4.3, though it provides the same information. I have added a companion command to the DOS TS command called WTS. WTS (Write Track/Sector) allows the user to modify a single byte at a time on any sector of a disk volume. And, DOS 4.3 introduces the DOS TOUCH command that will update any file's date and time stamp. Of course, if a file is locked nothing about the file can be changed nor can the file be deleted, unless there is an override available. DOS 4.3 provides that override for the DOS RENAME, TOUCH, and DELETE commands. Thus, DOS 4.3 introduces two additional File Manager opcodes to support WTS and TOUCH. DOS 4.3 introduces the DOS PHASE command which allows the user to set the number of Disk][stepper motor half-phases between adjacent tracks. Finally, DOS 4.3 introduces the CONFIG command which gives the user ultimate control over many DOS 4.3 display and input functions. Not that I allowed a single error to reside in any DOS 4.1 build, there are sometimes better programming methodologies. DOS 4.3 does contain many of the DOS 4.1 routines rewritten having a far better design in subverting virtually all possible DOS command programming consequences due to user naiveté. Let's begin with some software design strategies.

3. DOS 4.3 Software Development

In order to design reliable software for a particular machine or platform, one must understand the machine's complete architecture. I believe this design approach is fully applicable to the Apple][computer: either code or data occupies fixed addressable memory where some defined memory locations are reserved for the stack, text, graphics, control, and peripheral slot cards. Code is further restricted in the Apple][by the rather limited 6502-microprocessor Instruction Set. My obvious goal strategy is to design software in such a way as to create the most functionality with the least amount of code and data space. I believe this methodology will yield the highest degree of code effectiveness.

I use Gerard Putter's application Virtual][, Version 9.3, to create my software applications, and that is the platform I use to perform the initial, though simulated testing. Once I am satisfied with a program or a utility operating within the Virtual][application, I transfer the volume image containing that program or utility to an Enhanced Apple //e. I have found some discrepancies between Virtual][and my Enhanced Apple //e particularly in enabling Language Card memory: two successive writes to memory address 0xC083 does **not** write enable Language Card Bank 2 memory in my Enhanced Apple //e as it does in Virtual][. Two successive reads of memory address 0xC083 functions the same in both my Enhanced Apple //e and in Virtual][as they should. I have brought this to the attention of Mr. Putter. Also, Main memory is not initialized at power-up in quite the same way in my Enhanced Apple //e as it is in Virtual][. I believe DOS 3.3 always assumed that an Apple][will power-up with all of page-zero memory set to 0xFF. Virtual][also makes this same assumption. I know I have been caught unaware that all of Auxiliary page-zero memory is not always set to 0xFF at power-up. Therefore, I have included a call to SETNORM during Boot Stage 2 to ensure that page-zero memory location 0x32 is, indeed, set to 0xFF. I have used AUXMOVE to manually "hide" some ProDOS code in Auxiliary memory within Virtual][. The code disappears (is overwritten) when I boot with DOS 4.3. This does not happen in the Enhanced Apple //e: the code can still be safely found in Auxiliary memory after a reboot. Always, always, always make final tests on **real** hardware.

Before beginning any discussion of a complicated subject like a disk operating system or file management system for the Apple][, it is usually easier to understand such a system if each component of that system is shown as part of a Big Picture. That Big Picture is shown in Table I.3.1. Though certainly not to any scale, Table I.3.1 shows how memory is utilized in the Apple][and where the basic hardware and software components are found in Main memory. I exclude any discussion of Auxiliary memory as found in the Apple //e at this time. The basic components shown in Table I.3.1 are the 6502 microprocessor memory requirements, the DOS vectors and routines, text and LORES graphic pages, HIRES graphic pages, DOS file buffers, DOS software manager locations, Soft Switches, peripheral-card memory, Read/Write Track/Sector (RWTS) and HELP routines, Applesoft interpreter, and the ROM and RAM Monitor. The following pages will discuss the Apple][memory utilization in great detail. It may be helpful to refer to Table I.3.1 occasionally in order to fully understand how those details relate to the entire hardware and software management of the Apple][computer by the DOS 4.3 File Management System.

If any of the components shown in Table I.3.1 are unfamiliar, it would be to your advantage now to locate one or more Apple publications and refresh your understanding of that component. Even the *Apple][Reference Manual* that came with my Apple][+ computer contains invaluable information applicable to the entire family of Apple][computers. I even own a few **SAMS** Publications that have provided me with enhanced understanding of many of the components shown in Table I.3.1.

Memory Page	Description	Description
0x00	Page-zero variables, pointers, routines, and special addressing modes	
0x01	Stack for the 6502 microprocessor	
0x02	Input buffer, Applesoft interpretation buffer	
0x03	User buffer, DOS vectors and routines	
0x04-0x07	Text or LORES graphics Page 1	
0x08-0x0B	Applesoft program start, Text or LORES graphics Page 2, or available for software	
0x0C-0x1F	Available for software	
0x20-0x3F	HIRES graphics Page 1, or available for software	
0x40-0x5F	HIRES graphics Page 2, or available for software	
0x60-0xBD	Available for software	
0xBE-0xBF	DOS 4.3 HIMEM, DOS 4.3 Language Card interface, DOS 4.3 bootstrap routines	
0xC0	System Soft Switches	
0xC1-0xC7	Peripheral-card ROM memory for slots 1-7, or CX ROM	
0xC8-0xCF	Peripheral-card expansion ROM memory for slots 1-7, or CX ROM	
0xD0-0xDF	Bank 2, ROM Applesoft Interpreter, DOS 4.3 Command and File Managers	Bank 1, DOS 4.3 RWTS and HELP
0xE0-0xEB	ROM Applesoft Interpreter, DOS 4.3 Command and File Managers	
0xEC-0xEF	ROM Applesoft Interpreter, DOS 4.3 working variables and file buffers	
0xF0-0xF7	ROM Applesoft Interpreter, DOS 4.3 file buffers	
0xF8-0xFF	ROM Monitor and RAM Monitor	

Table I.3.1. Apple][Memory Utilization with DOS 4.3

The Apple][computer is truly a brilliant machine and it has a magnificent architecture. I hope you find my presentation of DOS 4.3 vis-à-vis the Apple][computer interesting, enlightening, and useful in view of your own hardware and software experiences with this delightful computer.

4. Page-Zero Utilization

The Instruction Set for the 6502-microprocessor (and the 65C02 processor as well) includes special processor instructions that utilize variables located in the first 256 bytes, or page, of addressable memory, that is, locations `0x0000` to `0x00FF`. I designate this area of memory "page-zero." When Steve Wozniak designed the Apple Monitor, he allocated a number of page-zero locations for its variables and pointers. Similarly, Applesoft, DOS, and virtually all other user assembly language programs use page-zero locations in order to utilize those special instructions. The 6502-microprocessor contains an accumulator, the A-register, and two index registers, the X-register and the Y-register. Page-zero instructions using these registers include load and store instructions, indexed load and store instructions, indexed indirect addressing instructions using the X-register, and indirect indexed addressing instructions using the Y-register. Page-zero wraparound occurs with page-zero indexed addressing and indexed indirect addressing instructions using the X-register and page-zero indexed addressing instructions of the X-register using the Y-register, but not with indirect indexed addressing instructions using the Y-register. Yes, it is a little confusing, but not too complicated.

When developing a user assembly language program, it is critical to select page-zero locations that do not conflict with the Apple Monitor, Applesoft, or DOS depending on whether those ROM and language card applications are important to the user program. Knowing which page-zero locations are used by or critical to resident applications can greatly simplify the selection of unused or available page-zero locations. Because DOS 3.3 supports Integer BASIC, a few page-zero locations were used to process that file type. DOS 4.3 also uses those same page-zero locations for processing the Applesoft `CHAIN` command, for example, and other DOS command enhancements. There are definitely obvious page-zero locations that cannot be used except for how they were intended, like the horizontal and vertical cursor locations `CH` and `CV`, respectively. Then, there are less obvious, rather dubious page-zero locations that are used by some Applesoft commands from `0x00` to `0x1F`. These page-zero locations are fair game for user programs that do not use the Applesoft interpreter or Steve Wozniak's *SWEET16* interpreter. Figure I.4.1 shows all the used and the unused page-zero locations and the applications that use those particular locations according to my references and the best of my ability to decipher the code that uses those locations. The shaded locations in Figure I.4.1 are unused page-zero locations that probably are not used by the Apple //e Monitor or Applesoft, so they are more than likely the better locations to select. Tables I.4.1 and I.4.2 lists all the page-zero locations utilized by DOS 4.3. Table I.4.3 summarizes all the available page-zero locations not utilized by the ROM routines and DOS 4.3. Keep in mind that indirect indexed addressing instructions using the Y-register do require a page-zero byte-pair, so it is even more critical that neither address byte is clobbered by software external to a user's assembly language program.

There are certainly common page-zero locations that all software routines can use as temporary variables and pointers. The 6502-microprocessor is not time-shared and there is no context switching between routines, so if a routine uses some common page-zero locations, it should complete all processing using those locations and not expect to find its results sometime later. Examples of common page-zero locations would be `A1L`/`A1H` at `0x3C`/`0x3D`, `A2L`/`A2H` at `0x3E`/`0x3F`, `A3L`/`A3H` at `0x40`/`0x41`, `A4L`/`A4H` at `0x42`/`0x43`, `OPRND` at `0x44`, and the first three bytes of `DSCTMP` at `0x9D:0x9F`. Using these page-zero locations to move or copy data would be safe and not interfere with the Monitor, Applesoft, or DOS processing. Actually, several Monitor routines require that some of these locations just mentioned contain your data before using those routines. The Monitor routine `MOVE` at `0xFE2C` is one such example. It is really up to the user to confirm and verify that the selected page-zero memory locations do not interfere with other routines external to and required by the user software.

5

0x	0	1	2	3	4	5	6	7	8	9	A	B	C	D	E	F
00	12 34	134	34	34	34	4					4	4	4	4	4	4
10	4	4	4	4	4	4	4	4	4	4	4	4	4	24	2	3
20	134	134	134	134	13 46	134	14 56	14 56	13 46	13 46	13 456	13 456	14 56	14 56	123 456	123 456
30	14	12	134	12 46	123	12 36	136	136	136	136	123	123	12 345	12 345	123 456	123 456
40	156	156	12 36	12 36	12 36	1	1	1	1	1	56	56	6	6	13	13
50	346	346	4	4	4	4	24	24	24	24	46	6	6	6	4	4
60	4	4	4	4	4	4	4	46	46	46	46	46	46	346	346	346
70	346	4	4	346	346	4	46	4	4	4	4	4	4	4	4	4
80	4	4	4	4	4	4	4	4	4	4	4	4	4	4	4	4
90	4	4	4	4	34	34	4	4	4	4	4	34	34	4	4	4
A0	4	4	4	4	4	4	4	4	4	4	4	4	4	4	4	46
B0	46	4	4	4	4	4	4	4	4	4	4	4	4	4	4	4
C0	4	4	4	4	4	4	4	4	4	4	4	4	4			
D0	4	4	4	4	4	4	46		46	6	4	4	4	4	4	4
E0	4	4	4		4	4	4	4	34	34	4					
F0	4	4	4	14	14	4	4	4	4	4						34

Figure I.4.1. Page-Zero Memory Utilization

Key

1 – used by the Monitor
2 – used by the Mini Assembler
3 – used by the Apple //e CX ROM
4 – used by Applesoft
5 – used by RWTS
6 – used by DOS 4.3

Address	Parameter	Description
0x24	CH	horizontal cursor location
0x25	CV	vertical cursor location
0x26	BUFRADRZ	ROM boot data field buffer address
0x26	TEMPZ	RWTS temporary 8-bit variable
0x27	TEMP2Z	RWTS temporary 8-bit variable
0x28	BASEZ	text screen line address
0x2A	ASPTRSAV	DOS CHAIN array descriptor addresses
0x2A	CURTRKZ	RWTS requested track
0x2B	DRVFLAG	RWTS data-changing drive flag
0x2B	SLOT16Z	boot slot * 16
0x2B	SYNCNT	RWTS format sync byte count
0x2C	DATAFNDZ	RWTS address field address
0x2D	SECFNDZ	RWTS address field sector found
0x2E	TRKFNDZ	RWTS address field track found
0x2F	VOLFNDZ	RWTS address field volume found
0x32	INVFLG	text screen inverse/normal flag
0x33	PROMPT	text screen prompt character
0x35	PAGECNT	boot/initialization DOS image page count
0x36	CSWL	output device handler address
0x38	KSWL	input device handler address
0x3C	ROMTEMPZ	ROM boot temporary 8-bit variable
0x3C	MOTORTIM	RWTS motor on-time 16-bit count
0x3C	A1	general purpose temporary 16-bit variable
0x3D	ROMSECTR	ROM boot requested sector
0x3E	BUFADR2Z	RWTS data field buffer address
0x3E	ODDBITSZ	RWTS temporary 8-bit variable
0x3E	A2	general purpose temporary 16-bit variable
0x3F	SECTORZ	RWTS address field sector
0x40	ROMDATA	ROM boot address field track found
0x40	FILEBUFZ	file context block parameter buffer address
0x40	TRACKZ	RWTS address field track
0x41	ROMTRACK	ROM boot requested track
0x41	VOLUMEZ	RWTS address field volume
0x42	A4	general purpose temporary 16-bit variable
0x42	BUFADRZ	general purpose sector data buffer address
0x44	DIRINDX	VTOC and TSL data index
0x4A	IOBADR	RWTS IOCB buffer address
0x4C	DOSPTR	DOS general purpose pointer address

Table I.4.1. DOS 4.3 Page-Zero Utilization – Part 1

0x50	LINNUM	Applesoft line number 16-bit variable
0x5A	DOSTEMP1	DOS general purpose 8-bit variable
0x5B	DOSTEMP2	DOS general purpose 8-bit variable
0x5C	DOSBUFR	DOS general purpose buffer address
0x67	ASPGMST	Applesoft program start address
0x69	ASVARS	Applesoft simple variables pointer
0x6B	ASARYS	Applesoft array pointer
0x6D	ARYEND	Applesoft end of array pointer
0x6F	ASSTRS	Applesoft end of string storage pointer
0x73	ASHIMEM	Applesoft HIMEM address
0x76	ASRUN	Applesoft RUN flag
0x9D	DSCTMP	Applesoft temporary string descriptor
0xAF	ASPEND	Applesoft end of program address
0xD6	PROTECT	Applesoft program write-protect flag
0xD8	ASONERR	Applesoft ONERR error flag
0xD9	RKEYWORD	DOS R keyword 8-bit variable

Table I.4.2. DOS 4.3 Page-Zero Utilization – Part 2

Start	End	Description
0x06	0x09	4 bytes free
0x1E	0x1E	1 byte free
0xCE	0xCF	2 bytes free
0xD7	0xD7	1 byte free
0xE3	0xE3	1 byte free
0xEB	0xEF	5 bytes free
0xFA	0xFE	5 bytes free

Table I.4.3. Available Page-Zero Locations Summary

5. DOS 4.3 VTOC Structure

How I agonized over how to best implement date and time stamping for disk volumes and files! Preferably, I only wanted to update a date and time stamp when either the Volume Table Of Contents (VTOC) of a disk volume or a file has changed. I also wanted to date and time stamp a disk volume (or disk image) when that volume is first created. However, creating or updating a date and time stamp is only half the task: the date and time stamp needs to be displayed appropriately. And, when the contents of a volume's Catalog directory are displayed, the file's date and time stamp need to be listed along with its filename, and either a 40-column or 80-column display can be used. Since the VTOC is basically the heart of the disk volume, it is best to begin there and show its organization and content in DOS 4.3.

The VTOC is defined to be located on track 0x11 and it uses sector 0x00, though it could be located on any sector of any track. The volume Catalog sectors may be any group of sectors on any other track, but typically they are defined to be on track 0x11 as well, and they are usually the lower sectors of that track just above the VTOC sector for optimal access. Figure I.5.1 shows the VTOC for a "data" volume that uses five sectors for its volume Catalog. A data volume is defined as volume type D for Data volume. A bootable volume that contains a DOS 4.3 image on its first three tracks is defined as volume type B for Boot volume. Table I.5.1 defines each entry in the VTOC, Table I.5.2 defines the free sector bitmap for each track, and Table I.5.3 defines the bytes of the six-byte date and time stamp in the order those bytes are stored. There is more information in Section I.6 about the free sector bitmap definition as it is used in DOS 4.3.

0x	0	1	2	3	4	5	6	7	8	9	A	B	C	D	E	F
00	00	11	05	43	08	C8	12	C4								
10	Volume Name (24 characters)															
20	D&T Volume was created						04	7A	Lib Num		D&T VTOC last changed					
30	11	01	00	00	24	10	00	01	FF	FF	00	00	FF	FF	00	00
40	FF	FF	00	00	FF	FF	00	00	FF	FF	00	00	FF	FF	00	00
50	FF	FF	00	00	FF	FF	00	00	FF	FF	00	00	FF	FF	00	00
60	FF	FF	00	00	FF	FF	00	00	FF	FF	00	00	FF	FF	00	00
70	FF	FF	00	00	FF	FF	00	00	FF	FF	00	00	FF	00	00	00
80	FF	FF	00	00	FF	FF	00	00	FF	FF	00	00	FF	FF	00	00
90	FF	FF	00	00	FF	FF	00	00	FF	FF	00	00	FF	FF	00	00
A0	FF	FF	00	00	FF	FF	00	00	FF	FF	00	00	FF	FF	00	00
B0	FF	FF	00	00	FF	FF	00	00	FF	FF	00	00	FF	FF	00	00
C0	FF	FF	00	00	FF	FF	00	00	00	00	00	00	00	00	00	00
D0	00	00	00	00	00	00	00	00	00	00	00	00	00	00	00	00
E0	00	00	00	00	00	00	00	00	00	00	00	00	00	00	00	00
F0	00	00	00	00	00	00	00	00	00	00	00	00	00	00	00	00

Figure I.5.1. DOS 4.3 Data Disk Volume VTOC

Byte	Name	Value	Description
0x00	VTOCSB	0x00	VTOC Structure Block
0x01	FRSTTRK	0x11	Track number of first catalog sector
0x02	FRSTSEC	0x05	Sector number of first catalog sector
0x03	DOSVRSN	0x43	Version number used to initialize this volume
0x04	DOSBUILD	0x08	Build number used to initialize this volume
0x05	DOSRAM	0xC8	RAM DOS used to initialize this volume (H)
0x06	DISKVOL	0x12	Volume number (0x00-0xFF)
0x07	DISKTYPE	0xC4	Volume Type (B or D)
0x08-0x1F	DISKNAME	~	Volume Name (24 ASCII characters)
0x20-0x25	INITIME	~	Date and Time when volume was initialized
0x26	VTOCPHAS	0x04	Number of Half-Phases per track (1-16)
0x27	NUMTSENT	0x7A	Maximum number of T/S pairs in one TSL sector
0x28-0x29	DISKSUBJ	~	Volume Library (subject) (0x0000-0xFFFF) (Lo/Hi)
0x2A-0x2F	VTOCTIME	~	Date and Time VTOC was initialized or last changed
0x30	NXTTOALC	0x11	Last Track used to allocate a sector
0x31	ALLOCDIR	0x01	Direction of Track Allocation (0x01 or 0xFF)
0x32	DOSCONFG	0x00	DOS Configuration byte (0x00-0xFF)
0x33	DISKLOCK	0x00	Disk Lock flag (0x00 for unlock and 0x80 for lock)
0x34	NUMTRKS	0x24	Number of tracks in volume (maximum is 50)
0x35	NUMSECS	0x10	Number of sectors per track (16 or 32)
0x36-0x37	BYTPRSEC	0x100	Number of bytes per sector (256) (Lo/Hi byte order)
0x38-0x3B	BITMAP	~	Bitmap of free sectors for track 0
0x3C-0x3F	:::	~	Bitmap of free sectors for track 1
0x40-0xC7	:::	~	Bitmap of free sectors for tracks 2-35 (to NUMTRKS-1)
0xC8-0xFF		0x00	reserved for additional tracks

Table I.5.1. DOS 4.3 VTOC Structure Block Definition

Byte	Sectors	Sector Order	Initial Value
0	0F-08	FEDCBA98	0xFF
1	07-00	76543210	0xFF
2	1F-18	FEDCBA98	0x00
3	17-10	76543210	0x00

Table I.5.2. Free Sector Bitmap for Each Track Having 16 Sectors

In DOS 3.3 much code and valuable data space was dedicated to the manipulation of Volume number beginning in the Command Manager, through the File Manager, and on to RWTS, and then back through the File Manager. Since most positional parameters such as Volume, Address, and Length are initialized to 0x00 by the Command Manager after a DOS 4.3 command has been parsed, the default VOLVAL for the Volume number keyword is always 0x00. DOS 4.3 passes Volume number through the File Manager to RWTS **unchanged**. Therefore, the **default** Volume number that is displayed by DOS 4.3 is 000 and not 254 (i.e. 0xFE) as it is by DOS 3.3. The Volume number at byte 0x06 in the VTOC is the **official** Volume number for the volume in DOS 4.3, not the volume number RWTS finds encoded in the Address Field header for a volume sector. Throughout this book it will be shown that VOLVAL plays a critical role in many file systems external to DOS 4.3.

Byte	Value Range	Value
0	0x00 — 0x59	second
1	0x00 — 0x59	minute
2	0x00 — 0x23	hour
3	0x00 — 0x99	year
4	0x01 — 0x31	day
5	0x01 — 0x12	month

Table I.5.3. DOS 4.3 Date and Time Definition in Variable Order

Referring to Figure I.5.1 bytes 0x01 and 0x02 of the VTOC are the track and sector numbers, respectively, for the first Catalog sector. As in DOS 3.3, DOS 4.3 uses byte 0x03 of the VTOC for the DOS Version Number, but unlike DOS 3.3, DOS 4.3 uses the unused byte at byte 0x04 for the DOS Build Number. Byte 0x05 is used to show that "H" (i.e. 0xC8) RAM DOS was in memory when the volume was created, and byte 0x07 is used for the Disk Volume Type, either B (i.e. 0xC2) or D (i.e. 0xC4). RAM DOS does not have any further use in DOS 4.3 except to remind the user that DOS 4.3 does reside in Language Card memory. Bytes 0x08 through 0x1F are used for the 24-character Disk Volume Name or Disk Title, bytes 0x20 through 0x25 are used for the Disk Volume Date and Time stamp when the volume was created, and bytes 0x2A through 0x2F are used for the VTOC Date and Time stamp, and this time stamp is updated whenever DOS 4.3 changes the VTOC for any reason. Byte 0x26 is the Phase number and bytes 0x28 and 0x29 are used for a 16-bit (Lo/Hi byte order) Disk Library value. Byte 0x32 is used for the system CONFIG value and byte 0x33 is used for the Disk Lock flag. All other VTOC variables are still at their original, DOS 3.3 location. The number of Bytes per Sector at bytes 0x36 and 0x37 is retained but it has no further internal use in DOS 4.3.

6. The VTOC Bitmap Definition

The free sector bitmap of a volume is located in the volume's VTOC starting at byte 0x38 as shown in Figure I.5.1. Four bytes are reserved for each track of a volume whose bits determine whether a sector on that track is utilized or not utilized for a Catalog sector, a Track/Sector List (TSL) sector, or a data sector. There are two routines where DOS 3.3 **uses** NUMSECS as shown in Table I.5.1, the VTOC variable equal to the number of sectors comprising a track: ALLOCSEC and RORBITMP. ALLOCSEC is a routine that will find, allocate, and reserve a disk track that contains an available sector. It uses the VTOC bitmap to locate and reserve this track. RORBITMP is a routine used by FREESECT that will set or clear a sector's assigned bit within the 4-byte bitmap of its track as shown in Table I.5.2. The ramifications of limiting these routines to the value found in NUMSECS causes the definition of the bit assigned to sector 0x00 to be different in 16-sector and 32-sector tracks. In DOS 3.3 sector 0x00 is assigned to the first bit (the LSB, or bit 0) in the **second** byte of the 4-byte bitmap for its track when NUMSECS is equal to 16 as shown in Table I.5.2. When NUMSECS is equal to 32, sector 0x00 is assigned to the first bit in the **fourth** byte of the 4-byte bitmap of its track as shown in Table I.6.1. Furthermore, *FID* has always assumed that NUMSECS is equal to 16 and has always rotated the bitmap of a track accordingly. *FID*, as published by Apple, cannot copy files onto a volume that contains 32-sector tracks because it does not rotate the bitmap properly for 32-sector tracks!

Here is a confounded situation where the VTOC, presumably designed by Apple, is not fully supported even by Apple designed utilities. I wonder if Apple thought as early as 1979 when it published *FID* that there would never be a device that would support 32-sector tracks? Were 32-sector tracks merely a placeholder? Did Apple give up on DOS 3.3 in preference to ProDOS earlier than anyone suspected? As an aside, I have never been convinced that the family of Apple][computers was necessarily the right platform for the hierarchal directory structures created in ProDOS. I am even less convinced now. I maintain that ProDOS performs better on a platform that uses a 16-bit processor at a minimum.

ALLOCSEC and RORBITMP manipulate the free sector bitmap for each track as shown in Table I.5.2 consistently in DOS 4.3 without regard to the value found in NUMSECS: 32-sector tracks is always implied even when a volume contains 16-sector tracks. DOS 4.3 only interacts with the VTOC bitmap by means of the variable NEXTSECR XOR'd (that is, exclusively OR'd) with the value of 0x10 in the routines FREESECT and ALLOCSEC. In other words, the bitmap is manipulated as if it looks like what is shown in Table I.6.1, but the bitmap appears in the VTOC as if it looks like what is shown in Table I.5.2. Whether a volume contains 16-sector or 32-sector tracks does not matter to the DOS 4.3 routines that utilize the bitmap values. When the bitmap is manipulated consistently in this fashion, sector 0x00 will always be assigned to the first bit in the **second** byte of the four-byte bitmap of its track as shown in Table I.5.2.

For volumes having 16-sector tracks, the 4-byte bitmap of such a track having all 16 sectors available would be set to "FF FF 00 00". For volumes having 32-sector tracks the 4-byte bitmap of such a track having all 32 sectors available would be set to "FF FF FF FF". When the 4-byte bitmap of a track is not used consistently for 16-sector and 32-sector volumes, it puts an unnecessary burden on the DOS INIT command handler to determine exactly which bit is assigned to sector 0x00 and which bit is assigned to sector 0x10.

Utilizing and manipulating the 4-byte bitmap of a track consistently puts no further throughput burden onto DOS 4.3. I have also incorporated the necessary bitmap utilization changes into my modified version of *FID* that models how DOS 4.3 defines the 4-byte bitmap of a track and how the bitmap must be correctly manipulated. As to be expected, DOS 4.3 and my modified version of *FID* can fully read, copy, and write to a DOS 3.3 volume that has 16-sector tracks, or to any other volume for that matter, without exception, even to a DOS 4.3 volume, whether that volume has 16-sector or 32-sector tracks.

One of the most interesting aspects of the RORBITMP routine is that it plays a crucial role in undeleting a file. Not only does RORBITMP reserve or unreserve a sector for file use, its intended purpose, but it can be equally used to reserve a sector for a file when that file is undeleted. I pay humble respects to my professor of Boolean Algebra and to Ken Williams at Sierra for showing me the power of the XOR instruction. I believe it is one of the most powerful instructions in the repertoire, for it certainly is most powerful when used in the RORBITMP routine. In normal processing the Carry flag is used to allocate a sector when the flag is **clear** or to deallocate a sector when the flag is **set**. Identifying the intended sector and either clearing or setting its respective bit in DOS 4.3's cache copy of the track's 4-byte bitmap completes the first step of normal processing in RORBITMP. The next step is to update the 4-byte bitmap of this sector's track in the actual VTOC. The RORBITMP routine simply OR's the cache copy with the actual 4-byte bitmap of the track. I do not recall where the inspiration came from, but after the cache and actual bytes have been OR'd, and if the URMFLAG is set signaling that the file is to be undeleted, that sum is then XOR'd with the cache bytes: simple, elegant, and powerful! With just eight additional bytes of code not only are a file's data sectors, but all of its TSL sectors are fully reserved in the VTOC and restored in the Catalog.

Whenever one analyzes a mathematical function, the end-points of that function present the most difficulty, and perhaps the most interest. In a similar fashion the routine ALLOCSEC presents some difficulty in processing sectors to allocate if NXTTOALC (next to allocate) happens to equal either the first track (track 0x00) or the last track (track NUMTRKS-1) of the operational range of the VTOC. Furthermore, track 0x00 needs to be processed as track 0x40 as will be explained in Section I.7. DOS 4.3 initially assigns the value of 0x11 (the catalog track) to NXTTOALC and the value of 0x01 (i.e. forward) to ALLOCDIR (allocate direction). Once ALLOCSEC searches forward for free sectors in the VTOC bitmap and reaches the last track, NXTTOALC is reassigned the value of 0x11 and ALLOCDIR is reassigned the value of 0xFF (i.e. backward). So, whenever NXTTOALC is either the first track or the last track initially, an extra count is decremented from ALLOCNTR (allocate loop counter) which basically counts for nothing. DOS 3.3 utilized the variable ALLCFLG for its two-state counter which was sufficient because DOS 3.3 was not required to process track 0x00 as a possible data track. Therefore, to ensure that the entire VTOC bitmap is searched for free sectors in DOS 4.3, and to process the first track or last track correctly if they happen to be the initial search track, three half-passes through the VTOC bitmap must be counted. When ALLOCNTR is decremented to 0x00, the error message "Volume Full" is correctly issued.

Byte	Sector	Bitmap
0	1F-18	FEDCBA98
1	17-10	76543210
2	0F-08	FEDCBA98
3	07-00	76543210

Table I.6.1. Free Sector Bitmap for Each Track Having 32 Sectors in DOS 3.3

0x	0	1	2	3	4	5	6	7	8	9	A	B	C	D	E	F
00	-	11	04	-	-	-	-	-	-	-	-	Trk 1	Sec 1	Type 1	Name 1->	-
10	-	-	-	-	-	-	-	-	-	-	-	-	-	-	-	-
20	-	-	-	-	-	Name <-1	Time 1->	-	Time <-1	Date 1->	-	Date <-1	LenL 1	LenH 1	Trk 2	Sec 2
30	Type 2	Name 2->	-	-	-	-	-	-	-	-	-	-	-	-	-	-
40	-	-	-	-	-	-	-	-	Name <-2	Time 2->	-	Time <-2	Date 2->	-	Date <-2	LenL 2
50	LenH 2	Trk 3	Sec 3	Type 3	Name 3->	-	-	-	-	-	-	-	-	-	-	-
60	-	-	-	-	-	-	-	-	-	-	-	Name <-3	Time 3->	-	Time <-3	Date 3->
70	-	Date <-3	LenL 3	LenH 3	Trk 4	Sec 4	Type 4	Name 4->	-	-	-	-	-	-	-	-
80	-	-	-	-	-	-	-	-	-	-	-	-	-	-	Name <-4	Time 4->
90	-	Time <-4	Date 4->	-	Date <-4	LenL 4	LenH 4	Trk 5	Sec 5	Type 5	Name 5->	-	-	-	-	-
A0	-	-	-	-	-	-	-	-	-	-	-	-	-	-	-	-
B0	-	Name <-5	Time 5->	-	Time <-5	Date 5->	-	Date <-5	LenL 5	LenH 5	Trk 6	Sec 6	Type 6	Name 6->	-	-
C0	-	-	-	-	-	-	-	-	-	-	-	-	-	-	-	-
D0	-	-	-	-	Name <-6	Time 6->	-	Time <-6	Date 6->	-	Date <-6	LenL 6	LenH 6	Trk 7	Sec 7	Type 7
E0	Name 7->	-	-	-	-	-	-	-	-	-	-	-	-	-	-	-
F0	-	-	-	-	-	-	-	Name <-7	Time 7->	-	Time <-7	Date 7->	-	Date <-7	LenL 7	LenH 7

Figure I.7.1. DOS 4.3 First Volume Catalog Sector

7. DOS 4.3 Catalog

The first volume Catalog sector for DOS 4.3 is shown in Figure I.7.1. Bytes `0x01` and `0x02` of each catalog sector point to the next catalog sector as they do in the `VTOC` sector. The last catalog sector, typically sector `0x01` on track `0x11`, contains `0x00` for these two bytes. A catalog sector may define up to a maximum of seven file entries. Table I.7.1 shows the content for a file entry. This table defines the first two bytes of a file's entry to be the track and sector values that point to that file's `TSL`. The `TSL` lists all the track/sector pairs for all the data sectors that comprise the contents of that file. The third byte of a file's entry defines the file's Type, and that byte is followed by the file's 24-character upper ASCII filename. The 3-byte time and 3-byte date stamp when the file was created or last modified follow the file's filename. The last two bytes of a file's catalog entry defines the size of the file's data content in sectors including all `TSL` sectors in low/high byte order. Table I.7.2 lists the volume Catalog data locations for each of the seven files defined in a Catalog sector. Table I.7.3 lists each file Type byte, its disk Catalog representation, and a brief description.

Item	Offset	Length	Format	Description
Track	0x00	0x01	%DZTT TTTT	'D'elete bit, track 'Z'ero bit, TSL 'T'rack bits
Sector	0x01	0x01	%000S SSSS	TSL 'S'ector bits
Type	0x02	0x01	%LTTT TTTT	'L'ock bit, 'T'ype bits
Name	0x03	0x18	upper ASCII	24-character ASCII filename
Time	0x1B	0x03	0xSS MM HH	'S'econds byte, 'M'inute byte, 'H'our byte
Date	0x1E	0x03	0xYY DD MM	'Y'ear byte, 'D'ay byte, 'M'onth byte
Size	0x21	0x02	0xLL HH	2-byte file size in sectors, 'L'ow/'H'igh order

Table I.7.1. DOS 4.3 Volume Catalog Entry

File	Track*	Sector	Type**	Name	Time	Date	Size
1	0x0B	0x0C	0x0D	0x0E−0x25	0x26−0x28	0x29−0x2B	0x2C−0x2D
2	0x2E	0x2F	0x30	0x31−0x48	0x49−0x4B	0x4C−0x4E	0x4F−0x50
3	0x51	0x52	0x53	0x54−0x6B	0x6C−0x6E	0x6F−0x71	0x72−0x73
4	0x74	0x75	0x76	0x77−0x8E	0x8F−0x91	0x92−0x94	0x95−0x96
5	0x97	0x98	0x99	0x9A−0xB1	0xB2−0xB4	0xB5−0xB7	0xB8−0xB9
6	0xBA	0xBB	0xBC	0xBD−0xD4	0xD5−0xD7	0xD8−0xDA	0xDB−0xDC
7	0xDD	0xDE	0xDF	0xE0−0xF7	0xF8−0xFA	0xFB−0xFD	0xFE−0xFF

* If MSB is set the file shown is Deleted   ** If the MSB is set the file shown is Locked

Table I.7.2. DOS 4.3 Catalog Sector Data Offsets for File Entries

DOS 4.3 does not process file Type `0x01` (i.e. Integer BASIC) files, and file Type `0x40` is used by DOS 4.3 to process *Lisa* files natively (DOS 3.3 referred to these as `B` type files). DOS 4.3 will process an `A` type (i.e. `0x20`) file as an Applesoft file. DOS 4.3 does not process `S` type or `R` type files natively until a suitable definition for those file types can be determined. In DOS 4.3 a file is marked "deleted" when the most significant bit (i.e. MSB, or bit 7) of its `TSL`'s track number is set, that is, in bytes `0x0B`, `0x2E`, `0x51`, `0x74`, `0x97`, `0xBA`, or `0xDD` from Table I.7.2. DOS 4.3 stipulates there will always be less than 64 tracks (i.e. `0x3F` or less) in a volume, so bit 7, the MSB of the `TSL`'s track number is certainly available to signify the delete status of a file. Furthermore, that definition still leaves bit 6 of a track number available to signify track `0x00` as track `0x40`. Using bit 6 of a track number to represent physical track `0x00` allows all of the File Manager logic testing for "last track/sector pair" in a `TSL` to remain unchanged. This representation for track `0x00` also allows track `0x00` to be used for file data like any other track. I have updated my version of *FID* to include this representation for track `0x00` and how a deleted file is determined and marked in the catalog.

File Type	Catalog	Description
00	T	Text file
01	I	Integer BASIC file (not supported in DOS 4.3)
02	A	Applesoft file
04	B	Binary file
08	S	S type file (not supported in DOS 4.3)
10	R	Relocatable object file (not supported in DOS 4.3)
20	A	A type file (processed as an Applesoft file)
40	L	L (*Lisa*) type file (formally B type)
80	*	File lock bit

Table I.7.3. DOS 4.3 File Type Byte Description

If an attempt is made to load (i.e. `LOAD` or `BLOAD`) a nonexistent file into memory when the volume Catalog is full, DOS 3.3 erroneously prints the "`DISK FULL`" error message rather than the "`FILE NOT FOUND`" error message. If an attempt is made to save (i.e. `SAVE` or `BSAVE`) a file when the volume Catalog is full, DOS 3.3 again erroneously prints the "`DISK FULL`" error message even when there are sufficient sectors available in the volume for the file's data. Even though this situation is rarely encountered where the volume Catalog is full, having DOS issue the wrong or inappropriate error message could lead one to make wrong conclusions.

DOS 4.3 provides a default volume Catalog consisting of five sectors that can define up to thirty-five files. However, the volume Catalog may be made as small as one sector or as large as fifteen sectors by using the `B` keyword with the DOS `INIT` command. If the volume Catalog consists of one or two sectors, the volume Catalog will only support seven or fourteen files, respectively, and an erroneous "`DISK FULL`" error message can have significant consequences in this instance. I have identified and rewritten the flawed DOS 3.3 routines, and DOS 4.3 now prints the correct error message "`File Not Found`" when a file does not exist in a volume Catalog regardless whether the Catalog is full or not full. Also, DOS 4.3 now prints the new error message "`Catalog Full`" when attempting to save a file to a volume whose Catalog is full regardless whether there are sufficient sectors available in the volume for the file's data.

At the heart of every file is its Track/Sector List. This list of track/sector entries is contained in the sector that every file's catalog entry defines. If a file exceeds 122 (i.e. 0x7A) sectors of data (see NUMTSENT from Table I.5.1) the TSL sector has provisions to define another TSL sector in order to contain additional track/sector entries. And, for every increment of 0x7A data sectors DOS 4.3 creates another TSL sector for that file.

0x	0	1	2	3	4	5	6	7	8	9	A	B	C	D	E	F
00	00	Next	TSL			Offset							T/S 01		T/S 02	
10	T/S 03		T/S 04													
20																
30																
40																
50																
60																
70																
80																
90																
A0																
B0																
C0																
D0																
E0																
F0															T/S 7A	

Figure I.7.2. DOS 4.3 TSL Sector

Byte	Name	Value	Description
0x00	TSLSB	0x00	unused, start of TSL structure block
0x01	TSTRKOFF	0x00	Track to next TSL; 0x00 if no more TSL sectors
0x02	TSSECOFF	0x00	Sector to next TSL; 0x00 if no more TSL sectors
0x03–0x04		0x00	unused
0x05–0x06	TSRECOFF	0x00	TSL record offset (RELSLAST); 0x00/0x00 first TSL
0x07–0x0B		0x00	unused
0x0C–0x0D	TSLTSOFF	~	T/S for data sector 0x01; at least one entry is required
0x0E–0x0F		~	T/S for data sector 0x02; 0x00/0x00 if at end
0x10–0x11		~	T/S for data sector 0x03; 0x00/0x00 if at end
0x12–0xFD		~	T/S for data sectors 0x04–0x79
0xFE–0xFF		~	T/S for data sector 0x7A

Table I.7.4. DOS 4.3 TSL Structure Block Definition

Figure I.7.2 shows a typical TSL sector and Table I.7.4 defines each entry in the TSL sector. "Next TSL" at bytes 0x01/0x02 point to the next TSL sector if it exists, otherwise these bytes are set to 0x00/0x00. "Offset" at bytes 0x05/0x06 is equal to 0x00/0x00 for the first TSL sector, and "Offset" increases by 0x007A for each succeeding TSL sector in Lo/Hi byte order. The track/sector list begins with the first entry at bytes 0x0C/0x0D, and all files will have at least one entry. Regardless whether the TSL contains additional track/sector entries from previous file modifications and file saves, DOS only loads into memory the number of bytes specified by an Applesoft or binary file. The DOS TLOAD command, for example, reads into memory **all** data sectors listed in the TSL for a TEXT file irrespective of the file's actual size which is demarcated by a NULL (i.e. 0x00) byte. The TSL officially concludes when the DIRINDX index pointer becomes 0x00 and when TSTRKOFF is 0x00. If the next track value in a track/sector entry is equal to 0x00 or is negative, that entry is simply skipped. I believe byte pairs 0x08/0x09 or 0x09/0x0A could have been utilized for the value of the L keyword instead of requiring the L keyword to OPEN a random-access Data file as shown in Table III.6.1 and Figure III.6.1. At least that is what I would have done.

Address	Variable	Instruction	Value
0xBFF0	BLDVRSN	BYT VERSION	0x43
0xBFF1	BLDNMBR	BYT BUILD	0x08
0xBFF2	MNGDISK	ADR EXMNGDSK	0xBE4D
0xBFF4	MNGVALS	ADR EXMNGVAL	0xBE56
0xBFF6	MNGUSER	ADR EXMNGUSR	0xBE5F
0xBFF8	INITDOS	ADR DOSINIT	0xBF5E
0xBFFA	INITVAL	ADR INITVALS	0xBEE2
0xBFFC	BCFGNDX	BYT BOOTCFG	0xC4
0xBFFD	NBUF1PG	HBY NBUF1	0xDE
0xBFFE	BOOTADR	HBY RWTSTART	0xD0
0xBFFF	BOOTPGS	HBY BOOTEND-RWTSTART	0x0F

Table I.8.1. DOS 4.3 Boot and Data Management Structure Definition

Offset	Variable	Size	Value	Description
0x00	DNUM	0x01	0x01	Drive number
0x01	VOLEXPT	0x01	0x00	Volume number expected
0x02	TNUM	0x01	0x02	Track number
0x03	SNUM	0x01	0x09	Sector number
0x04	DCTADR	0x02	0x0000	DCT address (unused)
0x06	USRBUF	0x02	0xF000	DOS initial start address
0x08	CFGPHASE	0x01	0x04	Half-phases per track

Table I.8.2. DOS 4.3 Boot Configuration Structure

8. Booting DOS 4.3

DOS 4.3 occupies the first two tracks, tracks 0x00 and 0x01, and an additional ten sectors on track 0x02 of a volume, whether the volume has 16 or 32 sectors per track. The remaining six sectors on track 0x02 (for a 16 sector per track volume) are available in the VTOC. The Disk][controller slot card firmware always loads the bootstrap code from sector 0x00 on track 0x00 into memory address 0x0800-0x08FF. This starts the Stage 0 boot process and the X-register always contains the value of the slot number of the controller card times sixteen. The first byte of this bootstrap code must equal 0x01 for the boot process to continue and read another sector into memory. Therefore, the Stage 0 boot instructions actually begin at address 0x0801 to initialize the Stage 1 boot software already in memory. Bytes 0x08FE and 0x08FF are known as BOOTADR and BOOTPGS as shown in Table I.8.1, and they direct the Stage 1 boot software to read sectors 0x0F to 0x02 into memory address 0xD000 to 0xDD00 and sectors 0x01 and 0x00 into memory address 0xBE00 to 0xBFFF.

A 16-byte sector interleave table is available to the Stage 1 boot software as well as to the RWTS routine whose interface is now in memory page 0xBF. Transfer of control passes to the Stage 2 boot software which is also in memory page 0xBF, and that software can now use RWTS located in Language Card Bank 1 memory to access any track and sector in the volume. The initial RWTS Input/Output Context Block (IOCB) values are specified in a BOOTCFG structure in memory page 0xBF. These values are used by the routine RWPAGES which is called by Boot Stage 2 software to read the remaining twenty-six sectors starting with sector 0x09 on track 0x02 and ending with sector 0x00 on track 0x01, in ascending order of memory pages. The DOS 4.3 BOOTCFG table is shown in Table I.8.2. When all of DOS 4.3 is in memory, ROM initialization is done, the main video and character set are selected, XMODE, CSWL, and KSWL are initialized, a search is made for a clock card, and DOS is cold-started and is now ready to execute the DOS CMDVAL command, a topic that will be discussed further in Section I.9. As an aside, the DOS INIT command also uses the RWPAGES routine to write DOS onto a newly initialized volume in the same order DOS was booted and read into memory. The complete volume track/sector mapping to memory address is shown in Table I.8.3.

Once DOS 4.3 is in memory and has initialized, other Input/Output (I/O) disk or disk-emulating devices can easily attach their slot card handler address to DOS 4.3. Table I.8.1 shows where the RWTS disk management routine MNGDISK is located in DOS 4.3 (i.e. 0xBFF2) to set or restore a DISKADRS table entry. To attach a slot card handler, simply make an indirect call to MNGDISK with the slot card number in the X-register, the address of the slot card handler in the Y- and A-registers in Lo/Hi byte order, and the Carry flag **set**. The X-register may also contain the slot card number times sixteen, and the register will be returned unchanged. RWTS will transfer control to the correct slot card handler for the requested I/O based entirely on the slot-number-times-sixteen value found in the IOCB. Figure I.8.1 shows an example assembly language routine that attaches the RAM Disk handler to DOS 4.3. The handler's low byte address value is that of the routine RDENTRY, its high byte address is its CX page (i.e. 0xC7 for slot 7) and that value is found in RDPAGECX, and its slot number is found in RDSLOT. Figure I.8.2 shows an example assembly language routine that first requests the address of the handler assigned to a particular slot into the Y- and A-registers because it initializes the A-register to 0x00 and **sets** the Carry flag. Then the routine calls MNGDISK again with the Carry flag **clear** in order to disconnect that handler from DOS 4.3. Unlike DOS 4.1, it is not necessary to know where the DISKADRS table is in DOS 4.3 memory nor how to properly index into that table. MNGDISK takes care of all that protocol which had to be done entirely by the DOS 4.1 user. MNGDISK always returns the Carry flag clear.

Track	Sector	Address	Code	Track	Sector	Address	Code
0x00	0x00	0xBF00	BOOT	0x01	0x05	0xE400	MNGR
0x00	0x01	0xBE00	XFER	0x01	0x06	0xE300	MNGR
0x00	0x02	*0xDD00	HELP	0x01	0x07	0xE200	MNGR
0x00	0x03	*0xDC00	HELP	0x01	0x08	0xE100	MNGR
0x00	0x04	*0xDB00	HELP	0x01	0x09	0xE000	MNGR
0x00	0x05	*0xDA00	HELP	0x01	0x0A	0xDF00	MNGR
0x00	0x06	*0xD900	HELP	0x01	0x0B	0xDE00	MNGR
0x00	0x07	*0xD800	HELP	0x01	0x0C	0xDD00	MNGR
0x00	0x08	*0xD700	HELP	0x01	0x0D	0xDC00	MNGR
0x00	0x09	*0xD600	INRF	0x01	0x0E	0xDB00	CMD
0x00	0x0A	*0xD500	RWTS	0x01	0x0F	0xDA00	CMD
0x00	0x0B	*0xD400	RWTS	0x02	0x00	0xD900	CMD
0x00	0x0C	*0xD300	RWTS	0x02	0x01	0xD800	CMD
0x00	0x0D	*0xD200	RWTS	0x02	0x02	0xD700	CMD
0x00	0x0E	*0xD100	RWTS	0x02	0x03	0xD600	CMD
0x00	0x0F	*0xD000	RWTS	0x02	0x04	0xD500	CMD
0x01	0x00	0xE900	DATA	0x02	0x05	0xD400	CMD
0x01	0x01	0xE800	DATA	0x02	0x06	0xD300	CMD
0x01	0x02	0xE700	DATA	0x02	0x07	0xD200	CMD
0x01	0x03	0xE600	DATA	0x02	0x08	0xD100	CMD
0x01	0x04	0xE500	SPCL	0x02	0x09	0xD000	CMD

Table I.8.3. DOS 4.3 Disk Track/Sector Mapping to Memory Address

```
     :                :               :
    0800              4               enz
     :                :               :
    BFF2              7     MNGDISK    equ $BFF2
    C020              8     RDENTRY    equ $C020      ; $C720
    C900              9     RDPAGECX   equ $C900      ; $C7
    C901             10     RDSLOT     equ $C901      ; $07
     :                :               :
    0940             24     ; Attach handler address.
    0940 AE 01 C9    25                ldx RDSLOT
    0943 A0 20       26                ldy #RDENTRY
    0945 AD 00 C9    27                lda RDPAGECX
    0948 38          28                sec
    0949 20 90 09    29                jsr GETDISK
     :                :               :
    0990 6C F2 BF    45     GETDISK    jmp (MNGDISK)
     :                :               :
```

Figure I.8.1. Attaching a Disk Controller Slot Card Handler in DOS 4.3

```
:               :           :
0800            4           enz
:               :           :
0000            7    ZERO    equ $00
:               :           :
BFF2            9    MNGDISK  equ $BFF2
C020           10    RDENTRY  equ $C020      ; $C720
C900           11    RDPAGECX equ $C900      ; $C7
C901           12    RDSLOT   equ $C901      ; $07
:               :           :
0940           24    ; Request handler address.
0940 AE 01 C9  25           ldx RDSLOT
0943 AD 00 C9  27           lda #ZERO
0946 38        28           sec
0947 20 90 09  29           jsr GETDISK
:               :           :
0960           39    ; Detach a handler.
0960 AE 01 C9  40           ldx RDSLOT
0963 18        41           clc
0964 20 90 09  42           jsr GETDISK
:               :           :
0990 6C F2 BF  65    GETDISK jmp (MNGDISK)
:               :           :
```

Figure I.8.2. Requesting and Detaching a Slot Card Handler in DOS 4.3

The file image of DOS 4.3 and how that image maps to memory is shown in Table 1.8.4. This table correlates file offset to memory address page, and gives the basic function of the code found there, such as DOS Command routine handlers (CMD), DOS File Manager routine handlers (MNGR), Data buffers, tables, and variables (DATA), DOS Read/Write Track/Sector routine (RWTS), and the Stage 0, Stage 1, and Stage 2 boot routines (BOOT). The asterisk before those entries in Tables 1.8.3 and 1.8.4 indicate that these DOS 4.3 routines or structures reside in Language Card Bank 1 memory; the CMD and MNGR routines and DATA reside in Language Card Bank 2 memory.

Having DOS 4.3 as a file image can be very useful. The image could be read from a quikLoader, for example, and placed into memory according to Table I.8.4. Getting DOS 4.3 started is as easy as using an indirect JMP, such as "JMP (INITDOS)". Refer to Table I.8.1 for the address of the variable INITDOS. DOS 4.3 will initialize and then transfer control to Applesoft. If, on the other hand, you do not wish to lose control of DOS 4.3 to Applesoft after DOS initialization, there is a DOS 4.3 command that is not part of the normal DOS command repertoire, and this command directs DOS to transfer its control back to your program or to any Main memory location less than 0xC800. CMDUSER is that command and its use is implemented by employing the function MNGUSER to set and/or reset the address found at USERADR shown in Table I.8.5. When enabled, CMDUSER simply does an indirect jump to USERADR. Figure I.8.3 shows an example assembly language program that totally manages the initialization of DOS 4.3. Once DOS 4.3 has initialized and Applesoft no longer has control, MNGUSER can be used again to restore the default values for USERADR and CMDVAL from within the USERADR routine. This will essentially restore DOS 4.3 to its initial CMDVAL state.

Offset	Address	Code	Offset	Address	Code
0x0000	0xD000	CMD	0x1500	0xE500	SPCL
0x0100	0xD100	CMD	0x1600	0xE600	DATA
0x0200	0xD200	CMD	0x1700	0xE700	DATA
0x0300	0xD300	CMD	0x1800	0xE800	DATA
0x0400	0xD400	CMD	0x1900	0xE900	DATA
0x0500	0xD500	CMD	0x1A00	*0xD000	RWTS
0x0600	0xD600	CMD	0x1B00	*0xD100	RWTS
0x0700	0xD700	CMD	0x1C00	*0xD200	RWTS
0x0800	0xD800	CMD	0x1D00	*0xD300	RWTS
0x0900	0xD900	CMD	0x1E00	*0xD400	RWTS
0x0A00	0xDA00	CMD	0x1F00	*0xD500	RWTS
0x0B00	0xDB00	CMD	0x2000	*0xD600	INRF
0x0C00	0xDC00	MNGR	0x2100	*0xD700	HELP
0x0D00	0xDD00	MNGR	0x2200	*0xD800	HELP
0x0E00	0xDE00	MNGR	0x2300	*0xD900	HELP
0x0F00	0xDF00	MNGR	0x2400	*0xDA00	HELP
0x1000	0xE000	MNGR	0x2500	*0xDB00	HELP
0x1100	0xE100	MNGR	0x2600	*0xDC00	HELP
0x1200	0xE200	MNGR	0x2700	*0xDD00	HELP
0x1300	0xE300	MNGR	0x2800	0xBE00	XFER
0x1400	0xE400	MNGR	0x2900	0xBF00	BOOT

Table I.8.4. DOS 4.3 File Image Mapping to Memory Address

```
      :                    :              :
   0800               6            enz
   0000                    :
   03D0               9    DOSWARM   equ $3D0
   BFF6              10    MNGUSER   equ $BFF6
   BFF8              11    INITDOS   equ $BFF8
      :                    :              :
   0900 38           20            sec
   0901 A0 80        21            ldy #SPCLCODE
   0903 A9 09        22            lda /SPCLCODE
   0905 20 F6 BF     23            jsr DOUSER
   0908 6C F8 BF     24            jmp (INITDOS)
      :                    :              :
   0980 18           43    SPCLCODE clc
   0981 20 F6 BF     44            jsr DOUSER
   0984 4C D0 03     45            jmp DOSWARM
      :                    :              :
   09B0 6C F6 BF     59    DOUSER   jmp (MNGUSER)
      :                    :              :
```

Figure I.8.3. Using MNGUSER in DOS 4.3

Address	Offset	Variable	Size	Description
0xBEE2	0x00	WARMADR	0x02	ROM soft entry handler address
0xBEE4	0x02	COLDADR	0x02	ROM hard entry handler address
0xBEE6	0x04	ERRORADR	0x02	ROM error handler address
0xBEE8	0x06	RESETADR	0x02	ROM set/reset handler address
0xBEEA	0x08	USERADR	0x02	USERCMD handler address
0xBEEC	0x0A	CMDVAL	0x01	DOS first-time cold-start command
0xBEED	0x0B	NMAXVAL	0x01	MAXFILES at initialization
0xBEEE	0x0C	YEARVAL	0x01	Year value for Thunderclock card
0xBEEF	0x0D	FIRSTCAT	0x01	First catalog sector
0xBEF0	0x0E	LASTRACK	0x01	Number of tracks in volume
0xBEF1	0x0F	SECVAL	0x01	First catalog sector
0xBEF2	0x10	ENDTRK	0x01	Number of tracks in volume
0xBEF3	0x11	SUBJCT	0x02	Volume Library value (subject number)
0xBEF5	0x13	TRKVAL	0x01	Catalog track number
0xBEF6	0x14	VRSN	0x01	DOS Version number
0xBEF7	0x15	BLD	0x01	DOS Build number
0xBEF8	0x16	RAMTYP	0x01	DOS RAM type
0xBEF9	0x17	VALSPHAS	0x01	Half-phases per track
0xBEFA	0x18	TSPARS	0x01	Number of T/S pairs per sector
0xBEFB	0x19	ALCTRK	0x01	Sector to allocate next
0xBEFC	0x1A	ALCDIR	0x01	Sector allocation direction
0xBEFD	0x1B	VALSCNFG	0x01	DOS Configuration byte
0xBEFE	0x1C	ENDSEC	0x01	Number of sectors per track
0xBEFF	0x1D	SECSIZ	0x01	(Bytes per sector) / 256

Table I.8.5. DOS 4.3 INITVALS Structure Definition

The DOS 4.3 Boot and Data Management Structure shown in Table I.8.1 contains a wealth of other values and vectors not yet discussed. Ever since the publication of the DOS 4.1 Manual and during the development of DOS 4.3 I thought there should be a far more convenient procedure in order to obtain the current DOS Version and Build information. One could parse the version and build values from the data string supplied by the RDCLKVSN function shown in Table I.9.1, for example. But it is far more convenient to obtain these values directly, and BLDVRSN and BLDNMBR at 0xBFF0 and 0xBFF1, respectively, provide this information. MNGVALS, similar in function to MNGDISK, provides a very convenient interface to access or change the CMDVALS structure variables. This is fully discussed in Section I.12.

The address found at INITVAL shown in Table I.8.1 is used to read or change the variables in the INITVALS structure shown in Table I.8.5. One should reference the variables in this structure indirectly and, therefore, more generally using the address found at INITVAL and the offsets shown in Table I.8.5. Because the INITVALS structure resides in Main memory, the variables in this structure are somewhat easier to access in order to read and change directly than those variables found in CMDVALS. The example assembly language routine shown in Figure I.8.4 copies the address found at

INITVAL to a page-zero pointer. The Y-register is used to hold the desired offset found in Table I.8.5. The example routine first reads RESETADR, saves it, then changes it to another address.

```
  :                       :           :
00EE                      4   PTR        epz $EE
  :                       :           :
0800                      8            enz
  :                       :           :
0006                     13   RESETOFF equ $06
008D                     14   RETURN   equ $8D
  :                       :           :
BFFA                     20   INITVAL  equ $BFFA
  :                       :           :
0940                     26   ; Setup pointer.
0940 AD FA BF            27            lda INITVAL
0943 85 EE               28            sta PTR
0945 AD FB BF            19            lda INITVAL+1
0948 85 EF               30            sta PTR+1
094A                     31   ;
094A                     32   ; Get current entry and save.
094A A0 06               33            ldy #RESETOFF
094C B1 EE               34            lda (PTR),Y
094E 8D 90 09            35            sta RESETSAV
0951 C8                  36            iny
0952 B1 EE               37            lda (PTR),Y
0954 8D 91 09            38            sta RESETSAV+1
0957                     39   ;
0957                     40   ; Change entry.
0957 A9 09               41            lda /MYRESET
0959 91 EE               42            sta (PTR),Y
095B 88                  43            dey
095C A9 80               44            lda #MYRESET
095E 91 EE               45            sta (PTR),Y
  :                       :           :
0980                     50   ; My RESET handler location.
0980 A9 8D               51   MYRESET  lda #RETURN
  :                       :           :
0990 00 00               66   RESETSAV hex 0000
  :                       :           :
```

Figure I.8.4. Accessing and Changing INITVALS in DOS 4.3

Table I.8.1 contains the offset BCFGNDX for the BOOTCFG Structure shown in Table I.8.2. This structure may be accessed indirectly similar to the INITVAL table knowing that this table resides in page 0xBF. A page-zero pointer to access this structure would be necessary as shown in Figure 1.8.5. The CFFA firmware I developed is one example that dynamically modifies the DNUM and VOLEXPT variables. Drive and volume numbers are critical parameters to the CFFA boot process, and being able to change those variables makes it possible for the CFFA to boot any of the volumes on any of its drives.

```
 :               :        :
00EE            4   PTR         epz $EE
 :               :        :
0800            7               enz
 :               :        :
0000           11   DNUMOFF     equ $00
 :               :        :
BFFC           16   BCFGNDX     equ $BFFC
 :               :        :
0940           24   ; Setup pointer.
0940 AD FC BF  25               lda BCFGNDX
0943 85 EE     26               sta PTR
0945 A9 BF     27               lda /BCFGNDX
0947 85 EF     28               sta PTR+1
0949          29   ;
0949          30   ; Change DNUM.
0949 A0 00    31               ldy #DNUMOFF
094B 85 12    32               lda #$12
094D 91 EE    33               sta (PTR),Y
094F          34   ;
094F          35   ; Change VOLEXPT.
094F C8       36               iny
0950 85 A7    37               lda #$A7
0952 91 EE    38               sta (PTR),Y
 :               :        :
```

Figure I.8.5. Changing the Boot Configuration Structure in DOS 4.3

Table I.8.1 also contains the most significant byte of the memory address for NBUF1. NBUF1 is 256 bytes of memory on a page boundary. This buffer resides in Language Card Bank 1 memory in DOS 4.3. This most significant address byte was included in order to provide easy access to a temporary page of memory as long as RWTS is not invoked, which would obviously overwrite the contents of this particular buffer. The firmware I developed for the Rana disk drive makes excellent use of the NBUF1PG address byte. The CFFA firmware I developed also uses this buffer to temporarily save either the lower half or the upper half of a 512-byte data block.

9. DOS 4.3 Initialization

DOS 4.3 initialization is a very complex procedure, and it begins immediately after the boot process has read track 0x00 into memory and before the Monitor routines have performed their initialization. The peripheral-card firmware on the controller card for the Disk][must generate a RDNIBLBT table from 0x36C to 0x3D5 in order for the firmware to process the 342 "disk" bytes it reads for a sector of 256 "memory" bytes. This process is called "6 and 2" decoding or Data Field Decoding, and this subject is thoroughly discussed in many publications on Apple DOS 3.3. DOS 3.3, DOS 4.1, and even ProDOS load the Read Translate (RDNIBL) and Write Translate (WRNIBL) tables into memory from the volume that is booted. The RDNIBL table is 0x6A bytes in size and the WRNIBL table is 0x40 bytes in size. The companion buffer to NBUF1, whose MSB is listed in Table I.8.1, is NBUF2, and the size of NBUF2 is 0x56 bytes. When NBUF1 and NBUF2 are filled, 342 "disk" bytes have been read.

```
   :              :           :
C019 98           57          tya
C01A 9D 56 03     58          sta RDNIBLBT-$16,X
   :              :           :
```

Figure I.9.1. Generating RDNIBLBT in Disk][Firmware

```
   :              :           :
D60C 8A           326         txa
D60D 09 80        327         ora #$80
D60F 99 56 DF     328         sta WRNIBL,Y
D612              329     ;
D612 98           330         tya
D613 9D 80 DF     331         sta RDNIBL-$16,X
   :              :           :
```

Figure I.9.2. Generating RDNIBL and WRNIBL in DOS 4.3

It is fortunate that NBUF2, WRNIBL, and RDNIBL all fit on one 256-byte page exactly. One could consider simply copying the firmware RDNIBLBT table to the RDNIBL address after the boot process, but that still leaves having to read in the WRNIBL table. I was fascinated to discover that I could programmatically generate both tables at the same time. In other words, I could save having to read in 0xAA bytes of data at the expense of 0x25 bytes of code, which is a savings of over one-half page of disk space that could be used for other DOS functionality. The firmware code snippet to generate the RDNIBLBT table is shown in Figure I.9.1. The DOS 4.3 code snippet to generate both the WRNIBL and the RDNIBL tables is shown in Figure I.9.2. The BLDNIBL routine incorporates only six additional bytes to generate 0x40 bytes of essential data.

One of the design limitations in having two banks of memory in the Language Card, Bank 1 and Bank 2, at the same address, 0xD000, is that it is not possible to execute code in one bank and read or write data in the other bank. Once RWTS is located in Bank 1 after Boot Stage 1 has finished, Boot Stage 2 reads the remaining twenty-six pages into memory in two sections: sixteen pages to 0xF0-0xFF and ten pages to 0xE0-0xE9. Those sixteen pages in 0xF0-0xFF need to be moved to 0xD0-0xDF in Bank 2. The ten pages at 0xE0-0xE9 are already where they need to be. This is how DOS 4.3 reads data in one bank and writes data to the other bank. Incidentally, just prior to moving pages 0xF0-0xFF, the CMDVALS structure shown in Table I.12.1 is initialized to 0x00. Once DOS 4.3 is properly placed in memory Monitor initialization can be performed.

Monitor initialization has slightly changed as Apple introduced new computers such as the Apple //e and the Apple //c. Now, Monitor initialization includes initializing the variable XMODE to 0xFF for proper CX ROM space functionality and accessing the variables VID80OFF and ALTCHOFF to select 40-column display and to engage the main video character set. I added a call to SETNORM to ensure normal screen character display (not inverse or not blinking) along with the usual calls to INIT, SETVID, and SETKBD. I do not believe the order these Monitor routines are called matter much, but this is the order DOS 4.3 calls these Monitor initialization routines. Now that the ROM Monitor is in focus, DOS 4.3 can verify the presence of ROM Applesoft. DOS 4.3 will not continue its initialization process if it does not find a JMP (i.e. 0x4C) instruction at 0xE000.

DOS 4.3 initialization continues with copying the entire Monitor that is in ROM from 0xF800 to 0xFFFF to the same location in RAM. Obviously, having the Monitor in RAM saves DOS 4.3 having to manage memory using Soft Switches in order to gain access to common Monitor routines. Unlike the Monitor routines in ROM, however, the Monitor routines in RAM can be modified, so DOS 4.3 copies the DOSWARM and DOSCOLD addresses shown in Table I.9.1 to the Monitor in RAM: 0xFEB0 is the cold-start location and 0xFEB3 is the warm-start location for Applesoft. Once the RAM Monitor is in place, DOS 4.3 can begin its search for a clock card in one of the peripheral slots. Section I.13 is devoted entirely to clock card access in DOS 4.3. At this time DOS 4.3 prepares for cold-start initialization by initializing the Command Manager with the booted slot, drive, and volume variables from the RWTS IOCB.

Software developers of my favorite utilities like *ADT*, *Big Mac*, *FID*, *Lisa*, *PGE*, *GPLE*, and *Sourceror*, made use of the DOS 3.3 Initial Address table at 0x9D00 to 0x9D0F, 0x9D56 to 0x9D83, and, unfortunately, direct entry points to many other internal DOS variables and routines. One can directly modify the DOS 4.3 INITVALS table values shown in Table I.8.5 to tailor a DOS boot image specific to one's needs: CMDVAL specifies the "HELLO" file type (i.e. 0x06 for RUN, 0x14 for EXEC, and 0x34 for BRUN), NMAXVAL specifies what the initial MAXFILES value will be, and YEARVAL specifies the current year in order to support the Thunderclock card which lacks a year register. SECVAL defines how many sectors will be used for the file catalog, ENDTRK specifies how many tracks are in the volume, and ENDSEC specifies whether a track has 16 or 32 sectors. In order to support hardware providing 40 tracks per volume, simply change ENDTRK to 40 (i.e. 0x28). If hardware supports 32 sectors per track, change ENDSEC to 32 (i.e. 0x20). Modify some or all of these parameters in memory directly or use the INIT keywords and initialize another disk volume with the appropriate HELLO file. A file catalog will be created on this new volume according to the values you specify.

When DOS 4.3 performs a cold-start it sets MAXFILES equal to NMAXVAL, it initializes the file buffers, it makes EXEC inactive, and it copies the contents of Table I.9.1 into memory beginning at memory address `0x3D0`. It is this interface where the important entry addresses and vectors for DOS routines are found, such as `RWTS` and the File Manager. This interface is the same as that found in DOS 3.3 in order to maintain compatibility with virtually all previous software, but with some important additions: read DOS version or read clock routine (i.e. `RDCLKVSN`) at memory address `0x3E1`, the error printing routine (i.e. `PRTERROR`) at memory address `0x3E8`, and the Apple //e `DOXFER` routine (i.e. `XFERADR`) at memory address `0x3ED`. All four routines can be accessed using an indirect `JMP` instruction such as "`JMP (RDCLKVSN)`". The two routines `GETFMCB` and `GETIOCB` are changed in DOS 4.3, but return the same information: the address of the `RWTS IOCB` in the Y- and A-registers in Lo/Hi byte order, and similarly, the address of the File Manager Context Block in the Y- and A-registers. These two context blocks are shown in Tables I.10.1 and I.11.1, respectively.

Address	Variable	Instruction	Description
0x3D0	DOSWARM	JMP EXTWARM	DOS warm-start JMP
0x3D3	DOSCOLD	JMP DOSINIT	DOS cold-start JMP
0x3D6	CALLFM	JMP EXTFM	File Manager JMP
0x3D9	CALLRWTS	JMP EXTRWTS	RWTS handler JMP
0x3DC	GETFMCB	LDY #FMVALS	Puts File Manager Context Block
0x3DE		LDA /FMVALS	address in #Y/A
0x3E1	RDCLKVSN	ADR EXCLKVSN	address in #Y/A, Clock CLC, Version SEC
0x3E3	GETIOCB	LDY #TBLTYPE	Puts RWTS I/O Context Block
0x3E5		LDA /TBLTYPE	address in #Y/A
0x3E8	PRTERADR	ADR EXTPRERR	Prints error message for error # in X-register
0x3EA	HOOKDOS	JMP EXTPTRS	DOS reconnect JMP
0x3ED	XFERADR	ADR *-*	Used for the Apple //e DOXFER routine
0x3EF	AUTOBRK	JMP OLDBRK	ROM break handler JMP
0x3F2	AUTORSET	ADR EXTWARM	ROM auto-reset routine address
0x3F4	PWRSTATE	BYT 0xA5^(0x3F3)	Power up byte
0x3F5	USRAHAND	JMP RPEATCMD	& handler JMP
0x3F8	USRYHAND	JMP AUXMOVE	Ctrl-Y handler JMP to 0xC311
0x3FB	NMASKIRQ	JMP MON	Non-maskable IRQ JMP to 0xFF65
0x3FE	MASKIRQ	ADR MON	Maskable IRQ routine address at 0xFF65

Table I.9.1. DOS 4.3 Page 0x03 Interface Routines and Vectors

The routine `RDCLKVSN` reads the current DOS version, a 19-byte upper ASCII text string (i.e. "`DOS4.3.08H 01/01/20`"), into a buffer whose address is in the Y- and A-registers with the `Carry` flag **set**. The routine `RDCLKVSN` reads the current date and time into a 6-byte buffer as shown in Table I.5.3 whose address is in the Y- and A-registers with the `Carry` flag **clear**. The routine `PRTERROR` prints the error messages as shown in Table I.11.7 whose index error number is in the X-register. Example code segments to read the current DOS version into a 20-byte buffer and the current date and time into a 6-byte buffer are shown in Figures I.9.3 and I.9.4, respectively. Figure I.9.5 shows how *Big Mac* prints all of its File Manager error codes.

```
:                       :                   :
03E1                    5       RDCLKVSN equ $3E1
:                       :                   :
0900 A0 43              13               ldy #VSNBUFR
0902 A9 09              14               lda /VSNBUFR
0904 38                 15               sec
0905 20 40 09           16               jsr READVSN
:                       :                   :
0920 60                 20               rts
:                       :                   :
0940 6C E1 03           40      READVSN  jmp (RDCLKVSN)
0943 00 00 00           41      VSNBUFR  dfs 20,0
:                       :                   :
```

Figure I.9.3. Reading the DOS Version in DOS 4.3

```
:                       :                   :
03E1                    5       RDCLKVSN equ $3E1
:                       :                   :
0900 A0 43              13               ldy #CLKBUFR
0902 A9 09              14               lda /CLKBUFR
0904 18                 15               clr
0905 20 40 09           16               jsr READCLK
:                       :                   :
0920 60                 20               rts
:                       :                   :
0940 6C E1 03           40      READCLK  jmp (RDCLKVSN)
0943 00 00 00           41      CLKBUFR  dfs 6,0
:                       :                   :
```

Figure I.9.4. Reading the Date and Time in DOS 4.3

It is worthwhile to note that the DOS 4.3 RWTS only supports the Disk][type hardware since there was no other device manufactured that was substantially different. The Device Characteristics Table (DCT) was originally designed so that RWTS could support devices having different stepper motor phases per track in order to support half-tracking for example, or even different motor on-time requirements. I saw no need for DOS 4.3 to support something that simply does not, nor will ever exist. I am aware that the RanaSystems EliteThree is a dual-headed disk drive with the ability to access 80 half-tracks on both sides of a double-sided, double-density diskette. Of course, the DCT for the Rana is different, but the Rana uses its own interface handler with its own PHASEON/PHASEOFF tables for its stepper motor operation, and its own number of stepper motor phases to accomplish its half-tracking capabilities. I even developed my own firmware for the Rana that formats a diskette with forty tracks on both sides of the diskette, with the first sixteen sectors on side one and the next sixteen sectors on side two, effectively creating a volume where each track has thirty-two sectors. I was absolutely successful and, by design, the firmware attached to the DOS 4.3 RWTS DISKADRS table. I

29

was able to obtain double-sided, double-density 5.25-inch floppy diskettes from floppydisk.com. As a word of caution, double-sided, double-density 5.25-inch floppy diskettes are manufactured with an inner reinforcement ring. Significantly better performance will be achieved from those diskettes whether half-tracking is employed or not. In summary, DOS 4.3 does not utilize the DCT, and it ignores any DCT address found in any RWTS IOCB for a Disk][or for any other Disk][-like drive.

```
    :                   :                :
   0044                 18   A5L         epz $44
   0045                 19   A5H         epz $45
    :                   :                :
   0800                 24               enz
    :                   :                :
   03D6                 27   CALLFM      equ $3D6
   03DC                 28   GETFMCB     equ $3DC
   03E8                 29   PRTERADR    equ $3E8
    :                   :                :
   D0B0 6C E8 03       101   PRTERROR    jmp (PRTERADR)
    :                   :                :
   D12D 20 DC 03       131               jsr GETFMCB
   D130 84 44          132               sty A5L
   D132 85 45          133               sta A5H
    :                   :                :
   E58A A2 01          316               ldx #1
   E58C 20 D6 03       317               jsr CALLFM
   E58F 90 40          318               bcc HE5D1
   E591 A0 0A          319               ldy #10
   E593 B1 44          320               lda (A5L),Y
   E595 AA             321               tax
    :                   :                :
   E5BC 8A             361               txa
   E5BD 48             362               pha
    :                   :                :
   E5C1 E8             366               inx
   E5C2 20 B0 D0       367               jsr PRTERROR
   E5C5 68             368               pla
   E5C6 AA             369               tax
   E5C7 20 B0 D0       370               jsr PRTERROR
   E5CA 20 8E FD       371               jsr CROUT
    :                   :                :
   E5D1 A2 0E          394   HE5D1       ldx #$0E
    :                   :                :
   FD8E A9 8D          586   CROUT       lda #$8D
    :                   :                :
```

Figure I.9.5. Big Mac Printing a File Manager Error in DOS 4.3

10. The DOS 4.3 RWTS Interface

The DOS 4.3 RWTS interface is very straightforward and simple to use. When a call is made to GETIOCB, shown in Table I.9.1, the Y- and A-registers point to the RWTS IOCB as shown in Table I.10.1. Any other address space may be used for an RWTS IOCB as well. Once the IOCB has been initialized, a call to CALLRWTS with the address of an IOCB, or the address of the IOCB within DOS, in the Y- and A-registers will begin RWTS processing. The RWTS handler pushes the current processor status onto the stack, disables interrupts, and saves the Y- and A-registers to the IOB address at zero-page address 0x4A/0x4B. Next, the handler extracts the supplied buffer address from the IOCB and saves the address to BUFADR2Z at zero-page address 0x3E/0x3F. The handler also extracts the SNUM16 value, copies it to the X-register, saves it to SLOTFND in the IOCB, and calculates the low-order address byte for DISKJMP based on the SNUM16 value divided by eight. The RWTS handler then indirectly jumps to the routine whose address is located in the Disk Address DISKADRS table for the specified slot number. The assembler initializes all seven DISKADRS table entries to the address of RWTSENT so that it does not matter which slot or slots a DISK][-like controller card is using.

Offset	Name	Size	Description
0x00	TBLTYPE	0x01	IOCB structure block
0x01	SNUM16	0x01	Slot * 16
0x02	DNUM	0x01	Drive number
0x03	VOLEXPT	0x01	Volume number expected; 0x00 for any
0x04	TNUM	0x01	Track number
0x05	SNUM	0x01	Sector number
0x06	DCTADR	0x02	Address of Device Characteristics Table
0x08	USRBUF	0x02	Data buffer address
0x0A	IOCBPHAS	0x01	Half-phases per track
0x0B	BYTCNT	0x01	Bytes to read/write; 0x00 means 256 bytes
0x0C	CMDCODE	0x01	Command
0x0D	ERRCODE	0x01	Return error code
0x0E	VOLFND	0x01	Return volume found
0x0F	SLOTFND	0x01	Return slot found
0x10	DRVFND	0x01	Return drive found

Table I.10.1. RWTS Input/Output Context Block Definition

Command	Value	Description
RWTSSEEK	0x00	Seek to track/sector command code
RWTSREAD	0x01	Read track/sector command code
RWTSWRIT	0x02	Write track/sector command code
RWTSFRMT	0x04	Format volume command code

Table I.10.2. RWTS Command Codes

Error	Value	Description
RWNOERR	0x00	RWTS No error
RWINITER	0x08	RWTS Initialization error
RWPROTER	0x10	RWTS Write protect error
RWVOLERR	0x20	RWTS Volume number error
RWSYNERR	0x30	RWTS Syntax error (out of range)
RWDRVERR	0x40	RWTS Drive error
RWREADER	0x80	RWTS Read error (obsolete)

Table I.10.3. RWTS Error Codes

The MOVEHD routine handles the placement of the record/playback head and masks all track values it encounters with TRKMASK, or 0x3F, in order to remove the value of TRKZERO, or 0x40. When RWTS completes its processing, it is required to save its results in the supplied IOCB: ERRCODE, VOLFND, and DRVFND. The RWTS handler will restore the original processor status and either clear or set the Carry flag based on the return status from its handler processing. If interrupts were initially enabled before the call to the RWTS handler, interrupts will be re-enabled when the RWTS handler exits. Table I.10.2 shows the four command codes that are valid RWTS commands and Table I.10.3 shows the seven possible error codes that RWTS can generate. I added the RWSYNERR error code for IOCBPHAS range checking and for the RAM Disk, Rana, and Sider firmware that performs its own range checking of their IOCB variables.

The astute reader will assuredly notice that I have utilized the spare byte in the RWTS IOCB for the IOCBPHAS variable. Furthermore, I have used the spare byte in the File Manager Context Block for FMPHASE as shown in Table I.11.1. Both variables, when encountered during their specific routine utilization, are range checked and copied to VALSPHAS as shown in Table I.8.5. The value entered with the DOS PHASE command is also copied to VALSPHAS. VALSPHAS is the key variable that is used to multiply the target track number to obtain the number of half-phases the R/W head needs to be moved before any data I/O can occur.

All physical tracks on a "normal" DOS diskette are separated by four half-phases, the equivalent of rotating the cam of the stepper motor 180 degrees as I prefer to imagine its operation. The stepper motor is used to move the R/W head along the diskette's radius towards or away from the center of the diskette. A simplified representation of the R/W head mechanics in the Disk][is shown in Figure I.10.1. The R/W head is connected to the Carriage Rod and that rod travels along the radius of the diskette as the Cam Table is rotated by the Stepper Motor. The Cam Rider is also attached to the Carriage Rod and it essentially "rides" the Cam Channel. As the Cam Table rotates the Cam Rider follows the Cam Channel, thereby pulling or pushing the Carriage Rod towards or away from the center of the diskette. The Stepper Motor can rotate both clockwise and counter-clockwise in order to move the R/W head from track 0x00 to track 0x23, and then back to track 0x00.

About one year after the Disk][drive was first introduced, the Cam Table and supporting hardware were slightly modified in order to access thirty-six tracks rather than thirty-five tracks. For one reason or another this information never found its way into the Apple user community.

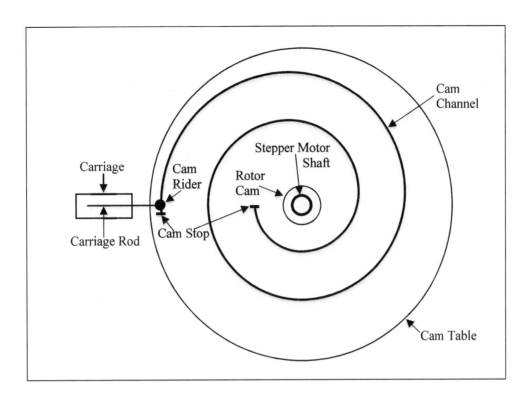

Figure I.10.1. Disk][Carriage and Cam Table

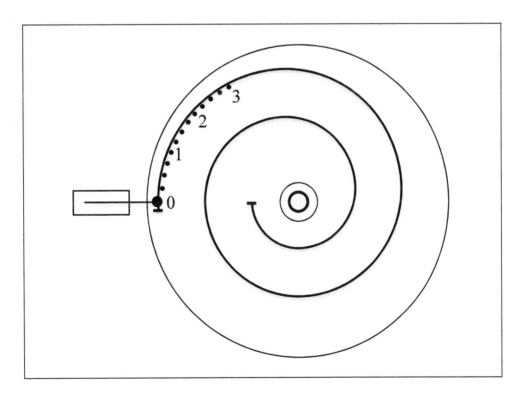

Figure I.10.2. Four Half-Phase Track Separation

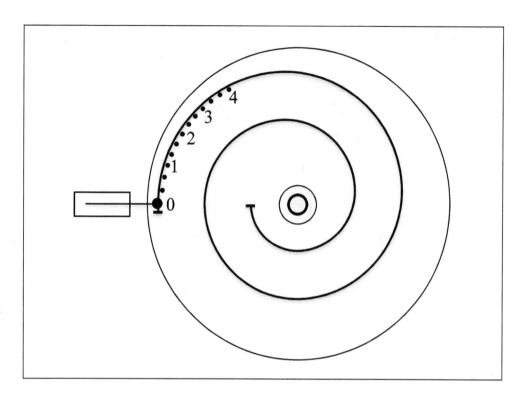

Figure I.10.3. Three Half-Phase Track Separation

The motor used to rotate the Cam Table in the Disk][is a general purpose 4-phase, 12-volt DC stepper motor. Each electromagnet or phase coil inside the stepper motor can be energized individually or in pairs, as well as de-energized, in such a way as to cause the Cam Table to rotate. The illustration shown in Figure I.10.2 gives the location of the first twelve half-phases as well as the location where tracks 0x00, 0x01, 0x02, and 0x03 would occur along the Cam Channel as the Cam Table is rotated clockwise or counter-clockwise. These tracks conform to the normal spacing of four half-phases like the tracks found on a DOS Master diskette. On the other hand, the Rana Elite has the ability to space tracks as close as two half-phases because the gap length of its record/playback head is smaller than the gap length of the record/playback head found in the Disk][. Actually, the gap length of the record/playback head in the Disk][is somewhat equal to the size of three half-phases. Manufacturing record/playback heads with this specification helps to minimize cross-talk between adjacent tracks that are spaced four or more half-phases apart.

In order to move the R/W head from track 0x00 to track 0x23, the stepper motor will need to rotate through 144 half-phases, that is, 36 * 4 half-phases. If tracks are separated by only three half-phases, it is conceivable that a diskette could support up to forty-eight tracks. Figure I.10.3 shows the same location of those first twelve half-phases as shown in Figure I.10.2, only now the tracks are spaced every three half-phases. Of course, this is merely an illustration until it can actually be achieved. There are a number of parameters to consider when designing software to actuate the stepper motor in the Disk][, or in any other similar disk drive. These parameters may include direction of movement, distance of movement, desired acceleration, desired deceleration, desired velocity, induced vibration, and controlled damping. The routine that moves the R/W head on behalf of RWTS may consider all these parameters in order to consistently place the R/W head at the correct location as efficiently as possible without regard to direction, and to negate any induced angular momentum. In other words, the R/W head must be totally stopped and it must be held at the right place before any data I/O can be obtained with any reliability.

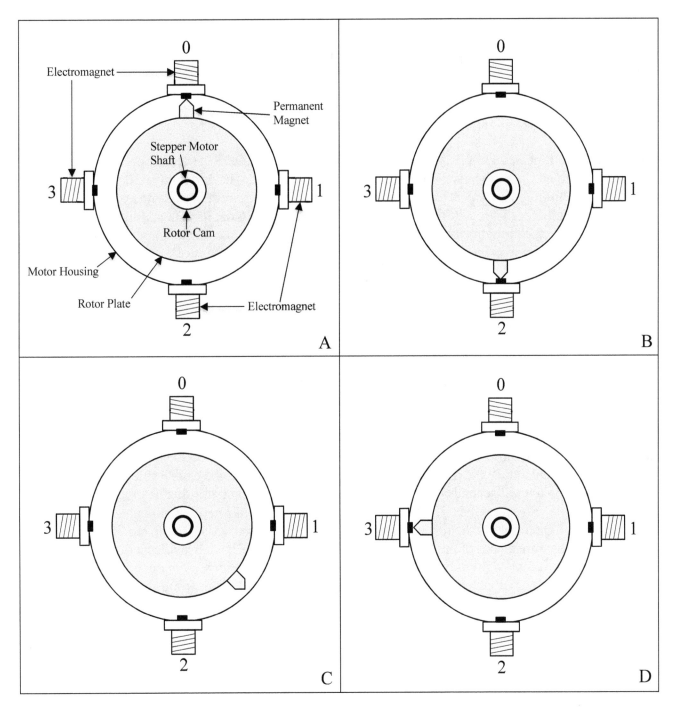

Figure I.10.4. Inside View of a Stepper Motor

For the sake of simplicity, I like to imagine the mechanical operation of a stepper motor as that represented by the illustrations shown in Figure I.10.4. The main functional components of this stepper motor are labeled in Figure I.10.4A. The permanent magnet that is attached to the Rotor Plate is attracted to each one of the four electromagnetic or phase coils as each coil is energized in succession. By design, the stepper motor is always at Phase 0 when the Cam Rider hits the outer Cam Stop, the location of track 0x00. Figure I.10.4B shows the Cam Rotor positioned clockwise at Phase Coil 2, effectively positioning the R/W head precisely over track 0x01 as shown in Figure I.10.2 where each track is separated by four half-phases. Every rotation of four half-phases will move the R/W head to the next or previous adjacent track. Figure I.10.4C shows the Cam Rotor positioned at three half-phases clockwise from Phase 0. This would position the R/W head precisely over track 0x01 as shown in Figure I.10.3 where each track is separated by three half-phases. Figure I.10.4D shows the Cam Rotor positioned clockwise at Phase Coil 3 which would position the R/W head precisely over track 0x02, again for tracks separated by three half-phases.

The MOVEHD routine in DOS 4.1 is similar to the routine found in DOS 3.3 in that both routines move the R/W head to and from the even numbered phase coils 0 and 2. The odd numbered phase coils 1 and 3 assist in turning the Cam Table as smoothly as possible. Both routines use an acceleration and deceleration algorithm that reaches maximum velocity after moving the R/W head through eight phases. That is, the current track and the target track are first doubled so that a computation is made every time the current track counter in incremented, and that would be for every phase: either a coil is energized or deenergized. The time to leave a coil energized or deenergized is determined by an entry from either an ONTBL or an OFFTBL of eight values in each table. One can just as easily view the distance between two adjacent tracks as being two phases rather than being four half-phases for DOS 3.3 and in DOS 4.1. However, since an individual half-phase is attainable, it is the more general expression, and Occam's Razor would select the "half-phase" as the preferred designation.

The MOVEHD routine in DOS 4.3 is radically different from the routine found in DOS 4.1 in that a computation must be made every half-phase, and the time a coil is energized or deenergized is determined by an entry from a single ONOFFTBL table of twelve values. This table also provides the MOVEHD routine with an acceleration and deceleration component that reaches maximum velocity after moving the R/W head through twelve half-phases. The resulting movement of the Cam Table is smooth and efficient. Once the R/W head is located at its destination, the Cam Table is held in place for nearly twenty-six milliseconds to ensure all vibration transients and torque due to its angular momentum has been suppressed. The last coil or coils can then be deenergized to guarantee that the R/W head is held precisely at the requested track. The Carriage Rod and Carriage are designed to inhibit any further movement of the R/W head once the coil or coils have been deenergized. Some disk manufactures employ a tension band that can be adjusted to restrict movement of the Carriage Rod, but obviously not enough restriction that cannot be overcome by the strong startup torque of the stepper motor.

The direction of Cam Table movement in the DOS 4.3 MOVEHD routine determines the values for the NEXTON and NEXTOFF variables. One or the other variable is used every time the current track counter is incremented or decremented and a new computation is made: either NEXTON is subtracted from or NEXTOFF is added to the track counter. When the R/W head has reached its final destination and held in place, and if the Permanent Magnet is at rest between two coils as shown in Figure I.10.4C, the coils are deenergized in a specific order. It does not matter whether the Cam Table was turned clockwise or counterclockwise: these two coils are always deenergized in the same order. Doing this minimizes any possible slewing of the R/W head. Understand that it is not physically possible to deenergize two coils of a stepper motor at precisely the same moment in time. Depending on which microprocessor instructions are used, an absolute addressing instruction will be faster and induce less slew than any indexed addressing instruction regardless whether the X- or Y-register(s) are used.

Managing disk phase in RWTS is an exceedingly complex process particularly when copying files from diskette volumes that have been initialized with different phase values. Beginning with the initial boot of a volume, the start location of the R/W head for both drive 1 and drive 2 is set to track 0x00 in Boot Stage 0: the Disk][slot card firmware forces the movement of the R/W head to track 0x00 in drive 1. As soon as drive 2 is accessed sometime later, its initial track location for its R/W head will be adjusted to the track number that is first obtained. Unlike DOS 3.3 during Boot Stage 0, DOS 4.3 initializes the DRV0TRK and DRV1TRK variables as well as the DRV0PHAS and DRV1PHAS variables to 0x00. DRV0TRK and DRV1TRK use the base addresses 0x0478 and 0x04F8, respectively, and DRV0PHAS and DRV1PHAS use the base addresses 0x0678 and 0x06F8, respectively. Of course, the slot number for the Disk][is used as an index from these base addresses. As an aside, the Rana uses 0x0578 and 0x05F8 as the base addresses for DRV2TRK and DRV3TRK, respectively.

In RWTS processing just prior to extracting the requested IOCB command, the IOCB phase is extracted and compared to one of the DRV0PHAS or DRV1PHAS values depending upon drive number. If the values are the same, command extraction begins. If the phase values differ, the requested phase value is range checked and put aside, the R/W head is moved to track 0x00 using the previously saved phase value, and then the R/W head is moved to the requested track number using the new phase value that was put aside. All further access to that drive will now utilize the new phase value. The additional logic to manage disk phase when the phase value does not change is still within the window established by the required number of 40 μsec sync bytes between an address field and its data field. Establishing a new phase value for a Disk][or a Disk][-like drive occurs once, so the impact to a disk copying session is extremely minimal. This re-phasing process happens so fast, so smoothly, most users would probably never even notice.

The illustration shown in Figure I.10.3 suggests that a Disk][in pristine working order can conceivably access up to forty-eight tracks on a double-sided double-density diskette using a half-phase value of three. The DOS 4.3 INIT command can certainly initialize a diskette with that format flawlessly. And *FID*, after being modified to request Phase number as well as Volume number, can be used to copy files from a phase-four diskette to a phase-three diskette. The new phase-three diskette will boot effortlessly because the INIT handler copied its value of VALSPHAS to CFGPHASE before creating the new DOS image. CFGPHASE is copied to IOCBPHAS at the beginning of Boot Stage 2. I have even created bootable phase-five and phase-six diskettes. A phase-five diskette can only access at most twenty-eight tracks (i.e. 144 / 5) and a phase-six diskette can only access at most twenty-four tracks. Why would one desire this capability? First and foremost an odd-phased initialized diskette would be difficult to copy and probably thwart a number of diskette copy applications. Because PHASE is a DOS command in DOS 4.3, its value can be changed at any given moment while this "special" diskette is booting and loading its first application. Actually, it could be the Application Loader that could "adjust" phase to ensure its copy-protection routines are well protected and difficult to access while also loading the primary application. I have no doubt that John K. Morris can perfectly copy any DOS 4.3 phased diskette using his Applesauce floppy drive controller. And that is okay.

11. The DOS 4.3 File Manager Interface

The DOS 4.3 File Manager interface is not as straightforward as the RWTS interface, and it is somewhat more difficult to use. One look at the File Manager Context Block shown in Table I.11.1 demonstrates how convoluted it is. Essentially, the Context Block is totally command driven and it is intended to be used with that in mind. So many of the Context Block entries are overloaded and the entry definitions and their usage strictly depends on the command in question. Table I.11.2 shows all seventeen command codes available to the File Manager in DOS 4.3. The first thirteen command codes are the same as in DOS 3.3 in order to maintain compatibility with all previous software utilizing the external File Manager interface. The last four command codes are new and unique in DOS 4.3.

The command codes new in DOS 4.3 include the FMURMCD, the FMTCHCD, the FMTSCD, and the FMWTSCD codes. The FMURMCD command code can be used to undelete a file that has been previously deleted from the volume Catalog by the FMDELECD command code. **There is no harm in undeleting a file that already exists in the file Catalog**. The FMTCHCD command code can be used to update the timestamp of a file. Processing a file with the FMTCHCD command does not update the VTOC timestamp since nothing is changed in the VTOC, including the bitmap. The FMTSCD command code can be used to read the desired volume sector into the catalog buffer where it is processed for display. The FMWTSCD command code can be used to read the desired volume sector into the catalog buffer where one selected byte is changed, and the result written back to the same volume sector. The catalog buffer is simply a convenient buffer to use for the DOS TS and WTS commands. The Command Manager utilizes the FMTSCD and FMWTSCD command codes primarily because the File Manager has the capability to gracefully handle any volume access error or I/O processing error.

Offset	Name	Size	Description
0x00	FMOPCOD	0x01	File Manager opcode
0x01	SUBCODE	0x01	File Manager subcode
0x02	RECNUM	0x02	Record number
	or FN2ADR	0x02	Secondary filename address
0x04	BYTOFFSET	0x02	Byte offset
	or VOLUME	0x01	Volume number
0x05	DRIVE	0x01	Drive number
0x06	BYTRANGE	0x02	Range length
	or SLOT	0x01	Slot number
0x07	FILETYPE	0x01	File type or SEC32 Flag
0x08	DATADR	0x02	Data byte address
	or FNADR	0x02	Primary filename address
	or DATBYTE	0x01	Data byte
0x0A	RTNCODE	0x01	Return code
0x0B	FMPHASE	0x01	Half-phases per track
0x0C	WBADR	0x02	Workarea buffer address
0x0E	TSLTSADR	0x02	Track/sector list buffer address
0x10	DATASADR	0x02	Data buffer address

Table I.11.1. File Manager Context Block Definition

Command	Value	Handler	Description
FMNOERR	0x00	NOERR2	File Manager No Operation code
FMOPENCD	0x01	OPNHNDLR	File Manager OPEN code
FMCLOSCD	0x02	CLSHNDLR	File Manager CLOSE code
FMREADCD	0x03	RDHNDLR	File Manager READ code
FMWRITCD	0x04	WRHNDLR	File Manager WRITE code
FMDELECD	0x05	DELHNDLR	File Manager DELETE code
FMCATACD	0x06	CATHNDLR	File Manager CATALOG code
FMLOCKCD	0x07	LCKHNDLR	File Manager LOCK code
FMUNLKCD	0x08	UNLKHNDL	File Manager UNLOCK code
FMRENMCD	0x09	RNMHNDLR	File Manager RENAME code
FMPOSICD	0x0A	POSHNDLR	File Manager POSITION code
FMINITCD	0x0B	INITHNDL	File Manager INIT code (modified)
FMVERICD	0x0C	VFYHNDLR	File Manager VERIFY code
FMURMCD	0x0D	URMHNDLR	File Manager URM code
FMTCHCD	0x0E	TCHHNDLR	File Manager TOUCH code
FMTSCD	0x0F	TSHNDLR	File Manager TS code
FMWTSCD	0x10	WTSHNDLR	File Manager WTS code

Table I.11.2. File Manager Command Codes

Command	Value	Description
FMNOOPSC	0x00	File Manager No Operation subcode
FMRW01SC	0x01	File Manager Read/Write 1-byte subcode
FMRWNBSC	0x02	File Manager Read/Write Range subcode
FMPOS1SC	0x03	File Manager Position and Read/Write 1-byte subcode
FMPOSRSC	0x04	File Manager Position and Read/Write Range subcode

Table I.11.3. File Manager Read and Write Command Subcodes

Some File Manager commands require a subcode to specify how the command is to be used. Table I.11.3 lists the five subcodes, one of which must be used with the READ and WRITE command codes FMREADCD and FMWRITCD, respectively. Table I.11.4 shows the other parameters that are required when using one of the five subcodes. For example, to read or write a range of bytes the Subcode at offset 0x01 must be set to 0x02 and the Range Size and Range Address of the data must be entered into offsets 0x06/0x07 and 0x08/0x09 of the Context Block, respectively. Using the FMREADCD and FMWRITCD commands may appear difficult at first, but once the Context Block is setup these two commands can be quite powerful. I added a subcode to FMCATACD command code in order to optionally display what the R keyword provides to the Command Manager. Simply save a non-zero value to the Subcode offset in the File Manager Context Block if that additional CATALOG information is desired. The FMINITCD command code uses the Subcode for the Boot Type information. The

FMWTSCD command code uses the subcode for its Buffer Index parameter. The buffer index is where the data byte (located at offset 0x07 in the context block) will be placed in the catalog buffer.

The File Manager Context Block entries for the FMURMCD command code are used in the same way as they are for the FMDELECD command code where bytes 0x08/0x09 contain the address of the filename to be undeleted. The sectors in the file's TSL(s) as well as all the TSL sectors associated with the file are marked as used in the VTOC free sector bitmap. It is always prudent to undelete a deleted file before subsequent files use those sectors made available when the file was deleted. A volume can be rendered unusable if a data sector should ever be interpreted as a TSL sector.

Subcode	File Manager Command Parameter List				Description
0x01	0x02/0x03	0x04/0x05	0x06/0x07	0x08/0x09	
0x00					No operation
0x01				Byte Data	R/W 1-byte
0x02			Range Size	Range Address	R/W Range
0x03	Record Number	Byte Offset		Byte Data	Position, R/W 1 byte
0x04	Record Number	Byte Offset	Range Size	Range Address	Position, R/W Range

Table I.11.4. File Manager Subcode Utilization

Boot Type	DOS Installed	Description
0x00	No	Data Disk D, all of track 0x00 can be used for data
0x06	Yes	Boot Disk B, RUN; value 0x06 put into CMDVAL
0x10	Yes	Boot Disk B, CLOSE; value 0x10 put into CMDVAL
0x14	Yes	Boot Disk B, EXEC; value 0x14 put into CMDVAL
0x34	Yes	Boot Disk B, BRUN; value 0x34 put into CMDVAL
0xN, 0x00≤N≤0x62	Yes	Boot Disk B, any even value valid within the DOS command table can be put into CMDVAL

Table I.11.5. File Manager FMINITCD Boot Type (SUBCODE)

The File Manager Context Block entries for the FMINITCD command code have been substantially modified from its DOS 3.3 version. Before the FMINITCD command code is even processed, the Command Manager initializes the Context Block to 0x00 except for the FMOPCOD and SUBCODE values. The Command Manager initializes the subcode to one of the example values shown in Table I.11.5 for Boot Type. In order to create a fully bootable DOS B type volume, the subcode must contain a non-zero value, the signal to the INIT handler to write DOS to the volume. If the INIT handler finds a 0x00 value in the subcode, a DOS D type volume will be created that does not contain a DOS. A D type volume will not boot, but all of track 0x00 will be available for data. The Command Manager initializes bytes 0x02/0x03 with the address of the Volume Title SFNAME (FN2ADR), and it updates the SECVAL, ENDTRK, and SUBJCT values in the VTOCVALS structure directly. The File Manager initializes bytes 0x08/0x09 of the Context Block with the address of FNAME (FNADR).

```
:             :        :
1300          394   FMVALS:
1300          395   ;
1300 0B       396   OPCODE    byt FMINITCD
1301 06       397   SUBCODE   byt BOOTYPE
1302          398   ;
1302 2A 13    399   FN2ADR    adr VTITLE
1304          400   ;
1304 00       401   VOLUME    hex 00
1305 01       402   DRIVE     hex 01
1306          403   ;
1306 06       404   SLOT      hex 06
1307 80       405   FILETYPE  hex 00
1308          406   ;
1308 12 13    407   FNADR     adr FNAME
130A          408   ;
130A 00       409   RTNCODE   hex 00
130B          410   ;
130B 00       411   FMPHASE   hex 00
130C          412   ;
130C 0E 13    413   WBADR     adr SECVAL
130E 05       414   SECVAL    hex 05
130F 23       415   ENDTRK    hex 23
1310 34 12    416   SUBJCT    hex 3412
1312          417   ;
0012          418   FMPLEN    equ *-FMVALS
1312          419   ;
1312 E8 E5 EC 420   FNAME     asc "hello"
1315 EC EF
1317          421             dfs FNLEN-5,SPACE
132A          422   ;
132A D4 E5 F3 423   VTITLE    asc "Test Disk"
     F4 A0 C4
     E9 F3 EB
1342          424             dfs FNLEN-9,SPACE
:             :        :
```

Figure I.11.1. Using the File Manager Context Block in DOS 4.3

When the INIT handler begins its processing, it knows whether it is processing on behalf of an external user or on behalf of the Command Manager by checking the MSB of the value found in KEYWORD1 (i.e. 0xEC04). If an external user is calling the File Manager, the INIT handler uses the address at bytes 0x0C/0x0D to copy four bytes of data to the VTOCVALS structure as shown in Table

41

I.11.6. The `INIT` handler then begins its generic processing for both an external user and the Command Manager. If the value of the `SEC32` Flag is negative at offset `0x07` (i.e. `FILETYPE`), a volume will be initialized with 32 sectors per track, otherwise the volume will be initialized with 16 sectors per track. The handler uses the address at offset `0x02/0x03` to copy a 24-character upper ASCII Volume Title to the `VTOC` and uses the address at offset `0x08/0x09` to copy a 24-character upper ASCII filename to `FNAME`. The volume is timestamped and the `VTOC` bitmap is created.

Offset	Name	Size	Normal Range	Description
0x00	SECVAL	0x01	0x01–0x0F	number of sectors in catalog
0x01	ENDTRK	0x01	0x12–0x30	number of tracks in volume
0x02	SUBJCT	0x02	0x0000–0xFFFF	volume library (subject) value

Table I.11.6. File Manager VTOCVALS Structure Initialization Data

In the ideal situation the File Manager knows nothing about the Command Manager and the values it parses from the command line keywords. All the information the File Manager requires for processing its commands **must** come from its Context Block and from its workarea buffer. And this is particularly true for `INIT` handler processing. For internal File Manager `INIT` processing the addresses or data found at offsets `0x0C` through `0x11` in the Context Block are not used. However, for external users of the File Manager, `WBADR` must contain an address of a 4-byte `VTOCVALS` structure block containing the values for `SECVAL`, `ENDTRK`, and `SUBJCT` as shown previously in Table I.11.6. Recall that `SECVAL` defines how many sectors will be used for the file catalog, `ENDTRK` specifies the number of tracks in the volume, and `SUBJCT` is the two-byte Volume Library value. The 4-byte `VTOCVALS` structure block, the address for `FNAME`, the address for Volume Title, the Boot Type, and the `SEC32` Flag provide the same information the Command Manager obtains when it parses the A, B, L, and R keywords for the DOS `INIT` command. Figure I.11.1 shows an Assembly Language listing of a File Manager Context Block where bytes `0x0C/0x0D` contain the address of a `VTOCVALS` structure which is located at offsets `0x0E` through `0x11` in the very same Context Block. The structure includes `SECVAL`, `ENDTRK`, and the two-byte variable `SUBJCT`. Yes, surprise! It's a thoroughly good use of the Context Block variables `TSLTSADR` and `DATASADR` that normally reside at offsets `0x0E` through `0x11` but are otherwise unused by the `FMINITCD` command code.

Understand that the File Manager uses only its **own** Context Block that resides within DOS memory on page `0xBF`. `GETFMCB` can be called to obtain the address of that Context Block so that its individual parameters can be modified. *FID* maintains its own copy of the 18-byte Context Block, modifies it as needed, and then copies it back in its entirety into DOS address space before calling `CALLFM`. Upon return from the File Manager, *FID* copies the entire Context Block again into its own address space before looking at the return code `RTNCODE` value. The File Manager Context Block resides in the interface area of DOS 4.3, the address space that is **not** within the Language Card memory, so the use of Soft Switches is unnecessary to read and to overwrite this Context Block.

Table I.11.7 shows all the possible error codes that can be reported by DOS 4.3, and the source or sources of those error codes: Command Manager (`CMD`), File Manager (`FM`), or `RWTS`. In DOS 4.3 the

42

File Manager uses a table lookup algorithm to translate an RWTS error code into a File Manager error code that can be reported by DOS. The actual value of the RWTS error code is shown in parenthesis. An RWTS Initialization Error message "Volume Format Error" was added to the Error and Display Message Text table as well as the "Catalog Full" and "Volume Locked" error messages.

Error #	CMD	FM	RWTS	Error Message Text
0	√	√	√	Ring bell and print two <rtn>
1	√			Clock Not Found
2	√	√		Range Error
3			√ (0x08)	Volume Format Error
4	√		√ (0x10)	Volume Write Protected
5	√	√		End of Data
6		√		File Not Found
7	√		√ (0x20)	Volume Number Mismatch
8			√ (0x40)	I/O Error
9		√		Volume Full
10		√		File Locked
11	√		√ (0x30)	Syntax Error
12	√			No Buffers Available
13	√			File Type Mismatch
14	√			Program Too Large
15	√			Not Direct Command
16		√		Catalog Full
17		√		Volume Locked

Table I.11.7. DOS 4.3 Error Messages and Sources

It is always the responsibility of the user to utilize the RWTS I/O Context Block and the File Manager Context Block rationally and with great care. If any context block value is not within its normal value range, unpredictable results should be expected. By design, the Command Manager always supplies values for these context blocks that are within their normal operational range. But the external user carries the full burden in selecting context block values that will provide the intended results. For example, if SECVAL is initialized to 0x00 or to any value greater than 0x0F, and the File Manager Context Block OPCODE is set to the FMINITCD command code, the target volume's VTOC will never initialize and DOS 4.3 will likely hang. Table I.11.6 shows that setting SECVAL to a value greater than 0x0F is not within its normal range and there may very well be unexpected results.

To what extent does an external user of RWTS or of the File Manager expect in "hand holding" vis-à-vis the values he selects for a context block entry? That is the question I grapple with in trying to decide whether I should try and "fix" a user's value, refuse to continue processing with that value, or simply allow the processing to continue knowing full well that something will undoubtedly break. There is only so much code space and "hand holding" is expensive code depending upon its depth. DOS 4.3 is designed to provide its intended results when its context blocks contain rational values that are within their normal operational range. That is all a user can and should expect. If a user is intent on breaking RWTS or the File Manager nothing will stand in his way.

It is always a good policy to test and experiment on diskette volumes that are clearly identified as "Test Disk #nnn" when testing a new program whether that program is written in Applesoft, assembly language, Fortran, or even Pascal. Even an EXEC file should be tested first on volumes that are exclusively used for experimentation. No one is immune to mistakes, but carelessly using either one of these context blocks irrationally will surely cause very unwanted results, perhaps even the complete loss of data. Therefore, I say again, it is always the responsibility of the user to utilize both of these context blocks rationally and with very great care.

The complete list of File Manager commands and the parameters and buffers that are needed or required by these commands is shown in Figure I.11.2.

0x Offset:	00	01	02	03	04	05	06	07	08	09	0A	0B	0C	0D	0E	0F	10	11
Command	Op-code	Sub-code	Record Length / Record Number / Filename Address		Volume	Drive	Slot	File Type	Filename Address / One Data Byte / Range Address		Return Status	Phase	Workarea Buffer Address		T/S List Buffer Address		Date Sector Buffer Address	
NO OPERATION	0x00										Return Status	Phase Value						
OPEN	0x01		Record Length or 0x0000		V	D	S	File Type	Filename Address									
CLOSE	0x02																	
READ	0x03	See Table I.11.4	Record Number		Byte Offset		Range Length		One Data Byte or Range Address						T/S List Buffer Address		Data Sector Buffer Address	
WRITE	0x04																	
DELETE	0x05				V	D	S		Filename Address				Workarea Buffer Address					
CATALOG	0x06	R KEYWORD				D	S											
LOCK	0x07				V	D	S		Filename Address						T/S List Buffer Address			
UNLOCK	0x08				V	D	S											
RENAME	0x09		New Filename Address		V	D	S											
POSITION	0x0A		Record Number		Byte Offset													
INIT	0x0B	Boot Type	Volume Title Address		V	D	S	SEC32 Flag					VTOCVALS Address		SECVAL Value	ENDTRK Value	SUBJCT Value	
VERIFY	0x0C				V	D	S		Filename Address				Workarea Buffer Address		T/S List Buffer Address		Data Sector Buffer Address	
URM	0x0D				V	D	S											
TOUCH	0x0E				V	D	S											
TS	0x0F	Sector Index	Track Value	Sector Value	V	D												
WTS	0x10				V	D	S	Data Byte										

Figure I.11.2. File Manager Command Parameter List

12. DOS 4.3 Data Structures

The Data Structures, or areas where data is found in DOS 3.3 are spread out between the various managers. Those variables used by the Command Manager are found after the Command Manager. Those variables used by the File Manager are found after the File Manager. The RWTS IOCB is found in the middle of all the RWTS routines. I thought DOS 4.3 should have better organization of the various collections of variables and data structures, and therefore reduce the number of addresses required to indirectly access any single variable or data structure if that is what is desired.

The CMDVALS Data structure and File Manager Workarea Data structure reside after the two pages of memory that is needed for the working VTOC and Catalog buffers in DOS 4.3. These two structures require nearly a half page of memory. The five File Manager file buffers follow the Workarea Data structure. Quite a few software tools such as *Big Mac* and *Lisa* require access to several internal variables from the CMDVALS structure. *Big Mac* requires the internal values of LOADLEN and DRVAL, and it needs the addresses of what DOS considers to be the true CSWL and KSWL handlers. *Lisa* also requires the internal values of LOADLEN and DRVAL. There is no telling how many other software utilities and programs that exist which require values from these DOS internal data structures in order to complete their processing functions. DOS 4.3 provides easy access to any variable within the CMDVALS and the Workarea Data structures shown in Tables I.12.1 and I.12.2, respectively. Even though these variables are in Language Card Bank 2 memory, the MNGVALS routine shown in Table I.8.1 can be used to access or change any of these values. Figure I.12.1 shows an example assembly language routine to access and change the DRVAL variable within CMDVALS.

```
   :              :          :
 0800            8          enz
   :              :          :
 002A           19   DRVALOFF equ $2A
 BFF4           20   MNGVALS  equ $BFF4
   :              :          :
 094A           32   ; Get the DRVAL value.
 094A 18        33          clc
 094B A0 2A     33          ldy #DRVALOFF
 094D 20 91 09  35          jsr MNGVAL
 0950 8E 90 09  36          stx DRIVE
 0952           37   ;
 0952           38   ; Change the DRVAL value.
 0952 38        39          sec
 0953 A0 2A     40          ldy #DRVALOFF
 0955 AD 90 09  41          lda DRIVE
 0958 20 91 09  42          jsr MNGVAL
   :              :          :
 0990           65   DRIVE    hex 00
 0991 B8        66   MNGVAL   clv
 0992 6C F4 BF  67          jmp (MNGVALS)
   :              :          :
```

Figure I.12.1. Accessing and Changing CMDVALS in DOS 4.3

Offset	Name	Size	Description
0x00	CURSTATE	0x01	0x00 = warm-start state 0x01 = READ state 0x02 = VALUE state 0x80 = cold-start state
0x01	CSWSTATE	0x01	CSWL intercept state number
0x02	CMDLNIDX	0x01	Apple command line offset
0x03	CMDINDX	0x01	Index of last command * 2
0x04	KEYWORD1	0x01	First keyword table byte
0x05	KEYWORD2	0x01	Second keyword table byte
0x06	ASAVE	0x01	A-register save
0x07	XSAVE	0x01	X-register save
0x08	YSAVE	0x01	Y-register save
0x09	SSAVE	0x01	S-register save
0x0A	BUFRADR	0x02	Current file buffer address
0x0C	EXECBUFR	0x02	EXEC file buffer address
0x0E	CSWLSAV	0x02	True CSWL handler address
0x10	KSWLSAV	0x02	True KSWL handler address
0x12	MAXFILES	0x01	MAXFILES value
0x13	MONFLAGS	0x01	0x10 = Output 0x20 = Input 0x40 = Command
0x14	DIRTS	0x02	Catalog track and sector values
0x16	TSSAV	0x02	TS and WTS track and sector values
0x18	FRESPC	0x02	Last catalog free space value
0x1A	FILELAST	0x02	File end address
0x1C	FILESTRT	0x02	File start address
0x1E	FILELEN	0x02	File length in bytes
0x20	CLKSLOT	0x01	Clock slot
0x21	CLKINDEX	0x01	Clock data index
0x22	CLKTIME	0x06	See Table I.5.3 for variable order
0x28	SLOTVAL	0x02	S keyword, slot value
0x2A	DRVAL	0x02	D keyword, drive value
0x2C	VOLVAL	0x02	V keyword, volume value
0x2E	ADRVAL	0x02	A keyword, address value
0x30	LENVAL	0x02	L keyword, length value
0x32	RECVAL	0x02	R keyword, record value
0x34	BYTVAL	0x02	B keyword, byte value
0x36	LOADLEN	0x02	LOAD and BLOAD length
0x38	MONVAL	0x01	MON/NOMON value
0x39	STKSAVE	0x01	Stack save
0x3A	ALLOCNTR	0x01	Allocation counter
0x3B	URMFLAG	0x01	Undelete flag
0x3C	NEXTON	0x01	Offset to calculate next ON phase
0x3D	NEXTOFF	0x01	Offset to calculate next OFF phase

Table I.12.1. CMDVALS Data Structure Definition

Offset	Name	Size	Description
0x3E	FRTSTRK	0x01	First T/S track
0x3F	FRTSSEC	0x01	First T/S sector
0x40	CURTSTRK	0x01	Current T/S track
0x41	CURTSSEC	0x01	Current T/S sector
0x42	CURDATRK	0x01	Current data track
0x43	CURDASEC	0x01	Current data sector
0x44	DSKFLAGS	0x01	0x02 = VTOC has changed 0x40 = DATA buffer has changed 0x80 = T/S buffer has changed
0x45	DIRSECIX	0x01	Directory sector index
0x46	DIRBYTIX	0x01	Directory byte index
0x47	SECPERTS	0x01	T/S entries in a sector
0x48	FILEBYTE	0x01	Current file byte
0x49	RELSFRST	0x02	Relative sector to first sector
0x4B	RELSLAST	0x02	Relative sector to last sector
0x4D	RELSLRD	0x02	Relative sector to just read sector
0x4F	FILEPOSN	0x02	Current file position
0x51	OPNRCLEN	0x02	File open record length
0x53	RECNUMBR	0x02	Current record number
0x55	BYTEOFFS	0x02	Current byte offset
0x57	SECCNT	0x02	Sector count
0x59	CURTRACK	0x01	Current track
0x5A	NEXTSECR	0x01	Next sector
0x5B	SECBTMAP	0x04	Sector bitmap
0x5F	FYPTE	0x01	File Type (^0x80 = locked)
0x60	SLOT16	0x01	Slot number times 16
0x61	DRVNUMBR	0x01	Drive number
0x62	VOLNUMBR	0x01	Volume number
0x63	TRKNUMBR	0x01	Track number

Table I.12.2. File Manager Workarea Data Structure Definition

DOS 4.3 must have at least one File Manager File buffer allocated, which is all that *Lisa* actually requires and uses, surprisingly. Even the DOS CATALOG command requires one free file buffer. However, reducing the number of file buffers in DOS 4.3 using the DOS MAXFILES command does not provide the user with any additional program memory as it does in DOS 3.3 and DOS 4.1L. Table I.12.3 shows the contents of a file buffer which is 582 (0x246) bytes in size: one memory page (256 bytes) for the data buffer DATABUFR, one memory page for the track/sector buffer TSBUFFER, 38 bytes for the working variables buffer WORKAREA, 24 bytes for the filename buffer FILNAMBF, and 8 bytes for the addresses of WORKAREA, TSBUFFER, DATABUFR, and NXTFNADR. NXTFNADR holds the address of FILNAMBF for the next (not necessarily following) file buffer, much like a single-direction linked-list address. If the address in NXTFNADR is 0x0000, there are no more next-linked file buffers.

Offset	Name	Size	Description
Data and Track/Sector Buffers			
0x000	DATABUFR	0x100	I/O data buffer
0x100	TSBUFFER	0x100	T/S buffer
WORKAREA – File Manager Workarea Variables			
0x200	TSFRSTTS	0x02	T/S of first T/S List for file
0x202	TSCURRTS	0x02	T/S of current T/S List for file
0x204	TSCURDAT	0x02	T/S of current data sector
0x206	WAFLAGS	0x01	0x02 = VTOC has changed 0x40 = DATA buffer has changed 0x80 = T/S buffer has changed
0x207	SECATOFF	0x01	Sector offset into catalog
0x208	BYCATOFF	0x01	Byte offset into catalog
0x209	MAXTSECR	0x01	Maximum entries in one T/S list
0x20A	BYSECOFF	0x01	Current sector byte offset
0x20B	SECFRSTS	0x02	Offset of first sector in current T/S List
0x20D	SECLASTS	0x02	Offset of last sector in current T/S List
0x20F	SECLSTRD	0x02	Relative sector number last read
0x211	SECRPOST	0x02	Current relative position in sector
0x213	RECDLNGH	0x02	Fixed record length
0x215	RECURNUM	0x02	Current record number
0x217	BYRECOFF	0x02	Byte offset into current record
0x219	SECFILEN	0x02	Length of file in sectors
0x21B	CURALOTR	0x01	Current track that is allocated
0x21C	SECALOTR	0x01	Next sector to allocate in track
0x21D	SECFRETR	0x04	Bitmap of free sectors in CURALOTR
0x221	WAFILTYP	0x01	File Type (^0x80 = locked)
0x222	WASLTNUM	0x01	Slot number times 16
0x223	WADRVNUM	0x01	Drive number
0x224	WAVOLNUM	0x01	Volume number
0x225	WATRKNUM	0x01	Track number
Filename Buffer			
0x226	FILNAMBF	0x18	Upper ASCII filename
Addresses of Buffer Locations			
0x23E	WABUFADR	0x02	Address of WORKAREA
0x240	TSBUFADR	0x02	Address of TSBUFFER
0x242	DABUFADR	0x02	Address of DATABUFR
0x244	NXTFNADR	0x02	Address of next FILNAMBF

Table I.12.3. File Manager File Buffer Definition

I have changed the order and the size of some of the variables in the workarea buffer shown in Tables I.12.2 and I.12.3 from the order they are found in DOS 3.3. As long as the workarea definition is consistent in both tables there will be no processing problems. I made those changes in order to reduce the number of routines necessary to copy variables to and from a file's workarea buffer and the File Manager's copy of the workarea buffer. I provided *FID* with the same changes to its copy of the workarea buffer as well.

I found it absolutely necessary to add two additional variables to the INITVALS Data Structure found in DOS 4.1 as shown in Table I.8.5. These two variables are FIRSTCAT and LASTRACK at offsets 0x0D and 0x0E, respectively. At first glance these two variables look exactly like SECVAL and ENDTRK which are part of the VTOCVALS structure. In the DOS 4.3 source code FIRSTCAT and SECVAL are set to the same value as are LASTRACK and ENDTRK. SECVAL and ENDTRK are working variables in that their values can be changed by the Command Manager or by an external user of the File Manager Context Block. FIRSTCAT and LASTRACK are reference variables in that their values are transferred to SECVAL and ENDTRK, respectively, when the Command Manager determines that the values it finds in the A keyword or in the B keyword are out of range. Now, the user can set FIRSTCAT and LASTRACK to any default value without having to reassemble DOS 4.3. Figure I.12.2 shows another example assembly language routine that is used in *Lisa* to obtain the value of LOADLEN that is added to BUFR to obtain the address where the data ends that was just read into memory. MNGVALS always returns the requested value in the X-register and the next value in the A-register whether it is used or not. However, MNGVALS can only write the value in the A-register as shown in Figure I.12.1. As long as the value in the Y-register is less than CVALSLEN (0x64), MNGVALS will return the Carry flag clear.

```
  :              :              :
0002           3   BUFR      epz $02
0800           4             enz
  :              :              :
000E           9   LDLENNDX  equ $36
BFF4          10   MNGVALS   equ $BFF4
  :              :              :
0917 18       32             clc
0918 A0 36    33             ldy #LDLENNDX
091A 20 91 09 34             jsr MNGVAL
091D 48       35             pha
091E 8A       36             txa
091F 65 02    37             adc BUFR
0921 85 02    38             sta BUFR
0923 68       39             pla
0924 65 03    40             adc BUFR+1
0926 85 03    41             sta BUFR+1
  :              :              :
0991 B8       66   MNGVAL    clv
0992 6C F4 BF 67             jmp (MNGVALS)
  :              :              :
```

Figure I.12.2. Lisa Reading LOADLEN Value in DOS 4.3

13. DOS 4.3 Clock Access

I applaud the individual (rarely, if at all, do teams of individuals do anything significant) who designed the concept of using signature and identification bytes in firmware in order to identify the hardware of a peripheral slot card. All clock cards made for the Apple][conform to the policy of using a `PHP` instruction for the first byte, an `SEI` instruction for the second byte, and either `0x03` or `0x07` for the clock ID which is the last byte of its peripheral-card ROM memory, or firmware. DOS 4.3 uses this policy to determine if a peripheral slot contains a clock card, and it starts looking in slot 7 and stops looking after slot 1 if a clock card has not been found. When the `FINDCLK` search routine finds a clock card, the routine issues a "Clock Colon Command" which commands the clock card to produce its most generic date and time data output, i.e. "`mo/dd hh:mi:ss`" or "`mo/dd/yy hh:mi:ss`". In this data `mo` is month, `dd` is day, `yy` is year, `hh` is hour, `mi` is minute, and `ss` is second. Some clock firmware includes the number of the week's day "`w`" before the date and time, or some firmware might include a period and a three-digit millisecond suffix to the seconds' data.

Clock cards from different manufactures differ only in the number of space characters (i.e. `0xA0`) that are used at the beginning of the data stream. In order to increase the efficiency of the `READCLK` routine, the `FINDCLK` search routine parses the clock data output and determines an index value where the Month data begins. The clock card I designed and built as well as the TimeMaster clock card both model the "Clock Colon Command" after the Thunderclock card. These two clock cards produce a year value whereas the Thunderclock card does not. (Why the Thunderclock slot card became the de facto standard is beyond my comprehension. Maybe it was the first clock card marketed for the Apple? So, what! Maybe it was well integrated into ProDOS. Again, so what! Not being able to produce a year value was just wrong, and definitely shortsighted.)

As mentioned above, in order to efficiently process the clock data generated by a Clock card, an index to the Month data is initially determined: there must be either no data before the month value or there must be at least one space before the month value. It does not matter what precedes that space, or what the separators are between the date and the time values. The separators can be " ", "/", ":", or even ";". Table I.13.1 lists the known clock cards that are supported by DOS 4.3, the raw data string the card generates when a "Clock Colon Command" is issued (where "`x`" can be any data), and the index that the `FINDCLK` routine determines for that data string. The `READCLK` routine uses that index to begin extracting the date and time values, and substituting in `YEARVAL` (see Table I.8.5) if it is parsing Thunderclock slot card data. If `READCLK` is not parsing Thunderclock slot card data, `READCLK` assumes the date data contains a year value.

Clock Card	Index Value	Raw Data String
Thunderclock card	0	`mo/dd hh;mi;ss`
unknown clock card	1	`mo/dd/yy hh:mi:ss`
unknown clock card	2	`x mo/dd/yy hh:mi:ss`
Vrbancic Clock card	3	`"w mo/dd/yy hh:mi:ss`
TimeMaster Clock card	3	`"w mo/dd/yy hh:mi:ss`
unknown clock card	4	`xxx mo/dd/yy hh:mi:ss`
unknown clock card	5	`xxxx mo/dd/yy hh:mi:ss`

Table I.13.1. Supported Clock Cards in DOS 4.3

14. DOS 4.3 Error Processing

Whether an Applesoft or Binary program is executing instructions, if Applesoft is **not** running, or if Applesoft is running and the ASONERR (page-zero 0xD8) flag has its MSB **clear**, the first step in DOS 4.3 error processing is to beep the speaker and print the error message text as shown in Table I.11.7. Applesoft is defined to be running when ASRUN (page-zero 0x76) is **not** equal to 0xFF **and** PROMPT (page-zero 0x33) is **not** equal to the "]" character. Conversely, Applesoft is defined to be **not** running when ASRUN equals 0xFF **or** when PROMPT equals "]". If Applesoft is running and the MSB of ASONERR is **set**, the error message is not printed and DOS exits indirectly into Applesoft at ROM address 0xD865 by means of ERRORADR. If an error message is printed, the next step in error processing is started where DOS restores its keyboard and video intercepts, and exits indirectly into Applesoft at ROM address 0xD43C by means of WARMADR. See Table I.8.5 for the offsets of WARMADR, COLDADR, ERRORADR, and RESETADR in the INITVALS structure.

Applesoft programs can handle their own DOS error processing by using the "ONERR GOTO <*line number*>" command in order to prevent instant program termination. Assembly language programs need to do a little more work: store 0xFF to ASONERR, 0x00 to ASRUN and PROMPT, and replace the address stored at ERRORADR with the address of your own error handler. DOS 4.3 will load the X-register with the appropriate DOS error number as shown in Table I.11.7 before exiting indirectly to ERRORADR (or WARMADR for that matter if Applesoft is **not** running). As shown previously in Table I.9.1, calling PRTERADR using an indirect JMP instruction with the appropriate DOS error number stored in the X-register will print the corresponding DOS error message text without beeping the speaker and without printing a carriage return after the error message text. *Big Mac*, for example, utilizes PRTERADR for printing all DOS errors it encounters as shown previously in the assembly language routine of Figure I.9.5. In that code example *Big Mac* sets the X-register to 0x00 before the first call to PRTERROR in order to beep the speaker and print two carriage returns. Then *Big Mac* loads the X-register with the actual error number, calls PRTERROR, and then prints a final carriage return. There is absolutely no need to duplicate the PRTERROR routine into the *Big Mac* source code because the Page 0x03 vector for PRTERADR is so conveniently located at memory address 0x3E8.

Section I.6 introduced the error message "Volume Full" in terms of the status of the VTOC bitmap and Section I.7 introduced the error message "Catalog Full" in terms of the status of the catalog sectors. Both of these error conditions were reported as a "DISK FULL" error in DOS 3.3. Not that DOS 3.3 was seriously wrong in combining both error conditions into a single error message, I simply believe the user is far better off knowing what actually triggered the error condition. DOS 4.3 accurately provides meaningful error messages when error conditions develop.

Both the Video Intercept routine and the Keyboard Intercept routine in the Command Manager save the contents of the registers and the current stack pointer into the CMDVALS structure before those routines do any processing. The File Manager also saves the current stack pointer into its own variable in the CMDVALS structure before it does any of its processing. However, the supporting routines for both these managers in DOS 3.3 strive to maintain the integrity of the stack pointer throughout their processing even though the stack pointer will eventually be restored once the processing completes. Many unnecessary instructions such as PLA are utilized in order to maintain stack pointer integrity. Even when error conditions occur great effort is made in order to maintain stack pointer integrity. Why? Why bother saving the stack pointer in the first place if it isn't going to be utilized? Error conditions in DOS 3.3 as well as in DOS 4.3 are terminal conditions. There is simply no reason to continue any further processing because whatever intermediate results that have been obtained thus far are probably wrong anyway. If Applesoft does not handle the DOS error, the DOS 4.3 Command Manager resets the stack pointer and performs a DOS warm-start. The File Manager restores its stack pointer due to any error condition it encounters. This is how both managers avoid stack overflow.

Pointer Addresses	Start Program	Smaller Program	Problematic Program	Bigger Program
	0x0000	0x0000	0x0000	0x0000
PRGTAB — 0x67/0x68	0x0801 Start Applesoft Program	0x0801 Small Chained Applesoft Program	0x0801 Problematic Chained Applesoft Program	0x0801 Big Chained Applesoft Program
PRGEND — 0xAF/0xB0 VARTAB — 0x69/0x6A	Simple Variables			
ARYTAB — 0x6B/0x6C	Array Variables			
STREND — 0x6D/0x6E				
	Free Space			
FRETOP — 0x6F/0x70				
	Character String Pool			
HIMEM — 0x73/0x74				
	0xFFFF	0xFFFF	0xFFFF	0xFFFF

Figure I.15.1. Example Applesoft Program Layout in Memory

15. DOS 4.3 Chain Command

DOS 4.3 includes a real CHAIN command in its command repertoire that is designed specifically for Applesoft programs. Having a native CHAIN command is far more convenient than having to include an assembly language utility on each and every application volume for those programs requiring this capability. However, careful considerations must be made when designing Applesoft programs that chain to each other.

The purpose of the DOS CHAIN command is to move two areas of memory where they reside for the "Start" program to where they need to reside for the "Chained" program. These two areas of memory include the Simple Variables and the Array Variables, or SAVs for short. Figure I.15.1 shows a typical Start Applesoft program residing in memory. In that figure Free Space exists because the Start Program, its SAVs, and its Character String Pool memory area do not exceed the value stored in HIMEM at page-zero 0x73/0x74 minus 0x0801, the memory address where the Start program begins. The Start program must never chain to another program whose size will exceed its available Free Space.

Applesoft uses a very large number of page-zero memory locations for its use. Many of these locations are to store addresses in low/high byte order that can easily be used as pointers in memory management routines. DOS always loads an Applesoft program into memory at address 0x0801, which is the value found in PRGTAB at page-zero 0x67/0x68. The DOS LOAD command knows the program's size in bytes before it actually loads the file into memory because it reads the file's first data sector and examines the first two bytes of that sector, the program size. Using the program size DOS can calculate the end address of the program, and save that information in PRGEND at page-zero 0xAF/0xB0. Initially, DOS will set VARTAB to PRGEND and Applesoft will set ARYTAB and STREND to PRGEND and FRETOP to HIMEM. The DOS MAXFILES command cannot be used to change HIMEM and FRETOP in DOS 4.3. Thus, all Applesoft programs written for DOS 4.3 should consider setting CONFIG Bit 3 (see Table III.1.2) or not use the DOS MAXFILES command.

When the Applesoft program starts to execute its instructions, the program will begin to create simple variables that include real numbers, integers, and string pointers. These variables and pointers reside in the Simple Variables area of memory as simple descriptors starting in VARTAB at page-zero 0x69/0x6A. The definition of the descriptors for these variables and pointers that comprise the content of the Simple Variables is shown in Table I.15.1. As more and more Simple Variable descriptors are added, the Array Variables area is pushed higher and higher up in memory reducing the size of Free Space. Simple variable descriptors are always seven bytes in size, and depending upon the variable type, some of the descriptor bytes may not even be used. Table I.15.1 shows that real variables require all seven bytes for the variable name, the exponent, and its 4-byte mantissa. Integers require only four bytes for the variable name and its value in **high/low** byte order, leaving the remaining three bytes set to 0x00. Finally, simple strings require five bytes for the variable name, the length of the string in bytes, and the address where the string resides in **low/high** byte order, leaving the remaining two bytes set to 0x00. Obviously, a simple string cannot contain more than 255 bytes since only a single byte is used to define the length of the simple string.

The definition of the descriptors for Applesoft Array Variables is shown in Table I.15.2. As seen in Figure I.15.1 the Array Variables area of memory begins in ARYTAB at page-zero 0x6B/0x6C and ends in STREND at page-zero 0x6D/0x6E. This area of memory contains single and multi-dimensioned array variable descriptors for real numbers, integers, and string pointers. Table I.15.2

shows example variable descriptors having two dimensions. Successive array element dimension sizes **precede** each other with the first-dimension size (**high/low** byte order) always coming **last**. The array variable descriptor grows as the number of dimensions increase in value. The nominal size of an array variable descriptor is seven bytes for a single dimension array. The descriptor increases in size by two additional bytes for each added dimension. Therefore, the dimension value (in Byte 5) becomes a critical piece of information that is used to calculate where the array elements begin relative to the address of the beginning of their array variable descriptor.

Variable Type	Byte Definitions						
	Byte 1	Byte 2	Byte 3	Byte 4	Byte 5	Byte 6	Byte 7
Real Numbers	name1 +ASCII 65	name2 +ASCII 66	Exponent	Mantissa Byte 1	Mantissa Byte 2	Mantissa Byte 3	Mantissa Byte 4
Integer Numbers	name1 -ASCII 195	name2 -ASCII 196	High Value	Low Value	0	0	0
Simple Strings	name1 +ASCII 69	name2 -ASCII 198	String Length	Low Address	High Address	0	0

Table I.15.1. Applesoft Simple Variable Descriptor Definitions

Variable Type	Byte Definitions							
	Byte 1	Byte 2	Byte 3	Byte 4	Byte 5	Byte 6	Byte 7	Byte 8	Byte 9
Real Array	name1 +ASCII 65	name2 +ASCII 66	Low Byte Offset	High Byte Offset	Number of Dimensions K	Size of Kth Dim High Byte	Size of Kth Dim Low Byte	Size of K-1 Dim High Byte	Size of K-1 Dim Low Byte
Integer Array	name1 -ASCII 195	name2 -ASCII 196	Low Byte Offset	High Byte Offset	Number of Dimensions K	Size of Kth Dim High Byte	Size of Kth Dim Low Byte	Size of K-1 Dim High Byte	Size of K-1 Dim Low Byte
String Array	name1 +ASCII 69	name2 -ASCII 198	Low Byte Offset	High Byte Offset	Number of Dimensions K	Size of Kth Dim High Byte	Size of Kth Dim Low Byte	Size of K-1 Dim High Byte	Size of K-1 Dim Low Byte

Table I.15.2. Applesoft Array Variable Descriptor Definitions

Many times, an Applesoft program will contain the text of some string variable. As long as there is no text operation on that string variable such as "A$ = A$ + B$", for example, the text pointer address found in the Simple Variable or in the Array Variable descriptor element will point to the actual string text within the contents of the Applesoft program. In this case the string can never be available to a Chained program. In order for a simple string variable or a string element to be available to a Chained program, the actual string text of that string variable must be relocated into the Character String Pool memory area. A simple way to force this string relocation is to perform some menial text operation on that string variable, such as "A$ = A$ + " "". This simple operation does nothing to string A$ except to cause the actual text of A$ to be copied from within the contents of the Applesoft program into the contents of the Character String Pool memory area.

The purpose of the DOS CHAIN command is to move the SAVs of the Start program to the end of the Chained program, and to update PRGEND, VARTAB, and ARYTAB with their new addresses so that the Chained program may access those variables and strings of the Start program. Because of some required Applesoft calls, even FRETOP needs to be reinitialized. When the Chained program is smaller than the Start program or when the Chained program is larger than the Start program plus the size of the SAVs area, there is no problem in copying the SAVs directly to their new location. However, if the end of the Chained program occurs somewhere within the SAVs area of the Start program, there will be disaster if the SAVs are copied directly. Due to how the Monitor memory move routine is implemented, if the SAVs area of memory is copied in this particular situation, the move routine will begin to overwrite the same area of memory it is attempting to copy. And this will certainly lead to disaster for the Chained program because some of the variable descriptors of the Start program will be overwritten and, therefore, destroyed. If the SAVs area is copied in reverse order (high memory to low memory) to the end of this problematic Chained program, disaster will also occur when that algorithm is used to copy the SAVs area for a Chained program that is smaller than the Start program. The CHAIN routine can either refuse to perform the chain operation and signal an error message in those situations, or it can utilize another algorithm to copy the SAVs.

Another algorithm is to copy the SAVs to the address in STREND for the Start program and set PRGEND and VARTAB to that address as long as there is enough memory in Free Space. PRGEND does not necessarily have to be exactly the address where the Chained program ends in memory, technically at its triple-nulls. In fact, an Applesoft program may include attached assembly language subroutines that follow the Applesoft triple-null ending giving the program a different physical length and end address. The DOS SAVE command uses PRGTAB and PRGEND to calculate the number of bytes to save, and not necessarily the address where the triple-nulls occur in memory minus 0x0801. However, this option does potentially waste a good deal of memory if the SAVs area is large in size and there is adequate Free Space.

The better algorithm would be to always copy the SAVs up in memory to FRETOP and then copy them again down in memory to the new PRGEND. Unfortunately, the first memory copy would require a negatively-indexed memory move algorithm (the pointers are decremented, not incremented), which is not for the faint-of-heart due to its difficulty and complexity. Also, a negatively-indexed memory move algorithm requires more CPU instructions than a simple positively-indexed memory move algorithm. The second memory copy would require a straight-forward positively-indexed memory move algorithm like the one found in the Monitor ROM. Fortunately, there was enough code space in DOS 4.3 to implement this far superior and correct algorithm. The user can utilize the DOS 4.3 CHAIN command to their heart's content and rest assured that CHAIN will always place the SAVs fully intact precisely where the Chained program ends with the single caveat already mentioned: the Start program must never chain to a Chained program whose size will exceed the available Free Space.

If the R keyword is **not** used with the CHAIN command, CHAIN will call the Applesoft ROM routine GARBAG at memory address 0xE484 before it moves the Simple Variable and Array Variable descriptors to their new location at the end of the Chained program. The GARBAG routine utilizes an algorithm similar in concept to a basic bubble sort algorithm to remove all unreferenced string data from the Character String Pool memory area, thus compacting the Character String Pool before CHAIN relocates the SAVs in memory. The processing time for GARBAG to collect all the little bits and pieces of unreferenced strings is proportional to the square of the number of strings in use. That is, if there are 100 active strings it will take four times longer to process those strings than if there had been only 50 active strings.

Many Garbage Collection algorithms have been previously published that accomplish the same results as GARBAG in far less time, but there can be a number of caveats when using some of these algorithms. For instance, normal Applesoft programs save all string data in lower ASCII, i.e. with the MSB of each string byte cleared. Furthermore, normal Applesoft programs never allow more than one string descriptor to point to the same exact copy of that string data in memory. Multiple string descriptors may each point to identical string data, but those sets of string data must reside at different memory addresses. Some Garbage Collection algorithms depend upon these constraints. If either constraint is not true, a catastrophe will happen during the course of subsequent Applesoft processing! Of course, if the Applesoft program's string data is normal, there will be no subsequent problems. Only if assembly language appendages to the Applesoft program or other code segments perform exotic manipulations to string descriptors or to the Character String Pool data might these constraints be violated. The Applesoft Garbage Collector is discussed in more detail in Section II.4.

If an efficient Garbage Collection routine is available, the user should invoke that routine before using the DOS CHAIN command, and utilize the R keyword to bypass calling GARBAG from within chain processing. There is always the dilemma in finding that balance between making the Applesoft Start program and Chained programs smaller in order to accommodate an external and complex assembly language Garbage Collection routine, or enlarging the Applesoft Start program and Chained programs and strategically placing many Applesoft FRE(aexpr) commands throughout the programs. The FRE(aexpr) command calls GARBAG which will process the Character String Pool more efficiently if there are fewer inactive strings or little unreferenced string data. Again, there is always the dilemma in finding that balance for the best strategy in ensuring that memory is utilized as efficiently as possible.

Routine, Table, or Buffer	DOS 4.3		ProDOS	
	Bytes	Cycles	Bytes	Cycles
PRENIBL	36	10557	172	6331
POSTNIBL	23	9524	n/a	
READSCTR	84	11207	206	11248
WRITSCTR	128	11419	222	11420
RDNIBL	106		106	
WRTNIBL	64		n/a	
BITNIBL	n/a		256	
NBUF1	256		n/a	
NBUF2	86		86	
Total	783	42707	1048	28999

Table I.16.1. Comparison of DOS 4.3 and ProDOS RWTS

16. ProDOS Disk I/O Algorithm

I have no idea whether Apple or Axlon, the manufacture of the RAM Disk 320, developed the fast disk read algorithm. As described in section V.11, the RAM Disk software can transfer the contents of an entire 35-track diskette to one of the RAM Disk drives in only seven seconds, the time to make thirty-five revolutions, one revolution for each track of a Disk][volume. The Axlon software locates track 0x00 on the Disk][volume, clears a sixteen byte "sector read" table, and reads the first sector data header it encounters. It does not matter which sector data header the routine finds first. The software notes the sector number and proceeds to read the sector data putting the first eighty-six bytes it reads into a buffer called NBUF2 as shown in Table I.16.1. These eighty-six bytes contain the lower two bits for each of the next three groups of data bytes about to be read. The first group of data bytes is comprised of eighty-six bytes, where each byte is OR'd with its lower two bits obtained from a BITNIBL table indexed by the respective byte from NBUF2, and stored directly into the designated RAM Disk sector. The second group of data bytes is comprised of another eighty-six bytes, similarly processed, and stored in the designated RAM Disk sector. The last eighty-four data bytes are similarly processed and stored in the designated RAM Disk sector, now totaling 0x100 data bytes. The final byte read is the checksum byte. If the checksum calculation is 0x00 then no read error is flagged and the "sector read" table is updated with this sector number marked as read. Once the "sector read" table is complete the Axlon software moves on to the next Disk][volume track, clears the "sector read" table, and processes that track. The Axlon software is finished when it has read and processed track 0x34.

The ProDOS version of the fast disk read algorithm is essentially the same as the Axlon version except that ProDOS incorporates the contents of the WRTNIBL table into the unused portion of the ProDOS BITNIBL table. Since only three of every four bytes are needed for NBUF2 processing, it made sense to utilize the unused fourth byte for its WRTNIBL table. Axlon did not provide a fast disk write algorithm so there was no need to incorporate the WRTNIBL table in the Axlon BITNIBL table. Closer inspection of the two algorithms indicates to me that the Axlon version is a little cleaner programmatically. Perhaps Axlon obtained the ProDOS version and tweaked it some? If I had seen the ProDOS version initially I would have made the same modifications Axlon did. I cannot imagine the reverse taking place where Apple obtained the Axlon version and purposefully sabotaged it. I could be wrong. Whatever the case, the algorithm is clever and it works well, and there is no need for a POSTNIBL routine in either algorithm. However, the READSCTR routine that implements the ProDOS fast disk read algorithm is nearly twice the size of the combined DOS 4.3 READSCTR and POSTNIBL routines: 206 bytes versus 107 bytes, respectively. The ProDOS READSCTR routine also takes a few more startup processing cycles than the DOS 4.3 READSCTR routine. ProDOS requires the BITNIBL table for its data processing and DOS 4.3 requires the NBUF1 buffer for its data processing. The ProDOS BITNIBL table and the DOS 4.3 NBUF1 buffer are the same size, but the BITNIBL table also includes the WRTNIBL table, a table that is a standalone table in DOS 4.3. To read and process a DOS 4.3 sector takes 20,731 cycles, or 20.73 milliseconds. ProDOS takes 11.25 milliseconds to read and process a sector. In order for ProDOS to read a block of data it must read two sectors sequentially.

The processing time for the ProDOS version of its fast disk write algorithm is essentially the same as the DOS 4.3 algorithm, and this is to be expected. Both algorithms must write five 40-μsec sync bytes, three 32-μsec prologue bytes, 343 32-μsec data bytes and checksum, three 32-μsec epilogue bytes, and a final 32-μsec sync byte. However, their algorithm sizes are substantially different and that is because NBUF1 lies on a page boundary for DOS 4.3 and the user data buffer may or may not lie on a page boundary for ProDOS. ProDOS must prenibblize its buffer data in the same way and for the same reason that DOS 4.3 prenibblizes its buffer data. However, ProDOS must modify its WRITSCTR code "on the fly" because it does not utilize an intermediary NBUF1 buffer. ProDOS must determine whether the data buffer address lies on a page boundary, and if not, then which pages contain what portion of the data buffer. There is one exception the ProDOS algorithm must also handle, and that is when the data buffer falls off a page boundary by just one byte. The ProDOS fast disk write algorithm requires 394 bytes for its PRENIBL and WRITSCTR routines, and gets its WRITNIBL table for free. On the other hand, DOS 4.3 requires a mere 164 bytes for its PRENIBL and WRITSCTR routines, but it requires a WRITNIBL table, for a total of 228 bytes which is still 58% the size of the ProDOS memory requirements. To process and write a DOS 4.3 sector takes 21,976 cycles, or 21.98 milliseconds. ProDOS takes 17,751 cycles to process and write a sector, or 17.75 milliseconds. In order for ProDOS to write a block of data it must write two sectors sequentially.

I have been referring to the data in Table I.16.1 that I collected for the information in the above sizing and timing comparison. Overall, the amount of software, table data, and buffer space required by DOS 4.3 to read and write data to and from a diskette totals 783 bytes. ProDOS requires 1048 bytes, a difference of 265 bytes, or an additional page of memory plus nine bytes. This difference in code/data amounts to a 25% increase in memory requirements by ProDOS. The time to read and write a sector of data takes 42.71 milliseconds for DOS 4.3 and 29.00 milliseconds for ProDOS. The ProDOS algorithms are 32% faster than the DOS 4.3 algorithms overall. With these results it is obvious that the extensive use of table data and of self-modifying code alone cannot account for the visible differences the two operating systems demonstrate when reading and writing files.

ProDOS achieves its significant speed difference by employing a sector interleaving (or skewing) such that only two revolutions are required to read all eight data blocks on a track, similar to the technique Apple Fortran and Apple Pascal use for reading their data diskettes. The sectors are arranged such that there is one sector between each of the sectors that comprise a block, and there is one sector between each successive block. Data blocks are read and written in ascending block number (i.e. "2 ascending" skew) in ProDOS and sectors are read and written in descending sector number (i.e. "2 descending" skew) in DOS 4.3. DOS 4.3 employs a sector interleaving such that it is possible to read all 16 sectors on a track in two revolutions, but typically three revolutions are more realistic. For a more complete discussion on sector interleaving refer to Worth's and Lechner's *Beneath Apple DOS*, *Beneath Apple ProDOS*, and *Bag of Tricks*. These references provide the reader with a complete understanding of this rather complicated subject.

One may ask whether DOS 4.3 could benefit from the disk I/O routines in ProDOS. To test this very question, I temporarily removed the code that supports the DOS HELP command and inserted the ProDOS disk I/O routines in place of the DOS 4.3 disk I/O routines. ProDOS also uses the Language Card memory for its disk I/O routines so I thought this would be a fair match. I was astonished, though I should not have been, to learn there was absolutely **no** benefit. Without these disk I/O routines coupled with a "2 ascending" skew sector interleave table, the overall disk I/O throughput did not benefit. DOS 4.3 still uses the "2 descending" skew sector interleave table from DOS 3.3 in order to maintain compatibility to that operating system. The DOS 4.3 disk I/O routines are still perfectly matched for the best data I/O performance possible using its required sector interleave table.

17. Building and Installing DOS 4.3 Images

The source code for DOS 4.3 and its object code `SEGnn` files fit onto two DOS 4.3 volumes. The Image volume called `DOS.4.3.Image` boots *Lisa80* directly, and the volume contains four of the twenty-two DOS 4.3 source files, the six object code files, and the DOS 4.3 linked image file. The *Lisa* `ctrl-P` command is used to create this linked image file from the six object code files so that the complete linked image file can easily be saved onto the Image volume. The Image volume also contains a utility that can install the DOS 4.3 linked image file onto the boot tracks of any volume, and a utility that can copy the DOS 4.3 linked image file onto any other volume simply as a file. For example, `INSTALL` reads the DOS 4.3 linked image file `DOS4.3` from the Image volume in disk drive 1 and installs that image directly onto the boot tracks of any volume in disk drive 2 as if the DOS 4.3 image had been written onto those tracks by the DOS `INIT` command. The utility `DOS1TO2` copies the DOS 4.3 linked image file `DOS4.3` from the Image volume in disk drive 1 onto a volume in disk drive 2 as `DOS4.3`. It is assumed that both disk drives are connected to the disk controller card in slot 6.

It is quite a simple matter to assemble the DOS 4.3 source code found on the DOS 4.3 Source data volume `DOS.4.3.Source`. I imagine it would take some effort to adapt this source code and its directives to another assembler other than *Lisa*. *Lisa* provides all the enhancements and directives necessary as well as the addition of a few new directives that provide a straightforward assembly. The source code is sectioned into many consecutive input files that are linked using a directive, and the generated object code stream is saved into many consecutive output files. In other words, the DOS 4.3 source code does not have to reside in memory *in toto*, and the generated object code files can be linked together at a later time using the *Lisa* `ctrl-P` command. The `ctrl-P` command is not a Linker as found in a compiler; it merely combines into memory a series of object code files sequentially. As discussed in Section V.8, *Lisa* uses Main memory above `0x0800` for object code, source code, and its complete symbol list.

To assemble the DOS 4.3 source code, place the DOS 4.3 Image volume `DOS.4.3.Image` in disk drive 1 and boot. *Lisa80* is automatically started. Enter the `SE` command-line command to select the *SETUP80* utility in order to verify or set the `Start of Source Code` to `0x4000` and the `Start of Symbol List` to `0x7800`. Place the DOS 4.3 Source volume `DOS.4.3.Source` in disk drive 2. Load the `DOS4.3.L` file into memory from disk drive 1 and start the assembler by entering either the `A` or the `Z` command-line command. If a printed version of the screen output is desired simply preface the `A` or the `Z` command with the `P1` command-line command. Six object code files will be created on the DOS 4.3 Image volume named `SEG01` to `SEG06`. The six object code files can be combined in memory sequentially starting at `0x1000` using the `ctrl-P` command. The complete binary image can be saved to the DOS 4.3 Image volume or to any other volume as `DOS4.3` or any other suitable filename.

18. Using DOS 4.3 Commands

I have enhanced many of the original DOS 3.3 commands primarily using the R keyword as a command switch since this keyword has very limited usage other than in the commands EXEC, POSITION, and the Random-Access Data file commands READ and WRITE. All DOS 4.3 commands may be entered in lowercase and/or uppercase. Filenames may also be entered in a mixture of lowercase and uppercase text, and the filenames are treated as case sensitive. For example, the filenames "HELLO" and "Hello" are treated as two different files. In order to make full use of lowercase and uppercase in DOS 4.3, an Apple //e is preferred. DOS 4.3 does function quite nicely on an Apple][or an Apple][+ if it has a character generator ROM (for example, Dan Paymar's *Lowercase Adaptor Interface PROM*) that can display the complete lowercase and uppercase Latin character set. DOS 4.3 does print error messages in mixed case. The enhanced Apple //e ROM also supports lowercase and/or uppercase entry for Applesoft commands. However, in my opinion this ROM continues to have at least two substantial deficiencies: no native DELETE key utilization and the HLIN drawing algorithm is flawed.

There is no consistency in DOS 3.3 in whether to print one or two carriage returns after DOS completes its processing for a command when that command is issued from the Apple command line. Certainly, it would be a mistake to print any additional carriage returns after DOS completes its processing for a command when that command is issued from an Applesoft program or during the processing of an EXEC file. DOS 4.3 does print **one** carriage return after DOS completes its processing for a command when that command is issued from the Apple command line. This policy is to ensure that there will be at least one blank line between all DOS commands issued from the Apple command line. Having this blank line helps to keep each DOS command and its output data as legible as possible on the display screen. Of course, DOS 4.3 does not print any additional carriage returns after DOS completes its processing for a command when that command is issued from an executing Applesoft program or during the processing of an EXEC file. However, DOS commands that are issued from assembly language programs using COUT will appear with the additional carriage return. One way to prevent DOS 4.3 from printing that additional carriage return is to store 0x00 for the variables ASRUN (page-zero 0x76) and PROMPT (page-zero 0x33). When DOS 4.3 checks these variables after DOS completes its processing for a command, it will appear to DOS that Applesoft is running, and therefore, DOS will not print the additional carriage return.

Both DOS 3.3 and DOS 4.3 save files to a disk volume using the file's TSL resources if the file already exists. For example, if the file TEMP already exists and its TSL contains eight track/sector entries, those same entries will be used to save TEMP again whether TEMP is larger or smaller than its initial size. If TEMP is larger, the File Manager will simply request additional data sectors and add them to the file's TSL. If TEMP is edited and the file now uses only three data sectors, the first three track/sector entries in the TSL will be used to save the file and the remaining entries will go unused. In other words, the last five TSL entries in this example will remain allocated to the file and these data sectors will be unavailable for use by any other file. This inherent resource wastefulness for both DOS 3.3 and DOS 4.3 is perpetuated by programs like *FID*. *FID* uses the File Manager to copy files in total, and it assumes that all track/sector entries in a file's TSL belong to that file. But DOS 4.3 introduces a new strategy called "File Delete/File Save". The DOS commands BSAVE, LSAVE, SAVE, and TSAVE can now utilize the B keyword to implement the "File Delete/File Save" strategy. This strategy first deletes the file from the volume Catalog and then saves the file to the same volume in order to ensure that the file's TSL contains only those track/sector entries that are actually required by that file.

II. Apple][ROM Modifications

I presented all my modifications to the Apple CX and D0:F0 ROM space in the DOS 4.1 Manual. These modifications include the correct HLIN Drawing Algorithm, Delete Key Utilization, Apple //e 80-Column Text Card, Apple //e ROM Monitor, and the Apple Character Generator ROM. The DOS 4.1 Manual is available at applecored.net as a PDF. If anyone is interested in exploring the benefits of the modifications I made to the Apple][ROM that I presented in the DOS 4.1 Manual, those ROM images are also available at applecored.net.

The topics I have include in this section are important to DOS 4.3 and they are particularly important to me. I have edited those topics with DOS 4.3 in mind.

In my version of the Apple //e firmware (or ROM) source code, I use the variable HLINMOD for a conditional assembly directive that is used to optionally assemble the original, flawed ROM code or the modified, corrected ROM code. The generated object code can be programmed into either a single 27128 EPROM as found in the Enhanced and Platinum Apple //e or programmed into two 2764 EPROMs for the earlier versions of the Apple //e. The modified contents of the Apple //e character generator ROM that defines each ASCII character in pixels can be programmed into a 2732 EPROM. An EPROM programmer is needed in order to program new EPROMs in order to replace the Apple //e firmware ROM or ROMs (depending on the motherboard) and the character generator ROM. I have not sourced the Apple][+ Autostart ROM. I have no doubt that the contents of the Autostart ROM was the basis for the *Lisa* and the *Big Mac* Monitors, which I have sourced. I do not believe much was changed in the Applesoft interpreter for the Apple //e, except to support the CX ROM space.

```
0xF57A:
        .if HLINMOD
        bcs HF580           ; branch to 0xF580 if set
        asl                 ; times 2
        jsr HF465           ; call 0xF465
HF580   clc                 ; prepare for delta, not diff
        lda ZPGD4           ; 0xD4
        .el
        bcs HF581           ; branch to 0xF581 if set
        asl                 ; times 2
        jsr HF465           ; call 0xF465
        sec                 ; prepare for diff, not delta
HF581   lda ZPGD4           ; 0xD4
        .fi
```

Figure II.1.1. First HLIN Code Adjustment

1. Correct HLIN Drawing Algorithm

I have always disliked the unsymmetrical look of a HIRES diagonal line in either the horizontal or the vertical direction ever since acquiring my Apple][+. And this same HLIN code resides in the Apple //e ROM unchanged, which is shameful. When I was assigned the task to provide all the icons for HomeWord Speller at Sierra On-Line, I analyzed the HLIN algorithm and found that the algorithm does not correctly calculate the delta difference of the horizontal and vertical end points before drawing a line. It is easy to demonstrate this error before and after installing my ROM modifications.

```
0xF5A5:
        .if HLINMOD
        sec                     ; prepare for diff, not delta
        .el
        clc                     ; prepare for delta, not diff
        .fi
```

Figure II.1.2. Second HLIN Code Adjustment

```
10 HOME                      300 HPLOT 100,110
20 HGR                       310 HPLOT TO 101,151
30 HCOLOR= 3                 320 HPLOT TO 139,150
40 HPLOT 10,10               330 HPLOT TO 140,111
50 HPLOT TO 50,10            340 HPLOT TO 100,110
60 HPLOT TO 50,50            350 GOSUB 1000
70 HPLOT TO 10,50            400 HPLOT 200,15
80 HPLOT TO 10,10            410 HPLOT TO 260,10
90 GOSUB 1000                420 HPLOT TO 265,30
100 HPLOT 100,10             430 HPLOT TO 250,35
110 HPLOT TO 140,11          440 HPLOT TO 270,55
120 HPLOT TO 139,50          450 HPLOT TO 255,75
130 HPLOT TO 101,51          460 HPLOT TO 275,100
140 HPLOT TO 100,10          470 HPLOT TO 245,115
150 GOSUB 1000               480 HPLOT TO 215,117
200 HPLOT 10,110             490 HPLOT TO 200,15
210 HPLOT TO 10,150          500 GOSUB 1000
220 HPLOT TO 50,150          900 TEXT : END
230 HPLOT TO 50,110          1000 POKE - 16368,0
240 HPLOT TO 10,110          1010 WAIT - 16384,128
250 GOSUB 1000               1020 RETURN
```

Figure II.1.3. Applesoft HLIN Demonstration Program

There are two locations that require a small code adjustment. The first code adjustment is located at `0xF57A` and that is shown in Figure II.1.1. In that figure `ZPGD4` is the page-zero location `0xD4` and `HF465` is a label for a routine at memory address `0xF465`.

The second code adjustment is located at `0xF5A5` and that is shown in Figure II.1.2. You will be simply amazed at how "lovely" and symmetrical diagonal lines are drawn either left to right, right to left, top to bottom, or bottom to top. And I am appalled that the old code passed any sort of testing and/or code review vis-à-vis how trivial these two modification are and how elegant the results appear.

Figure II.1.3 shows a simple Applesoft program that can be used to demonstrate the visual differences between the original `HLIN` drawing algorithm and the modified drawing algorithm. Figure II.1.4 shows what this Applesoft program visually produces when it runs on an Apple //e without the `HLIN` modification to its ROM firmware.

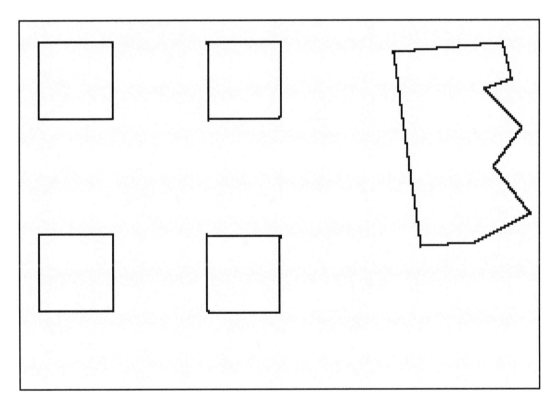

Figure II.1.4. Original ROM HLIN Routine Display

In Figure II.1.4 the two boxes on the left are square boxes and they draw perfectly no matter which direction the lines are drawn. The two middle boxes are nearly square boxes except that the horizontal and vertical line end points differ by one pixel. They show different anomalies depending upon which direction the lines are drawn: the upper middle box is drawn clockwise and the lower middle box is drawn counterclockwise. The shape on the right is drawn clockwise and it shows many odd corner anomalies as the direction and angle of the lines change.

Figure II.1.5 shows what this same Applesoft program produces visually when this program runs on the same Apple //e with the HLIN modification included in its ROM firmware. All corner anomalies disappear without regard to drawing direction, and when the lines are drawn diagonally, the lines are segmented equally. It is obvious from Figure II.1.5 that having the HLIN modifications allows one to draw any shape in any direction and in any order without having to worry about corner anomalies and inconsistent line segmentation.

Obviously, the two middle boxes are for demonstration purposes only in order to visually see what precise line segmentation looks like; otherwise, these two boxes have no other practical use. The shape at the right is far more representative of a very complex shape that shows precise corner detail as well as precise line segmentation. Even double-high-resolution graphics will show some degree of line roughness for diagonal lines due to line segmentation that is inherent in the relatively low pixel density of the Apple //e screen. In its day Apple high-resolution graphics were totally awesome.

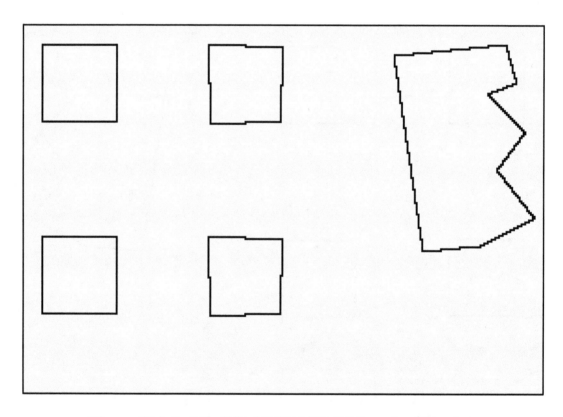

Figure II.1.5. Modified ROM HLIN Routine Display

2. Soft Switches in the Apple //e

My parents purchased their Apple //e while I was working at Sierra On-Line with the understanding that I would set up their system, teach them how to use its capabilities, fix and/or repair any software or hardware problems, and perform any regular maintenance as required. I didn't fully realize what I was getting myself into particularly when I attempted to teach my father how to use VisiCalc: his hands were quite large so his fingers were not keyboard-nimble, he had poor close-up vision, and he could not remember repetitive key-entry sequences very well. I developed his VisiCalc daily expense report (requiring the wide paper in their Epson MX-100 printer) and an Applesoft program to strip his monthly totals from his VisiCalc data files in order to create his annual summary VisiCalc data file. I provided him detailed instructions on how to begin his VisiCalc session and how to enter his data into each row and column. When he made mistakes or skipped instructions, he became rather agitated and blamed the computer for making his errors. My mother would then enter the data for him to keep everyone calm. I should say that these were our typical family dynamics!

My parents purchased their Apple //e when it first became available, probably three or four years before the enhanced version was developed. I have no recall if we were even aware of an Enhanced Apple //e while I was at Sierra around 1983 and 1984. Because I was assisting another engineer in porting ScreenWriter to the Apple //e, I became very familiar with the 80-column text card, the routines `AUXMOVE` and `XFER`, and a whole gamut of new Soft Switches. Also, Ken Williams asked me to extract the database from *the Dic-tio-nary*, the companion spell checker to ScreenWriter. He wanted this database for his new product called HomeWord Speller, the companion spell checker to HomeWord which he had already released. HomeWord and HomeWord Speller were both developed in-house. I utilized calls to `XFER` within a printer driver I developed for *the Dic-tio-nary*, its only vulnerable access location at `0x300`. My special driver sent specific sections of the product's database to Auxiliary memory instead of to a printer. Once I took control of the computer after the data transfer, I was able to copy that database section from Auxiliary memory to Main memory, and then into a file on a disk volume. It is important to note that the `XFER` starting address is found at `0x3ED` and `0x3EE` in the Page `0x03` Interface Routines and Vectors as shown in Table I.9.1.

I believe the enhanced version of the Apple //e provides MouseText characters in place of the alternate uppercase inverse characters, and it also introduced double-high-resolution graphics. This Apple also provides lowercase input for Applesoft and its new Monitor allows lower ASCII input data to be stored in memory locations, it has a search command, and it contains the phenomenal Mini-Assembler from the very old Apple][. The new Monitor also supports a very sophisticated interrupt handler that captures any Apple //e memory configuration before the interrupt is processed. This is done by saving the current memory configuration state onto the stack at the time of the interrupt, placing the Apple in a standard memory configuration before calling the requested interrupt handler, and then restoring the memory configuration state after the requested interrupt handler is finished. However, I firmly believe Apple fell way short in not providing the ability to fully utilize the Mini-Assembler in order to enter and to display the complete 65C02 Instruction Set since the computer was designed to use and was shipped with a 65C02 processor. What was Apple thinking? Any fool knows that the Mini-Assembler is dynamite when coupled with the Monitor's `STEP` and `TRACE` commands.

What was Apple thinking when it continues to provide and to support the use of a cassette tape recorder to store and retrieve programs, multi-dimensioned integer and real arrays, and shape tables? I know of no software engineer in my professional career or among my personal friends who ever used a cassette tape recorder with any Apple computer for any reason. I did develop a communication protocol with a programmable keyboard by means of a wire, which was similar to the tape output data to a cassette tape recorder. Other than programming a keyboard using an annunciator, I have never used a cassette tape recorder with any of my Apple computers. I have never used the Applesoft LOAD, RECALL, SAVE, STORE, or SHLOAD commands in any of my Applesoft programs, nor have I seen these commands used in any professional or commercial Applesoft programs. And, I have never used the Monitor's READ or WRITE commands at any time. Why would I use such a ridiculous and incredibly slow data archiving method when I have the Disk][, the Rana, the RAM Disk 320, the Sider, or the CFFA card to save programs and data in the form of files, visible within its media, and time and date stamped? Honestly, I derive no personal satisfaction in knowing that one can read data into an Apple][computer from a cassette tape recorder port. I do have a few suggestions for what could replace the useless Monitor's READ and WRITE commands with something rather quite useful.

The Apple //e Main and Auxiliary memory together total 128 KB, and each can be controlled by means of an MMU and an IOU device using Soft Switches. By design, the memory of a 65C02 processor within the Apple //e hardware architecture can be naturally divided into four strategic areas: page-zero and the stack, 0x200 to 0xBFFF, 0xC000 to 0xCFFF, and 0xD000 to 0xFFFF that includes the bank-switched 0xD000 to 0xDFFF memory space. These memory areas can be individually activated from Main or Auxiliary memory resources using the appropriate Soft Switches. What is also unique to the Apple //e is that the Monitor firmware has been expanded to include additional ROM memory that is mapped to the 0xC100 to 0xCFFF address space. This address space is enabled or disabled using the appropriate Soft Switches. If there is a display slot card residing in Slot 3, that card's firmware can be activated rather than using the internal 80-column text card firmware. Table II.2.1 summarizes the new memory management and video Soft Switches used to control Main and Auxiliary memory. Some data must be written to all these Soft Switches in order to invoke their action. It does not matter what that data is because that data is not stored anywhere. Table II.2.2 summarizes the new Soft Switch status flags. It is by means of these status flags that one may determine the complete memory and video configuration of the Apple //e.

Address	Access	Name	Description	Notes
0xC000	W	STR80OFF	Disable 80-column store	1
0xC001	W	STR80ON	Enable 80-column store	1
0xC002	W	RAMRDOFF	Read enable Main RAM, 0x0200-0xBFFF	2
0xC003	W	RAMRDON	Read enable Auxiliary RAM, 0x0200-0xBFFF	2
0xC004	W	RAMWROFF	Write enable Main RAM, 0x0200-0xBFFF	2
0xC005	W	RAMWRON	Write enable Auxiliary RAM, 0x0200-0xBFFF	2
0xC006	W	CXROMOFF	Enable slot ROMs, slots 1-7, or 0xC100-0xC7FF	3
0xC007	W	CXROMON	Enable internal CX ROM, or 0xC100-0xCFFF	3
0xC008	W	AUXZPOFF	Enable Main ZP, stack, language card, Av1 BSR RAM	4
0xC009	W	AUXZPON	Enable Auxiliary ZP, stack, lang. card, Av1 BSR RAM	4
0xC00A	W	C3ROMOFF	Enable internal CX3 ROM, 0xC300-0xC3FF	
0xC00B	W	C3ROMON	Enable Slot ROM, 0xC300-0xC3FF	
0xC00C	W	VID80OFF	Disable 80-column video	
0xC00D	W	VID80ON	Enable 80-column video	
0xC00E	W	ALTCHOFF	Enable normal Apple character set	
0xC00F	W	ALTCHON	Enable alternate character set (no flash)	

Table II.2.1. New Memory Management and Video Soft Switches

Address	Access	Name	Description	Clear	Set	Notes
0xC000	R/R7	KEY	Read keyboard for keypress	None	Yes	
0xC010	R/R7	CLRKEY	Clear keyboard strobe, keypress	None	Yes	
0xC011	R7	RDBANK2	Which LC bank in use	BANK1	BANK2	
0xC012	R7	RDLCRAM	LC RAM or ROM read-enabled	ROM	RAM	
0xC013	R7	RDRAMRD	Main, AUX RAM read-enabled	AUX	Main	
0xC014	R7	RDRAMWR	Main, AUX RAM write-enabled	AUX	Main	
0xC015	R7	RDCXROM	Slot or internal ROM enabled	Slot	Internal	
0xC016	R7	RDAUXZP	Which ZP & LC enabled	Main	AUX	
0xC017	R7	RDC3ROM	Slot or CX ROM enabled	Slot	CX3	
0xC018	R7	RDSTR80	State of STR80 switch	Off	On	
0xC019	R7	RDVRTBLK	State of vertical blanking	Off	On	
0xC01A	R7	RDTEXT	State of TEXT switch	Graphics	Text	
0xC01B	R7	RDMIXED	Read MIXED switch	Off	On	
0xC01C	R7	RDPAGE2	State of PAGE2 switch	Main	AUX	
0xC01D	R7	RDHIRES	State of Graphics resolution	LOWRES	HIRES	
0xC01E	R7	RDALTCH	State of Alternate Character Set	Off	On	
0xC01F	R7	RDVID80	State of VID80 video	Off	On	
0xC07E	R7	RDIOUDIS	Read IOUDIS switch	On	Off	5
0xC07F	R7	RDDHIRES	Read DHIRES switch	Off	On	5

Table II.2.2. New Soft Switch Status Flags

Address	Access	Name	Description	Notes
0xC020	R	TAPEOUT	Cassette output Toggle	
0xC030	R	SPKRTOGL	Speaker output Toggle	
0xC040	R	UTILTOGL	Utility Strobe; 1 Ms. pulse Game I/O pin 5	
0xC050	R/W	TEXTOFF	Display Graphics	
0xC051	R/W	TEXTON	Display Text	
0xC052	R/W	MIXEDOFF	Full Screen graphics	6
0xC053	R/W	MIXEDON	Text with graphics	6
0xC054	R/W	PAGE1ON	Display Page 1 or Main video memory	7
0xC055	R/W	PAGE2ON	Display Page 2 or Auxiliary video memory	7
0xC056	R/W	HIRESOFF	Select low resolution Graphics	6
0xC057	R/W	HIRESON	Select high resolution Graphics	6
0xC058	R/W	ANN1OFF	Annunciator 1 off (active if IOUDIS off)	
0xC059	R/W	ANN1ON	Annunciator 1 on (active if IOUDIS off)	
0xC05A	R/W	ANN2OFF	Annunciator 2 off (active if IOUDIS off)	
0xC05B	R/W	ANN2ON	Annunciator 2 on (active if IOUDIS off)	
0xC05C	R/W	ANN3OFF	Annunciator 3 off (active if IOUDIS off)	
0xC05D	R/W	ANN3ON	Annunciator 3 on (active if IOUDIS off)	
0xC05E	R/W	ANN4OFF	Annunciator 4 off (active if IOUDIS off)	
0xC05E	R/W	DHRESON	Double HIRES on (active if IOUDIS on)	
0xC05F	R/W	ANN4ON	Annunciator 4 on (active if IOUDIS off)	
0xC05F	R/W	DHRESOFF	Double HIRES off (active if IOUDIS on)	

Table II.2.3. Original Input/Output Control Soft Switches, Part 1

Address	Access	Name	Description	Notes
0xC060	R	TAPEIN	Cassette input	8
0xC061	R	PB1IN	Push Button 1 input	8
0xC062	R	PB2IN	Push Button 2 input	8
0xC063	R	PB3IN	Push Button 3 input	8
0xC064	R	GC1IN	Game Controller 1 input	9
0xC065	R	GC2IN	Game Controller 2 input	9
0xC066	R	GC3IN	Game Controller 3 input	9
0xC067	R	GC4IN	Game Controller 4 input	9
0xC070	R	GCTOGL	Game Controller Strobe; resets GC1-GC4	
0xC073	W	BANKSEL	RamWorks Bank Select; 64 KB bank select	
0xC07E	W	IODISON	Disable annunciators, enable double HIRES	
0xC07F	W	IODISOFF	Enable annunciators, disable double HIRES	

Table II.2.4. Original Input/Output Control Soft Switches, Part 2

For completeness I have included Tables II.2.3, II.2.4, II.2.5, and II.2.6 showing the original Input/Output, memory management, and Disk][control Soft Switches. In all cases the names of each Soft Switch are those that I use within the *Lisa* assembler because *Lisa* has an eight-character limitation for labels. Figure II.2.1 contains all notes referenced by Tables II.2.1 to II.2.6.

Address	Access	Name	Description	Notes
0xC080	R	RAM2WP	Select Bank 2; write protect RAM	
0xC081	R | RR	ROM2WE	Deselect Bank 2; enable ROM | write enable RAM	
0xC082	R	ROM2WP	Deselect Bank 2; enable ROM; write protect RAM	
0xC083	R | RR	RAM2WE	Select Bank 2 | write enable RAM	
0xC084			See 0xC080	
0xC085			See 0xC081	
0xC086			See 0xC082	
0xC087			See 0xC083	
0xC088	R	RAM1WP	Select Bank 1; write protect RAM	
0xC089	R | RR	ROM1WE	Deselect Bank 1; enable ROM | write enable RAM	
0xC08A	R	ROM1WP	Deselect Bank 1; enable ROM; write protect RAM	
0xC08B	R | RR	RAM1WE	Select Bank 1 | write enable RAM	
0xC08C			See 0xC088	
0xC08D			See 0xC089	
0xC08E			See 0xC08A	
0xC08F			See 0xC08B	

Table II.2.5. Original Memory Management Soft Switches

Address	Access	Name	Description	Notes
0xC080	R	PHAS0OFF	Turn stepper motor phase 1 off	
0xC081	R	PHAS0ON	Turn stepper motor phase 1 on	
0xC082	R	PHAS1OFF	Turn stepper motor phase 2 off	
0xC083	R	PHAS1ON	Turn stepper motor phase 2 on	
0xC084	R	PHAS2OFF	Turn stepper motor phase 3 off	
0xC085	R	PHAS2ON	Turn stepper motor phase 3 on	
0xC086	R	PHAS3OFF	Turn stepper motor phase 4 off	
0xC087	R	PHAS3ON	Turn stepper motor phase 4 on	
0xC088	R	MOTOROFF	Turn motor off	
0xC089	R	MOTORON	Turn motor on	
0xC08A	R	DRV0EN	Select Drive 1	
0xC08B	R	DRV1EN	Select Drive 2	
0xC08C	R	STROBE	Strobe data latch for I/O	
0xC08D	R/W	LATCH	Load data latch	
0xC08E	R	DATAIN	Prepare latch for input	10
0xC08F	W	DATAOUT	Prepare latch for output	11

Table II.2.6. Original Disk][Control Soft Switches

1) If STR80OFF, then access PAGE1/PAGE2 and use RAMRD and RAMWR; if STR80ON, then access Main or Auxiliary display page (0x400) using PAGE2.
2) If 80STORE is ON these switches do not affect video memory.
3) If INTCXROM is ON, then switch SLOTC3ROM is available; otherwise Main ROM is accessed.
4) Use bank enable and write protect switches to control 0xD000-0xFFFF.
5) Triggers paddle timer and resets VBLINT.
6) This mode is only effective when TEXT switch is OFF.
7) This switch changes function when 80STORE is ON.
8) Data is on MSB only.
9) Read 0xC070 first, then count until MSB is zero.
10) DATAIN with STROBE for Read and DATAIN with LATCH for Sense Write Protect.
11) DATAOUT with STROBE for Write and DATAOUT with LATCH for Load Write Latch.

Figure II.2.1. Notes for Tables II.2.1 to II.2.6

Table II.2.7 shows the Soft Switches that are used to control the *Zip Chip* if it is used in place of the 65C02 processor. The *Zip Chip* includes a 65C02 processor along with cache memory and a cache memory controller in order to execute processor instructions and to manage memory data faster. Table II.2.8 shows the Soft Switches that are used to control the CFFA and Table II.2.9 shows the Soft Switches that are used to control the quikLoader. Table II.2.10 shows the Soft Switches that are used to control the Sider, RAM Disk 320, RAM Card, and Rana drives. Typically, the X-register contains the slot number in which the device resides times sixteen and this register is used in combination with the addresses shown in Tables II.2.8, II.2.9, and II.2.10. Or, if speed is critical and the address space where the device driver is writable, the slot number of the device times sixteen can be added to the base addresses shown in these tables.

Address	Access	Name	Description
0xC05A	W	ZIPCTRL	4 writes of 0x5A unlocks *Zip Chip*; 0xA5 locks *Zip Chip*
0xC05B	W	ZIPSTATS	Any byte written enables *Zip Chip*
0xC05B	R	ZIPSTATS	Bits 0 and 1 is RAM size: 0–8K, 1–16K, 2–32K, 3–64K; bit 3 for memory delay: 0 = fast mode (no delay), 1 = sync mode (delay); bit 4 is ZIP enable: 0 = enabled, 1 = disabled; bit 5 is paddle speed: 0 = fast, 1 = normal; bit 6 is cache update: 0 = no, 1 = yes; bit 7 is clock pulse every 1.0035 milliseconds
0xC05C	R/W	ZIPSLOTS	read/write speaker/slot 0 = fast, 1 = normal. Bit 0 = speaker, bits 1 to 7 for slots 1 to 7
0xC05D	W	ZIPSPEED	Write speed: bit 2 = clk2/3, bit 3 = clk3/4, bit 4 = clk4/5, bit 5 = clk5/6, bit 6 = clk/2, bit 7 = clk/4
0xC05E	W	ZIPDELAY	Bit 7: 0 = enable delay, 1 = disable and reset delay
0xC05E	R	ZIPDELAY	0 = OFF; 1 = ON: bit 0 = ROMRD, bit 1 = RAMBNK, bit 2 = PAGE2, bit 3 = HIRES, bit 4 = 80STORE, bit 5 = MWR, bit 6 = MRD, bit 7 = ALTZP
0xC05F	W	ZIPCACHE	Bit 6 paddle delay: 0 = disable, 1 = enable; bit 7 language card cache: 0 = enable, 1 = disable

Table II.2.7. Zip Chip Control Soft Switches

Address	Access	Name	Description
0xC080	R/W	ATADATAH	Read or write high data byte register
0xC081	R	SETCSMSK	Disable pre-fetch register
0xC082	R	CLRCSMSK	Enable pre-fetch register
0xC086	W	ATADEVCT	Write device control register
0xC086	R	ATASTAT2	Read alternate status register
0xC088	R/W	ATADATAL	Read or write low data byte register
0xC089	R	ATAERROR	Read error register
0xC08A	W	ATASECCT	Write sector count register
0xC08B	W	ATASECTR	Write LBA3 (07:00) address register
0xC08C	W	ATACYLNL	Write LBA2 (15:08) address register
0xC08D	W	ATACYLNH	Write LBA1 (23:16) address register
0xC08E	W	ATAHEAD	Write drive/head configuration register
0xC08F	W	ATACMD	Write command register
0xC08F	R	ATASTAT	Read primary status register

Table II.2.8. CFFA Control Soft Switches

Address	Access	Name	Description
0xC080	W	QLSELC0	Select banks 0 or 1, ON/OFF, USR, EPROM number
0xC081	W	QLSELC1	Select banks 2 or 3, ON/OFF, USR, EPROM number
0xC082	W	QLSELC2	Select banks 4 or 5, ON/OFF, USR, EPROM number
0xC083	W	QLSELC3	Select banks 6 or 7, ON/OFF, USR, EPROM number

Table II.2.9. quikLoader Control Soft Switches

Address	Access	Name	Description
0xC080	R	SDINPUT	Sider read status
0xC080	W	SDINPUT	Write drive number, DCB data, input data
0xC081	R	SDOUTPUT	Sider read output data
0xC081	W	SDOUTPUT	Write start, flush, and stop commands
0xC080	W	RDSECTR	RAM Disk sector number
0xC081	W	RDTRACK	RAM Disk track number
0xC084	W	RAMCARD	RAM Card ON/OFF, track*2, sector/8
0xC800	W	ROMCODE1	Select Rana drive pairs 1 and 2
0xC801	W	ROMCODE2	Select Rana drive pairs 3 and 4

Table II.2.10. Sider, RAM Disk, RAM Card, and Rana Control Soft Switches

In addition to what is shown in Table II.2.10, the Rana controller card also uses the original Disk][control Soft Switches shown in Table II.2.6. The Rana controller card uses a complicated algorithm where some of the PHASEON and PHASEOFF control Soft Switches are used to select its upper or lower recording head and the 0xC800/0xC801 addresses are used to select a pair of drives, either drives 1 and 2 or drives 3 and 4.

The Apple][+ Monitor disabled the STEP and TRACE commands. Even though the Apple //e has additional ROM memory in the CX ROM (0xC100 to 0xCFFF) space, the original STEP and TRACE entry points are still disabled and cannot be used in conjunction with the enabled Mini-Assembler command (the ! command). And, this ROM also contains a silly SEARCH command (the S command). In my opinion the SEARCH command is pretty lame for it can find at most two consecutive bytes in low/high byte order. And I am still annoyed that the cassette tape recorder READ and WRITE commands were retained in the Apple //e ROM. What disturbs me the most is that the Monitor cannot even display the additional opcodes in the 65C02 Instruction Set that pertains to the specific 65C02 processor supplied in the Apple //e and used by the Apple //e. As an aside, the 65C02 Instruction Set was expanded even further in the Rockwell and WDC versions of the processor to include the BBR, BBS, RMB, and SMB mnemonics adding 32 additional opcodes. These opcodes are not available in the Apple //e supplied 65C02 processor.

In summary, it makes no sense to me to provide a computer to a user that utilizes a particular processor and its firmware cannot display the complete set of its processor's mnemonics. What I would have done is to recommend to Apple to retire the Monitor's READ and WRITE commands and reintroduce the Monitor's STEP and TRACE commands, and to provide a more useful Monitor command in addition to the SEARCH command if there was sufficient room. And, of course, the Monitor must be able to display all of its useable 65C02 mnemonics. Will retiring the Monitor's READ and WRITE commands provide enough room for all my suggestions? Can the Monitor's new lower ASCII data input routine be further enhanced? Let's find out. The Monitor software begins at 0xF800. The CX ROM space support routines and 80-column routines are found in memory from 0xC100 to 0xCFFF.

3. SWEET16 Metaprocessor

The *SWEET16* Metaprocessor is a "pseudo microprocessor" implemented in 6502 assembly language. Originally conceived and written by Steve "Woz" Wozniak, *SWEET16* and Integer BASIC were included in the ROM firmware of the early Apple II computers. *SWEET16* is a really smart and useful extension to a 6502 based computer and it can be ported to other 6502 based systems to provide useful 16-bit functionality. It can be thought of as a virtual machine that gives the 6502 programmer a 16-bit extension to the 8-bit microprocessor. *SWEET16* utilizes sixteen 16-bit registers/pointers at the beginning of page-zero and it provides new opcodes to use those registers. Although *SWEET16* instructions are not as fast as native 6502 instructions, *SWEET16* can reduce the code size of programs and ease some programming difficulties.

Steve Wozniak wrote "While writing Apple BASIC for the 6502 microprocessor, I repeatedly encountered a variant of Murphy's Law. Briefly stated, any routine operating on 16-bit data will require at least twice the code that it should. Programs making extensive use of 16-bit pointers such as compilers, editors, and assemblers are included in this category. In my case, even the addition of a few double-byte instructions to the 6502's Instruction Set would have only slightly alleviated the problem. What I really needed was a hybrid of the MOS Technology 6502 and RCA 1800 architectures: a powerful 8-bit data handler complemented by an easy to use processor with an abundance of 16-bit registers and excellent pointer capability. My solution was to implement a non-existent 16-bit "metaprocessor" in software, interpreter style, which I call *SWEET16*. *SWEET16* is based around sixteen 16-bit registers called R0 to R15, which are actually implemented as 32 memory locations. R0 doubles as the *SWEET16* Accumulator (ACC), R15 as the Program Counter (PC), and R14 as the Status Register. R13 holds compare instruction results and R12 is the Subroutine Return stack pointer if *SWEET16* subroutines are used. All other *SWEET16* registers are at the user's unrestricted disposal.

"*SWEET16* instructions fall into register and non-register categories. The register instructions specify one of the sixteen registers to be used as either a data element or as a pointer to data in memory, depending on the specific instruction. For example, the instruction INR R5 uses R5 as a data register and ST @R7 uses R7 as a pointer register to data in memory. Except for the SET instruction, register instructions require one byte. The non-register instructions are primarily 6502 style branch operations with the second byte specifying a +/- 127-byte displacement relative to the address of the following instruction. If a Prior Register (PR) operation result meets a specified branch condition, the displacement is added to the *SWEET16* Program Counter, thus effecting a branch. *SWEET16* is intended as an enhancement package to the 6502 processor, not as a standalone processor. A 6502 program switches to *SWEET16* mode with a subroutine call, and subsequent code is interpreted as *SWEET16* instructions. The non-register instruction RTN returns the user program to the 6502's direct execution mode after restoring the A, X, Y, P, and S internal registers. Even though most opcodes are only one byte long, *SWEET16* runs approximately ten times slower than equivalent 6502 code, so it should be employed only when code is at a premium or execution is not. As an example of its usefulness, I have estimated that about 1K byte could be weeded out of my 5K byte Apple][BASIC interpreter with no observable performance degradation by selectively applying *SWEET16*."

SWEET16 was probably the least used and least understood seed in the original Apple][. In exactly the same sense that the Integer and Applesoft BASICs are languages, *SWEET16* is a language, too. Compared to the BASICs, however, it would be classified as lower level with a strong likeness to conventional 6502 assembly language. Obviously, to use *SWEET16*, you must learn the language. And according to "Woz", "The opcode list is short and uncomplicated." *SWEET16* was ROM based in every early Apple][and it resided in memory from 0xF689 to 0xF7FC. It uses the SAVE and

RESTORE routines in the Apple's Monitor to preserve the 6502 registers during its use, allowing *SWEET16* to be used as a subroutine. Table II.3.1 lists the *SWEET16* registers and the function of each register. The complete *SWEET16* Instruction Set is shown in Tables II.3.2 and II.3.3. These tables list each opcode, its mnemonic, and a brief description of the opcode and what it does. Table II.3.2 lists the non-register opcodes and Table II.3.3 lists the register opcodes.

Register	Description
R0	*SWEET16* Accumulator (ACC)
R1-R11	*SWEET16* user registers
R12	*SWEET16* subroutine return Stack Pointer (SP)
R13	*SWEET16* compare instruction results
R14	*SWEET16* Status Register (PR & Carry flag)
R15	*SWEET16* Program Counter (PC)

Table II.3.1. SWEET16 Register Descriptions

Opcode	Mnemonic	Opcode Description
0x00	RTN	Return to 6502 mode to process native 6502 instructions
0x01	BR rel	Branch always to PC+rel+2→PC
0x02	BNC rel	Branch if prior operation left carry clear to PC+rel+2→PC
0x03	BC rel	Branch if prior operation left carry set to PC+rel+2→PC
0x04	BP rel	Branch if Prior Register is positive to PC+rel+2→PC
0x05	BM rel	Branch if Prior Register is negative to PC+rel+2→PC
0x06	BZ rel	Branch if Prior Register is zero to PC+rel+2→PC
0x07	BNZ rel	Branch if Prior Register is not zero to PC+rel+2→PC
0x08	BM1 rel	Branch if Prior Register is minus one to PC+rel+2→PC
0x09	BNM1 rel	Branch if Prior Register is not minus one to PC+rel+2→PC
0x0A	SOUT chr	Send character chr to COUT (originally the BK opcode)
0x0B	RS	Return from Subroutine, and POPD @SP→PC, SP=SP-2
0x0C	BS rel	Branch to Subroutine, and PC→STD @SP, SP=SP+2, PC+rel+2→PC
0x0D	RSNS	Return from Subroutine without stack, and SP→PC (originally unassigned opcode)
0x0E	BSNS rel	Branch to Subroutine without stack, and PC→SP, PC+rel+2→PC (originally unassigned opcode)
0x0F	SJMP adr	Jump to 16-bit address adr and adr-1→PC (originally unassigned opcode)

Table II.3.2. SWEET16 Non-Register Opcodes

Opcode	Mnemonic	Opcode Description
0x1n	SET Rn,val	Load Rn with 16-bit value val
0x2n	LD Rn	Load ACC from Rn, PR=n
0x3n	ST Rn	Store ACC into Rn, PR=n
0x4n	LD @Rn	Load LO ACC indirectly using Rn, HO ACC=0, Rn=Rn+1, PR=0
0x5n	ST @Rn	Store LO ACC indirectly using Rn, Rn=Rn+1, PR=0
0x6n	LDD @Rn	Load ACC indirectly using Rn, Rn=Rn+2, PR=0
0x7n	STD @Rn	Store ACC indirectly using Rn, Rn=Rn+2, PR=0
0x8n	POP @Rn	Rn=Rn-1, load LO ACC indirectly using Rn, HO ACC=0, PR=0
0x9n	STP @Rn	Rn=Rn-1, store LO ACC indirectly using Rn, PR=0
0xAn	ADD Rn	ACC = ACC + Rn, status = carry, PR=0
0xBn	SUB Rn	ACC = ACC – Rn, status = carry, PR=0
0xCn	POPD @Rn	Rn=Rn-2, load ACC indirectly using Rn, PR=0
0xDn	CPR Rn	R13 = ACC – Rn, status = carry, PR=13
0xEn	INR Rn	Rn = Rn + 1, PR=n
0xFn	DCR Rn	Rn = Rn – 1, PR=n

Table II.3.3. SWEET16 Register Opcodes

Glen Bredon utilized *SWEET16* extensively in his *Big Mac* software by incorporating the *SWEET16* interpreter within its source code since the interpreter did not exist in the Apple][+ or Apple //e ROMs. Mr. Bredon re-coded the NUL (not shown) and BNM1 opcodes to provide other functions specific to his needs. He also did not use the R12 register as a Return from Subroutine stack pointer and he did not use the R14 register for the PR and Status. Rather than using a stack pointer at all, he simply saved the Return from Subroutine address at page-zero 0xDA/0xDB and the PR and Status at page-zero 0xFF. I am simply astounded at how easy it is to utilize the *SWEET16* instructions for any task that processes large sets of data, like an assembler. In fact, the early versions of the S-C (Sander-Cederlof) Assembler II used *SWEET16* in several locations within its code. The TED/ASM assembler and all its descendants, including the DOS Tool Kit, TED II+, Merlin, and many others, used *SWEET16* heavily. Several of the programs in the Apple Programmer's Aid ROM used *SWEET16* including the Integer BASIC Renumber/Append programs.

As Tables II.3.2 and II.3.3 show, the *SWEET16* opcode list is short and uncomplicated. Except for relative branch displacements, hand assembly is trivial. All register opcodes are formed by combining two hexadecimal digits, one for the opcode and one to specify a register. For example, opcodes 0x15 and 0x45 both specify register R5 while opcodes 0x23, 0x27, and 0x2B are all LD Rn instructions. Most register instructions are assigned in complementary pairs to facilitate remembering them. Thus, "LD Rn" and "ST Rn" are opcodes 0x2n and 0x3n, while "LD @Rn" and "ST @Rn" are opcodes 0x4n and 0x5n, respectively.

Opcodes 0x00 through 0x0F are assigned to the sixteen Non-Register Opcodes and opcodes 0x1n through 0xFn opcodes are assigned to the fifteen Register Opcodes. Except for the opcodes RTN (0x00), SOUT (0x0A), RS (0x0B), RSNS (0x0D), and SJMP (0x0F), the non-register opcodes are basic 6502 style branches. The second byte of a branch instruction contains a +/- 127-byte displacement value (in two's complement form) relative to the address of the instruction immediately following the branch. The SOUT (0x0A) opcode sends its second byte to COUT at ROM address 0xFDED. Of course, the SJMP opcode, like the SET opcode, takes its second and third byte to form a 16-bit address, or a 16-bit value in the case of SET.

Before the BS/RS opcodes can be used, R12 must be initialized with the address of a stack buffer that will be used to contain return-from-subroutine 16-bit addresses. The stack buffer must be of sufficient size to hold n-levels of subroutine calls, or n-number of 16-bit addresses.

If a specified branch condition is met by using the PR instruction result, the displacement is added to the Program Counter effecting a branch. Except for the BR (BRanch always) opcode, the BS (Branch to a Subroutine) opcode, and the BSNS (Branch to a Subroutine using No Stack) opcode, the branch opcodes are assigned in complementary pairs like the register opcodes, thus rendering them easily remembered for hand coding. For example, Branch if Plus and Branch if Minus are opcodes 0x04 and 0x05 while Branch if Zero and Branch if Not Zero are opcodes 0x06 and 0x07, respectively.

The original *SWEET16* software left the last three non-register opcodes unassigned, where any of them could be used as a NUL opcode, and the BK (BreaK, 0x0A) opcode simply executed a 6502 BRK instruction. The PR and the Carry flag were both combined in the high order (HO) byte of R14. I chose to separate the PR and Carry flag into separate bytes of the R14 register in order to reduce the code size and number of execution cycles for all of the non-register operations. Doing this allowed the inclusion of three additional opcodes within the limited, single memory page boundary that must contain all of the *SWEET16* routines: send character to COUT, Branch to Subroutine using No Stack, Return from Subroutine using No Stack, and JuMP to address. Incidentally, one can jump to an address using other *SWEET16* opcodes, but it requires using two of them (SET and ST), and the address must already be decremented by one, or decremented using a third opcode, DCR. The new instruction, SJMP adr, will load the *SWEET16* Program Counter directly with adr-1.

My implementation of *SWEET16* saves the register number (PR) of the register receiving the value or change in value into the low order (LO) byte of R14 when a register opcode is processed. If the register opcode is ADD, SUB, or CPR, I chose to save the state of the Carry flag in bit 0 of the HO byte of R14. The reasons for doing this are quite compelling. Originally the LO byte of R14 was not utilized by the SWEET16 interpreter, so it was available to the user. Personally, I found that that unused byte to be virtually useless. So, if there was a way to transform that byte into a more useful function, I was more inclined to adopt that strategy. Each time a non-register opcode is encountered, the original code used nine cycles in five bytes for part of the setup code, and ten additional bytes were used for five of the branch instructions. My implementation requires only eight cycles in five bytes for the setup code, and no additional bytes for the same five branch instructions. This does not seem like very much of a savings; that is, one cycle for every invocation of a non-register opcode, but in data processing loops that execute many, many times, a single cycle in savings adds up. Mr. Bredon chose to use sixteen cycles in seven bytes for the same capability.

The SET command is another example where a few cycles can be saved just by using a different strategy. The original code used thirteen cycles in ten bytes to increment the *SWEET16* Program Counter by two, not including its RTS instruction. My implementation requires only eleven cycles in ten bytes every time the SET command is utilized. Mr. Bredon requires thirty-five cycles in seven bytes for the same functionality. To me, that seems like a lot of overhead just to save three bytes of code. This simply exemplifies the observable fact that when code is made extremely compact, the price paid is usually slower execution time.

As stated above the original image of *SWEET16* was located in ROM from `0xF689` to `0xF7FC`, so it was 372 bytes in size, though the last three bytes of the `0xF7` page were set to `0xFF`. My implementation of *SWEET16* is exactly 400 bytes in size, though it includes four additional, and very useful opcodes in my opinion. I believe having the *SWEET16* Metaprocessor located in the Apple //e `CX` ROM space rather than having the `RESET` diagnostic routines consume that code space certainly makes far more sense to me. And, what's more, there is more than sufficient room for the *SWEET16* interpreter to reside in the `CX` ROM space if, and only if, there is sufficient room for a calling and a return location in the `0xF0` Monitor firmware. I believe a suitable ROM entry point for *SWEET16* is at `0xFA72`. And, the *SWEET16* return address follows at `0xFA78`. The DOS 4.1 Manual provides the details for why I chose those ROM addresses for *SWEET16*. The Apple //e ROM image that contains *SWEET16* may be found at applecored.net.

4 Applesoft Garbage Collector

The Applesoft Garbage Collector routine GARBAG is located in ROM from 0xE484 to 0xE597, and that routine moves all currently active string variables up in String Pool memory as far as possible. There are several routines in ROM that rely on the garbage collector, as well as the Applesoft command FRE(aexpr), to consolidate the Character String Pool when there is not enough Free Space memory as shown in Figure I.15.1 to perform any requested string variable manipulation. When certain conditions are met while these Applesoft ROM routines process character string data, GARBAG is called. Depending upon how many string variables are active, the processing time for GARBAG is proportional to the square of the number of active strings currently in use. This processing time may be a few seconds if there are less than fifty active strings, or many minutes if there are hundreds of active strings. It may even appear as if the Applesoft program has literally stopped, or hanged for no apparent reason. In Section I.15 it was even suggested that strategically placing multiple Applesoft FRE(aexpr) statements throughout an Applesoft program may help to alleviate processing delays.

Many years ago, Cornelis Bongers of Erasmus University in Rotterdam, Netherlands, published a brilliant Garbage Collector algorithm for Applesoft strings in *Micro*, August, 1982. According to an article in *Apple Assembly Line*, March, 1984, the speed of his program was incredible when compared to the GARBAG algorithm in ROM. And the processing time for his algorithm was directly proportional to the number of active strings, rather than to the number of active strings squared. The only problem with his algorithm was that the magazine that published it owned the algorithm. Worse yet, the algorithm was tied to a program called Ampersoft, marketed by Microsparc, then publishers of *Nibble* magazine. It was reported that a license to use Bongers' algorithm was very costly at that time.

Recall that Table I.15.1 shows the definition of a simple string variable descriptor as it is found in the Simple Variables memory area and Table I.15.2 shows the definition of an array string variable descriptor as it is found in the Array Variables memory area. After analyzing these tables, Bongers introduced the idea of marking active strings that are located in the Character String Pool memory area: he set the third byte in the string data to its upper ASCII value and swapped in the address of the string descriptor in place of the first two bytes of the string data. Also, during this first pass through the Simple Variables and Array Variables memory area he saved those first two bytes of the string data safely in the address field of its descriptor or string element. The address previously in the address field would be changed anyway after all the strings are moved up in memory to their final destination. The second pass through the Character String Pool memory area moved all active strings as high in memory as they could go, it retrieved the first two characters from storage in its descriptor or string element, and it updated the address field to the new memory location for that string.

Bongers' algorithm is most efficient when the active strings are a least three bytes in length, so one- and two-character strings require different handling. On the first pass through the Simple Variables and Array Variables memory area, the first byte of string data pointed to by these "short" descriptors is stored in the string length byte of its descriptor. If the string length is two, the second data byte is stored in the low address byte of its descriptor. For single character strings the low address byte is flagged with an 0xFF value. The high address byte in all "short" descriptors is flagged with an 0xFF value since no string can have an address greater than 0xFF00. If "short" strings are found during the first pass, a third pass returns them to the string pool with their descriptors updated to their new memory location. "Short" strings do slow down Bongers' algorithm a little. However, the processing time is still directly proportional to the number of active strings, and not to the number of active strings squared. Tables II.4.1 and II.4.2 illustrate Bongers' algorithm during the first pass.

ADL/ADH Descriptor Before Pass 1							⇒	ADL/ADH Descriptor After Pass 1						
+AS	−AS	1	LSB	MSB	0	0	⇒	+AS	−AS	41	FF	FF	0	0

LSB/MSB Memory Before Pass 1							⇒	LSB/MSB Memory After Pass 1						
41							⇒	41						

ADL/ADH Descriptor Before Pass 1							⇒	ADL/ADH Descriptor After Pass 1						
+AS	−AS	2	LSB	MSB	0	0	⇒	+AS	−AS	41	42	FF	0	0

LSB/MSB Memory Before Pass 1							⇒	LSB/MSB Memory After Pass 1						
41	42						⇒	41	42					

ADL/ADH Descriptor Before Pass 1							⇒	ADL/ADH Descriptor After Pass 1						
+AS	−AS	>2	LSB	MSB	0	0	⇒	+AS	−AS	LEN	41	42	0	0

LSB/MSB Memory Before Pass 1							⇒	LSB/MSB Memory After Pass 1						
41	42	43	44	45	46	47	⇒	ADL+2	ADH	C3	44	45	46	47

Table II.4.1. Simple Variable Descriptor Processing in Bongers' Pass 1

ADL/ADH Element Before Pass 1			⇒	ADL/ADH Element After Pass 1		
1	LSB	MSB	⇒	41	FF	FF

LSB/MSB Memory Before Pass 1			⇒	LSB/MSB Memory After Pass 1		
41			⇒	41		

ADL/ADH Element Before Pass 1			⇒	ADL/ADH Element After Pass 1		
2	LSB	MSB	⇒	41	42	FF

LSB/MSB Memory Before Pass 1			⇒	LSB/MSB Memory After Pass 1		
41	42		⇒	41	42	

ADL/ADH Element Before Pass 1			⇒	ADL/ADH Element After Pass 1		
>2	LSB	MSB	⇒	LEN	41	42

LSB/MSB Memory Before Pass 1							⇒	LSB/MSB Memory After Pass 1						
41	42	43	44	45	46	47	⇒	ADL	ADH	C3	44	45	46	47

Table II.4.2. Array Variable Element Processing in Bongers' Pass 1

Pass two in Bongers' algorithm uses only the information in the String Pool to move all currently active string variables up in String Pool memory as far as possible. This is accomplished by initializing a pool pointer and a string pointer to `HIMEM` and searching down to `FRETOP` for any upper ASCII bytes. Once an upper ASCII byte has been found, its string descriptor is located at the memory location two bytes prior to the upper ASCII byte. That string descriptor contains the length of the string and the first two ASCII characters of the string. Those two characters may be safely moved back to the string and the upper ASCII byte changed to a lower ASCII byte. The string length can now be subtracted from the current string pointer address, the new string address can be copied to the second and third byte in its string descriptor, and the string data can be copied to its new string address. However, the string must be copied from its last character backward to prevent possibly overwriting part of the string if the string were to be copied from its first character forward. Once the pool pointer reaches the original address in `FRETOP`, the current string pointer address becomes the new address in `FRETOP` if the "short" descriptors flag is clear.

If the "short" descriptors flag is set then a third pass must be made through the Simple Variables and Array Variables memory area. A memory pointer is initialized to `VARTAB` and the `0xFF` flag is searched for in either the fifth byte of a Simple Variable descriptor or the third byte of an Array Variable element. If there is an `0xFF` flag in the prior byte then the descriptor is for a single character string, otherwise the descriptor is for a two-character string. The current string pointer is adjusted for one or two characters, the string data is copied from its descriptor to the string pool, and the string pointer address is copied to its string descriptor. Once the memory pointer reaches `STREND`, the current string pointer address becomes the new address in `FRETOP`.

It must be emphasized that Bongers' algorithm depends on two important caveats: normal Applesoft programs save all string data in **lower** ASCII, i.e. with the MSB of each byte cleared, and normal Applesoft programs never allow more than one string descriptor to point to the same exact copy of that string data in memory. If a user should program something like "`A$ = CHR$( 193 )`", Bongers' algorithm will **fail**. If an assembly language program should modify two string descriptors to point to the same string in the String Pool, Bongers' algorithm will **fail**. Therefore, reasonable care must be given to creating Applesoft programs and/or assembly language programs that take the above caveats seriously in order to exact the stupendous benefit in using a garbage collector routine that is based on Bongers' algorithm.

Armed with only the initial details of Bongers' algorithm and my analysis of those details, my attempt to recreate his algorithm resulted in an assembly language program that was `0x200` bytes in size. This necessitated creating a suitable Applesoft test program that would verify the accuracy of my algorithm and confirm that no character string was altered in length, modified in content, or destroyed. My ultimate goal would be to replace `GARBAG` in ROM with my version of Bongers' algorithm. `GARBAG` occupies `0x113` bytes of ROM memory and there was `0x70` bytes of memory available in the `CX` ROM space from `0xC600` to `0xC66F` (`0xC670` is where I put the *SWEET16* program code). If the `CX` ROM space is used then `CX` ROM memory management must also be incorporated in the routine. All totaled my garbage routine must fit within `0x183` bytes if it is to be located in ROM. On the other hand, my garbage routine, after some adjustment, could be attached to an Applesoft program and simply called prior to issuing the DOS `CHAIN` command providing that the `R` keyword is utilized with `CHAIN`. At least that would mitigate having to call `GARBAG` in this particular instance. Periodically, the Applesoft program could check the remaining Free Space and call its attached garbage routine based on reasonable criteria. There is still much indeterminacy whether a particular character string manipulation will trigger a call to `GARBAG`. If that should happen Applesoft processing could come to a grinding pause until the Character String Pool has been processed without regard to my attached garbage routine.

In order to compact an assembly language routine certain decisions must be made that, hopefully, will not cause the introduction of more processor cycles than absolutely necessary. Example strategies would be to limit subroutine calls in the inner-most loops and to limit the pushing and popping of variables onto the stack. Sometimes simply reorganizing the order of a number of processing loops can greatly simplify the code and eliminate having to re-initialize registers. Keeping a variable's MSB address in a register when addresses need to be compared can often help simplify and accelerate the code as well. I have no doubt that Mr. Bongers could have condensed his algorithm down to `0x183` bytes (where six of those bytes are required for `CX` ROM memory management). My initial attempt to condense my garbage routine could not meet the goal of `0x183` bytes unless I removed the flag that signaled whether a third pass was necessary, and so the routine always made a third pass. Many times, it is helpful to just take a break from a difficult programming task like this one, and work on something else. Thus, when I returned to my garbage routine, I took a fresh look and I found several additional strategies that could condense the code even further, and allow the reintroduction of the third pass flag. Hurray! I was able to fit one segment of the routine into the `0x70` bytes located in `CX` ROM space and the other segment into the `0x113` bytes where `GARBAG` normally resides. All that was left to do was the testing, the timing, and the verification of the routine after it was installed in the ROM (actually an EPROM to be precise).

As mentioned earlier a verification test must prove that no character string is altered in length, modified in content, or destroyed by the garbage collector algorithm. The test results of the new algorithm must be **identical** to the results obtained using the `GARBAG` algorithm. And since there is a DOS 4.3 `DATE` command available, each pass through the string array variables can be easily time stamped. The Applesoft test created three two-dimension character string arrays where both dimensions were set to twenty-six. Each string array element was initialized with a single character that was "forced" into the String Pool. On each successive pass another character was added to each element within the dimension that was being processed, from one to twenty-six. This caused the utilization of memory to grow larger on each successive pass. Before each pass I captured the size of Free Space. If Free Space was less than 15,000 bytes, I issued the Applesoft `FRE( aexpr )` command forcing the garbage collector to process the String Pool. I obtained identical memory results for each and every pass in my Applesoft test program whether I used the original `GARGAG` in ROM or my new garbage routine in ROM. The timing results for my test program are shown in Table II.4.3. The left three columns of timings summarize the results obtained from the original `GARBAG` routine. The time each pass began is shown in the first of the three columns. If the Free Space fell below 15,000 bytes another timestamp was recorded after I made another call to `FRE( aexpr )`. This timestamp is shown in the middle of the three columns. The delta time the routine required for its processing is shown in the third of the three columns. The right three columns of timings contain the same information for my new garbage collector routine.

My implementation of Bongers' algorithm shows how amazing this routine actually is. Table II.4.3 shows only a peek at the capacity of this routine. When I changed the Free Space parameter from 15,000 to 5,000 bytes the Applesoft program calling the original `GARBAG` routine did not complete, even after an hour, because I finally terminated it. The Applesoft program using my new garbage collector routine completed in 06:54 minutes, and twenty-four of the twenty-six possible passes finished before I terminated it (due to impatience). Table II.4.3 shows that only the first eighteen of the twenty-six possible passes finished before insufficient memory remained when calling the original

GARBAG routine. After every pass a verification routine was called that simply confirmed that the contents of all arrays still contained the ASCII data that was expected to be there, and no other data. Therefore, this verification test routine confirmed and verified that no character string was altered in length, modified in content, or destroyed for both the original GARBAG routine and for my new garbage collector routine. I give complete credit to Cornelis Bongers for creating the concept of this brilliant Garbage Collector algorithm. I would be fascinated to know if my implementation is anything like Mr. Bongers' implementation for his algorithm. Someone may someday discover the answer to that question.

Pass Number	Original Garbage Collector			New Garbage Collector		
	Time	<15000	Delta	Time	<15000	Delta
0	00:00			00:00		
1	00:02			00:02		
2	00:05			00:05		
3	00:09			00:09		
4	00:14			00:14		
5	00:21			00:20		
6	00:28			00:28		
7	00:37			00:36		
8	00:47	01:26	00:39	00:46	00:47	00:01
9	02:37			00:58		
10	02:49	04:55	02:06	01:10	01:12	00:02
11	05:11			01:25		
12	05:25	07:57	02:32	01:39	01:41	00:02
13	08:13	11:08	02:55	01:56	01:58	00:02
14	11:29	14:31	03:02	02:15	02:16	00:01
15	14:59	18:12	03:13	02:34	02:36	00:02
16	18:36	21:59	03:23	02:55	02:56	00:01
17	22:27	26:00	03:33	03:17	03:19	00:02
18	30:27	34:14	03:47	03:42	03:43	00:01
	34:40			03:43		

Table II.4.3. Garbage Collector Comparison and Verification Timing Results

5. Building a New Apple //e ROM

The DOS 4.1 Manual includes an in-depth analysis of the Apple //e ROM including the CX ROM space and the Apple //e 80-column text card. That Manual explains and shows where some of the 0xF0 ROM routines were incorrectly coded using example code segments. The analysis began with the BASCALC routine and my Delete Key handler in order to provide sufficient room for the new 65C02 16-byte FMT2 table and its new content. The GETFMT routine was also presented along with the TBLC and TBLL tables, as well as the MNEML and MNEMR tables which grew to be 0xA6 bytes larger in size. STEP and TRACE were introduced along with GETNSP to where these routines must now reside. Also, an enhancement to the SEARCH routine was presented along with a new Monitor routine called ZAPMEM that could initialize a range of memory to any single value. These enhancements required changes to the LOOKASC routine that now offers both lower ASCII and upper ASCII data input support. Part of the RESET handler was moved to the CX ROM space in order to make additional room in the 0xF0 ROM for the entry and exit of the *SWEET16* metaprocessor. Even the NXTCHR and OLDRST routines were discussed.

In the DOS 4.1 Manual I explained why the Applesoft LOAD, RECALL, SAVE, STORE, and SHLOAD commands were useless without the cassette tape TAPEOUT and TAPEIN routines, which I removed from the 0xC500 page in favor of the STEP and TRACE routines. Instead of replacing the calls to the TAPEOUT and TAPEIN routines with a call to IORTS at 0xFF58, for example, I instead replaced the addresses to these Applesoft commands with that of IORTS. This frees a total of 0xAE bytes for other processing and/or other Applesoft commands. The entry addresses for Applesoft commands are located from 0xD000 to 0xD0CF, and the ASCII text for Applesoft commands is located from 0xD0D0 to 0xD25F. Table II.5.1 shows the available ROM spaces and their locations when the Applesoft LOAD, RECALL, SAVE, STORE, and SHLOAD commands are disabled and effectively removed from Applesoft processing. As I said in that Manual, I have no doubt that I will innovate a terrific use for these ROM memory spaces in the next development cycle. So far that innovation has yet to happened. Someone is bound to create a terrific new Applesoft command and use this valuable ROM memory to implement that command.

Table II.5.2 shows the migration, removal, and insertion of various routines and tables of data to transform the stock Apple //e ROM and CX ROM space into a new and more powerful Apple //e ROM in my opinion. I call this new Apple //e ROM ROM2E.SW16GC.3 because Build 3 contains the *SWEET16* metaprocessor, the STEP and TRACE routines, the display and logic for all 65C02 mnemonics, the Delete Key handler, and the incredible Garbage Collector based on the algorithm developed by Cornelis Bongers. What this ROM does not contain are the Apple //e diagnostic DIAGS routines and the cassette tape recorder TAPEOUT and TAPEIN routines.

Start	End	Length	Applesoft Commands
0xD8B0	0xD900	0x51	LOAD and SAVE
0xF39F	0xF3D7	0x39	STORE and RECALL
0xF775	0xF786	0x12	SHLOAD
0xF7D5	0xF7E6	0x12	GETARYPT

Table II.5.1. Disabled Applesoft Commands

ROM2E		ROM2E.SW16GC.3		Description
Start	End	Start	End	
0xC1B6	0xC1BD	0xC1B6	0xC1BC	add BASCALC support
0xC204	0xC209	0xC203	0xC207	modify VTAB support; saves Y-reg in BASL
0xC230	0xC230	0xC22E	0xC22E	add CLD before address calculation
0xC298	0xC29F	0xC297	0xC2A4	change DELETE (0xFF) to LARROW (0x88)
0xC2B0	0xC2ED	0xC2B5	0xC2EA	modify RESET support, remove DIAGS support
0xC2F2	0xC2FD	0xCE15	0xCE1E	move XRDKEYX routine near INVERT
0xC600	0xC66F	0xC600	0xC66F	remove DIAGS, add Bongers' algorithm Part 2
0xC670	0xC7FF	0xC670	0xC7FF	remove DIAGS, add *SWEET16*
0xC849	0xC84B	0xC849	0xC84B	add jump to CONTKEY
0xC9A4	0xC9A9	0xC2EF	0xC2F4	move KBDOUT
0xCA71	0xCA88	0xC5E7	0xC5FE	form mnemonic table index; put TBLC and TBLL
0xCC90	0xCC95	0xC9A4	0xC9A9	move XFF, put CONTKEY here
0xCE14	0xCE1E	0xCE15	0xCE1E	remove duplicate UPRCASE, put KRDKEYX here
0xCF16	0xCF16	0xCF16	0xCF18	fix logic for X-register
0xCF37	0xCF39	0xCF39	0xCF39	change 3 unused bytes to 1 unused bytes
0xD034	0xD035	0xD034	0xD035	use IORTS for SHLOAD address
0xD04E	0xD04F	0xD04E	0xD04F	use IORTS for RECALL address
0xD050	0xD051	0xD050	0xD051	use IORTS for STORE address
0xD06C	0xD06D	0xD06C	0xD06D	use IORTS for LOAD address
0xD06E	0xD06F	0xD06E	0xD06F	use IORTS for SAVE address
0xD8B0	0xD8C8	0xD8B0	0xD8C8	remove SAVE code; empty (0x19 bytes)
0xD8C9	0xD8EF	0xD8C9	0xD8EF	remove LOAD code; empty (0x27 bytes)
0xD8F0	0xD900	0xD8F0	0xD900	remove SAVE, LOAD code; empty (0x11 bytes)
0xE484	0xE596	0xE484	0xE596	replace GARBAG with Bongers' algorithm Part 1
0xF39F	0xF3BB	0xF39F	0xB3BB	remove STORE code; empty (0x1D bytes)
0xF3BC	0xF3D7	0xF3BC	0xF3D7	remove RECALL code; empty (0x1C bytes)
0xF57A	0xF582	0xF57A	0xF582	add HLINMOD
0xF5A5	0xF5A5	0xF5A5	0xF5A5	add HLINMOD
0xF775	0xF786	0xF775	0xF786	remove SHLOAD code; empty (0x12 bytes)
0xF7D5	0xF7E6	0xF7D5	0xF7E6	remove STORE, RECALL code; empty (0x12 bytes)
0xF9A6	0xF9B3	0xFBC7	0xFBD6	move FMT2 table, add (zpage), (absolute,X) modes
0xF9B4	0xF9BF	0xFA30	0xFA3B	move CHAR1 and CHAR2 tables
0xF9C0	0xFA3F	0xF9A6	0xFA2F	move MNEML and MNEMR tables (0xA6 added), CXOFF/RTN
0xFA62	0xFA81	0xFA62	0xFA81	modify RESET; add SWEET16, SW16RTN
0xFB08	0xFB18	0xFB08	0xFB18	remove Apple text; put RSETINIT, move XLTBL
0xFBC1	0xFBD8	0xFBC1	0xFBD8	use BASCALC in CX ROM (Y-reg=2), add FMT2 table
0xFC5D	0xFC5F	0xFC5D	0xFC5F	unused bytes, add STEPRTN2
0xFCC9	0xFCD1	0xFCC9	0xFCD1	remove HEADR (rts); add STEPRTN
0xFEC2	0xFEC3	0xFEC2	0xFEC3	add TRACE
0xFEC4	0xFEC9	0xFA3C	0xFA3F	add STEP, move CXOFF add CXRTN
0xFECD	0xFED6	0xFECD	0xFED6	remove WRITE, add ZAPMEM
0xFEF1	0xFEF5	0xFEFD	0xFF04	move MINIASM, modify SEARCH2
0xFEFD	0xFF12	0xFEFD	0xFF0E	remove READ, add MINIASM, modify TITLE
0xFF13	0xFF1A	0xC500	0xC507	move GETNSP to CX ROM
0xFF1B	0xFF2C	0xFF18	0xFF2C	enhance LOOKASC, add "X" search command
0xFFCC	0xFFE2	0xFFCC	0xFFE2	remove "W" & "R", add "T" & "Z", "S" for STEP

Table II.5.2. Transformations to Build a New Apple //e ROM

The `ROM2E.SW16GC.3` ROM image has no provisions to write to or to read from an external cassette tape recorder. The `TAPEOUT` soft switch at `0xC020` as shown in Table II.2.3 and the `TAPEIN` soft switch at `0xC060` as shown in Table II.2.4 can certainly be used for other crafty external devices. Both cassette tape recorder external ports are unique in that they can be used to write and read a stream of electrically buffered digital data, respectively. `TAPEOUT` is the electrically buffered output of a 74LS74 D-type flip flop. There is no way to know whether the output signal is high or low at any given moment when the `0xC020` soft switch is read. This behavior is more like the `SPKRTOGL` soft switch at `0xC030` than any of the four annunciators whose output follow address bit `A0`. `TAPEIN` is a capacitor filtered and electrically buffered input whose signal is amplified by a 741 op amp. This op amp requires a minimum input threshold voltage to create an `ON` state for data bit `D0`, otherwise data bit `D0` is `OFF`. The value for data bit `D0` is obtained by reading the `0xC060` soft switch. This behavior is totally unlike the four paddle inputs that are Resistor/Capacitor (R/C) filtered and connected to a 558 quad timer device whose output is capable of sinking up to 100 mA of current.

I have been using the `ROM2E.SW16GC.3` ROM image for nearly a year with Virtual][as well as this image programmed into EPROM for an early Apple //e, for an Enhanced Apple //e, and for a Platinum Apple //e. In all instances the ROM image has been totally stable. All Applesoft routines that rely on the `TAPEOUT` and `TAPEIN` routines simply return immediately and without error to the caller.

I have no doubt that the individuals or the engineering teams that designed the Apple //e ROM firmware, and subsequently the Enhanced Apple //e ROM firmware were given a momentous task. That task was to preserve sixteen "classic" ROM entry points and to introduce a few new Monitor entry points in order to support 40-column and 80-column screen displays. This ROM also had to support most all previously written software for the Apple][and the Apple][+. Obviously, one can no longer expect to use any previous Monitor code "within" these classic entry points and expect reliable results. For example, the `IRQ` interrupt vector at `0xFFFE` and `0xFFFF` no longer uses the old `BREAK` vector at `0xFA40`. The useless snippet of code left at `0xFA40` only saves the A-register to `0x45` (AREG) before jumping to the new `IRQ` interrupt handler at `0xC3FA` instead of to the address found at `0x3FE` and `0x3FF` (usually the address of the Monitor, `0xFF65`). It appears that it may be no longer necessary to clear the page-zero `0x48` location after making a call to `RWTS` if DOS 3.3 is being utilized. It must be understood and accepted that the location of some data tables in this new Monitor is not sacrosanct and that these tables have been moved to other locations. I believe it is fair to say that ROM memory is very, very precious. I believe the Apple engineers did a remarkable job in building a quality 80-column text card firmware product that performs simply and elegantly.

To assemble the third build of the `ROM2E.SW16GC.3` ROM source code, place the `ROM2E.SW16GC.3` ROM Image volume `ROM2E.SW16GC.3.Image` in disk drive 1 and boot. *Lisa80* will start automatically into the 80-column display mode. Enter the `SE` command-line command to select the *SETUP80* utility in order to verify or set the `Start of Source Code` to `0x4000` and the `Start of Symbol List` to `0x7000`. Place the `ROM2E.SW16GC.3` ROM Source volume `ROM2E.SW16GC.3.Source` in disk drive 2, load the `ROM2E.L` file into memory, and start the assembler by entering either the `A` or the `Z` command-line command. If a printed version of the screen output is desired simply preface the `A` or the `Z` command with the `P1` command-line command. Four object code files will be created on the `ROM2E.SW16GC2` ROM Image volume named `C0ROM`, `D0ROM`, `E0ROM`, and `F0ROM`. These four object code files along with `ZEROPAGE`, `PAGE3`, and `PAGE6` need to be extracted from the `ROM2E.SW16GC.3` ROM Image volume into an empty directory using the C Language routines found at applecored.net. In that same directory copy or create the UNIX command file shown in Figure II.5.1 and execute that command file to generate the `APPLE2E.SW16GC.3.ROM` file.

```
cat d0rom e0rom f0rom > romA
cat zeropage zeropage zeropage page3 > rom1
cat zeropage zeropage page6 zeropage > rom2
cat zeropage zeropage zeropage zeropage > rom3
cat rom1 rom2 rom3 rom3 romA > rom4
cat rom4 c0rom romA > APPLE2E.SW16GC.3.ROM
rm rom1 rom2 rom3 rom4 romA
```

Figure II.5.1. UNIX Command File to Build the APPLE2E.SW16GC.3.ROM

Copy the newly generated `APPLE2E.SW16GC.3.ROM` ROM image file into the Virtual][folder for Application Support. Then manually configure Virtual][with this ROM image file. The virtual machine will need to be restarted for this ROM image file to take effect. To build the ROM images for a real Apple //e computer, `BRUN` the `BLDROM` program on the `ROM2E.SW16GC.3` ROM Image volume `ROM2E.SW16GC.3.Image`. `BLDROM` will create the ROM images `SW16GC.CF.ROM`, `SW16GC.CD.ROM`, and `SW16GC.EF.ROM`. The `SW16GC.CF.ROM` ROM image can be programmed into a 27128 EPROM for an Enhanced Apple //e and a Platinum Apple //e. The `SW16GC.CD.ROM` and `SW16GC.EF.ROM` ROM images can each be programmed into 2764 EPROMs for an earlier Apple //e. The PROmGRAMER, for example, could be used to program an EPROM with these ROM images.

6. Apple //e Character Generator ROM

Virtual][, Gerard Putter's MacOS application to emulate the Apple][computer, provides the capability to use a personally designed ASCII display character set. The input character set is defined by a character set bitmap that is either a PNG or TIFF file which is exactly 128 pixels wide and exactly 64 pixels high. The bitmap depth must be one or eight pixels. Each character in the bitmap is defined in a character cell that is eight pixels by eight pixels. Because characters displayed on the Apple][are only seven pixels wide, the right most column of the character cell is ignored by Virtual][. The black pixels within a character cell comprise the background of the character; all other pixels comprise the character itself. The "Users/<username>/Library/Application Support/Virtual][/CharacterSets" directory must contain this character set bitmap file. A filename suggested by the Virtual][documentation for this bitmap file is MyCharacters.tif. An XML file named International.plist must also be located in this directory and it defines the actual name of the character set bitmap file. This XML file may include the name of an icon bitmap file called MyCharSetIcon.tif whose size can be up to sixteen pixels wide by eleven pixels high, and it is displayed in the upper left corner of the Virtual][window. The XML file may also include a keyboard translation table if that is needed as well. The XML file I created is shown in Figure II.6.1 and it includes two different character set bitmap files.

Key	Type	Value
▼ Root	Dictionary	(2 items)
▼ My new character set	Dictionary	(3 items)
CharacterSet	String	MyNewCharacters.tif
Icon	String	MyCharSetIcon.tif
▶ KeyboardTranslation	Dictionary	(0 items)
▼ My old character set	Dictionary	(3 items)
CharacterSet	String	MyOldCharacters.tif
Icon	String	MyCharSetIcon.tif
▶ KeyboardTranslation	Dictionary	(0 items)

Figure II.6.1. International XML File

I used Xcode to easily create the XML file shown in Figure II.6.1. Any "Property List Editor" will work as well. To create the TIFF bitmap files I used the MacOS Paintbrush application because it was available for download at no charge. I am not an expert Paintbrush user and I had some difficulties with the application to produce what I wanted easily. Most of my difficulties occurred when I tried to save my work during incremental stages of testing. I found that if I used the Lasso tool to copy the entire bitmap area into the clipboard, I could save the contents of the clipboard into a new bitmap file of the same size, and then discard the original file. I do not know why the "save" or "save as" option failed to save my incremental work to the original file, and why I had to save my work in such a round-about way. I used the Line tool configured for a "stroke" of one to toggle a pixel from black to white or white to black. Paintbrush saved the bitmap file as a TIFF file having a Color Space of RGB, a Color Profile of Generic RGB Profile, and the Alpha Channel set to Yes. I have no idea what these specifications mean or imply, but Virtual][had no problem reading and utilizing all the TIFF files I created in this manner.

My greatest source of irritation came when I discovered that the "Library" directory specified in the above pathname for the CharacterSets directory is a hidden file by default. I lost more time putting the XML and TIFF files in the wrong location because I could not see the hidden Library directory in my personal Users account. Once I realized this directory was hidden, it was extremely easy to unhide it using XQuartz or the Terminal application found in the Utilities directory. Simply launch the Terminal application and enter bash on the command line. This will start the GNU "Bourne-Again SHell." Now, when you enter the UNIX command "ls -AF" at /Users/<username>, all files, including "." files and hidden files (i.e. directories), will be displayed. Now enter the command "chflags nohidden Library" and have a look at a Finder window for your personal Users account. You should now see a "Library" directory. Once you locate the XML and TIFF files properly and launch Virtual][, select Quick settings>Character Set>My character set. Be sure to save your Virtual][session when you are satisfied with the selected character set bitmap file: it will be loaded and selected every time Virtual][is launched.

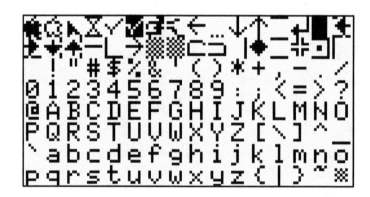

Figure II.6.2. Inverse of New Character Set Bitmap TIFF File

Figures II.6.2 shows the inverse of the MyNewCharacters.tif file and Figure II.6.3 shows the normal MyCharSetIcon.tif file I created for Virtual][. I modified quite a few of the characters to my preferences. Once I was satisfied with my character set bitmap, I created a simple tool using LORES graphics that allowed me to create a 4 KB binary character set ROM file. This file must also contain the inverse characters as well as the alternate keyboard characters which are not included in Figure II.6.2. I found that it was easier to read the stock character generator ROM using the PROmGRAMER, for example, into a binary file. I could display the data of each character using my LORES tool and edit a copy of each character which is displayed to the right of the original character as shown in Figure II.6.4. Once I made all the changes to the character set, I could save the data currently in memory to another binary ROM file and program an equivalent sized 2732 EPROM with that data. My Apple][+ and all three of my Apple //e computers use the character set shown in Figure II.6.2.

Figure II.6.3. Icon TIFF Bitmap File

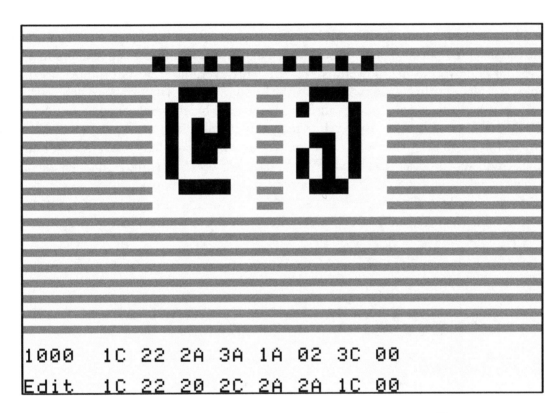

Figure II.6.4. Binary Character Set LORES Editor

7. Peripheral Slot Card Signature Bytes

More than likely Apple Computer designed the concept of Signature Bytes when the Disk][was first introduced to the Apple][consumer. The first eight bytes of the firmware that resides on the peripheral slot card that connects the Disk][drive to the Apple][computer are the Signature Bytes for this slot card. Other manufactures of peripheral slot cards adopted this scheme so that each slot card could be potentially identified by inspecting those first eight bytes. Other manufactures who designed slot cards for their disk drives used the same scheme developed by Apple Computer. Manufactures of real time clock cards also used the signature byte scheme developed by ThunderClock. Similarly, signature byte schemes were developed for printer interface slot cards, serial data interface slot cards, mouse interface slot cards, and display interface slot cards to list just a few examples. Each scheme has a general pattern that contains identical portions and unique portions of bytes. Table II.7.1 lists the signature bytes for a number of peripheral slot cards that I happen to own or know about.

All of the odd signature bytes for peripheral slot cards that interface disk drives must be the same. This is done purposefully because the Autostart ROM that Apple Computer copyrighted in 1978 checks those four odd bytes during powerup or restart. However, the Autostart routine was modified for the Apple //e Video Firmware, copyrighted in 1981 and in 1984. The firmware note is shown in Figure II.7.1. In other words, only the first three odd signature bytes are checked by the Apple //e Autostart ROM for a bootable disk drive. After analyzing the disk startup firmware that follows the first eight bytes for the Disk][peripheral slot card, it shows that upon entry the Y-register must be set to `0x00`, the X-register can be set to any value from `0x00` to `0x16`, and the A-register can contain any value. The page-zero location `0x3C` is a temporary storage location so any value can be stored there, which is done in the fourth instruction, "`STX $3C`". The first instruction, "`LDX #$20`", does nothing since the third, and critical instruction rewrites the value contained in the X-register.

```
Check 3 ID bytes instead of 4.  Allows devices
other than Disk II's to be bootable.
```

Figure II.7.1. Video Firmware Note for the Apple //e

Apparently, Applied Engineering used the same signature bytes for their TimeMaster II clock card as those found in the ThunderClock clock card. Only the first two bytes are significant as well as the last byte in its firmware page. The last byte, or `CLKID` for the ThunderClock firmware is `0x07` and the last byte for the TimeMaster II firmware is `0x03`. I set the last byte for my clock card firmware to `0x03`. It is these three bytes, the first two and the last, that DOS 4.3 checks for a valid clock card.

In many cases a peripheral slot card not only must be compatible with DOS, but possibly also with ProDOS, CP/M, Fortran, and Pascal as well. The peripheral-card ROM memory and the peripheral-card expansion ROM memory amounts to only nine pages of code space. Therefore, even the signature bytes must perform a necessary function besides being unique to the particular peripheral slot card. In some cases, the signature bytes provide multiple return entry points for input and output data control. If the peripheral slot card supports Pascal, the Pascal initialization, read, write, and status routine offsets closely follow the initial signature bytes.

Slot Card	Signature Bytes							
	0	1	2	3	4	5	6	7
Disk][	LDX	#$20	LDY	#$00	LDX	#$03	STX	$3C
	0xA2	0x20	0xA0	0x00	0xA2	0x03	0x86	0x3C
SCSI][	LDX	#$20	LDX	#$00	LDX	#$03	LDX	#$00
	0xA2	0x20	0xA2	0x00	0xA2	0x03	0xA2	0x00
RANA	LDX	#$20	LDY	#$00	LDX	#$03	LDX	#$3C
	0xA2	0x20	0xA0	0x00	0xA2	0x03	0xA2	0x3C
SIDER	LDA	#$20	LDA	#$00	LDA	#$03	LDA	$3C
	0xA9	0x20	0xA9	0x00	0xA9	0x03	0xA9	0x3C
RAM Disk	LDX	#$20	LDY	#$00	LDX	#$03	STY	$3C
	0xA2	0x20	0xA0	0x00	0xA2	0x04	0x84	0x3C
CFFA	LDA	#$20	LDX	#$00	LDA	#$03	LDA	#$00
	0xA9	0x20	0xA2	0x00	0xA9	0x03	0xA9	0x00
ThunderClock	PHP	SEI	PLP	BIT	$FF58		BVS	$Cs0D
	0x08	0x78	0x28	0x2C	0x58	0xFF	0x70	0x05
TimeMaster II	PHP	SEI	PLP	BIT	$FF58		BVS	$Cs0D
	0x08	0x78	0x28	0x2C	0x58	0xFF	0x70	0x05
My Clock	PHP	SEI	BIT	$CFFF		CLR	BCC	$Cs38
	0x08	0x78	0x2C	0xFF	0xCF	0x18	0x90	0x30
SuperSerial	BIT	$FF58		BVS	$Cs11	SEC	BCC	$Cs20
	0x2C	0x58	0xFF	0x70	0x0C	0x38	0x90	0x18
Grappler	CLC	BCS	$Cs3B	BCC	$Cs11	SEC	BCC	$Cs20
	0x18	0xB0	0x38	0x90	0x0C	0x38	0x90	0x18
Mouse	BIT	$FF58		BVS	$Cs20	SEC	BCC	$Cs20
	0x2C	0x58	0xFF	0x70	0x1B	0x38	0x90	0x18
80-Column	BIT	$CE43		BCS	$C317	SEC	BCC	CLC
	0x2C	0x43	0xCE	0x70	0x12	0x38	0x90	0x18

Table II.7.1. Peripheral Slot Card Signature Bytes

Since the operation of the first signature byte instruction is not used, any of the other ten 6502 Immediate Addressing Mode instructions can be used as a component identifier within the Disk][signature byte scheme. Once I realized which were the important and unimportant bytes within the signature byte data, I could design a very simple strategy to quickly identify a Disk][signature byte scheme by checking the first three odd bytes like the Apple //e Autostart ROM does, and use the first instruction byte to select the actual device. Table II.7.2 lists the revised signature bytes for my collection of Disk][, Disk][-like, and disk drive peripheral devices.

Slot Card	Signature Bytes							
	0	1	2	3	4	5	6	7
Disk][	LDX	#$20	LDY	#$00	LDX	#$03	STX	$3C
(no change)	0xA2	0x20	0xA0	0x00	0xA2	0x03	0x86	0x3C
SCSI][	LDX	#$20	LDX	#$00	LDX	#$03	LDX	#$00
(no change)	0xA2	0x20	0xA2	0x00	0xA2	0x03	0xA2	0x00
RANA	ORA	#$20	LDY	#$00	LDX	#$03	STX	$3C
	0x09	0x20	0xA0	0x00	0xA2	0x03	0x86	0x3C
SIDER	AND	#$20	LDY	#$00	LDX	#$03	STX	$3C
	0x29	0x20	0xA0	0x00	0xA2	0x03	0x86	0x3C
RAM Disk	EOR	#$20	LDY	#$00	LDX	#$03	STX	$3C
	0x49	0x20	0xA0	0x00	0xA2	0x03	0x86	0x3C
CFFA	ADC	#$20	LDY	#$00	LDX	#$03	STX	$3C
	0x69	0x20	0xA0	0x00	0xA2	0x03	0x86	0x3C
available	LDA	#$20	LDY	#$00	LDX	#$03	STX	$3C
	0xA9	0x20	0xA0	0x00	0xA2	0x03	0x86	0x3C
available	CMP	#$20	LDY	#$00	LDX	#$03	STX	$3C
	0xC9	0x20	0xA0	0x00	0xA2	0x03	0x86	0x3C
available	SBC	#$20	LDY	#$00	LDX	#$03	STX	$3C
	0xE9	0x20	0xA0	0x00	0xA2	0x03	0x86	0x3C
available	LDY	#$20	LDY	#$00	LDX	#$03	STX	$3C
	0xA0	0x20	0xA0	0x00	0xA2	0x03	0x86	0x3C
available	CPY	#$20	LDY	#$00	LDX	#$03	STX	$3C
	0xC0	0x20	0xA0	0x00	0xA2	0x03	0x86	0x3C
available	CPX	#$20	LDY	#$00	LDX	#$03	STX	$3C
	0xE0	0x20	0xA0	0x00	0xA2	0x03	0x86	0x3C

Table II.7.2. Revised Disk Drive Peripheral Slot Card Signature Bytes

III. DOS 4.3 Commands

DOS 4.3 commands comprise a set of commands in addition to the Applesoft ROM commands. As in Applesoft commands, DOS 4.3 commands and keywords may be entered in uppercase and/or lowercase. DOS 4.3 uses a number of data tables in order to process a valid DOS command when the command is found in the DOS Command Name Text table. This table consists of the DCI ASCII name for each DOS command in the order of command index value generally used in DOS 3.3. The Command Valid Keyword table is used to determine which keywords if any are required or may be used in conjunction with each DOS command based on command index. Each command has a two-byte table entry, thus providing 16 possible bit flags indicating which keywords are legal, or if a filename is expected, for example. The bit flag settings for the DOS Command Valid Keywords are defined in Table III.0.1. The legal keywords have been ordered in a more logical, hierarchical, and useful way than the order used in DOS 3.3. Before processing a valid DOS 4.3 command, the value of the R keyword is copied to the File Manager SUBCODE variable. This allows users of the external File Manager handler to utilize the SUBCODE in order to simulate the R keyword as in the case of the File Manager FMCATACD command code for the DOS CATALOG command. The DOS INIT command, however, overwrites the SUBCODE variable with BOOTYPE for its own specific use as shown previously in Figures I.11.1 and I.11.2.

Valid Keyword bits 10 and 11 are mutually exclusive in that no DOS 3.3 command uses these two bits together in any single command. I chose to identify a special non-keyword "value" category by setting both bits for the DOS SV, PHASE, and CONFIG commands. This special category of "value" commands may be easily identified and range-checked as appropriate.

Bit	Bit Position	Value	Flag Bit Description
15	%1000 0000 0000 0000	0x8000	Filename legal but optional
14	%0100 0000 0000 0000	0x4000	Command has no positional operands
13	%0010 0000 0000 0000	0x2000	Filename #1 is expected
12	%0001 0000 0000 0000	0x1000	Filename #2 is expected
11	%0000 1000 0000 0000	0x0800	Slot number positional operand is expected
11&10	%0000 1100 0000 0000	0x0C00	Non-keyword value number is expected
10	%0000 0100 0000 0000	0x0400	MAXFILES value positional operand is expected
9	%0000 0010 0000 0000	0x0200	Command is only issued from within a program
8	%0000 0001 0000 0000	0x0100	Command creates a new file if the file is not found
7	%0000 0000 1000 0000	0x0080	C, I, O keywords are legal
6	%0000 0000 0100 0000	0x0040	S keyword is legal but not necessarily expected
5	%0000 0000 0010 0000	0x0020	D keyword is legal but not necessarily expected
4	%0000 0000 0001 0000	0x0010	V keyword is legal but not necessarily expected
3	%0000 0000 0000 1000	0x0008	A keyword is legal but not necessarily expected
2	%0000 0000 0000 0100	0x0004	L keyword is legal but not necessarily expected
1	%0000 0000 0000 0010	0x0002	R keyword is legal but not necessarily expected
0	%0000 0000 0000 0001	0x0001	B keyword is legal but not necessarily expected

Table III.0.1. DOS 4.3 Command Valid Keyword Table

Command Name	Index	ASCII Text	S/W Handler	Keyword
CMDINIT	0x00	INIT	DOINIT	0x317F
CMDLOAD	0x02	LOAD	DOLOAD	0xA072
CMDSAVE	0x04	SAVE	DOSAVE	0xA173
CMDRUN	0x06	RUN	DORUN	0xA074
CMDCHAIN	0x08	CHAIN	DOCHAIN	0x2276
CMDDELET	0x0A	DELETE	DODELETE	0x2072
CMDLOCK	0x0C	LOCK	DOLOCK	0x6070
CMDUNLCK	0x0E	UNLOCK	DOUNLOCK	0x6070
CMDCLOSE	0x10	CLOSE	DOCLOSE	0x6000
CMDREAD	0x12	READ	DOREAD	0x2203
CMDEXEC	0x14	EXEC	DOEXEC	0x2073
CMDWRITE	0x16	WRITE	DOWRITE	0x2203
CMDPOSTN	0x18	POSITION	DOPSTION	0x2202
CMDOPEN	0x1A	OPEN	DOOPENTX	0x2374
CMDAPND	0x1C	APPEND	DOAPND	0x2270
CMDRENAM	0x1E	RENAME	DORENAME	0x3072
CMDCAT	0x20	CATALOG	DOCAT	0x4072
CMDMON	0x22	MON	DOMON	0x4080
CMDNOMAN	0x24	NOMON	DONOMON	0x4080
CMDPRNUM	0x26	PR#	DOPRNUM	0x4800
CMDINNUM	0x28	IN#	DOINNUM	0x4800
CMDMXFLS	0x2A	MAXFILES	DOMXFLS	0x4400
CMDDATE	0x2C	DATE	DODATE	0x4000
CMDLIST	0x2E	LIST	DOLIST	0x2077
CMDBSAVE	0x30	BSAVE	DOBSAVE	0x217F
CMDBLOAD	0x32	BLOAD	DOBLOAD	0x207A
CMDBRUN	0x34	BRUN	DOBRUN	0x2078
CMDVERFY	0x36	VERIFY	DOVERIFY	0x2072
CMDLSAVE	0x38	LSAVE	DOLSAVE	0x217F
CMDLLOAD	0x3A	LLOAD	DOLLOAD	0x207A
CMDTSAVE	0x3C	TSAVE	DOTSAVE	0x2173
CMDTLOAD	0x3E	TLOAD	DOTLOAD	0x207F
CMDDIFF	0x40	DIFF	DODIFF	0x3070
CMDGREP	0x42	GREP	DOGREP	0x3071
CMDMORE	0x44	MORE	DOLIST	0x2077
CMDCAT2	0x46	CAT	DOCAT	0x4072
CMDURM	0x48	URM	DOURM	0x2070
CMDCD	0x4A	CD	DOCD	0x4072
CMDLS	0x4C	LS	DOCAT	0x4072
CMDMV	0x4E	MV	DORENAME	0x3072
CMDRM	0x50	RM	DODELETE	0x2072
CMDSV	0x52	SV	DOSV	0x4C00
CMDTS	0x54	TS	DOTS	0x407F
CMDWTS	0x56	WTS	DOWTS	0x407F
CMDTW	0x58	TW	DOTW	0x2170
CMDPHASE	0x5A	PHASE	DOPHASE	0x4C00
CMDTOUCH	0x5C	TOUCH	DOTOUCH	0x2072
CMDCONFG	0x5E	CONFIG	DOCONFIG	0x4C00
CMDHELP	0x60	HELP	DOHELP	0x4000
CMDUSER	0x62	-	DOUSER	-

Table III.0.2. DOS 4.3 Command Table

Table III.0.2 is a comprehensive listing of all DOS 4.3 commands in processing order showing the command name, index, ASCII text, software handler, and valid keyword value. `CMDHELP` is available in DOS 4.3 because there is additional room in Language Card Bank 1 memory where `RWTS` is located. This additional memory seemed like an ideal location for placing a Help Command handler in order to provide instant syntactical usage information for all DOS 4.3 commands. DOS 4.3 needed two additional sectors for its interface and boot pages, so the DOS image required the use of track `0x02` anyway. Why not use a few more sectors on track `0x02` for something quite useful like the Help Command handler? Another DOS developer may choose to eliminate the Help Command handler and utilize the memory and/or disk sectors for something else entirely.

`CMDUSER` is designed and available for a user who needs to load DOS 4.3 into memory, initialize it, and then have DOS 4.3 return control back to that user instead of to Applesoft after Applesoft initialization. After DOS 4.3 has been copied into memory, all the user needs to do is to call the `MNGUSER` routine with the address of the routine that will take control after DOS 4.3 has initialized. `MNGUSER` simply sets or resets the address found at `USERADR` so that `CMDUSER` simply executes an indirect jump to `USERADR`. Figure I.8.3 shows an example assembly language program that totally manages the initialization of DOS 4.3. DOS 4.3 can always be restored to its initial state by calling `MNGUSER` with the `Carry` flag cleared.

Keyword Name	Bit Position - Value	Minimum Value	Maximum Value
C	%1100 0000 – 0xC0	–	–
I	%1010 0000 – 0xA0	–	–
O	%1001 0000 – 0x90	–	–
MON/NOMON	%1000 0000 – 0x80	–	–
S	%0100 0000 – 0x40	1 (0x01)	7 (0x0007)
D	%0010 0000 – 0x20	1 (0x01)	81 (0x0051)
V	%0001 0000 – 0x10	0 (0x00)	255 (0x00FF)
A	%0000 1000 – 0x08	0 (0x00)	65535 (0xFFFF)
L	%0000 0100 – 0x04	0 (0x00)	65535 (0xFFFF)
R	%0000 0010 – 0x02	0 (0x00)	32767 (0x7FFF)
B	%0000 0001 – 0x01	0 (0x00)	32767 (0x7FFF)

Table III.0.3. DOS 4.3 Keyword Name and Range Table

DOS 4.3 uses the following four tables to parse valid keywords, ascertain a keyword's bit position, and determine if a keyword is within a minimum and a maximum value: `PPARMS`, `PARMBITS`, `KWRANGEL`, and `KWRANGEH`. The content of these tables is summarized in Table III.0.3. Unlike DOS 3.3, DOS 4.3 will allow up to 81 drives in order to support CFFA Volume Manager software for a Compact Flash card up to 8 GB in size, allow default Volume numbers to be `0x00`, and allow `BSAVE` and `LSAVE` to write files greater than `0x7FFF` bytes. The Bit Positions for the keywords `C`, `I`, and `O` are actually used to generate the `MONVAL` variable once the MSB of the bit position value is cleared. The other Bit Positions are added to the variable `KYWRDFND` as each keyword is parsed. It is no accident that the Bit Position of each Keyword in Table III.0.3 is the same as it is in the lower byte of each command keyword shown in Table III.0.1.

The syntax of a DOS 4.3 command begins with the command, and the command is immediately followed by one or two filenames if they are required. All parameters whether they are required or optional follow the filename(s) or the command, and usually a comma must delineate each parameter. In all the following command definitions, optional parameters are contained in square brackets, as in [,Vv]. Commands and keywords are shown in CAPITAL letters and keyword values are shown in lowercase letters for ease of explanation and not in how they need to be used in a program or entered on the Apple command line. Keyword values may be entered as a decimal or as a hexadecimal number; hexadecimal numbers are always prefaced with the dollar sign as in $1234. However, DOS 4.3 usually prints hexadecimal values preceded with "0x" as in 0x1234 unless a Keyword precedes the hexadecimal number. The value of "zero" is shown as "0x00" for ease of explanation. Table III.0.4 lists all keywords and keyword value items.

In keeping with the original DOS 3.3 documentation, DOS 4.3 commands may be grouped into the six categories shown on the following page.

Keyword	Name	Description
S	Slot	Keyword followed by slot number
D	Drive	Keyword followed by drive number
V	Volume	Keyword followed by volume number
A	Address	Keyword followed by address number
L	Length	Keyword followed by length number
R	Record	Keyword followed by record number or nothing
B	Byte	Keyword followed by byte number
C	Command	Keyword to display or not display DOS commands
I	Input	Keyword to display or not display input data
O	Output	Keyword to display or not display output data
f	filename	Begins with "0" or greater and be 1-24 characters in length
f2	2nd filename	Begins with "0" or greater and be 1-24 characters in length
s	slot number	Slot number of a peripheral slot card, value range 1-7
d	drive number	Initialized to 1, value range 1-81 (for CFFA use)
v	volume number	Initialized to 0, value range 0-255
a	address number	Initialized to 0, value range 0-65535
l	length number	Initialized to 0, value range 0-65535
r	record number	Initialized to 0, value range 0-32767
b	byte number	Initialized to 0, value range 0-32767
n	number	Some numerical value required by some commands

Table III.0.4. DOS 4.3 Keywords and Keyword Value Items

System Commands

CONFIG	DATE	HELP	IN#
MAXFILES	MON	NOMON	PHASE
PR#	SV		

File System Commands

CAT	CATALOG	CD	DELETE
DIFF	GREP	INIT	LIST
LOCK	LS	MORE	MV
RENAME	RM	TOUCH	TS
UNLOCK	URM	VERIFY	WTS

Applesoft File Commands

CHAIN	LOAD	RUN	SAVE

Binary File Commands

BLOAD	BRUN	BSAVE	LLOAD
LSAVE			

Sequential Text File Commands

APPEND	CLOSE	EXEC	OPEN
POSITION	READ	TLOAD	TSAVE
TW	WRITE		

Random-Access Data File Commands

CLOSE	OPEN	READ	WRITE

Command	Command Syntax
CONFIG	[n]
DATE	
HELP	
IN#	s
MAXFILES	[n]
MON	[,C][,I][,O]
NOMON	[,C][,I][,O]
PHASE	[n]
PR#	s
SV	[n]

Table III.1.1. DOS 4.3 System Commands

1. System Commands

The DOS 4.3 System Commands manage the general operation of DOS 4.3, the Input/Output data streams, the display of commands and data items, the syntactical usage of DOS commands, the conversion of decimal and hexadecimal values, the track size in half-phases, and the number of active data buffers within DOS 4.3. The syntax of the System Commands is shown in Table III.1.1.

CONFIG   [n]

Example: CONFIG
            CONFIG $C7

This command is new to DOS 4.3 and it provides the means to change the operation of eight key processing elements in DOS 4.3. CONFIG values may be entered in either decimal or hexadecimal. If no value or 0x00 is entered with the CONFIG command, its current value is displayed on the Apple command line in decimal. Each of the eight available bits for CONFIG control one processing element. As shown in Table III.1.2, the LSB, or Bit 0 is the first command bit listed. In order to clear all CONFIG bits to zero, the value 0xFF or 255 must be entered with the CONFIG command.

CONFIG Bit 0, when set, will eliminate the extra carriage return between command entries on the Apple command line except when displaying the header for the DOS CATALOG command. Bit 1, when set, will eliminate the automatic verification of a file after it is saved to a volume when using the DOS SAVE, BSAVE, LSAVE, or TSAVE commands. Enabling this bit will visibly reduce the amount of time that is required to save a file to a volume, but it eliminates the verification that the file can be read into memory without error. Bit 2, when set, will eliminate printing the prompt character (usually "]") while EXEC is processing its file. Setting this bit will not change how EXEC processes DOS commands. Bit 3, when set, will bypass any DOS MAXFILES command when that statement is encountered in an Applesoft or assembly language program. However, if the DOS MAXFILES command is used without a value it will still function as normal without regard to CONFIG Bit 3.

It is important to understand that there is no benefit in changing the value of MAXFILES in DOS 4.3. DOS 4.3 builds five file buffers in Language Card memory that cannot be used for any other purpose. Reducing the number of file buffers in DOS 4.3 does not provide any additional memory to programs. HIMEM is always set to memory address 0xBE00 without regard to the number of file buffers.

Bit	Description
0	Do not print extra carriage returns between commands in local CROUT
1	Do not verify files after a SAVE, BSAVE, LSAVE, or TSAVE in WRITRNG
2	Do not print prompt character "] " during EXEC processing in CSWST1B
3	Bypass MAXFILES command processing in DOMXFLS
4	Bypass all disk and file locks
5	Bypass pushing DOSWARM-1 onto the stack before BRUN
6	Convert all output characters to uppercase in local COUT
7	Convert all input characters to uppercase in GNXTCHR

Table III.1.2. CONFIG Command Bit Summary

```
]config = 000

]config $ef
]CONFIG = 239
]SV 239 = 0X00EF = 00239
]LOAD HELLO
]LS

S=6 D=02 V=123 F=0508 01/01/20 08:28:48

 A 004 HELLO            01/01/20 08:28:48
]CONFIG $FF

]config = 000

]
```

Figure III.1.1. CONFIG Command Display

101

CONFIG Bit 4, when set, will bypass all disk and file locks. Bit 5, when set, will not push the DOSWARM-1 address onto the stack before jumping to a BRUN start address. Pushing this address onto the stack simply ensures that DOS will reconnect after the BRUNed file has finished its processing. Bit 6, when set, will convert all DOS 4.3 output characters to uppercase. For example, all DOS 4.3 error messages will appear in uppercase when Bit 6 is set. Even text printed using an Applesoft PRINT command will appear in uppercase. Essentially, everything printed to the display will appear in uppercase. Bit 7, when set, will convert all DOS 4.3 input filename characters to uppercase. In other words, whether the caps lock key is enabled or not, all input filenames will be converted to uppercase. This makes it possible to load or save uppercase file names while the keyboard is set for lowercase. Figure III.1.1 shows a few display results when using the DOS CONFIG command.

DATE

Example: DATE

This command was originally developed for DOS 4.1 and it displays on the screen the current date and time as shown in Figure III.1.2. DOS 4.3 supports at least three clock cards and possibly others: Thunderclock, TimeMaster, and the clock card I designed and built. The major difference in these clock cards is the index where the date and time data begin in the output raw data string each card generates. Figure III.1.2 also shows an example Applesoft program that displays the raw data string for a Thunderclock card residing in slot 4. The index where the date and time data begin for this clock card is 0x00 from Table I.13.1. The TimeMaster clock card and my clock card both have an index of 0x03. DOS 4.3 can support any clock card having the standard signature bytes, CLKID, and an index value from 0x00 to 0x05 where the date and time data begin in its output raw data string.

HELP

Example: HELP

This command was originally developed only for DOS 4.1H, and modified for DOS 4.3. The HELP command provides instant syntactical usage information for all DOS 4.3 commands. When HELP is entered on the Apple command line, Figure III.1.3 is displayed showing the entire DOS 4.3 command repertoire. Arrow keys must be used to navigate to the specific DOS command for which HELP is desired. The left/right arrow keys step through the command list either backwards or forwards, respectively. The up/down arrow keys step through a column of commands either upwards or downwards, respectively. Stepping backwards from the first command CONFIG navigates to the last command WRITE, and vice versa. Pressing the RTN key selects the command and displays its HELP content. Pressing the ESC key resumes normal DOS processing even while viewing HELP content. Figure III.1.4 shows the help content for HELP. Figure III.1.5 shows the help content for INIT.

```
]date = 01/01/20 08:28:48

]load read clock

]list

 10  D$ =  CHR$ (4)
 20  SLOT = 4
 30   PRINT D$;"pr#";SLOT
 40   PRINT D$;"in#";SLOT
 50   INPUT ":";A$
 60   PRINT D$;"pr#0"
 70   PRINT D$;"in#0"
 80   PRINT
 90   PRINT A$

]run

01/01  08;28;48.000

]※
```

Figure III.1.2. DATE Command for Thunderclock Card Display

```
            System Commands
CONFIG    DATE      HELP      IN#    MAXFILES
  MON     NOMON    PHASE      PR#      SV

         File System Commands
  CAT    CATALOG    CD      DELETE      DIFF
 GREP     INIT     LIST      LOCK        LS
 MORE      MV     RENAME      RM       TOUCH
  TS     UNLOCK    URM      VERIFY      WTS

        Applesoft File Commands
 CHAIN    LOAD      RUN      SAVE

         Binary File Commands
 BLOAD    BRUN     BSAVE     LLOAD     LSAVE

       Sequential Text File Commands
APPEND   CLOSE     EXEC      OPEN    POSITION
 READ    TLOAD     TSAVE      TW      WRITE

       Random-Access Data File Commands
 CLOSE    OPEN      READ     WRITE

            <+>   RTN   ESC
```

Figure III.1.3. HELP Command Display

```
                DOS 4.3 Management


*BE00G - enable RAM Bank2
*BE08G - enable RAM Bank1

0xBFF0 - BLDVRSN (DOS version number)
0xBFF1 - BLDNMBR (DOS build number)

0xBFF2 - MNGDISK (manage Disk Table)
0xBFF4 - MNGVALS (manage DOS values)
0xBFF6 - MNGUSER (manage DOS CMDUSER)

0xBFF8 - INITDOS (DOS init address)
0xBFFA - INITVAL (INIT values address)

0xBFFC - BCFGNDX (BOOTCFG Table offset)
0xBFFD - NBUF1PG (NBUF1 MSB Page)



                RTN   ESC
```

Figure III.1.4. HELP Content in HELP Command

```
INIT f, f2 [,Ss] [,Dd] [,Vv] [,An] [,Bn]
           [,Ln] [,R[n]]

INIT HELLO,<Title>,L$1234          (Boot)

INIT HELLO,<Title>,A40,B4,R        (Data)

INIT HELLO,<Title>,R$14            (EXEC)


A = volume tracks
B = catalog sectors|sectors/track flag
L = volume subject
R = volume type




                RTN   ESC
```

Figure III.1.5. INIT Content in HELP Command

It is certainly not possible with the limited memory resources and disk space of the Apple][to provide any further help content than what this command already provides. The HELP command is intended to display sufficient information in how each command is used and all the keywords associated with that command. Keywords that have been added to a DOS command are defined. At least one example is given for each command showing how the command can be used. If more information is required the DOS 4.3 File Management System Book is always available and is always the ultimate resource.

IN#   s

Example: IN#7

This command configures the KSWL interface to receive all subsequent data from the peripheral device residing in the specified slot s instead of from the Apple keyboard. Figure III.1.2 shows an example Applesoft program that uses the IN# command to configure the KSWL interface in order to communicate with the Thunderclock clock card.

MAXFILES [n]

Example: MAXFILES 4
           MAXFILES

This command specifies the number of file buffers n that can be active at any given time up to a maximum of five buffers. When DOS 4.3 boots, the default number of file buffers is configured using the NMAXVAL variable as shown in Table I.8.5. This value is set to five in the DOS 4.3 source code. Each file buffer requires 582 (or 0x246) bytes of memory, and DOS 4.3 builds its file buffers up in memory beginning at memory address 0xECA0. DOS 4.3 was designed this way such that setting MAXFILES to three will allow the installation of the MiniAssembler and its monitor at memory address 0xF500 and not perturb any of those three file buffers. Apple][memory is very precious, but specifying fewer than five file buffers does not provide any more memory for programs in DOS 4.3. HIMEM is always set to memory address 0xBE00 regardless how many file buffers are configured.

MAXFILES with no parameter n will display the current number of active file buffers on the Apple command line as shown in Figure III.1.6. This figure shows that changing the number of file buffers does not change the location of HIMEM: it remains set to 0xBE00. The number of file buffers can never be zero. Even the CATALOG command requires a file buffer for the CLOSOPEN routine used by the File Manager. Table III.1.3 shows the memory locations for the contents of all five file buffers. There is just enough room for the 32-byte SECMAP buffer at 0xEC80 to precede the DOS file buffers that end right before the ROM Monitor routines begin. As stated before, reducing the number of file buffers in DOS 4.3 does not provide any additional memory for software programs because all file buffers reside in Language Card memory. Before the MAXFILES command rebuilds the file buffers so that DOS can utilize them, DOS 4.3 terminates any active EXEC file and closes all open files.

If CONFIG Bit 3 is set as shown in Table III.1.2 the Command Manager in DOS 4.3 will bypass MAXFILES processing except if the MAXFILES statement is given without a parameter n. In this instance DOS 4.3 will display the current number of active file buffers on the Apple command line. Setting CONFIG Bit 3 is far easier than having to modify and edit an Applesoft program to eliminate all DOS MAXFILES statements thereby transforming the program to be far more suitable to the DOS 4.3 processing environment. Even assembly language programs could benefit from setting CONFIG Bit 3 in order to bypass MAXFILES processing and unnecessarily change the configuration of DOS to have a specific number of file buffers.

File Buffer	Data Buffer	TS Buffer	Workarea	Filename
1	0xECA0-0xED9F	0xEDA0-0xEE9F	0xEEA0-0xEEC5	0xEEC6-0xEEDD
2	0xEEE6-0xEFE5	0xEFE6-0xF0E5	0xF0E6-0xF10B	0xF10C-0xF123
3	0xF12C-0xF22B	0xF22C-0xF32B	0xF32C-0xF351	0xF352-0xF369
4	0xF372-0xF471	0xF472-0xF571	0xF572-0xF597	0xF598-0xF5AF
5	0xF5B8-0xF6B7	0xF6B8-0xF7B7	0xF7B8-0xF7DD	0xF7DE-0xF7F5

Table III.1.3. DOS 4.3 File Buffer Memory Locations

```
]MAXFILES = 5

]PRINT PEEK(116);",";PEEK(115)
190,0

]

]MAXFILES 4

]MAXFILES = 4

]PRINT PEEK(116);",";PEEK(115)
190,0

]

]SV 190 = 0x00BE = 00190

]
```

Figure III.1.6. MAXFILES Command Display

```
]MON C,I,O

]LIST EXECFILE
MON C,I,O
LIST TEXTFILE.TXT


]EXEC EXECFILE

]MON C,I,O

]LIST TEXTFILE.TXT

This is line 1.
This is line 2.
This is line 3.

]

]※
```

Figure III.1.7. MON Command Display

```
]NOMON C,I,O

]LIST EXECFILE2
NOMON C,I,O
LIST TEXTFILE.TXT

]EXEC EXECFILE2
]
]

This is line 1.
This is line 2.
This is line 3.
]

]※
```

Figure III.1.8. NOMON Command Display

```
MON          [,C][,I][,O]

Example:     MON C,I,O
             MON
```

This command enables the display of commands, input data, and output data to a DOS volume. If the C keyword is included all programmatically executed DOS Commands are displayed. If the I keyword is included all Input data from a volume is displayed. If the O keyword is included all Output data to a volume is displayed. Figure III.1.7 shows an example of using the MON command before processing an EXEC file. First, the EXEC file EXECFILE is listed to show its contents, and then the file is processed. Each data line in EXECFILE is echoed to the screen before that line is processed. If no keywords are included with the MON command, the CSWL and KSWL pointers are initialized and DOS enters the Apple Monitor at memory address 0xFF65. Entering a ctrl-C from within the Apple Monitor re-enables DOS's control over the CSWL and KSWL pointers.

```
NOMON        [,C][,I][,O]

Example:     NOMON C,I,O
             NOMON
```

This command disables the display of commands, input data, and output data to a DOS volume. If the C keyword is included all programmatically executed DOS Commands are no longer displayed. If the I keyword is included all Input data from a volume is no longer displayed. If the O keyword is included all Output data to a volume is no longer displayed. Figure III.1.8 shows an example of using the NOMON command before processing an EXEC file. First, the EXEC file EXECFILE2 is listed to show its contents, and then the file is processed. Now, each data line in EXECFILE2 is no longer echoed to the screen before that line is processed. If no keywords are included with the NOMON command, the CSWL and KSWL pointers are initialized and DOS enters the Apple Monitor at memory address 0xFF65. Entering a ctrl-C from within the Apple Monitor re-enables DOS's control over the CSWL and KSWL pointers.

```
PHASE        n

Example:     PHASE 4
```

This command is new to DOS 4.3 and it provides the means to change the number of half-phases between adjacent tracks of a DOS volume particularly when the volume is initialized. Once the volume is initialized with a particular phase value, that phase value must be used whenever the volume is accessed for I/O. The phase value for an Apple Master DOS diskette is four. It is quite possible to initialize a volume with multiple phase values where the software residing on this unique volume knows when to change the phase value before it accesses those particular tracks. Figure III.1.9 shows a volume initialized with a phase value of three so that this volume may contain forty-eight tracks within the same space that volumes having a phase value of four contain thirty-six tracks. Figure III.1.10 shows the VTOC of this same volume after the volume has been initialized.

```
]PHASE 3
]INIT HELLO,PHASE Figure,A48,B3,L$F00B
]LS
S=6 D=02 V=000 F=0716 01/01/20 08:28:48
 A 006 HELLO              01/01/20 08:28:48
]LSR
M=4308H P=03 T=PHASE Figure
B=4308H boot L=0xF00B 01/01/20 08:28:48
S=6 D=02 V=000 F=0716 01/01/20 08:28:48
 001 0x13,0x0F HELLO
]
```

Figure III.1.9. PHASE Command Display

I spent a significant amount of time once again analyzing the algorithm that DOS 3.3 and DOS 4.1 use to move the Disk][read/write head from one track to an adjacent track. This algorithm includes an acceleration and deceleration component to ensure movements to and from distant tracks occur smoothly in the least amount of time. When moving the R/W head to distant tracks it is necessary to account for all induced momentum and mechanical reluctance in the Cam Rider and Carriage Rod as shown in Figure I.10.1. I literally tore apart a Disk][and marked where tracks 0, 1, 2, 3, 4, and 5 were located along the Cam Channel on the Cam Table. Then I developed an algorithm to move the Cam Rider in half-phase steps perfectly in either direction. Lastly, I added in the acceleration and deceleration components that have sufficient electromagnetic holding time to buffer any induced momentum and mechanical reluctance, and to provide smooth track-to-track movements.

In order to obtain the highest signal-to-noise ratio for physical diskette recording, Apple designed the Disk][R/W head to be somewhat smaller than the width of a normal, four half-phase track. Actually,

Apple manufactured their R/W head just slightly smaller than three half-phases, but not as small as two half-phases like the R/W heads used in Rana drives. A Disk][is not capable of reading and writing tracks that are spaced two half-phases due to extreme crosstalk between adjacent tracks; however, it is capable of reading and writing tracks spaced three half-phases. The MOVHD algorithm I designed is capable of de-energizing two adjacent electromagnetic poles within four microseconds, and the position of the R/W head is maintained between those poles by mechanical reluctance of the Carriage Rod. The DOS PHASE command, normally set to four, can be set from one to sixteen half-phases.

Virtual][is capable of storing data in the WOZ 1.0 and WOZ 2.0 disk image formats. These formats were basically an offshoot of the Applesauce project started by John K. Morris, and they duplicate the way data is stored on a physical diskette A WOZ 2.0 volume can be initialized by DOS 4.3 using a PHASE value other than four to create unique volume images. Figures III.1.9 and III.1.10 were captured from a WOZ 2.0 volume image.

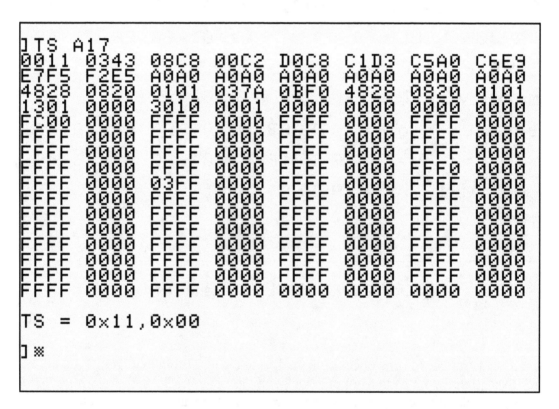

Figure III.1.10. PHASE 3 VTOC Using a TS Command Display

PR#   s

Example: PR#7

This command configures the CSWL interface to send all subsequent data to the peripheral device
residing in the specified slot s instead of to the Apple display. Previously, Figure III.1.2 shows an
example Applesoft program that uses the PR# command to configure the CSWL interface in order to
communicate with the Thunderclock clock card.


```
] SV $1234 = 0x1234 = 04660
] SV 1234 = 0x04D2 = 01234
]
] SV 0 = 0x0000 = 00000
] SV $ffff = 0xFFFF = 65535
] ▓
```

Figure III.1.11. SV Command Display

SV   [n]

Example: SV $1234
           SV 1234

This command was originally developed for DOS 4.1 and it displays on the Apple command line the
decimal and hexadecimal values of the requested number whether that number is entered as a decimal

111

or as a hexadecimal value. DOS 4.1 required the use of the A keyword to hold the decimal or hexadecimal number. Keyword bits 10 and 11 are mutually exclusive in that no DOS 3.3 command used those two bits together for any single command. DOS 4.3 uses these two bits together to identify a special non-keyword "value" category for the DOS CONFIG, PHASE, and SV commands. Figure III.1.11 shows the use of the DOS SV (i.e. Show Value) command. Using the SV command is a convenient way to convert numbers from decimal to hexadecimal or hexadecimal to decimal without having to reach for the calculator.

The Print Decimal PRTDEC routine was severely flawed in DOS 3.3, and it could only convert 8-bit hexadecimal values. DOS 4.3 requires the conversion of 16-bit hexadecimal values in order to selectively print numbers having up to five zero-prefaced decimal digits. The DOS SV command can print up to five zero-prefaced decimal digits to the display. The algorithm I designed for the DOS 4.3 PRTDEC routine requires one additional byte for the low-order bytes in its Decimal DECTBLL Table and five additional bytes for the added high-order bytes in its Decimal DECTBLH Table.

Command	Command Syntax
CAT	[,Ss][,Dd][Vv][,R]
CATALOG	[,Ss][,Dd][Vv][,R]
LS	[,Ss][,Dd][Vv][,R]
CD	[,Ss][,Dd][Vv][,R]
DELETE	f [,Ss][,Dd][,Vv][,R]
RM	f [,Ss][,Dd][,Vv][,R]
DIFF	f, f2 [,Ss][,Dd][,Vv]
GREP	f, f2 [,Ss][,Dd][,Vv][,Bn]
INIT	f, f2 [,Ss][,Dd][,Vv][,An][,Bn][,Ln][,R[n]]
LIST	f [,Ss][,Dd][,Vv][,Bb][,Ll][,R]
MORE	f [,Ss][,Dd][,Vv][,Bb][,Ll][,R]
LOCK	[f] [,Ss][,Dd][,Vv]
MV	f, f2 [,Ss][,Dd][,Vv][,R]
RENAME	f, f2 [,Ss][,Dd][,Vv][,R]
TOUCH	[f] [,Ss][,Dd][,Vv][,R]
TS	[,Ss][,Dd][,Vv][,An][,Bn][,L][,R]
UNLOCK	[f] [,Ss][,Dd][,Vv]
URM	f [,Ss][,Dd][,Vv]
VERIFY	f [,Ss][,Dd][,Vv][,R1]
WTS	Ln, Rn [,Ss][,Dd][,Vv][,An][,Bn]

Table III.2.1. DOS 4.3 File System Commands

2. File System Commands

The DOS 4.3 File System Commands manage the file system of a disk volume and manage the display of the contents of a disk volume. The syntax of the File System Commands is shown in Table III.2.1.

```
CAT      [,Ss][,Dd][,Vv][,R]          ; short version of CATALOG
CATALOG  [,Ss][,Dd][,Vv][,R]
LS       [,Ss][,Dd][,Vv][,R]          ; UNIX version of CATALOG

Example:  CAT D1
          CATALOG S6,D2
          LS R
```

This command displays on the screen a wealth of information for the specified volume: the current slot (S=), the drive (D=), and the volume number (V=) for the volume, the remaining free space (F=) on the volume, the date and time the VTOC was last modified, and a list of all files on the volume. Each file is displayed with its lock/unlock status, its file type, its size in sectors including all TSL sectors, the first fourteen characters of its filename, and the date and time the file was created or last modified. Table I.7.3 lists all file types that are native to DOS 4.3. Figure III.2.1 shows an example screen display of the CATALOG and the CAT commands. Notice that the asterisk before the file type shows that the files DOS4.3 and INSTALL are locked. DOS 4.3 commands may be entered in lowercase.

If the R keyword is included with the CATALOG command the screen displays the version of DOS that is currently in memory (M=), the number of half-phases (P=) for the width of tracks that were initialized on this volume, the twenty-four ASCII character volume title (T=), the version and build of the DOS that created this volume (B=), the volume type (boot or data), the volume library value (L=), and the date and time the volume was created, followed by the information above. The list of files on the volume also includes all deleted files shown by the x character.

Without the R keyword each file is displayed as shown in Figure III.2.1.

With the R keyword each file is displayed with its sequence number, the track and sector of its first TSL sector, and all twenty-four characters of its filename. Figure III.2.2 shows an example screen of the LS R command. Having the track and sector of a file's first TSL sector is absolutely necessary in order to begin any investigation of a file, its sector resources, and the location of all of its data on a volume.

113

```
]CATALOG S6,D2

S=6 D=02 V=000 F=0488 01/01/20 08:28:48

*B 044 DOS4.3          01/01/20 08:28:48
 L 013 INSTALL.L       01/01/20 08:28:48
*B 003 INSTALL         01/01/20 08:28:48
 L 006 MOVEDOS.L       01/01/20 08:28:48

]cat

S=6 D=02 V=000 F=0488 01/01/20 08:28:48

*B 044 DOS4.3          01/01/20 08:28:48
 L 013 INSTALL.L       01/01/20 08:28:48
*B 003 INSTALL         01/01/20 08:28:48
 L 006 MOVEDOS.L       01/01/20 08:28:48

]※
```

Figure III.2.1. CATALOG and CAT Command Display

```
]LS R

M=4308H P=04 T=CATALOG Figure

B=4308H data L=0xF001 01/01/20 08:28:48

S=6 D=02 V=000 F=0488 01/01/20 08:28:48

*001 0x12,0x0F DOS4.3
 002 0x15,0x0F INSTALL.L
*003 0x16,0x0F INSTALL
 004 0x17,0x0F MOVEDOS.L
x005 0x18,0x0F DOS2TO1

]※
```

Figure III.2.2. LS R Command Display

114

```
CD          [,Ss][,Dd][,Vv][,R]

Example:    CD S6,D2,V3
            CD
```

This command was originally developed for DOS 4.1 and it was expanded for DOS 4.3. The CD command can change the default slot, drive, and volume parameters used by the Command Manager and by the File Manager. If no keywords are used with the CD command the current default slot, drive and volume parameters are displayed on the Apple command line after the CD command. Figure III.2.3 shows two examples of using the CD command. When the CD command is used with keywords, the keyword values are stored in the CMDVALS structure. When the CD command is used without keywords, two values are displayed for volume. The first comes from DISKVOL as shown in Table I.5.1 and the second comes from VOLNUMBR as shown in Table I.12.2. DISKVOL is the actual volume number value in the VTOC and VOLNUMBR is the volume number value used by the File Manager. When these values differ and VOLNUMBR is not 000 then the "Volume Number Mismatch" error message is issued. When the R keyword is given with the CD command, the VTOC of the specified volume is read and the variable DOSCONFG as shown in Table I.5.1 is copied to the variable VALSCNFG as shown in Table I.8.5. Using the CD command in this way can restore the DOS CONFIG configuration that was used when this volume was initialized. The value of VALSCNFG can be displayed by entering the DOS CONFIG command without any arguments.

```
]CD S6,D2,V123
]LS
S=6 D=02 V=123 F=0518 01/01/20 08:28:48
 A 004 HELLO              01/01/20 08:28:48
]
]CD = S=6 D=02 V=123 123
]
]ls v23
Volume Number Mismatch
]cd = S=6 D=02 V=123 023
]※
```

Figure III.2.3. CD Command Display

```
DELETE    f [,Ss][,Dd][,Vv][,R]
RM        f [,Ss][,Dd][,Vv]                          ; UNIX version of DELETE

Example:  DELETE COPYDOS
          RM COPYDOS
```

This command removes the filename f from the catalog listing of the specified volume if the filename exists by setting the most significant bit of its TSL track byte, and marking the sectors in the TSL(s) of the file and all TSL sectors as available. Refer to Figure I.7.1 showing a volume catalog entry. Figure III.2.4 shows an example of a file being deleted. It is prudent to undelete a deleted file as soon as possible before the previous sectors in the TSL(s) of the file and all TSL sectors are utilized by another file. A locked file cannot be deleted unless the R keyword is used to override the lock status.

```
] DELETE DOS1TO2
] CAT
S=6 D=02 V=000 F=0510 01/01/20 08:28:49
  B 044 DOS4.3             01/01/20 08:28:48
]
] CAT R
M=4308H P=04 T=DELETE Figure
B=4308H data L=0xF005 01/01/20 08:28:48
S=6 D=02 V=000 F=0510 01/01/20 08:28:49
 001 0x12,0x0F DOS4.3
x002 0x15,0x0F DOS1TO2
] ※
```

Figure III.2.4. DELETE Command Display

```
DIFF      f, f2 [,Ss][,Dd][,Vv]
```

Example: `DIFF TEST1,TEST2`

This command was originally developed for DOS 4.1 and it compares any two files `f` and `f2` in the specified volume up to the end of `SECCNT-1` sectors for the second file, `f2`. The routine will display the number of bytes compared on the Apple command line, and the location(s) where the files differ and the differing bytes. **The two files must reside on the same volume.** The location(s) where the files differ are the number of bytes from the beginning of each file. The first differing byte comes from the first file, or file `f`, and the second differing byte comes from the second file, or file `f2`. Displayed values are all shown in hexadecimal. Figure III.2.5 shows an example of three pairs of files that are compared. The first pair of files are identical and the screen shows that `0x0100` bytes were compared even though the files themselves are only `0x0080` bytes in size. CF compares whole sectors. The second pair of files are exactly `0x1000` bytes in size but `CF` compared `0x1100` bytes. Because these are Binary files their address and length bytes occupy the first four bytes of the file, thus making the files actually `0x1004` bytes in length. Again, `CF` compares whole sectors, and the last four bytes of data reside in an additional sector. These files differed at only one location. The third pair of files are `0x300` bytes in size and they differ at five specific locations.

```
]DIFF F1,F2 = 0x0100

]DIFF N1,N2 = 0x1100
0x0F84 = 0x00,0xFF

]

]DIFF Z1,Z2 = 0x0400
0x0084 = 0x00,0xFF
0x0104 = 0x00,0xFF
0x0184 = 0x00,0xFF
0x0204 = 0x00,0xFF
0x0284 = 0x00,0xFF

]
```

Figure III.2.5. DIFF Command Display

```
]GREP HELLO,WINDOW = 0x0500

0x03FD

]

]GREP VOLMGR,Images,D2 = 0x3D00

0x076D
0x1557
0x183D
0x185C

]

]grep VOLMGR,Firmware to*,b$aa = 0x3D00

0x00C7
0x159E

]
```

Figure III.2.6. GREP Command Display

GREP   f, f2 [,Ss][,Dd][,Vv][,Bn]

Example: GREP HELLO,TEST
           GREP HELLO,Manage Test*,B$AA

This command was originally developed for DOS 4.1 and it searches file f for the single word ASCII string or the multiple word character-terminated string f2 in the specified volume up to the end of SECCNT-1 sectors for file f. The routine will display the number of bytes searched in file f on the Apple command line and the location(s) where string f2 occurs in the file. The location(s) where f2 is found is the number of bytes from the beginning of the file to the first character of f2. Displayed values are all shown in hexadecimal. Figure III.2.6 shows an example of three searches on two files. The first search is on an Applesoft file. The second and third searches are on a Binary file. The third search uses a multiple word character-terminated string for f2. GREP searches whole sectors. Regardless how many actual bytes that are associated with the file in its last sector, the entire last sector of the file is included in the search. GREP is case sensitive as shown in Figure III.2.6., and GREP masks out the MSB of all data read from file f so lower ASCII character 0x41 is the same as upper ASCII character 0xC1. DOS 4.3 expects the string contained in f2 to conform to the format and length of a filename, therefore the first character must be a "0" or greater ASCII character. Otherwise, Applesoft will process the Apple command line as if it contains a GR command and issue a "?SYNTAX ERROR" message. The maximum length of f2 is twenty-four characters, which includes the end, or termination character if it is used. Any ASCII character may be used for the end character

118

as long as it is unique within the characters comprising `f2`. If an end character is used it must be defined by the `B` keyword and set equal to its upper ASCII value, that is, with its MSB on.

```
]INIT HELLO,Boot Disk,S6,D2,V123,L$F007
]
]CAT R
M=4308H P=04 T=Boot Disk
B=4308H boot L=0xF007 01/01/20 08:28:48
S=6 D=02 V=123 F=0506 01/01/20 08:28:48
 001 0x12,0x0F HELLO
]
```

Figure III.2.7. INIT Command for Boot Disk

```
INIT     f, f2 [,Ss][,Dd][,Vv][,An][,Bn][,Ln][,R[n]]
```

Example: `INIT HELLO,<title>,V123,L$101`   ; creates Volume Type B
          `INIT EXECFILE,<title>,V123,R$14`   ; creates Volume Type B
          `INIT Hello,<title>,V123,r`   ; creates Volume Type D

This command initializes the specified volume with the filename `f`, and can write a DOS 4.3 image onto tracks `0x00`, `0x01`, and ten additional sectors onto track `0x02`. A **boot** volume, or Volume Type B, is created with a DOS image when the `R` keyword is **not** included or the value of the `R` keyword is **not** equal to `0x00` as shown in Figure III.2.7. All initialized volumes are titled with the required upper ASCII string in `f2`. The parameter `v` is assigned the volume number if the `V` keyword is included; otherwise, the disk is initialized with a volume number of `000`. A **data** volume, or Volume Type D, is created without a DOS image and with an empty volume catalog when the `R` keyword **is** included without a value or with a value of `0x00` as shown in Figure III.2.8. All volume sectors are available for data storage including track `0x00` in a `data` volume. The upper ASCII string in `f2` is still used for the volume Title, but the filename `f` is simply a placeholder and not utilized. If the `R` keyword is included with a nonzero value, that value is copied to `CMDVAL` and a `boot` volume is initialized with a DOS image. No boot file is saved to that volume if Boot Type (`SUBCODE`) does not equal `0x06` (DOS `RUN`), even if there is an Applesoft file in memory. This logic is new to DOS 4.3. It is up to the user to copy an `EXEC` file for `R$14` or a Binary file for `R$34` to the volume as its `HELLO`, or `f` filename. Other possible values for the `R` keyword could include `R$10` for `CLOSE`, `R$2C` for `DATE`, and `R$2E` for `LIST`, obtained from Table III.0.2.

```
] init hello,Data Disk,v101,l$f007,r
]
] cat r
M=4308H P=04 T=Data Disk
B=4308H data L=0xF007 01/01/20 08:28:48
S=6 D=02 V=101 F=0554 01/01/20 08:28:48

]
```

Figure III.2.8. INIT Command for Data Disk

The complete set of `INIT` initialization values is available at the address found in `INITVAL` at memory address `0xBFFA`. These initialization values can be modified directly or indirectly before invoking the DOS `INIT` command in order to tailor a DOS 4.3 volume specific to ones needs and that of the target hardware. See Table I.8.5 for a list of all of the possible initialization values.

If the `A` and `B` keywords are not used or are set to `0x00`, the default initialization values for `ENDTRK` and `SECVAL` come from `LASTRACK` and `FIRSTCAT`, respectively. The `A` keyword is used to specify a new `ENDTRK`, the "accepted" number of tracks in a DOS volume. The `B` keyword is used to specify a new `SECVAL`, the number of Catalog sectors from 1 to 15, and to select a new `ENDSEC`: 16-sector tracks if the `B` keyword's MSB is clear or 32-sector tracks if the MSB is set. The default value is 16-sector tracks. The `L` keyword is used to specify a Library Value (or, subject value) for the DOS volume if it is included, from `0x0000` to `0xFFFF`, otherwise the Library Value is set to `0x0000`. Once an initialization parameter has been changed, it remains equal to that value except for `CMDVAL`,

120

SECVAL, ENDTRK, SUBJCT, and ENDSEC. There is no reset to "default" settings for NMAXVAL, YEARVAL, TRKVAL, VRSN, BLD, RAMTYP, VALSPHAS, TSPARS, ALCTRK, ALCDIR, VALSCNFG, and SECSIZ as shown previously in Table I.8.5. Use common sense when modifying these values.

The value in SECVAL determines the number of sectors the catalog will contain not including the VTOC sector. The useable values for SECVAL are 0<SECVAL<16. If its value is greater than fifteen, no more than fifteen Catalog sectors will be created. Table III.2.2 shows the number of available data sectors in a volume based on Volume Type for volumes having thirty-six tracks with sixteen or thirty-two sectors per track. A few disk drives, either physical or solid state, were manufactured to access forty tracks for a volume. Set ENDTRK to 0x28 (use A40 or A$28) to provide access to all forty tracks, or set ENDTRK to 0x30 (use A48 or A$30) to access forty-eight tracks if they are available. The VTOC is designed to manage up to fifty tracks per volume as shown previously in Figure I.5.1. Table III.2.3 shows the total number of sectors in a volume having thirty-five, thirty-six, forty, or forty-eight tracks with sixteen or thirty-two sectors per track.

SECVAL	Catalog Sectors	16 Sectors/Track		32 Sectors/Track	
		B	D	B	D
0x01	1	532	574	1108	1150
0x02	2	531	573	1107	1149
0x03	3	530	572	1106	1148
0x04	4	529	571	1105	1147
0x05	5	528	570	1104	1146
0x06	6	527	569	1103	1145
0x07	7	526	568	1102	1144
0x08	8	525	567	1101	1143
0x09	9	524	566	1100	1142
0x0A	10	523	565	1099	1141
0x0B	11	522	564	1098	1140
0x0C	12	521	563	1097	1139
0x0D	13	520	562	1096	1138
0x0E	14	519	561	1095	1137
0x0F	15	518	560	1094	1136

Table III.2.2. Available Data Sectors for 36 Tracks, 16/32 Sectors/Track

Tracks/Volume	16 Sectors/Track	32 Sectors/Track
35	560	1120
36	576	1152
40	640	1280
48	768	1536

Table III.2.3. Total Sectors in Initialized Volumes

121

```
]LIST EXECFILE.T

MON CIO
BLOAD FOO
NOMON CIO

]

]LIST EXECFILE.T,L6

MON CI

]LIST EXECFILE.T,B9,L7

LOAD FO

]LIST EXECFILE.T,B9,L7,R

CFC1 C4A0 C6CF CF8D

] ※
```

Figure III.2.9. LIST Command Display

LIST   f [,Ss][,Dd][,Vv][,Bb][,Ll][,R]
MORE   f [,Ss][,Dd][,Vv][,Bb][,Ll][,R]   ; UNIX version of LIST

Example: LIST EXECFILE,B8,L10,R

This command was originally developed for DOS 4.1 and it displays on the screen the data of file f in the specified volume in ASCII if the file type is a Text file or in hexadecimal for all other file types. If the R keyword is included, the data of a Text file will be displayed in hexadecimal rather than in ASCII. If the B keyword is included, that number of bytes, b, into the file will be skipped. If the L keyword is included, that number of bytes, l, of data will only be displayed, or until the end of the file, whichever occurs first. LIST displays a complete sector of data at a time, and the LIST display can be terminated at any time by pressing the ESC key. Figure III.2.9 shows examples of using LIST on a Text file utilizing the various keywords. First, the entire file is displayed. Then, the first six bytes of the file are displayed. Then, the first nine bytes are skipped and the next seven bytes are displayed. Finally, those same seven bytes are displayed in hexadecimal. Hexadecimal data is displayed in even/odd byte-pairs from the beginning of the file, starting with byte 0x00. Thus, the "L" in the data word "BLOAD" is an odd byte in the file and that byte is skipped. The second "O" in the data word "FOO" and the carriage return that follows are added to the displayed byte-pairs. Remember to count the carriage return (i.e. 0x8D) as an ASCII character as well. LIST will not skip over a NULL byte (i.e. 0x00) like those found in Random Access Text Files when those files are displayed in ASCII.

122

Random Access Text files should only be displayed in hexadecimal in order to show the complete contents of the records that are contained in those type of text files.

```
]CAT

S=6 D=02 V=000 F=0486 01/01/20 08:28:48

 B 044 DOS4.3              01/01/20 08:28:48
 L 013 INSTALL.L           01/01/20 08:28:48
 B 003 INSTALL             01/01/20 08:28:48
 L 006 MOVEDOS.L           01/01/20 08:28:48
 B 002 DOS1TO2             01/01/20 08:28:48

]LOCK DOS4.3

]CAT

S=6 D=02 V=000 F=0486 01/01/20 08:28:48

*B 044 DOS4.3              01/01/20 08:28:49
 L 013 INSTALL.L           01/01/20 08:28:48
 B 003 INSTALL             01/01/20 08:28:48
 L 006 MOVEDOS.L           01/01/20 08:28:48
 B 002 DOS1TO2             01/01/20 08:28:48

]
```

Figure III.2.10. LOCK File Command Display

LOCK   [f] [,Ss][,Dd][,Vv]

Example: LOCK
           LOCK TEST

This command sets the most significant bit of the **Type** byte of the file **f** in the specified volume as shown in Tables I.7.1 through I.7.3. A locked file cannot be deleted, renamed, or touched until it is unlocked. The lock status of a file is indicated in the volume Catalog using an asterisk before the file's type character as shown in Figure III.2.10. The date and time stamp for the file is also updated but not the date and time stamp for the **VTOC** because nothing in the **VTOC** is changed.

When the **LOCK** command is used without specifying a filename and any keyword parameters the current Volume in focus is locked. The **TSL** and data buffers are flushed, the volume **DISKLOCK** byte is set as shown in Table I.5.1, and the **VTOC** is updated with a current date and time stamp. The volume may be read at any time but DOS 4.3 cannot write to the volume until the volume is unlocked. In order to specify a particular volume to be locked, precede the **LOCK** command with the DOS **CD** command. Figure III.2.11 shows the same volume from Figure III.2.10 after the Volume has been locked. Files may not be deleted, renamed, touched, or saved to a locked volume by DOS 4.3. In Figure III.2.11 the DISKLOCK byte status is shown in the "B=" data with an asterisk, as in "B=4308*". The date and time stamp for the VTOC is updated because the VTOC is changed by changing the DISKLOCK byte to lock. There is no harm in locking a volume that is already locked.

```
]LOCK

]LS R

M=4308H P=04 T=LOCK Figure

B=4308* data L=0xF00A 01/01/20 08:28:48

S=6 D=02 V=000 F=0486 01/01/20 08:28:49

*001 0x1B,0x0F DOS4.3
 002 0x1E,0x0F INSTALL.L
 003 0x1F,0x0F INSTALL
 004 0x20,0x0F MOVEDOS.L
 005 0x21,0x0F DOS1TO2

]DELETE DOS1TO2

Volume Locked

]
```

Figure III.2.11. LOCK Volume Command Display

```
RENAME    f, f2 [,Ss][,Dd][,Vv][,R]
MV        f, f2 [,Ss][,Dd][,Vv]                    ; UNIX version of RENAME

Example:   RENAME COPYDOS,COPYDOS.EXEC
```

This command changes the name of the file f to f2 in the specified volume if the file f exists. The date and time stamp of the renamed file is also updated as shown in Figure III.2.12. A locked file cannot be renamed unless the R keyword is used to override the lock status. A file cannot be renamed in a locked volume unless the volume is unlocked or CONFIG Bit 4 is set. The VTOC date and time stamp remains unchanged when a file is renamed because nothing in the VTOC is changed. Note that in Figure III.2.12 only the first 14 characters of a filename are shown in a volume catalog.

```
]LS

S=6 D=02 V=000 F=0488 01/01/20  08:28:48

  B 044 DOS4.3            01/01/20  08:28:48
  L 013 INSTALL.L         01/01/20  08:28:48
  B 003 INSTALL           01/01/20  08:28:48
  L 006 MOVEDOS.L         01/01/20  08:28:48
]RENAME INSTALL,install DOS 4.3

]ls

S=6 D=02 V=000 F=0488 01/01/20  08:28:48

  B 044 DOS4.3            01/01/20  08:28:48
  L 013 INSTALL.L         01/01/20  08:28:48
  B 003 install DOS 4.    01/01/20  08:28:49
  L 006 MOVEDOS.L         01/01/20  08:28:48

]
```

Figure III.2.12. RENAME Command Display

```
]LS

S=6 D=02 V=000 F=0494 01/01/20  08:28:48

*B 044 DOS4.3            01/01/20  08:28:48
 L 013 INSTALL.L         01/01/20  08:28:48
*B 003 INSTALL           01/01/20  08:28:48
]TOUCH DOS4.3

File Locked

]TOUCH DOS4.3,R

]LS

S=6 D=02 V=000 F=0494 01/01/20  08:28:48

*B 044 DOS4.3            01/01/20  08:28:49
 L 013 INSTALL.L         01/01/20  08:28:48
*B 003 INSTALL           01/01/20  08:28:48

]
```

Figure III.2.13. TOUCH Command Display

```
TOUCH     [f] [,Ss][,Dd][,Vv][,R]
```

```
Example:   TOUCH TEST
```

This command is new to DOS 4.3 and it updates the date and time stamp of the file f in the specified volume if the file f exists. Figure III.2.13 shows an example in using the TOUCH command. TOUCH cannot update the date and time stamp of a locked file unless the R keyword is used to override the lock status. The VTOC date and time stamp remains unchanged when the TOUCH command is used because nothing in the VTOC is changed. This command was implemented by adding the TCHHNDLR handler to the File Manager Subroutine table as shown in Table I.11.2. If the TOUCH command is used without specifying a file and keywords, the variable VALSCNFG as shown in Table I.8.5 is copied to the variable DOSCONFG as shown in Table I.5.1 and the date and time stamp of the VTOC is updated for the specified volume. Using the DOS TOUCH command in this way will save the current DOS CONFIG configuration to the specified volume.

```
TS        [,Ss][,Dd][,Vv][,An][,Bn][,L][,R]
```

```
Example:   TS
           TS A$11,B7
           TS L
```

This command was originally developed for DOS 4.1 and it displays on the screen the contents of the specified sector in hexadecimal of the specified track for the specified volume. The A keyword is used to specify a track value and the B keyword is used to specify a sector value, and if not given, their values are 0x00. The value n for these keywords may be entered in decimal or hexadecimal, and range checking is done against the specified volume's VTOC parameters NUMTRKS (i.e. number of tracks in the volume) and NUMSECS (i.e. number of sectors in a track). It is critical that a suitable DOS command, like CATALOG for example, has been previously issued to ensure that the volume's VTOC has been read and is currently in memory so that NUMTRKS and NUMSECS have relevant values. If the L or R keyword is included then any A or B keyword is ignored if they happen to be included, too. The R keyword takes precedence over the L keyword if both are included. The L keyword will display the previous sector (i.e. to the Left, or down) and the R keyword will display the next sector (i.e. to the Right, or up). Figure III.2.14 shows a typical TS view of an initialized data disk VTOC where the sector data is displayed in hexadecimal byte pairs followed by the TS command and the requested track and sector values. The TS command is designed to view two complete sectors of data when the 80-column display is in view. This command was implemented by adding the TSHNDLR handler to the File Manager Subroutine table as shown in Table I.11.2.

```
]TS A17
0011 0543 08C8 00C4 D4D3 A0C6 E9E7 F5F2
E5A0 A0A0 A0A0 A0A0 A0A0 A0A0 A0A0 A0A0
4828 0820 0101 047A 3412 4828 0820 0101
1101 0000 2310 0001 FFFF 0000 FFFF 0000
FFFF 0000 FFFF 0000 FFFF 0000 FFFF 0000
FFFF 0000 FFFF 0000 FFFF 0000 FFFF 0000
FFFF 0000 FFFF 0000 FFFF 0000 FFFF 0000
FFFF 0000 FFFF 0000 FFFF 0000 FFC0 0000
FFFF 0000 FFFF 0000 FFFF 0000 FFFF 0000
FFFF 0000 FFFF 0000 FFFF 0000 FFFF 0000
FFFF 0000 FFFF 0000 FFFF 0000 FFFF 0000
FFFF 0000 0000 0000 0000 0000 0000 0000
0000 0000 0000 0000 0000 0000 0000 0000
0000 0000 0000 0000 0000 0000 0000 0000
0000 0000 0000 0000 0000 0000 0000 0000

TS = 0x11,0x00

]
```

Figure III.2.14. TS Command of an Empty Data Disk VTOC Display

```
]LS

S=6 D=02 V=000 F=0486 01/01/20 08:28:48

*B 044 DOS4.3         01/01/20 08:28:48
 L 013 INSTALL.L      01/01/20 08:28:48
 B 003 INSTALL        01/01/20 08:28:48
 L 006 MOVEDOS.L      01/01/20 08:28:48
 B 002 DOS1TO2        01/01/20 08:28:48

]UNLOCK DOS4.3

]LS

S=6 D=02 V=000 F=0486 01/01/20 08:28:48

 B 044 DOS4.3         01/01/20 08:28:49
 L 013 INSTALL.L      01/01/20 08:28:48
 B 003 INSTALL        01/01/20 08:28:48
 L 006 MOVEDOS.L      01/01/20 08:28:48
 B 002 DOS1TO2        01/01/20 08:28:48

] ※
```

Figure III.2.15. UNLOCK File Command Display

```
UNLOCK    [f] [,Ss][,Dd][,Vv]

Example:  UNLOCK
          UNLOCK TEST
```

This command clears the most significant bit of the **Type** byte of the file **f** in the specified volume as shown in Tables I.7.1 through I.7.3. A locked file cannot be deleted, renamed, or touched until it is unlocked. The lock status of a file is indicated in the volume Catalog using an asterisk before the type character of the file. The date and time stamp of the file is updated when the file **f** is unlocked as shown in Figure III.2.15. The date and time stamp for the **VTOC** is not updated when a file is unlocked because nothing is changed in the **VTOC**.

When the **UNLOCK** command is used without specifying a filename and any keyword parameters the current volume in focus is unlocked. The **TSL** and data buffers are flushed, the volume **DISKLOCK** byte is cleared as shown in Table I.5.1., and the updated **VTOC** with a current date and time stamp is written to the volume. A locked volume may be read at any time but DOS 4.3 cannot write to the volume until the volume is unlocked. In order to specify a particular volume to be unlocked, precede the **UNLOCK** command with the DOS **CD** command. Figure III.2.16 shows a volume before and after the volume has been unlocked. Files may not be deleted, renamed, touched, or written to a locked volume by DOS 4.3. In Figure III.2.16 the **VTOC DISKLOCK** byte is shown in the "B=" data with an asterisk, as in "B=4308*", for lock and without an asterisk, as in "B=4308H", for unlock. The date and time stamp for the **VTOC** is updated because the **VTOC** is changed by changing the **DISKLOCK** byte to its unlock value. There is no harm in unlocking a volume that is already unlocked.

```
URM       f [,Ss][,Dd][,Vv]

Example:  URM MOVEDOS
```

This command was originally developed for DOS 4.1 and it restores the file **f** to the volume Catalog of the specified volume by clearing the most significant bit of its **TSL** track byte and marking the sectors in the **TSL**(s) of the file and all **TSL** sectors as used. It is prudent to restore a deleted file as soon as possible before the sectors in the **TSL**(s) of the file and all **TSL** sectors are utilized by another file. Even if a file requires multiple **TSL** sectors, all data sectors and all **TSL** sectors are restored by the **URM** command. There is no harm in attempting to undelete a file that is already displayed in the volume Catalog. Figure III.2.17 shows an example of a deleted file being restored using the **URM** command. The "**x**" before the deleted filename is now gone after the file is restored and free sectors are reduced. This command was implemented by adding the **URMHNDLR** handler to the File Manager Subroutine table as shown in Table I.11.2. The DOS 4.3 File Manager handles this command much like the **DELHNDLR** hander. The date and time stamp for the **VTOC** is updated because the **VTOC** is changed when a file is restored. The date and time stamp for the restored file is not updated even when the **URM** command is used to restore a file that is already displayed in the volume Catalog.

```
]LSR
M=4308H P=04 T=UNLOCK Figure 2
B=4308* data L=0xF00A 01/01/20 08:28:48
S=6 D=02 V=000 F=0510 01/01/20 08:28:48
 001 0x12,0x0F DOS4.3
]UNLOCK
]LSR
M=4308H P=04 T=UNLOCK Figure 2
B=4308H data L=0xF00A 01/01/20 08:28:48
S=6 D=02 V=000 F=0510 01/01/20 08:28:49
 001 0x12,0x0F DOS4.3
]※
```

Figure III.2.16. UNLOCK Volume Command Display

```
]cat r
M=4308H P=04 T=URM Figure
B=4308H data L=0xF00D 01/01/20 08:28:48
S=6 D=02 V=000 F=0510 01/01/20 08:28:48
 001 0x12,0x0F DOS4.3
x002 0x15,0x0F INSTALL
]urm INSTALL
]LS
S=6 D=02 V=000 F=0507 01/01/20 08:28:49
 B 044 DOS4.3          01/01/20 08:28:48
 B 003 INSTALL         01/01/20 08:28:48
]※
```

Figure III.2.17. URM Command Display

```
VERIFY    f [,Ss][,Dd][,Vv][,R1]

Example:   VERIFY DOS4.1,R1
```

This command reads into memory each sector listed in the TSL sector(s) of the file f in the specified
volume. The read routine in RWTS simply verifies the checksum for each sector read. No data is
copied to memory or modified, and the date and time stamp of the file is not changed. The TSL
sector(s) are indirectly verified since it they are read into a DOS TS buffer and used to obtain the track
and sector list for the file, but they are not included in the verified sector count. Only when a non-zero
R keyword is included will the number of verified sectors be displayed on the Apple command line as
shown in Figure III.2.18. If a non-zero R keyword is included with the DOS SAVE, BSAVE, LSAVE,
and TSAVE commands, not only is the address and length information displayed, but also the number
of verified sectors displayed as well. The VTOC and the time stamp of the file remain unchanged when
a file is verified because nothing in the VTOC or the file is changed.

If CONFIG Bit 1 is set as shown in Table III.1.2, DOS 4.3 will bypass the automatic verification of a
file after the file is saved to a volume when using the DOS SAVE, BSAVE, LSAVE, or TSAVE
command. Enabling this bit will visibly reduce the amount of time it takes to save a file to a volume,
but it eliminates the verification that the file can be read into memory without error.

```
] CAT

S=6 D=02 V=000 F=0507 01/01/20 08:28:48

  B 044 DOS4.3               01/01/20 08:28:48
  B 003 INSTALL             01/01/20 08:28:48

]

] VERIFY DOS4.3

] VERIFY DOS4.3,R1 = 043

] LS

S=6 D=02 V=000 F=0507 01/01/20 08:28:48

  B 044 DOS4.3               01/01/20 08:28:48
  B 003 INSTALL             01/01/20 08:28:48

]
```

Figure III.2.18. VERIFY Command Display

```
WTS        Ln, Rn [,Ss][,Dd][,Vv][,An][,Bn]

Example:   WTS A17,L4,R3
           WTS L0,R1
```

This command is new to DOS 4.3 and it provides the ability to modify a single byte on any sector of the specified volume. The L and R keywords are required for this command and they provide the sector index and the data byte value to WTS, respectively, that will be used to modify the specified sector. As in the TS command, the A keyword is used to specify a track value and the B keyword is used to specify a sector value, and if not given, their values are 0x00. The value n for all four keywords may be entered in decimal or hexadecimal. Range checking is done against the specified volume's VTOC parameters NUMTRKS (i.e. number of tracks in the volume) and NUMSECS (i.e. number of sectors in a track) for the A and B keywords, respectively. It is critical that a suitable DOS command, like CATALOG for example, has been previously issued to ensure that the specified volume's VTOC has been read and is currently in memory, and NUMTRKS and NUMSECS have relevant values. Figure III.2.19 shows a Boot Stage 0 sector (sector 0x00 on track 0x00) that has been modified using WTS such that this boot image will no longer be valid and the volume will not boot. Once WTS modifies the specified byte, WTS saves the sector to the specified volume and then displays the contents of the sector in hexadecimal byte pairs followed by the WTS command and its specified track and sector values. This command was implemented by adding the WTSHNDLR handler to the File Manager Subroutine table as shown in Table I.11.2.

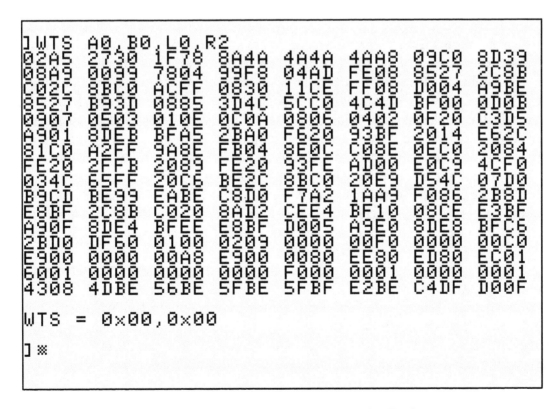

Figure III.2.19. WTS Command Display

Command	Command Syntax
CHAIN*	f [,Ss][,Dd][,Vv][,Ll][,R]
LOAD	f [,Ss][,Dd][,Vv][,R]
RUN	f [,Ss][,Dd][,Vv][,Ll]
SAVE	f [,Ss][,Dd][,Vv][,B][,R[1]]

Table III.3.1. DOS 4.3 Applesoft File Commands

3. Applesoft File Commands

The DOS 4.3 Applesoft File Commands manage Applesoft files. The syntax of the Applesoft File Commands is shown in Table III.3.1. The command shown with an asterisk cannot be used on the Apple command line.

CHAIN   f [,Ss][,Dd][,Vv][,Ll][,R]

Example: CHAIN TESTPART2, D2

This command was originally developed for DOS 4.1 and the command can only be used from within an Applesoft program. It LOADs and RUNs the Applesoft file f in the specified volume in a unique way: it does not clear the value(s) of any previous Applesoft program variable. Therefore, the file f can use the data and results from the previous program(s) and it can provide data and results to any following CHAINed program. If the L keyword is included, processing will begin at that line number only if that line number exists in program f, otherwise Applesoft reports an error and terminates processing. This capability opens up a myriad of programming possibilities. If the R keyword is **not** used CHAIN calls the Applesoft ROM routine GARBAG at memory address 0xE484 before CHAIN moves the Simple Variables and Array Variables descriptors to their new location found at the end of program f. Using the R keyword bypasses GARBAG and allows the user to utilize another method for string garbage collection before or after using the CHAIN command. It is critical that the program calling CHAIN move all of its simple string variables and string array variables that will be used in the next CHAINed program to the Character String Pool memory area where string data is safely stored. See Section I.15 for a more thorough discussion of the DOS CHAIN command.

Figure III.3.1 shows two Applesoft programs called START and PROGRAM2. START defines four simple variables D$, AB, CD%, and EF$. The string variable EF$ is defined in such a way as to force Applesoft to move it immediately into the Character String Pool memory area where string data is stored. Applesoft will also move the variable D$ to the Character String Pool memory area before it is used with the CHAIN command. All four variables will be available to the CHAINed program PROGRAM2 as shown in Figure III.3.2 when the program START is RUN.

```
]load START

]list

 10  D$ =   CHR$ (4):AB = 123:CD% =
         456:EF$ = "Test Chain" + ""
 20     PRINT : PRINT "This is the S
         TART program to test CHAIN":
         PRINT
 30     PRINT "AB = ";AB;", CD% = ";
         CD%;", EF$ = ";EF$: PRINT
 40     PRINT D$;"CHAIN PROGRAM2"

]load PROGRAM2

]list

 10     PRINT : PRINT "Now running p
         rogram PROGRAM2": PRINT
 20     PRINT "AB = ";AB;", CD% = ";
         CD%;", EF$ = ";EF$
 30     PRINT D$;"CATALOG": PRINT

]※
```

Figure III.3.1. Listing of START and PROGRAM2 CHAIN Display

```
]run START

This is the START program to test CHAIN

AB = 123, CD% = 456, EF$ = Test Chain

Now running program PROGRAM2

AB = 123, CD% = 456, EF$ = Test Chain


S=6 D=02 V=000 F=0550 01/01/20 08:28:48

 A 002 START            01/01/20 08:28:48
 A 002 PROGRAM2         01/01/20 08:28:48

]
```

Figure III.3.2. Output of START and PROGRAM2 CHAIN Display

133

Table I.15.1 shows the definition of the descriptor for the simple variables used in Applesoft programs. The string descriptor consists of only the first two characters of the string name (so care must be given in naming variables), the string length, the address in low/high byte order where the string resides in memory, and two 0x00 filler bytes. String descriptors for array variables are shown in Table I.15.2 and each string element contains the string length and the address in low/high byte order where the string resides in memory. The address in the string descriptor or string element will initially be the location where the actual string data exists within the contents of an Applesoft program. Once the next CHAINed file f replaces that Applesoft program, the actual string data will be overwritten and lost, and its address will become invalid. Therefore, caution must be exercised when using string variables and CHAIN if the string variables are not moved to the Character String Pool memory area.

LOAD   f [,Ss][,Dd][,Vv][,R]

Example   LOAD HELLO
            LOAD HELLO,R

This command reads into memory at 0x0801 the Applesoft file f in the specified volume. Applesoft program files are file type 0x02 as shown in Table I.7.3. This command will also process A type files (i.e. type 0x20) as an Applesoft file similarly as in DOS 3.3. If the R keyword is included the memory load address (i.e. 0x0801) and the number of bytes loaded (i.e. 0x0494) are displayed as shown in Figure III.3.3.

RUN   f [,Ss][,Dd][,Vv][,Ll]

Example: RUN START

This command reads into memory at 0x0801 the Applesoft file f in the specified volume and begins program execution. DOS initializes Applesoft pointers, calls ASROMCLR at ROM memory address 0xD665 to clear Applesoft variables, clears the PROMPT and ONERR flags, and finally calls ASROMNEW at ROM memory address 0xD7D2 to begin program execution. If the L keyword is included processing will begin at that line number only if that line number exists in program f, otherwise Applesoft reports an error and terminates processing. An example of using the RUN command was shown previously in Figure III.3.2.

```
]CATALOG
S=6 D=02 V=000 F=0506 01/01/20 08:28:48
 A 006 HELLO          01/01/20 08:28:48
]LOAD HELLO
]LOAD HELLO,R
A$0801,L$0494
]SAVE HELLO2
]SAVE HELLO2,R
A$0801,L$0494
]SAVE HELLO2,R1
A$0801,L$0494 = 005

]
```

Figure III.3.3. LOAD and SAVE Commands Display

```
]load HELLO
]save HELLO3
]save HELLO3,r1
A$0801,L$0494 = 005
]config 2
]save HELLO3,r1
A$0801,L$0494
]config $ff
]config = 000
]
```

Figure III.3.4. SAVE Commands Display

```
SAVE        f [,Ss][,Dd][,Vv][,B][,R[1]]

Example:    SAVE HELLO2
            SAVE HELLO2,R
            SAVE HELLO2,R1
```

This command saves the Applesoft file f to the specified volume. If the R keyword is included the save address (i.e. 0x0801) and the number of bytes saved (i.e. 0x0494) are displayed as shown previously in Figure III.3.3. If a non-zero R keyword is included, the number of verified sectors is also displayed as shown in Figure III.3.3. The B keyword can be used to implement the "File Delete/File Save" strategy. That is, the Applesoft file f will be deleted from the volume Catalog and then saved to the same volume in order to ensure that the file's TSL contains only those track/sector entries that are required by the file. If CONFIG Bit 1 is set the Applesoft file will not be verified after it is saved. Figure III.3.4 shows that even when a non-zero R keyword is used with the DOS SAVE command, no sectors are verified. The VALSCNFG variable as shown in Table I.8.5 can be cleared by using the DOS CONFIG command and setting it to 0xFF as shown in Figure III.3.4.

Command	Command Syntax
BLOAD	f [,Ss][,Dd][,Vv][,Aa][,R]
BRUN	f [,Ss][,Dd][,Vv][,Aa]
BSAVE	f [,Ss][,Dd][,Vv][,Aa][,B][,Ll][,R[1]]
LLOAD	f [,Ss][,Dd][,Vv][,Aa][,R]
LSAVE	f [,Ss][,Dd][,Vv][,Aa][,B][,Ll][,R[1]]

Table III.4.1. DOS 4.3 Binary File Commands

4. Binary File Commands

The DOS 4.3 Binary File Commands manage Binary, or assembly language files. The syntax of the Binary File Commands is shown in Table III.4.1.

```
BLOAD    f [,Ss][,Dd][,Vv][,Aa][,R]

Example:  BLOAD RD
          BLOAD RD,R
          BLOAD RD,A$1000,R
```

This command reads into memory at address a if the A keyword is included, the Binary file f in the specified volume. If the A keyword is not included the file is read into memory at the address the file was originally, or last BSAVEd. Binary files are file type 0x04 as shown in Table I.7.3. If the R keyword is included the memory load address and the number of bytes read into memory are displayed as shown in Figure III.4.1.

```
] BLOAD RD,R
A$4000,L$1B00
] BLOAD RD,A$1000,R
A$1000,L$1B00
] BSAVE RD2
] BSAVE RD3,R
A$1000,L$1B00
] BSAVE RD4,A$4000,L$1B00,R1
A$4000,L$1B00 = 028
] DIFF RD,RD4 = 0x1C00

]
```

Figure III.4.1. BLOAD and BSAVE Commands Display

```
BRUN        f [,Ss][,Dd][,Vv][,Aa]

Example:    BRUN INSTALL
            BRUN INSTALL,A$1000
```

This command reads the Binary file f in the specified volume into memory at address a if the A keyword is included, and begins program execution at that address. If the A keyword is not included, the Binary file f is loaded into memory at the address the file was originally, or last BSAVEd, and execution begins at that address. In DOS 4.3 the DOSWARM address is pushed onto the stack before executing an indirect JMP to ADRVAL, the Binary file memory load address, to guarantee that DOS will be in control after the Binary program exits. See Table III.1.2 for setting CONFIG Bit 5 before using the DOS BRUN command in order to bypass pushing the DOSWARM address onto the stack. An example of the BRUN command is shown in Figure III.4.2.

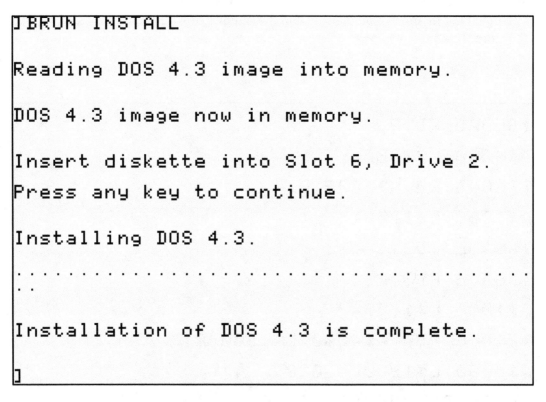

Figure III.4.2. BRUN Command Display

```
BSAVE      f [,Ss][,Dd][,Vv][,Aa][,B][,Ll][,R[1]]

Example:   BSAVE RD2
           BSAVE RD2,R
           BSAVE RD3,A$4000,L$1C00,R1
```

This command saves the Binary file `f` to the specified volume using the memory address `a` and the length `l` in bytes if the A and L keywords are included, respectively. In DOS 4.3 these keywords are optional, but if they are included, they are both required. If the A and L keywords are not included, the address `a` and the length `l` values of the previous BLOAD or BSAVE command are used. If the R keyword is included the memory save address and the number of bytes written to the specified volume are displayed as shown previously in Figure III.4.1. If a non-zero R keyword is included, the number of verified sectors is also displayed as shown in Figure III.4.1. If CONFIG Bit 1 is set the Binary file will not be verified after it is BSAVEd as shown previously for the DOS SAVE command in Figure III.3.4. Figure III.4.1 shows a byte comparison of the two files RD and RD4 using the DOS DIFF command. The DIFF command proves that both those files are identical because no differences are shown. The B keyword can be used to implement the "File Delete/File Save" strategy. That is, the Binary file `f` will be deleted from the volume Catalog and then saved to the same volume in order to ensure that the file's TSL contains only those track/sector entries that are required by the file.

```
]LLOAD README.L,R
A$3800,L$1627
]LLOAD README.L,A$1000,R
A$1000,L$1627
]LSAVE README2.L
]LSAVE README3.L,R
A$1000,L$1627
]LSAVE README4.L,A$3800,L$1627,R1
A$3800,L$1627 = 023
]DIFF README.L,README4.L = 0x1700

]
```

Figure III.4.3. LLOAD and LSAVE Commands Display

139

```
LLOAD      f [,Ss][,Dd][,Vv][,Aa][,R]
```

Example: LLOAD READM.L
           LLOAD READM.L,R
           LLOAD README.L,A$1000,R

This command was originally developed for DOS 4.1 and it reads into memory the *Lisa* Binary file `f` in the specified volume at memory address `a` if the A keyword is included. If the A keyword is not included the *Lisa* file is read into memory at the address the file was originally, or last `LSAVE`d. *Lisa* files are file type `0x40` as shown in Table I.7.3. If the R keyword is included the memory load address and the number of bytes read into memory are displayed as shown in Figure III.4.3.

```
LSAVE      f [,Ss][,Dd][,Vv][,Aa][,B][,Ll][,R[1]]
```

Example: LSAVE README2.L
           LSAVE README2.L,R
           LSAVE README3.L,A$2100,L$CED,R1

This command was originally developed for DOS 4.1 and it saves the *Lisa* Binary file `f` to the specified volume using the memory address `a` and length `l` if the A and L keywords are included. In DOS 4.3 these keywords are optional, but if they are included both values are required. If the A and L keywords are not included, the address `a` and the length `l` of the previous `LLOAD` or `LSAVE` command are used. If the R keyword is included the memory save address and the number of bytes saved to the specified volume are displayed as shown in Figure III.4.3. If a non-zero R keyword is included, the number of verified sectors is also displayed as shown in Figure III.4.3. If `CONFIG` Bit 1 is set the Binary file will not be verified after it is saved as shown previously for the DOS `SAVE` command in Figure III.3.4. Figure III.4.3 shows a byte comparison of the two files `README.L` and `README4.L` using the DOS `DIFF` command. The `DIFF` command proves that both files are identical because no differences are shown. The B keyword can be used to implement the "File Delete/File Save" strategy. That is, the *Lisa* Binary file `f` will be deleted from the volume Catalog and then saved to the same volume in order to ensure that the file's `TSL` contains only those track/sector entries that are required by the file.

Command	Command Syntax
APPEND*	f [,Ss][,Dd][,Vv]
CLOSE	[f]
EXEC	f [,Ss][,Dd][,Vv][,Rr]
OPEN*	f [,Ss][,Dd][,Vv]
POSITION*	f [,Rr]
READ*	f [,Bb]
TLOAD	f [,Ss][,Dd][,Vv][,A][,Bb][,Ll][,R]
TSAVE	f [,Ss][,Dd][,Vv][,B][,R[1]]
TW	f [,Ss][,Dd][,Vv]
WRITE*	f [,Bb]

Table III.5.1. DOS 4.3 Sequential Text File Commands

5. Sequential Text File Commands

The DOS 4.3 Sequential Text File Commands manage sequential Text files. The syntax of the Sequential Text File Commands is shown in Table III.5.1. The commands shown with an asterisk cannot be used on the Apple command line, whereas the other sequential Text file commands are permitted to be used on the Apple command line. Sequential Text files are comprised of sequential fields of ASCII characters where a RETURN (i.e. 0x8D) character terminates each field, and a NULL (i.e. 0x00) character terminates the file. DOS 4.3 differentiates between sequential Text files and random-access Data files in how the file is opened. If the L keyword is **not** included with the OPEN command the file is treated as a sequential Text file, and the READ and WRITE commands **must not use** the R keyword as shown in Table III.5.1. See Table III.6.1 that shows the DOS 4.3 random-access Data file commands in order to understand how those commands are syntactically different from the DOS 4.3 sequential Text file commands.

Data may be read from or written to a sequential Text file immediately after the file is opened, after the file pointer has been positioned to a particular byte location, or after the file pointer has been positioned to a particular field location. If the B keyword is included with the READ or WRITE command, that keyword will take precedence over any previous POSITION command. That is, even though the file pointer may be at the beginning of the rth field specified by a previous POSITION command, the B keyword, if it is included with a subsequent READ or WRITE command, will force the recalculation of the file pointer location so that the pointer will point to the bth byte relative to the beginning of the file.

Many DOS commands utilize the File Manager to open a Text file, which is handled by the Common Open routine CMNOPEN. This routine initializes the File Manager workarea, checks if the RECNUM value as shown in Table I.11.1 is 0x00, and allocates a file if the requested filename is not found in the volume Catalog. If RECNUM equals 0x00, DOS 3.3 sets the value of OPNRCLEN as shown in Table I.12.2 to 0x0001. If RECNUM equals 0x00, DOS 4.3 sets the value of OPNRCELN equal to BYTPRSEC as shown in Table I.5.1. For sectors that are 0x0100 bytes in size, BYTPRSEC would equal 0x0100. This is a far better and more logical design because Text file records are rarely, if ever, one byte in size, and using 0x0100 for an initial record size is far closer to reality.

```
APPEND    f [,Ss][,Dd][,Vv]

Example:   APPEND STEST.T
```

This command will open the sequential Text file f in the specified volume if it is not already open. The APPEND command must be followed by a WRITE command for the file f. The APPEND command will read the entire file f and then position the file pointer to the first NULL (i.e. 0x00) character it finds in the file. All subsequent input data will be written to the file beginning at that location. Figure III.5.1 shows an example Applesoft program that uses the OPEN, WRITE, and CLOSE commands in order to create the sequential Text file STEST.T. Figure III.5.2 shows another example Applesoft program that is similar to the program shown in Figure III.5.1 except that this program uses the sequential Text file APPEND command to add more information to the file STEST.T.

The APPEND command was flawed in several locations in DOS 3.3 which required patches to correct the manipulation of the internal variable BYTOFFST and the File Manager Context Block variable RECNUM. DOS 4.3 manipulates these variables correctly within the File Manager driver routine FMDRVR, in the Common Open routine CMNOPEN, and in the Calculate Position routine CALPOSN. The original DOS 3.3 Calculate Position routine failed to ensure that the Carry flag was clear before manipulating its variables in order to calculate the desired file position.

```
]LOAD STEST

]LIST

 10 D$ =   CHR$ (4):F$ = "STEST.T"
    : ONERR  GOTO 100
 20  PRINT D$;"OPEN ";F$
 30  PRINT D$;"WRITE ";F$
 40  PRINT "This is a sequential
    TEXT file."
 50  PRINT D$;"CLOSE ";F$
 100  END

]RUN

]LIST STEST.T

This is a sequential TEXT file.


] ▓
```

Figure III.5.1. OPEN, WRITE, and CLOSE Commands Display

```
]LOAD STEST2

]LIST

  10 D$ =  CHR$ (4):F$ = "STEST.T"
     : ONERR  GOTO 100
  20  PRINT D$;"OPEN ";F$
  30  PRINT D$;"APPEND ";F$
  40  PRINT D$;"WRITE ";F$
  50  PRINT "This is an appended l
     ine."
  60  PRINT D$;"CLOSE ";F$
  100  END

]RUN

]LIST STEST.T

This is a sequential TEXT file.
This is an appended line.

]
```

Figure III.5.2. APPEND Command Display

CLOSE   [f]

Example: CLOSE
           CLOSE STEST.T

This command will flush and de-allocate the file buffer associated with the sequential Text file f, thereby closing the file from any further data input or data output. If a filename is not supplied with the CLOSE command, all open files regardless of their file type will be closed except for an open EXEC file. If a file f is open for data input, a CLOSE command will cause all remaining data in its file buffer to be flushed to the file and then the file f will be closed. Figures III.5.1 and III.5.2 show examples of using the CLOSE command in an Applesoft program.

```
EXEC      f [,Ss][,Dd][,Vv][,Rr]

Example:  EXEC ETEST.T
          EXEC ETEST.T,R3
```

This command opens the file f in the specified volume with the expectation of reading either Applesoft commands or DOS 4.3 commands as if the commands had been issued from the Apple command line. There can be only one active EXEC file, but an EXEC file may transfer its control to another EXEC file. If the R keyword is included the file pointer is positioned that number of fields r from the beginning of the file. A field is a sequence of characters terminated with a RETURN (i.e. 0x8D) character. Figure III.5.3 shows an example of an EXEC file and its output.

There is one obvious and undesirable feature in Figure III.5.3, and that is the presence of the PROMPT character "]" on nearly every line of EXEC file output. I vividly remember my co-worker in 1982 asking me "Why? Why is that PROMPT character there?" Now, I can honestly answer that question: DOS always prepares the Apple command line for the next command to be typed in. The EXEC file proceeds to "type in" the data for the next command line. When CONFIG Bit 2 is set as shown in Table III.1.2, and when there is an active EXEC file, DOS 4.3 bypasses the instructions that prints the PROMPT character. The same EXEC file is processed again in Figure III.5.4 with CONFIG Bit 2 set.

```
]LIST ETEST.T

print "This is ETEST running."
mon c
brun BTEST
date


]EXEC ETEST.T
]
This is ETEST running.

]

]
This is an example Binary program.
Clock data:  01/01/20 08:28:48
End of Binary program.

] = 01/01/20 08:28:48
]

]
```

Figure III.5.3. EXEC Command Display

```
]CONFIG 4

]EXEC ETEST.T

This is ETEST running.


This is an example Binary program.
Clock data:  01/01/20 08:28:48
End of Binary program.

 = 01/01/20 08:28:48


]EXEC ETEST.T,R3
 = 01/01/20 08:28:49


]CONFIG $FF

]※
```

Figure III.5.4. No PROMPT, "EXEC,Rr" Command Display

Also shown in Figure III.5.4 is R keyword utilization: the file pointer is positioned at the first character after counting three RETURN characters, thus ignoring those fields, and all subsequent commands are issued from that point in the EXEC file. That is, the first three commands in the EXEC file ETEST.T are skipped.

If the DOS MAXFILES command is used in an EXEC file, EXEC command processing will terminate and the EXEC file will be closed. In both Figures III.5.3 and III.5.4 command line spacing is set to single spacing while an EXEC file is open. Once the EXEC file is closed DOS 4.3 will return to double spacing between successive DOS commands unless CONFIG Bit 0 is set.

OPEN   f [,Ss][,Dd][,Vv]

Example: OPEN STEST.T

This command will allocate one of the available file buffers, which is 582 (i.e. 0x246) bytes in size, for the sequential Text file f in the specified volume. This file buffer will be initialized to read from or write to the beginning of this file. If this file does not exist in the specified volume, the file is created and an entry is made in the volume Catalog. If this file is already open, the file is flushed so any remaining data in its file buffer is written to the file before the file is closed, and the specified file is again opened. Figures III.5.1 and III.5.2 show examples of using the sequential Text OPEN command in an Applesoft program. The L keyword must **not** be included with the OPEN command when reading and writing a sequential Text file.

```
POSITION f [,Rr]

Example:   POSITION STEST.T,R1
```

This command will position the file pointer for the file f that number of fields r ahead relative to the current file pointer position. A field is a sequence of ASCII characters terminated with a RETURN (i.e. 0x8D) character. Figure III.5.5 shows an example Applesoft program where the file pointer is positioned at the first character after counting one RETURN character relative to the beginning of the file STEST.T since this sequential Text file POSITION command directly follows a DOS OPEN command. Otherwise, the file pointer would be positioned ahead relative to the current file pointer position.

```
]LIST STEST.T

This is a sequential TEXT file.
This is an appended line.

]LOAD STEST3

]LIST

 10 D$ =  CHR$ (4):F$ = "STEST.T"
    : ONERR  GOTO 100
 20  PRINT D$;"OPEN ";F$
 30  PRINT D$;"POSITION ";F$;",R1
    "
 40  PRINT D$;"READ ";F$
 50  INPUT A$: PRINT A$
 60  GOTO 50
 100  PRINT D$;"CLOSE ";F$: END

]RUN
This is an appended line.

]
```

Figure III.5.5. POSITION and READ Commands Display

146

```
READ        f [,Bb]

Example:    READ STEST.T
```

This command will configure the sequential Text file buffer for file f such that all data will come from
that file. If the B keyword is included the file pointer position will be located that many actual bytes b
from the beginning of the file before any data is read from the file. Figure III.5.6 shows an example
Applesoft program that uses the sequential Text file READ command with a byte b offset. Any
previous POSITION command will be ignored when the B keyword is included with the READ
command.

```
]LIST STEST.T

This is a sequential TEXT file.
This is an appended line.


]LOAD STEST4

]LIST

 10 D$ =   CHR$ (4):F$ = "STEST.T"
    : ONERR  GOTO 100
 20   PRINT D$;"OPEN ";F$
 30   PRINT D$;"READ ";F$;",B3"
 40   INPUT A$:  PRINT A$
 50   GOTO 40
 100   PRINT D$;"CLOSE ";F$: END

]RUN
s is a sequential TEXT file.
This is an appended line.

]
```

Figure III.5.6. "READ,Bb" Command Display

147

```
TLOAD      f [,Ss][,Dd][,Vv][,A][,Bb][,Ll][,R]

Example:   TLOAD ETEST.T,L31
           TLOAD STEST,A,R
           TLOAD ETEST.T,A,B31
```

This command was originally developed for DOS 4.1 and it will read into memory the sequential Text file f in the specified volume at memory address 0x0900. If the A keyword is included in a subsequent TLOAD command, that sequential Text file f will be appended to the sequential Text file(s) already in memory as long as the internal variable FILELAST+1 is not 0x00. If FILELAST+1 is 0x00 (a sequential Text file is not in memory) and the A keyword is included, the Text file f will be read into memory at memory address 0x0900. If the B keyword is included, that number of bytes b will be skipped before reading the remaining contents of the file into memory. If the L keyword is included, that number of bytes l will be read into memory, or until the end of the file if that should occur first. If the R keyword is included the start address and total number of bytes of Text data currently in memory is displayed once the TLOAD command completes its processing.

In Figure III.5.7 the first thirty-one bytes of the file ETEST.T are read into memory at memory address 0x0900. The entire contents of the file STEST.T is read into memory next, and appended to the previous Text data already in memory because the A keyword was specified. The total Text data now in memory is shown to be 0x59 (i.e. 89) bytes. Finally, the first thirty-one bytes of the file ETEST.T are skipped and the remaining contents of the file ETEST.T is appended to all the previous Text data already in memory. The complete sequential Text data is written to the file TOTAL.T, and the entire file of 0x6F (i.e. 111) bytes is displayed using the DOS LIST command. It is quite apparent that a complete sequential Text file may be easily created by extracting pieces of other sequential Text files using the TLOAD command and its powerful set of keywords.

```
TSAVE      f [,Ss][,Dd][,Vv][,B][,R[1]]

Example:   TSAVE TOTAL.T,R
           TSAVE TOTAL2.T,R1
```

This command was originally developed for DOS 4.1 and it will save the sequential Text data currently in memory to the file f in the specified volume. The start address and total number of bytes of Text data currently in memory is internal to DOS 4.3. If the R keyword is included the start address and total number of bytes of sequential Text data currently in memory is displayed as shown in Figure III.5.7 once the TSAVE command completes its processing. If a non-zero R keyword is included, the number of verified sectors is also displayed. If CONFIG Bit 1 is set the Text file f will not be verified after it is saved. The B keyword can be used to implement the "File Delete/File Save" strategy. That is, the Text file f will be deleted from the volume Catalog and then saved to the same volume in order to ensure that the file's TSL contains only those track/sector entries that are required for the file.

148

```
]TLOAD ETEST.T,L31

]TLOAD STEST.T,A,R

A$0900,L$0059

]TLOAD ETEST.T,A,B31

]TSAVE TOTAL.T,R1

A$0900,L$006F = 001

]LIST TOTAL.T

print "This is ETEST running."
This is a sequential TEXT file.
This is an appended line.
mon c
brun BTEST
date


]
```

Figure III.5.7. TLOAD and TSAVE Command Display

```
]LIST TEST.T

PRINT "This is TEST.T running."
PRINT "Ready to run BTEST."
BRUN BTEST

]TW TEST.T

>DATE
>

]LIST TEST.T

PRINT "This is TEST.T running."
PRINT "Ready to run BTEST."
BRUN BTEST
DATE


] ※
```

Figure III.5.8. TW Command Display

```
TW          f [,Ss][,Dd][,Vv]
```

Example: `TW ETEST`

This command was originally developed for DOS 4.1 and it will record all keystrokes typed on the Apple command line into the sequential Text file f in the specified volume. If the file does not exist it is created, otherwise the file is always opened in `APPEND` mode. The file is flushed and closed when the `ESC` key is pressed. That is, when the `ESC` key is pressed all buffered data is written to file f, and then the file is closed. No line editing is provided and all keystrokes including arrow keystrokes (quasi editing) are recorded to the file as well. The sequential Text file `TW` (i.e. Text Write) command provides a convenient and expeditious way to create or append an `EXEC` file or any other sequential Text file as the example shows in Figure III.5.8.

```
WRITE       f [,Bb]
```

Example: `WRITE STEST.TXT`

This command will configure the sequential Text file buffer for file f such that all data will be written to that file. If the `B` keyword is included the file pointer position will be located that many actual bytes b from the beginning of the file before any data is written to the file. Figures III.5.1 and III.5.2 show examples of using the sequential Text file `WRITE` command in an Applesoft program. Any previous `POSITION` command will be ignored if the `B` keyword is included with the `WRITE` command

Command	Command Syntax
CLOSE	[f]
OPEN*	f, Ll [,Ss][,Dd][,Vv]
READ*	f, Rr [,Bb]
WRITE*	f, Rr [,Bb]

Table III.6.1. DOS 4.3 Random-Access Data File Commands

6. Random-Access Data File Commands

The DOS 4.3 Random-Access Data File Commands manage random-access Data files. The syntax of the Random-Access Data File Commands is shown in Table III.6.1. The commands shown with an asterisk, or OPEN, READ, and WRITE, cannot be used on the Apple command line, whereas the CLOSE command is permitted to be used on the Apple command line. Random-access Data files are composed of records having a specified size, or length in bytes. A record may be comprised of Text fields, numerical data fields, or both, and can be as small as one byte or as large as 32767 (i.e. 0x7FFF) bytes in size. The record size is established by the OPEN command. A Text field is any number of sequential ASCII characters terminated with a RETURN (i.e. 0x8D) character. A numerical data field may be any number of digits, either integer or floating point values, in decimal, hexadecimal, or expressed in scientific notation in the case of real and imaginary numbers. All fields must reside within the specified record size. All records comprising a file f are not required to contain the same number or order of fields; but all records within file f must be the same size. **Only those records that contain any data exist within file f**; all other records will be created whenever data is supplied for those records. DOS 4.3 allows the r value of the R keyword to be specified up to 32767, thus permitting up to 32768 records in a single file f. There is no mathematical or logical reason for this limitation; maximum number of records in DOS 4.3 was set only to be compatible with DOS 3.3.

DOS 4.3 differentiates sequential Text files and random-access Data files by how the file is opened. If the L keyword is **included** with the OPEN command the file is treated as a random-access Data file and the READ and WRITE commands **must use** the R keyword as shown in Table III.6.1. See Table III.5.1 that shows the DOS 4.3 sequential Text file commands in order to understand how those commands are syntactically different from the DOS 4.3 random-access Data file commands. Applesoft programs that access a random-access Data file must open this file with the same record size l using the L keyword, otherwise the results will be unpredictable and quite possibly disastrous as the file is processed. DOS 3.3 could have provided the value for l in the first TSL for a random-access Data file. There certainly is enough room for that value in the TSL, particularly at bytes 0x08 and 0x09.

Data sectors are created as necessary when a random-access record is supplied with data. The file pointer value is calculated based on record size l and record number r. Using the file pointer value, the necessary TSL index can be determined, and if there is no track/sector entry for the respective data sector, a data sector is obtained from the volume Catalog and an entry is made in the TSL sector. Any numerical remainder from the TSL index calculation plus any b index value determines the byte offset within the data sector where the record data is written. If the complete record requires additional sectors, those sectors will be obtained from the volume Catalog and added to the TSL sector.

CLOSE   [f]

Example: CLOSE RTEST.T

This command will de-allocate the file buffer associated with the random-address Data file f, thereby closing the file from any further data input or data output. If a filename is not supplied with the CLOSE command, all open files regardless of their file type will be closed except for an open EXEC file. If a file f was open for data input, a CLOSE command will cause all remaining data in its file buffer to be flushed to the file and then the file f will be closed. Figure III.6.1 shows an example of using the CLOSE command in an Applesoft program.

```
]LOAD RTEST
]LIST

 10  D$ =   CHR$ (4):F$ = "RTEST.T"
     :L = 32: ONERR  GOTO 60
 20     PRINT D$;"OPEN ";F$;", L";L
 30     PRINT D$;"WRITE ";F$;", R3"
 35     PRINT "This is Record 3."
 40     PRINT D$;"WRITE ";F$;", R2,
        B6"
 45     PRINT "This is Record 2."
 50     PRINT D$;"WRITE ";F$;", R1,
        B12"
 55     PRINT "This is Record 1."
 60     PRINT D$;"CLOSE ";F$: END
]RUN

]
```

Figure III.6.1. OPEN, WRITE, and CLOSE Commands Display

OPEN   f, Ll [,Ss][,Dd][,Vv]

Example: OPEN RTEST.T, L32

This command will allocate one of the available file buffers, which is 582 (i.e. 0x246) bytes in size, for the random-access Data file f in the specified volume, and set the record length to the number of bytes l specified by the required L keyword. If this file does not exist in the specified volume, the file is created and an entry is made in the volume Catalog. If this file is already open, the file is flushed so any remaining data in its file buffer is written to the file, the file is closed, and the specified file is again opened. Figures III.6.1 and III.6.3 show examples of using the random-access Data OPEN command in an Applesoft program. The L keyword **must** be included with the OPEN command when reading data from and writing data to a random-access Data file.

152

```
]LIST RTEST.T,R

0000 0000 0000 0000 0000 0000 0000 0000
0000 0000 0000 0000 0000 0000 0000 0000
0000 0000 0000 0000 0000 0000 D4E8 E9F3
A0E9 F3A0 D2E5 E3EF F2E4 A0B1 AE8D 0000
0000 0000 0000 D4E8 E9F3 A0E9 F3A0 D2E5
E3EF F2E4 A0B2 AE8D 0000 0000 0000 0000
D4E8 E9F3 A0E9 F3A0 D2E5 E3EF F2E4 A0B3
AE8D 0000 0000 0000 0000 0000 0000 0000
0000 0000 0000 0000 0000 0000 0000 0000
0000 0000 0000 0000 0000 0000 0000 0000
0000 0000 0000 0000 0000 0000 0000 0000
0000 0000 0000 0000 0000 0000 0000 0000
0000 0000 0000 0000 0000 0000 0000 0000
0000 0000 0000 0000 0000 0000 0000 0000
0000 0000 0000 0000 0000 0000 0000 0000

] ※
```

Figure III.6.2. Contents of RTEST.T Display

READ   f, Rr [,Bb]

Example: READ RTEST.T,R1,B12

This command will configure the random-access Data file buffer for the file f such that all data will come from that file. Data will be read from the specified Record r, one field at a time. If the R keyword is not included no error will be generated and the file pointer will simply be positioned at the beginning of the file. DOS 4.3 does not check for the presence or absence of the R keyword; it simply utilizes its value if it exists. However, even though the R keyword is initialized to 0x00 before a DOS command is parsed, the practice of not using the R keyword with the random-access READ command is strongly not advised. If the B keyword is included the file pointer will be positioned that many bytes b from the beginning of the specified Record r before any data is read from the file.

Figure III.6.2 shows a hexadecimal listing of the contents of RTEST.T using the DOS LIST command with the R keyword. The R keyword for the LIST command selects hexadecimal output rather than ASCII output for a Text file. It is easy to see that each record is thirty-two bytes in size from byte 0x00 to byte 0x1F. There is no data in the first record, Record 0, data in Record 1 begins at byte 0x0C, data in Record 2 begins at byte 0x06, and data in Record 3 begins at byte 0x00. Figure III.6.3 shows an example Applesoft program using the random-access READ command. The file records may be specified and their data will be read from the file in any order, hence the

153

descriptive term 'random-access'. Figure III.6.3 also shows the results of running the RTEST2 Applesoft program.

```
]LOAD RTEST2

]LIST

 10 D$ =  CHR$ (4):F$ = "RTEST.T"
    :L = 32: ONERR  GOTO 60
 20  PRINT D$;"OPEN ";F$;",  L";L
 30  PRINT D$;"READ ";F$;", R2, B
    6": INPUT D2$
 40  PRINT D$;"READ ";F$;", R3": INPUT
    D3$
 50  PRINT D$;"READ ";F$;", R1, B
    12": INPUT D1$
 60  PRINT D$;"CLOSE ";F$
 70  PRINT : PRINT D1$: PRINT D2$
    : PRINT D3$: END

]RUN

This is Record 1.
This is Record 2.
This is Record 3.
]
```

Figure III.6.3. READ and RUN Command Display

WRITE   f, Rr [,Bb]

Example: WRITE RTEST.T,R1,B12

This command will configure the random-access Data file buffer for file f such that all data will be written to that file. Data will be written to the specified Record r, one field at a time. If the R keyword is not included no error will be generated and the file pointer will simply be positioned at the beginning of the file. The practice of not using the R keyword with the random-access WRITE command is strongly not advised. If the B keyword is included the file pointer will be positioned that many bytes b from the beginning of the specified Record r before any data is written to the file. Previously, Figure III.6.1 showed an example of using the random-access WRITE command in an Applesoft program. The file records may be specified and their data will be written to the file in any order, hence the descriptive term 'random-access'.

154

```
]LOAD CREATE

]LIST

100  D$ = .CHR$ (4)
200  F$ = "BIGFILE"
300  L = 467
400   PRINT D$;"OPEN ";F$;",L";L
500  R = 32767
600   PRINT D$;"WRITE ";F$;",R";R

700   PRINT "RECORD ";R
800   PRINT D$;"CLOSE ";F$: END

]RUN

]LS

S=6 D=02 V=000 F=0061 01/01/20 08:28:49

  A 002 CREATE              01/01/20 08:28:48
  T 491 BIGFILE             01/01/20 08:28:49

]
```

Figure III.6.4. Random-Access Data File CREATE

Denis Molony, a citizen of Australia and author of *DiskBrowser*, provided me with an excellent example of an Applesoft program that creates a random-access Data file that will quickly become useless after a few records are written to the file. Figure III.6.4 shows Molony's Applesoft program. His program certainly looks simple enough until you realize that the program writes to the last possible record permitted by DOS 4.3, record 32767 (i.e. 0x7FFF), or the 32768th record. When DOS first creates a random-access Data file only the first TSL sector is created as in line 400 and the value of the L keyword, 467 in this example, is saved in the file's workarea in the RECDLNGH variable as shown in Table I.12.3 at offset 0x213. When this file is reopened sometime in the future, the file must be opened with the same L keyword value in order to accurately locate the desired records. When Molony's program writes to record 32767 in line 600 a file pointer is calculated and sufficient TSL sectors are created in order to save that particular record to its rightful data sector.

How many TSL sectors are created may seem puzzling at first, though easy to determine. Each TSL sector contains 122 (i.e. 0x7A) track/sector entries. These entries are for sectors of data, not for records of data. Each sector of data contains 256 (i.e. 0x100) bytes. Including record 0, therefore,

{ (467 bytes/record * 32768 records) / 256 bytes/sector } /

    122 sectors/TSL = <u>490 TSLs</u>

When the data is actually written to the file in line 700, an entry is made in the 490th TSL sector for the sector that is created to contain the provided data. The data is not necessarily written to the first byte of the sector, but in this instance to byte 46, which comes at the end of record 32766, or the 32767th

155

record. The entire record of 467 bytes is not written to the file but only the data provided in the Applesoft PRINT statement in line 700. This byte offset into the data sector is the remainder from the file pointer calculation:

```
( 467 bytes/record * 32767 records ) / 256 bytes/sector =

     59,774 sectors + 45 bytes
```

Figure III.6.4 shows that BIGFILE is 491 sectors in size, currently composed of 490 TSL sectors and one data sector. There are only sixty-one sectors free on this DOS 4.3 data volume which originally contained 554 sectors when it was first initialized. Why has DOS created all these TSL sectors? It seems rather ludicrous, because 59,774 sectors are required to contain all the data for all 32768 records if every record contained 467 bytes of data and all records were written to this file. But that would require a volume having at least 3,736 additional disk tracks. At the very least DOS has created the minimum number of required linked-list TSL sectors in order to write record 32767. It is rather obvious that the file BIGFILE is not at all suitable to contain all the data the program CREATE intended. Therefore, it is critical that random-access Data files are properly sized to the volumes on which they are stored.

Family Roots by Stephen C. Vorenberg and marketed by Quinsept, Inc., utilizes sequential Text files and random-access Data files for the *Family Roots* data base. Each data volume contains three files: CONTROL, NAMELIST, and FAMILY. The random-access Data file NAMELIST uses 26 sectors. The sequential Text file CONTROL uses 2 sectors, and it contains the Start and End record numbers that exist in the random-access Data file FAMILY whose records have been pre-initialized using a 256-byte empty buffer. The CONTROL file also contains the size of the FAMILY file records, and a few other operating parameters, so that the file FAMILY is always opened with the correct value 1 for the L keyword. Essentially, each FAMILY file contains 224 records, and each record can be utilized up to a maximum of 512 bytes. The equations required to verify whether there is sufficient disk space for this random-access Data file when all of its records are completely filled with data can be expressed as follows:

```
( 224 records * 512 bytes/record ) / 256 bytes/sector = 448 sectors

448 sectors / 122 sectors/TSL = 4 TSLs
```

Since *Family Roots* utilizes the DOS 3.3 disk operating system, tracks 0x00, 0x01, and 0x02 are not available for data (reserved for DOS 3.3), and the VTOC and Catalog combined require sixteen sectors. This leaves 496 sectors for data in a volume having thirty-five tracks. Using the above results, each data volume for *Family Roots* requires 26 + 2 + 448 + 4 = 480 sectors. Therefore, at least sixteen sectors should be left available in each data volume that could be used for additional files. A few data volumes did contain one or two additional files: LASTID and DATE. These files were only two sectors each in size and they appeared transitory. Vorenberg sized his data files such that 96.8% of each data volume is utilized giving the program *Family Roots* a little safety margin.

These two examples demonstrate how important it is to consider whether a single data volume can provide sufficient room to store the contents of a particular random-access Data file, or whether several volumes would be required to store all the generated data when using multiple random-access Data files. Performing the file sizing analysis upfront certainly saves much grief later on when and if a random-access Data file should exceed its storage media capacity. Certainly, a random-access Data file cannot grow endlessly and it must have limits built into its design. Given R for the number of records, L for the size of each record in bytes, and S for the number of available sectors where each sector contains 256 bytes, the general sizing equations incorporating TSL sector overhead can be expressed as follows:

```
S = ( R * L * 123 ) / ( 256 * 122 ) sectors        (always round up)

R = ( S * 256 * 122 ) / ( L * 123 ) records        (always round down)

L = ( S * 256 * 122 ) / ( R * 123 ) bytes          (always round down)
```

Inserting Vorenberg's parameters where R = 224 and L = 512:

```
S = ( 224 * 512 * 123 ) / ( 256 * 122 ) = 451.67 => 452 sectors
```

This is precisely the same value obtained above: 448 data sectors + 4 TSL sectors = 452 sectors.

For Molony's example program, the required number of sectors for his random-access Data file is:

```
S = ( 32768 * 467 * 123 ) / ( 256 * 122 ) => 60,266 sectors
```

A single, 35-track volume is hardly the appropriate media for this random-access Data file.

Assuming Molony's Data file can be spread over several 36-track volumes each providing 570 sectors when using DOS 4.3, the number of records on each volume would be:

```
R = ( 570 * 256 * 122 ) / ( 467 * 123 ) => 309 records  (round down)
```

And, the number of volumes required would be:

```
32768 records / 309 records/volume => 106 volumes          (round up)
```

A database of this magnitude would require quite a substantial programing effort, but easily managed on the CFFA using DOS 4.3 and the *VOLMGR*. Vorenberg strongly recommended using the Sider with *Family Roots* and that is precisely the hard drive my mother utilized with *Family Roots* in order to digitize the rather extensive size of our family tree.

IV. DOS 4.3 Assembly Language Routines

DOS 4.3 provides excellent support for assembly language routines that need to acquire or change the value of some or all of the operational variables used throughout the DOS software. DOS 4.3 also provides interface routines and vectors to handle error reporting, for obtaining the date and time, and for displaying the DOS version and build information easily. Even though the data management routines and Page 0x03 vectors have been previously discussed, I thought it would be informative to present all these routines and vectors in one section, together, showing their address, the registers they use, and the processor flag values that are required upon entry to these routines and vectors, and the values returned to the user.

There are two basic approaches a user can call an assembly language routine or vector: directly or indirectly. The direct approach is simply to use the JSR instruction. The indirect approach is to use the JSR instruction coupled with an indirect JMP instruction, or (JMP). Figure IV.0.1 shows both approaches a user can use to call a DOS 4.3 assembly language routine or vector. Depending upon how the assembly language routine or vector is entered (i.e. by a JMP instruction) or specified (i.e. by an address) usually determines which approach is more favorable.

```
 :              :           :
03E1           10    RDCLKVSN  equ  $3E1
03EA           11    HOOKDOS   equ  $3EA
 :              :           :
 :              :           :
1000          100    ; Direct subroutine approach.
1000 20 EA 03 101              jsr  HOOKDOS
 :              :           :
 :              :           :
2000          200    ; Indirect vector approach.
2000 A0 83    201              ldy  #VSNBUFR
2002 A9 20    202              lda  /VSNBUFR
2004 38       203              sec
2005 20 80 80 204              jsr  READVSN
 :              :           :
 :              :           :
2080 6C E1 03 300    READVSN   jmp  (RDCLKVSN)
2083 00 00 00 301    VSNBUFR   dfs  20,0
 :              :           :
```

Figure IV.0.1. Direct and Indirect Approach for a Subroutine Call

1. DOSWARM Routine

Function	Address	X-reg	Y-reg	A-reg	C-flag	Description
Entry	0x3D0	–	–	–	–	Enters (WARMADR) handler
Return	0xD43C	–	–	–	–	No return to caller

The DOSWARM routine at memory address 0x3D0 as shown in Table I.9.1 directly jumps to a page 0xBE routine in order to write enable Language Card Bank 2 memory and then jump to the WARMSTRT routine in DOS. WARMSTRT resets the state machine, initializes the MON flags and keyboard and video intercepts, turns ROM memory on, and then exits indirectly by means of the WARMADR vector in the page 0xBE INITVALS structure.

DOS 4.3 initially sets WARMADR to memory address 0xD43C, the address of ASROMWRM. ASROMWRM is the Applesoft soft entry address in ROM and does not return to the caller. The user is free to change the address at WARMADR in order to tailor the DOSWARM routine not to exit into Applesoft ROM, but into a user specific routine. Use the Direct approach to call the DOSWARM routine.

2. DOSCOLD Routine

Function	Address	X-reg	Y-reg	A-reg	C-flag	Description
Entry	0x3D3	–	–	–	–	Enters (COLDADR) handler
Return	0xE000	–	–	–	–	No return to caller

The DOSCOLD routine at memory address 0x3D3 as shown in Table I.9.1 directly jumps to DOSINIT in memory page 0xBF in order to initialize the stack pointer, select the main video and character set, initialize XMODE, CSWL, and KSWL, set the video output to normal, copy the ROM Monitor to RAM, search for a clock card, and then jump to the COLDSTRT routine in DOS. COLDSTRT resets the state machine, initializes the MON flags and keyboard and video intercepts, turns ROM memory on, and then exits indirectly by means of the COLDADR vector in the page 0xBE INITVALS structure.

DOS 4.3 initially sets the COLDADR vector to memory address 0xE000, the address of BASCLD. BASCLD is the Applesoft hard entry address in ROM that performs a complete reinitialization of Applesoft and does not return to the caller. The user is free to change the address at COLDADR in order to tailor the COLDSTRT routine not to exit into Applesoft ROM, but into a user specific routine. Use the Direct approach to call the DOSCOLD routine.

3. CALLFM Routine

Function	Address	X-reg	Y-reg	A-reg	C-flag	Description
Entry	0x3D6	File Flag	–	–	–	Enter File Manager handler
Return	–	Error	–	–	Status	Return to caller

The CALLFM routine at memory address 0x3D6 as shown in Table I.9.1 directly jumps to a page 0xBE routine in order to write enable Language Card Bank 2 memory and then jump to the FMHNDLR routine in DOS. FMHNDLR will allocate a new file if it does not exist when the X-register (File Flag) is set to 0x00 (otherwise a new file will **not** be created in the volume Catalog), it saves the registers, and then enters the internal FILEMNGR routine.

When processing is complete, FILEMNGR returns to the caller. For the external caller, FMHNDLR returns to page 0xBE, enables ROM memory, and then returns to the external caller. If the Carry flag is **set** the X-register will contain an error number, otherwise the Carry flag is **clear** and the X-register will be set to 0x00. The File Manager uses **only** its own context block to process either an internal or an external File Manager command. Use the Direct approach to call the CALLFM routine.

4. CALLRWTS Routine

Function	Address	X-reg	Y-reg	A-reg	C-flag	Description
Entry	0x3D9	–	#IOCB	/IOCB	–	Enter RWTS handler
Return	–	–	–	Error	Status	Return to caller

The CALLRWTS routine at memory address 0x3D9 as shown in Table I.9.1 directly jumps to a page 0xBE routine in order to write enable Language Card Bank 1 memory and then jump to the DORWTS routine in DOS. DORWTS disables interrupts, saves the Y- and A-registers that contain the address of the user's IOCB to IOBADR, extracts the BUFADR2Z address from the IOCB, extracts the slot-times-sixteen value from the IOCB, copies it to the X-register, and saves it back to the IOCB at SLOTFND, and then enters the requested slot handler.

When processing is complete, DORWTS restores the processor status, sets the Carry flag if the A-register contains an error code (otherwise it clears the Carry flag when the A-register contains 0x00), and returns to page 0xBE, enables ROM memory, and then returns to the external caller. RWTS can use any context block, even the DOS internal context block in page 0xBF as long as the Y- and A-registers contain the address of that context block. Use the Direct approach to call the CALLRWTS routine.

5. GETFMCB Routine

Function	Address	X-reg	Y-reg	A-reg	C-flag	Description
Entry	0x3DC	–	–	–	–	Gets FMCB address
Return	0x3E0	–	#FMCB	/FMCB	–	Return to caller

The GETFMCB routine at memory address 0x3DC as shown in Table I.9.1 loads the Y- and A-registers with the address of the File Manager Context Block FMVALS residing in page 0xBF. The File Manager uses **only** this context block to process either an internal or an external File Manager command. *FID* maintains its own copy of the 18-byte Context Block, modifies it as needed, and then copies it back in its entirety into DOS address space before calling CALLFM. Upon return from the File Manager, *FID* copies the entire Context Block again into its own address space before looking at the return code RTNCODE value. Use the Direct approach to call the GETFMCB routine.

6. RDCLKVSN Vector

Function	Address	X-reg	Y-reg	A-reg	C-flag	Description
Entry	0x3E1	–	#CLKBUF	/CLKBUF	clear	Gets date and time in 6-byte buf
Return	–	–	–	–	–	Return to caller
Entry	0x3E1		#VSNBUF	/VSNBUF	set	Gets DOS Version in 20-byte buf
Return	–					Return to caller

The RDCLKVSN vector at memory address 0x3E1 as shown in Table I.9.1 is used to indirectly jump to a page 0xBE routine in order to write enable Language Card Bank 2 memory and then jump to the dual-purpose routine DOCLKVSN routine in DOS.

If the Carry flag is **clear** when entering the DOCLKVSN routine, the Y- and A-registers must contain the address of a 6-byte clock buffer in order to obtain the current date and time values.

If the Carry flag is **set** when entering the DOCLKVSN routine, the Y- and A-registers must contain the address of a 20-byte version buffer to obtain the 19-byte DOS Version text string.

Once processing has completed in either routine, the DOCLKVSN routine returns to page 0xBE, enables ROM memory, and then returns to the external caller. Use the Indirect approach to call the RDCLKVSN vector.

162

7. GETIOCB Routine

Function	Address	X-reg	Y-reg	A-reg	C-flag	Description
Entry	0x3E3	–	–	–	–	Gets IOCB address
Return	0x3E7	–	#IOCB	/IOCB	–	Return to caller

The GETIOCB routine at memory address 0x3E3 as shown in Table I.9.1 loads the Y- and A-registers with the address of the Input/Output Context Block TBLTYPE variable residing in page 0xBF. RWTS uses this context block to process either an internal or an external RWTS command. RWTS can use virtually any writable memory space for its processing as long as the Y- and A-registers contain the address for that context block. Use the Direct approach to call the GETIOCB routine.

8. PRERRADR Vector

Function	Address	X-reg	Y-reg	A-reg	C-flag	Description
Entry	0x3E8	Error #	–	–	–	Print error message handler
Return	–	–	–	–	–	Return to caller

The PRERRADR vector at memory address 0x3E8 as shown in Table I.9.1 is used to indirectly jump to a page 0xBE routine in order to write enable Language Card Bank 2 memory and then jump to the DOPRTERR routine in DOS. DOPRTERR saves the registers, retrieves the error number in the X-register, range checks its value (i.e. X-register must be less than 0x12), and then prints the text string of the respective error number. No carriage return is printed after the text string. Once DOPRTERR completes its processing, it returns to page 0xBE, write enables Language Card Bank 2 memory, initializes the CSWL and KSWL pointers, enables ROM memory, and then returns to the external caller. Use the Indirect approach to call the PRERRADR vector.

9. HOOKDOS Routine

Function	Address	X-reg	Y-reg	A-reg	C-flag	Description
Entry	0x3EA	–	–	–	–	DOS reconnect handler
Return	–	–	–	–	–	Return to caller

The HOOKDOS routine at memory address 0x3EA as shown in Table I.9.1 directly jumps to a page 0xBE routine in order to write enable Language Card Bank 2 memory and then jump to the INITPTRS routine in DOS. INITPTRS restores DOS's control over the CSWL and KSWL pointers. Once INITPTRS completes its processing the routine returns to page 0xBE, enables ROM memory, and then returns to the external caller. Use the Direct approach to call the HOOKDOS routine.

10. XFERADR Address

Function	Address	X-reg	Y-reg	A-reg	C-flag	Description
Address	0x3ED	–	–	–	Direction	Target program starting address
Return	–	same	same	same	–	Return to caller

The XFERADR address at memory address 0x3ED as shown in Table I.9.1 is used by the built-in ROM routine XFER at memory address 0xC314 for the target program starting address. XFER jumps to DOXFER at memory address 0xC3C3 in order to transfer control to or from program segments in Auxiliary memory. Three parameters must be initialized before the user can jump to XFER (i.e. JMP XFER): the XFERADR address, the direction of transfer (Main to Auxiliary or Auxiliary to Main), and which page-zero/stack to use (Main or Auxiliary memory). The Carry flag controls the transfer direction and the Overflow flag controls the page-zero/stack selection. The A-, X-, and Y-registers are returned without change so their values are restored by XFER. Simply copy the target program start address to XFERADR in Lo/Hi byte order.

Set the Carry flag to transfer from Main to Auxiliary memory or clear the Carry flag to transfer from Auxiliary to Main memory. Set the Overflow flag to use page-zero/stack in Auxiliary memory or clear the Overflow flag to use page-zero/stack in Main memory. The 6502 (or 65C02) Instruction Set does not have a native "set Overflow flag" instruction.

Generally, one can use the "BIT IORTS" statement to achieve setting the Overflow flag. IORTS is the address for an RTS instruction in ROM at memory address 0xFF58. XFER saves the return address of the source program currently in focus onto the stack in order for XFER to return to that same source program with its previous page-zero/stack in focus.

11. AUTOBRK Routine

Function	Address	X-reg	Y-reg	A-reg	C-flag	Description
Entry	0x3EF	–	–	–	–	Enters OLDBRK (0xFA59)
Return	0xFA59	–	–	–	–	No return to caller

The AUTOBRK routine at memory address 0x3EA as shown in Table I.9.1 directly jumps to the Autostart ROM BRK handler OLDBRK at memory address 0xFA59. OLDBRK prints the current program counter and the contents of all processor registers, and then enters MON at memory address 0xFF65. MON is the normal entry address for the ROM Monitor and does not return to the caller. Use the Direct approach to call the AUTOBRK routine.

12. AUTORSET Vector

Function	Address	X-reg	Y-reg	A-reg	C-flag	Description
Entry	0x3F2	–	–	–	–	Enters (WARMADR) handler
Return	0xD43C	–	–	–	–	No return to caller

The AUTORSET vector at memory address 0x3F2 as shown in Table I.9.1 is the reset vector for the Autostart ROM. The AUTORSET vector contains the address of the page 0xBE routine in order to write enable Language Card Bank 2 memory and then jump to the WARMSTRT routine in DOS. WARMSTRT resets the state machine, initializes the MON flags and keyboard and video intercepts, turns ROM memory on, and then exits indirectly by means of the WARMADR vector in the page 0xBE INITVALS structure.

DOS 4.3 initially sets WARMADR to memory address 0xD43C, the address of ASROMWRM. ASROMWRM is the Applesoft soft entry address in ROM and does not return to the caller. The user is free to change the address at WARMADR in order to tailor the DOSWARM routine not to exit into Applesoft ROM, but into a user specific routine. Use the Indirect approach to call the AUTORSET vector.

13. PWRSTATE Variable

Function	Address	X-reg	Y-reg	A-reg	C-flag	Description
Verification	0x3F4	–	–	–	–	Power up byte

The PWRSTATE variable at memory address 0x3F4 as shown in Table I.9.1 verifies whether or not the Apple][is processing the RESET vector at memory address 0xFFFC during power up when the computer is first turned on. The NEWMON routine at memory address 0xFA81 calculates the power up state byte and compares its calculated value to PWRSTATE. If the values do not compare NEWMON branches to PWRUP at memory address 0xFAA6. There is a 1-in-256 probability that this logic will fail to sense a real power up condition. SETPWRC at memory address 0xFB6F calculates the power up state byte and saves it to PWRSTATE.

The assembler calculates PWRSTATE using the following statement:

    PWRSTATE BYT PWRUPBYT^EXTWARM/PAGESIZE

where PWRUPBYT is defined to be 0xA5, the EXTWARM interface routine resides on page 0xBE, and PAGESIZE is equal to 0x100. In DOS 4.3 PWRSTATE is calculated to be 0x1B. PWRSTATE is solely dependent on the address of EXTWARM and changes when the MSB of EXTWARM changes.

165

14. USRAHAND Routine

Function	Address	X-reg	Y-reg	A-reg	C-flag	Description
Entry	0x3F5	–	–	–	–	Enters REPEATCD
Return	–	–	–	–	–	No return to caller

The USRAHAND routine at memory address 0x3F5 as shown in Table I.9.1 directly jumps to a page 0xBE routine in order to write enable Language Card Bank 2 memory and then jump to the REPEATCD routine in DOS. REPEATCD saves the registers and calls the DOS REPEAT function to load the Y-register with the last DOS command DOS processed before entering the DOCMD routine.

The USRAHAND routine is known as the "Ampersand Handler" and it is a favorite routine vehicle for many software programs and utilities to utilize in order for its user to easily and quickly enter the software's main processing routine. USERAHAND, as initialized in DOS 4.3, is engaged when the AMPERSAND character is entered on the Apple command line followed by the RETURN character. USRAHAND does not return to the caller. Use the Direct approach to call the USRAHAND routine.

15. USRYHAND Routine

Function	Address	X-reg	Y-reg	A-reg	C-flag	Description
Entry	0x3F8	–	–	–	Direction	Enters AUXMOVE (0xC311)
Return	–	same	same	same	–	Return to caller

The USRYHAND routine at memory address 0x3F8 as shown in Table I.9.1 directly jumps to the AUXMOVE routine at memory address 0xC311. AUXMOVE is a built-in ROM routine that can copy blocks of data from Main memory to Auxiliary memory or from Auxiliary memory to Main memory. Before AUXMOVE can be called, three byte-pair locations in page-zero must be initialized with the starting and ending addresses of the source and the starting address of the destination. The Carry flag is used to select the direction of transfer.

If the Carry flag is **set** data is moved from Main to Auxiliary memory and if the Carry flag is **clear** data is moved from Auxiliary to Main memory. A1 at 0x3C/0x3D must contain the source starting address, A2 at 0x3E/0x3F must contain the source ending address, and A4 at 0x42/0x43 must contain the destination starting address. All three page-zero byte-pair locations expect the address to be saved in Lo/Hi byte order.

USRYHAND returns to the caller with the A-, X-, and Y-registers unchanged. Use the Direct approach to call the USRYHAND routine.

16. NMASKIRQ Routine

Function	Address	X-reg	Y-reg	A-reg	C-flag	Description
Entry	0x3FB	–	–	–	–	Enters MON (0xFF65)
Return	0xFF65	–	–	–	–	No return to interrupted code

The NMASKIRQ routine at memory address 0x3F8 as shown in Table I.9.1 is for the non-maskable IRQ handler and it directly jumps to MON at memory address 0xFF65. MON is the normal entry for the ROM Monitor. The address for NMASKIRQ, or 0x3FB, is coded in ROM at the 0xFFFA NIRQ vector. Whenever the processor receives a non-maskable IRQ interrupt, the processor indirectly jumps to the NMASKIRQ routine to handle the IRQ interrupt.

A non-maskable IRQ interrupt handler must initialize 0x3FC with the LSB and 0x3FD with the MSB of a handler's entry address. An intelligently written non-maskable IRQ handler **will** return to the instruction immediately following the instruction that was interrupted when the processor receives a non-maskable IRQ interrupt by means of the RTI instruction. Use the Direct approach to call the NMASKIRQ routine for testing.

17. MASKIRQ Vector

Function	Address	X-reg	Y-reg	A-reg	C-flag	Description
Entry	0x3FE	–	–	–	–	Enters (MON) (0xFF65)
Return	0xFF65	–	–	–	–	No return to interrupted code

The MASKIRQ vector at memory address 0x3FE as shown in Table I.9.1 contains the address for the maskable IRQ handler and it is used to indirectly jump to MON at memory address 0xFF65. MON is the normal entry for the ROM Monitor. The address for IRQRTN, or 0xC3FA, is coded in ROM at the 0xFFFE IRQ vector. Whenever the processor receives a maskable IRQ interrupt, the processor indirectly jumps to IRQRTN to handle the IRQ interrupt. IRQRTN read enables the internal CX ROM space so that ROM page 0xC4 is in focus for processing.

The Apple //e interrupt handler is highly complex and it begins its processing at memory address 0xC400. This handler creates a system status byte that is saved to page-zero 0x44. If a bit is turned on, that function is turned off during handler processing. Language Card RAM is always turned off. Table IV.17.1 summarizes the function of each bit for this status byte. There are two caveats to Table IV.17.1: 1) if Bit 3 is off, then bits 1 and 2 are both off; 2) if bit 3 is on, then bit 1 **or** bit 2 is on.

The Auxiliary and Main memory stack pointers are both saved as well as the system status byte at page-zero 0x44. The processor status is restored and the interrupt handler jumps to GOTOIRQ at memory address 0xFC74. GOTOIRQ enables slot ROMs (in other words it disables the CX ROM) and indirectly jumps to the address at MASKIRQ.

A maskable IRQ interrupt handler must initialize MASKIRQ with the handler's entry address in Lo/Hi byte order. An intelligently written maskable IRQ handler will return to the instruction immediately following the instruction that was interrupted when the processor receives a maskable IRQ interrupt by means of the RTI instruction. Use the Indirect approach to call the MASKIRQ routine for testing.

Bit	Name	Bit Off	Bit On	Function Address
0	RDCXROM	off	on	read 0xC015
1	RDBANK2	off	either bit 1	read 0xC011, Bank 1
2		off	or bit 2	read 0xC011, Bank 2
3	RDLCRAM	ROM	RAM	read 0xC012
4	RDRAMWR	off	on	read 0xC014
5	RDRAMRD	off	on	read 0xC013
6	RDPAGE2	off	on	read 0xC01C
7	RDAUXZP	Main	Auxiliary	read 0xC016

Table IV.17.1. Interrupt Handler System Status Byte Definition

18. GOTOMON2 Routine

Function	Address	X-reg	Y-reg	A-reg	C-flag	Description
Entry	0xBE00	–	–	–	–	Enters MON with Bank 2 on
Return	–	–	–	–	–	No return to caller

The GOTOMON2 routine at memory address 0xBE00 write enables Language Card Bank 2 memory and then directly jumps to the GOTOMON routine in page 0xBF. GOTOMON is an integral part of the DOS cold-start initialization routine that is used when DOS 4.3 boots or when a user utilizes the INITDOS vector to initialize DOS. GOTOMON initializes the stack pointer, it selects the main video and character set, it initializes XMODE, CSWL, and KSWL, and it sets the video output to normal.

Because Language Card RAM memory has been enabled, GOTOMON fails the Applesoft ROM verification check and a jump is made to RAM MON at memory address 0xFF65. RAM MON is the normal entry address for the RAM Monitor and it does not return to the caller. Language Card Bank 2 memory space will be in focus. Use the Direct approach to the call GOTOMON2 routine.

19. GOTOMON1 Routine

Function	Address	X-reg	Y-reg	A-reg	C-flag	Description
Entry	0xBE08	-	-	-	-	Enters MON with Bank 1 on
Return	-	-	-	-	-	No return to caller

The GOTOMON1 routine at memory address 0xBE08 write enables Language Card Bank 1 memory and then directly jumps to the GOTOMON routine in page 0xBF. GOTOMON is an integral part of the DOS cold-start initialization routine that is used when DOS 4.3 boots or when a user utilizes the INITDOS vector to initialize DOS. GOTOMON initializes the stack pointer, it selects the main video and character set, it initializes XMODE, CSWL, and KSWL, and it sets the video output to normal.

Because Language Card RAM memory has been enabled, GOTOMON fails the Applesoft ROM verification check and a jump is made to RAM MON at memory address 0xFF65. RAM MON is the normal entry address for the RAM Monitor and it does not return to the caller. Language Card Bank 1 memory space will be in focus. Use the Direct approach to call the GOTOMON1 routine.

20. BLDVRSN Variable

Function	Address	X-reg	Y-reg	A-reg	C-flag	Description
Identification	0xBFF0	-	-	-	-	DOS Version number

The BLDVRSN variable at memory address 0xBFF0 as shown in Table I.8.1 identifies the DOS version number that is currently in memory. Using this variable to identify the current DOS version number in memory is far more useful than having to extract the version number from the DOS Version text string provided by indirectly calling RDCLKVSN at memory address 0x3E1.

21. BLDNMBR Variable

Function	Address	X-reg	Y-reg	A-reg	C-flag	Description
Identification	0xBFF1	-	-	-	-	DOS Build number

The BLDNMBR variable at memory address 0xBFF1 as shown in Table I.8.1 identifies the DOS build number that is currently in memory. Using this variable to identify the current DOS build number in memory is far more useful than having to extract the build number from the DOS Version text string provided by indirectly calling RDCLKVSN at memory address 0x3E1.

22. MNGDISK Vector

Function	Address	X-reg	Y-reg	A-reg	C-flag	Description
Entry	0xBFF2	slot #	#handler	/handler	set	Attach slot card disk handler
Return	–	same	same	same	clear	Return to caller
Entry	0xBFF2	slot #	–	0x00	set	Request DISKADRS entry
Return	–	same	#handler	/handler	clear	Return to caller
Entry	0xBFF2	slot #	–	–	clear	Detach slot card disk handler
Return	–	same	#RWTSENT	/RWTSENT	clear	Return to caller

The MNGDISK vector at memory address 0xBFF2 as shown in Table I.8.1 contains the address of EXMNGDSK that is used to indirectly jump to a page 0xBE routine to write enable Language Card Bank 1 memory and then jump to the MNGEXDSK routine in DOS. MNGEXDSK sets or restores a DISKADRS Table entry. To attach a slot card disk handler to RWTS, indirectly jump to MNGDISK with the slot card number in the X-register, the address of the slot card handler in the Y- and A-registers in Lo/Hi byte order, and the Carry flag **set**. The X-register may also contain the slot-times-sixteen number, and the register will be returned unchanged. RWTS will transfer control to the slot card disk handler for the requested I/O based entirely on the slot number value found in the RWTS IOCB.

Figure I.8.1 shows an example assembly language routine that attaches the RAM Disk slot card handler to RWTS. Figure I.8.2 shows an example assembly language routine that calls MNGDISK to request the address of the handler currently assigned to a particular slot to be returned in the Y- and A-registers when the A-register is set to 0x00 and the Carry flag **set**. The same example calls MNGDISK again with the Carry flag **clear** in order to detach that slot handler from RWTS.

For all MNGDISK functions the X-register must contain a valid slot number or a valid slot-times-sixteen number. A valid slot number is any number in the range from one to seven. If MNGDISK processing determines that the X-register contains an invalid value, MNGDISK immediately returns to the caller with the Carry flag **set** before any further processing occurs. Otherwise, MNGDISK returns to the caller with the Carry flag **clear**.

Unlike DOS 4.1 it is not necessary to know where the DISKADRS Table resides in DOS 4.3 memory nor anything about how to properly index into that table. MNGDISK takes care of all the necessary protocol that had to be manually coded entirely by the DOS 4.1 user. MNGDISK always returns the Carry flag clear unless the X-register contains an invalid value. Once MNGEXDSK completes its processing the routine returns to page 0xBE, enables ROM memory, and then returns to the external caller. The X-register will be returned to the user unchanged. Use the Indirect approach to call the MNGDISK vector.

23. MNGVALS Vector

Function	Address	X-reg	Y-reg	A-reg	V-flag	C-flag	Description
Entry	0xBFF4	–	<0x64	variable	clear	set	Write CMDVALS variable
Return	–	same	same	same	clear	clear	Return to caller
Entry	0xBFF4	–	<0x64	–	clear	clear	Read CMDVALS byte pair
Return	–	variable	same	variable+1	clear	clear	Return to caller
Entry	0xBFF4	–	<0x1E	variable	set	set	Write INITVALS variable
Return	–	same	same	same	set	clear	Return to caller
Entry	0xBFF4	–	<0x1E	–	set	clear	Read INITVALS byte pair
Return	–	variable	same	variable+1	set	clear	Return to caller

The MNGVALS vector at memory address 0xBFF4 as shown in Table I.8.1 contains the address of EXMNGVAL that is used to indirectly jump to a page 0xBE routine to write enable Language Card Bank 1 memory and then jump to the MNGEXVAL routine in DOS. When the V-flag is **clear** MNGEXVAL reads or writes the CMDVALS variables and the File Manager Workarea structure which begin at memory address 0xEC00 as shown in Tables I.12.1 and I.12.2. In either case the Y-register is range checked and if it is greater than CVALSLEN (i.e. 0x64), MNGVALS returns with the Carry flag **set**.

In order to change a CMDVALS or Workarea variable the A-register must hold the desired data, the Y-register must hold the index for the desired variable to be changed, and the Carry flag must be **set**. Variable indices are shown in Tables I.12.1 and I.12.2. In order to access the value of a CMDVALS or Workarea variable the Y-register must hold the index for the desired variable and the Carry flag must be **clear**. The data for the desired variable will be returned in the X-register as well as data at the address following the desired variable in the A-register. In either case MNGVALS will return to the caller with the Carry flag **clear** unless the Y-register holds an invalid value. Figures I.12.1 and I.12.2 show example assembly language routines in how to access and change CMDVALS using the MNGVALS vector. Use the Indirect approach to call the MNGVALS vector.

When the V-flag is **set** the MNGEXVAL routine reads or writes the INITVALS variables which begin at memory address 0xBEE2 as shown in Table I.8.5. In either case the Y-register is range checked and if it is greater than IVALSLEN (i.e. 0x1E), MNGVALS returns with the Carry flag **set**.

In order to change an INITVALS variable the A-register must hold the desired data, the Y-register must hold the index for the desired variable to be changed, and the Carry flag must be **set**. Variable indices are shown in Table I.8.5. In order to access the value of an INITVALS variable the Y-register must hold the index for the desired variable and the Carry flag must be **clear**. The data for the desired variable will be returned in the X-register as well as data at the address following the desired variable in the A-register. In either case MNGVALS will return to the caller with the Carry flag **clear** unless the Y-register holds an invalid value. Use the Indirect approach to call the MNGVALS vector.

24. MNGUSER Vector

Function	Address	X-reg	Y-reg	A-reg	C-flag	Description
Entry	0xBFF6	–	#usradr	/usradr	set	Enable CMDVAL/USERADR
Return	–	#USERADR	same	same	clear	Return to caller
Entry	0xBFF6	–	–	–	clear	restore CMDVAL/USERADR
Return	–	#CMDRUN-CMDTBL	#GOTOMON	/GOTOMON	clear	Return to caller

The MNGUSER vector at memory address 0xBFF6 as shown in Table I.8.1 contains the address of EXMNGUSR that is used to indirectly jump to a page 0xBE routine to write enable Language Card Bank 1 memory and then jump to the MNGEXUSR routine in DOS. MNGEXUSR enables or disables USERADR and CMDVAL which are variables in the INITVALS Structure as shown in Table I.8.5. In either case MNGUSER returns to the caller with the Carry flag **clear**.

In order to manage the DOS CMDUSER command and enable CMDVAL and USERADR, the Y- and A-registers must hold the address of the DOS post-initialization routine in Lo/Hi byte order and the Carry flag must be **set**. MNGEXUSR will initialize CMDVAL with the value of the DOS CMDUSER command. If the Carry flag is clear MNGEXUSR will restore CMDVAL and USERADR and restore the variables to their initial states: CMDVAL holds the value of CMDRUN-CMDTBL which is 0x06 and USERADR holds the address of GOTOMON in page 0xBF.

The DOS 4.3 CMDUSER command is designed and available to a user who needs to load DOS 4.3 into memory, initialize it, and then have DOS 4.3 return control back to that user instead of returning control to Applesoft. Once DOS 4.3 has been copied into memory and MNGUSER has been called with the Carry flag set, an indirect jump to INITDOS will begin DOS 4.3 initialization. Instead of DOS processing the DOS RUN command normally found in CMDVAL, it will process the DOS CMDUSER command since CMDVAL now holds that command. All CMDUSER does is to enable ROM memory and indirectly jump to the memory address found in USERADR as a DOS post-initialization routine.

Once this DOS post-initialization routine begins its processing, it can simply restore DOS 4.3 to its initial state by utilizing the MNGUSER vector with the Carry flag **clear**. Figure I.8.3 shows an example assembly language routine in how to utilize MNGUSER. Use the Indirect approach to call the MNGUSER vector.

25. INITDOS Vector

Function	Address	X-reg	Y-reg	A-reg	C-flag	Description
Entry	0xBFF8	–	–	–	–	Enters (COLDADR) handler
Return	0xE000	–	–	–	–	No return to caller

The INITDOS vector at memory address 0xBFF8 as shown in Table I.8.1 contains the address of the DOSINIT routine that resides in memory page 0xBF. DOSINIT initializes the stack pointer, it selects the main video and character set, it initializes XMODE, CSWL, and KSWL, it sets the video output to normal, it copies the ROM Monitor to RAM, it searches the slots for a clock card, and it jumps to the COLDSTRT routine in DOS.

COLDSTRT resets the state machine, initializes the MON flags and keyboard and video intercepts, turns ROM memory on, and exits indirectly by means of the COLDADR vector in the page 0xBE routines. DOS 4.3 initially sets the COLDADR vector to memory address 0xE000, the address of BASCLD. BASCLD is the Applesoft hard entry address in ROM that performs a complete reinitialization of Applesoft and does not return to the caller.

The user is free to change the address at COLDADR, a variable in the INITVALS structure, to tailor the COLDSTRT routine not to exit into Applesoft ROM, but into a user specific routine. Figure I.8.3 shows an example assembly language routine in how to utilize INITDOS. Use the Indirect approach to call INITDOS.

26. INITVAL Address

Function	Address	X-reg	Y-reg	A-reg	C-flag	Description
Address	0xBFFA	–	–	–	–	Address of INITVALS Table
Return	–	–	–	–	–	

The INITVAL address at memory address 0xBFFA as shown in Table I.8.1 contains the address of the INITVALS Structure as shown in Table I.8.5. The INITVALS Structure resides in page 0xBE so its variables can be modified directly without having to manage any Language Card Soft Switches or enable a particular memory bank. However, accessing and changing the values of the variables in the INITVALS Structure is far easier and more general as shown in the example assembly language routine in Figure I.8.4. The address at INITVAL is simply copied to a page-zero pointer in Lo/Hi byte order and any of the variables can be accessed using the offsets (or indices) for those variables as shown in Table I.8.5. The address of INITVAL will not change, but the address it holds for the INITVALS Structure may, indeed, change. The INITVALS Structure may also be accessed using the MNGVALS vector if that interface is more suitable to the specific assembly language program environment being used.

27. BCFGNDX Variable

Function	Address	X-reg	Y-reg	A-reg	C-flag	Description
#Address	0xBFFC	–	–	–	–	BOOTCFG Table offset

The `BCFGNDX` variable at memory address `0xBFFC` as shown in Table I.8.1 is the offset for the DOS 4.3 Boot Configuration `BOOTCFG` Structure that resides in memory page `0xBF` as shown in Table I.8.2. This table may be accessed indirectly by using a page-zero pointer as shown in Figure I.8.5.

The Boot Stage 1 process can be easily monitored, and at the appropriate time, the `BOOTCFG` Table can be tailored specifically for the Boot Stage 2 process. As Figure I.8.5 shows the variables `DNUM` and `VOLEXPT` are dynamically modified with the CFFA drive and volume values, respectively, that is currently booting.

Boot Stage 1 sectors are directly copied into memory by the CFFA firmware. However, Boot Stage 2 is unique for each volume and that boot process must be handled by its DOS. When its Boot Stage 2 process begins its `RWPAGES` routine is now correctly configured from the contents of its `BOOTCFG` Table. Once DOS is loaded into memory it can initialize and execute its initial `HELLO` program.

28. NBUF1PG Variable

Function	Address	X-reg	Y-reg	A-reg	C-flag	Description
/Address	0xBFFD	–	–	–	–	NBUF1 MSB Address

The `NBUF1PG` variable at memory address `0xBFFD` as shown in Table I.8.1 is the most significant byte of the memory address for `NBUF1`. `NBUF1` is a buffer that is 256 bytes in size that starts on a page boundary. This buffer resides in Language Card Bank 1 memory in DOS 4.3. This most significant address byte is included in order to provide easy access to a temporary page of memory as long as `RWTS` is not invoked, which would obviously overwrite the contents of this buffer.

To utilize this page of memory would require write enabling Language Card Bank 1 and copying the `NBUF1PG` variable to the MSB of a page-zero pointer. The LSB of this pointer would be set to `0x00`. Oftentimes having access to a buffer that is a full page in size can alleviate a difficult programming situation. This memory buffer can also be used to temporally hold a page of data that is being swapped for another page of data. In order to write enable `NBUF1` the soft-switch `0xC08B` must be read twice. In the *Lisa* assembler this would be coded as:

```
BIT $C08B
BIT $C08B
```

29. BOOTADR Variable

Function	Address	X-reg	Y-reg	A-reg	C-flag	Description
/Address	0xBFFE	–	–	–	–	Boot Stage 1 MSB Address

The BOOTADR variable at memory address 0xBFFE as shown in Table I.8.1 is set to the most significant byte of the memory address for the data contained in the first sector that is read from track 0x00 during Boot Stage 1. BOOTADR is copied to the page-zero pointer BUFRADRZ+1 at page-zero address 0x27. This pointer is incremented in the Disk][firmware at 0xCnEB, where n is the slot number of the Disk][interface card. DOS 4.3 is unique in that as BUFRADRZ+1 is incremented the next sector to be read is decremented in Boot Stage 1 as shown in Table I.8.3.

30. BOOTPGS Variable

Function	Address	X-reg	Y-reg	A-reg	C-flag	Description
Sectors	0xBFFF	–	–	–	–	Boot Stage 1 sectors read

The BOOTPGS variable at memory address 0xBFFF as shown in Table I.8.1 is set to the number of sectors that will be read from track 0x00 during Boot Stage 1. BOOTPGS serves as a counter for Boot Stage 1 and its value determines when to begin two important processing steps during Boot Stage 1: when to change the value in BUFRADRZ+1 and when to begin Boot Stage 2. Table I.8.3 shows the relationship of track 0x00 sector value and the memory page MSB for the DOS 4.3 boot image.

V. DOS 4.3 Operational Environment

DOS 4.3, like DOS 4.1 previously, provides a far more advanced operational environment for the entire genre of Apple][software design be it for tools, utilities, or games, particularly when they make full use of its open architecture. I have developed my own software such as *Applesoft Formatter*, Binary File Installation (*BFI*), *Real Time Clock* (my own hardware, too), *Disk Window*, EPROM Operating System (*EOS*), Volume Manager for the CFFA card (*VOLMGR, BOOTVOL, BOOTDOS*), and VTOC Manager (*VMGR*). On the other hand, I have created source files for commercial programs that include Asynchronous Data Transfer (*ADT*), *Big Mac*, PROmGRAMER, CFFA card firmware, File Developer (*FID*), Lazer's Interactive Symbolic Assembler (*Lisa*), Program Global Editor (*PGE*), Global Program Line Editor (*GPLE*), RAM Disk 320 firmware, RanaSystems EliteThree firmware, Sider firmware, and *Sourceror* to utilize the features of DOS 4.3.

Because so much time has passed since these commercial programs were published, I did not even consider requesting permission from the respective authors of this commercial software, the object code, to "source" their software: sadly, many of these authors have already passed on. My intent was to learn the internal dependencies on DOS 3.3 from these programs. Collectively, these dependencies partially drove my design of DOS 4.1, and now DOS 4.3, to best provide enough visibility into the DOS 4.3 processing internals and data structures these authors required.

As is said, "The proof is in the pudding." I have successfully modified all the above-mentioned commercial programming tools, utilities, and firmware to be fully DOS 4.3 compliant as if DOS 4.3 is some black box with a few special access points: there should be no need to directly access any of the DOS 4.3 internal routines. I created these source code files for my own intellectual edification and for my own use. I am simply showing the effort and time I have invested to modify what I consider to be valuable software programs written by other brilliant Apple][software programmers to function successfully along with the operational environment of DOS 4.3.

I did spend considerable time attempting to relocate DOS 4.3 to Auxiliary memory. I was absolutely successful in this exercise. However, I could not successfully interface this DOS with either *Big Mac* or *Lisa*. The interface code became unwieldy and started to consume precious code space in Main memory that became too significant. Next, I chose to leave DOS 4.3 in Main Language Card memory and relocate *Lisa* to Auxiliary memory. This proved to be far easier than I thought given the previous interface challenges. Now that I have developed the interface routines for *Lisa* and have considerable experience working with Auxiliary memory, I attempted to relocate *Big Mac* to Auxiliary memory as well. Of course, this proved to be easier to accomplish, and the interface routines for *Big Mac* were very similar to the ones I developed for *Lisa*. Furthermore, I buckled down and developed all the remaining code in both *Sourceror* and *Big Mac* to fully support the *SWEET16* Metaprocessor Instruction Set I presented in Section II.3.

After successfully using recursive code in the DOS 4.3 HELP command, I employed similar techniques for the CFFA firmware error messages in order to reduce its code space. Having more code space allowed me to add a DOS 4.3 interface to the CFFA without having to remove either the DOS 3.3 interface or the DOS 4.1 interface. Now, there is enough room in the CFFA firmware to support DOS 3.3, DOS 4.1L, DOS 4.1H, and DOS 4.3 volumes. There is also enough room in a Compact Flash card for *VOLMGR* to install two more experimental DOS images.

1. Disk Window

I have no doubt Don Worth and Pieter Lechner inspired thousands of computer hobbyists with their Example Programs found in their book *Beneath Apple DOS*, for these authors certainly inspired me. The learning curve was a bit steep if I recall, diskettes were expensive at that time, and I had some preconceived underlying fears that I would destroy something precious, be it hardware or software, if I casually started messing around with RWTS back in 1981. Patience was certainly a virtue, and when one is examining the sectors and tracks of a diskette, it was like peering through some sort of digital microscope. The idea of reading a specific sector on a diskette and displaying that data was awe-inspiring. Furthermore, having a utility that could edit those data bytes and write those edits back to that same sector, or to any other sector for that matter, was totally mind blowing: what can of worms would that capability open? Worth's and Lechner's utility Zap did inspire me to design *Disk Window*, what I call my fancy Zap program. It is like having a digital window focused on any device, track, sector, or Logical Block Address (LBA) of my choosing.

The current version of *Disk Window* now supports the reading and writing of any valid LBA sector on a CFFA card. If a CFFA card is detected in the selected slot, LBA mode will be used for reading and writing block data. If a Disk][interface or similar peripheral card is detected in the selected slot, track-sector mode will be used for reading and writing sector data. Regardless which mode is used to read and write data, the appropriate LBA for the selected volume-track-sector will be displayed according to the conversion algorithm I developed. The startup screen for *Disk Window* is displayed as shown in Figure V.1.1. The four commands at the bottom of the screen `Configure`, `Select LBA`, `Select D/V`, and `Select T/S` utilize the respective variables at the top of the screen. The commands `Forward` and `Backward` simply increment or decrement the track/sector values if in track-sector mode or LBA value if in LBA mode. The commands `Edit`, `Write`, and `Print` display a respective screen for their particular function.

Figure V.1.2 shows the display of the VTOC data for the diskette in Drive 2 of a Disk][whose peripheral interface card resides in Slot 6. The data is displayed both in hexadecimal and in ASCII, unless the data is a control character. The hexadecimal values from 0x00 to 0x1F and 0x80 to 0x9F are displayed as an ASCII PERIOD character. Lower ASCII values from 0x20 to 0x7F are displayed in inverse text and upper ASCII values from 0xA0 to 0xFF are displayed in normal text. If `Edit` is selected the same VTOC data is displayed as shown in Figure V.1.3, and the cursor is initially placed on row 0x70 and column 0x07. After all edits have been applied the `Write` command will write the sector data to the selected sector or to any other sector (or LBA) as shown in Figure V.1.4. It must be noted that LBA blocks are 512 bytes in size. "Page 0" refers to the first 256 bytes and "Page 1" refers to the second 256 bytes of a LBA block. Thus, CFFA sectors 0x00-0x0F reside on Page 0 and CFFA sectors 0x10-0x1F reside on Page 1. The 256-byte sector data may be saved to any available LBA, either on Page 0 or on Page 1. Page 0 is selected by pressing the 0 or L key and Page 1 is selected by pressing the 1 or H key. The data contents of the screen can also be printed using the `Print` command as shown in Figure V.1.5. The command `Configure` in Figure V.1.5 allows the user to change the `Printer Slot` value if desired without having to return to the main menu screen as shown in Figure V.1.1. If an RWTS error should occur it is prominently printed in the center of the hexadecimal data display window as shown in Figure V.1.6. I purposefully opened the Disk][drive 2 door to cause a disk drive error before writing data to the diskette. According to Table I.9.4 an error value of 0x40 is an RWTS Drive error. The error message will remain until any key is pressed on the keyboard.

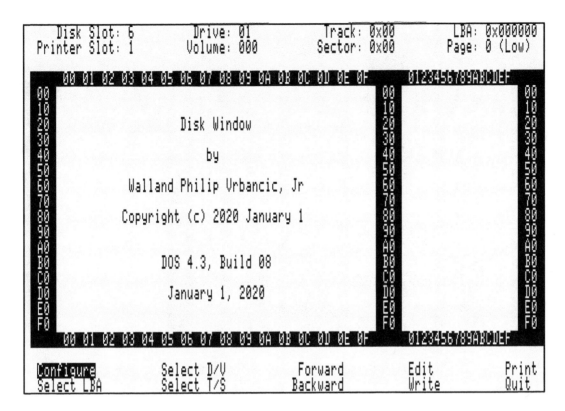

Figure V.1.1. Disk Window Startup Screen

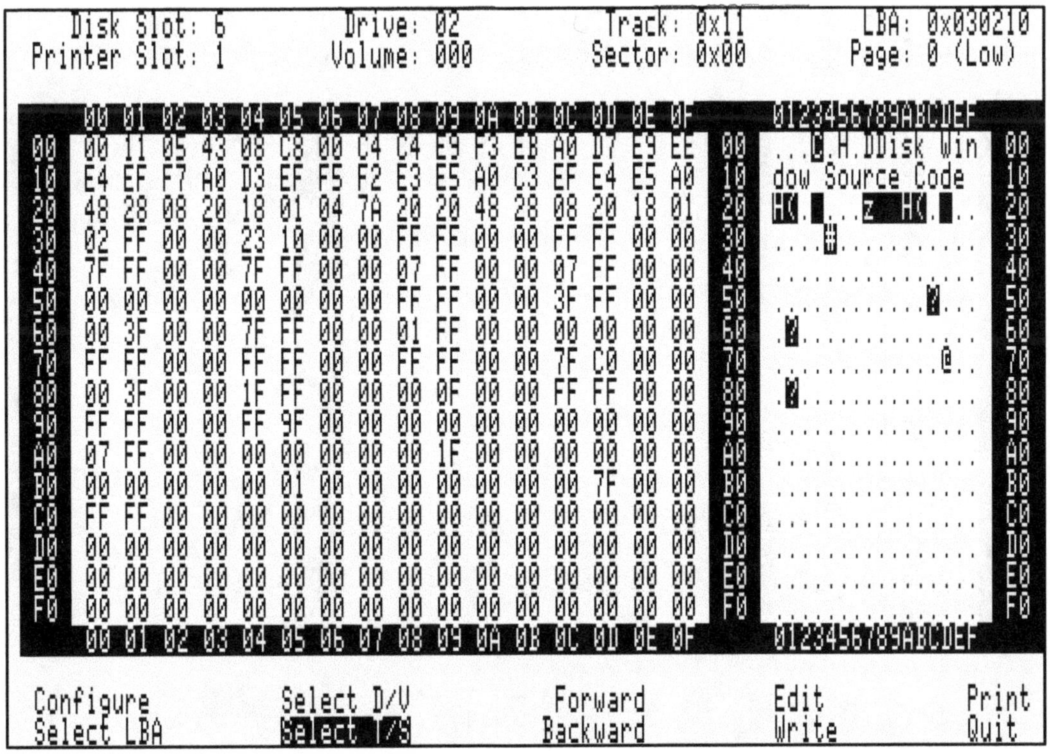

Figure V.1.2. Select T/S Mode

179

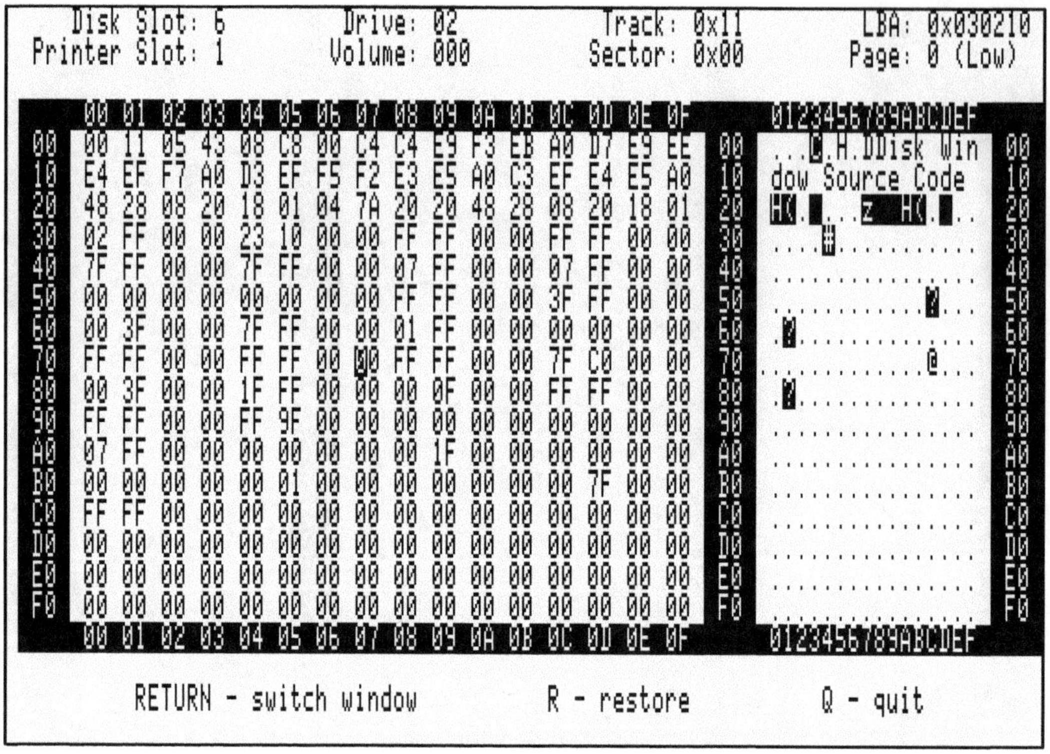

Figure V.1.3. Edit Data Screen

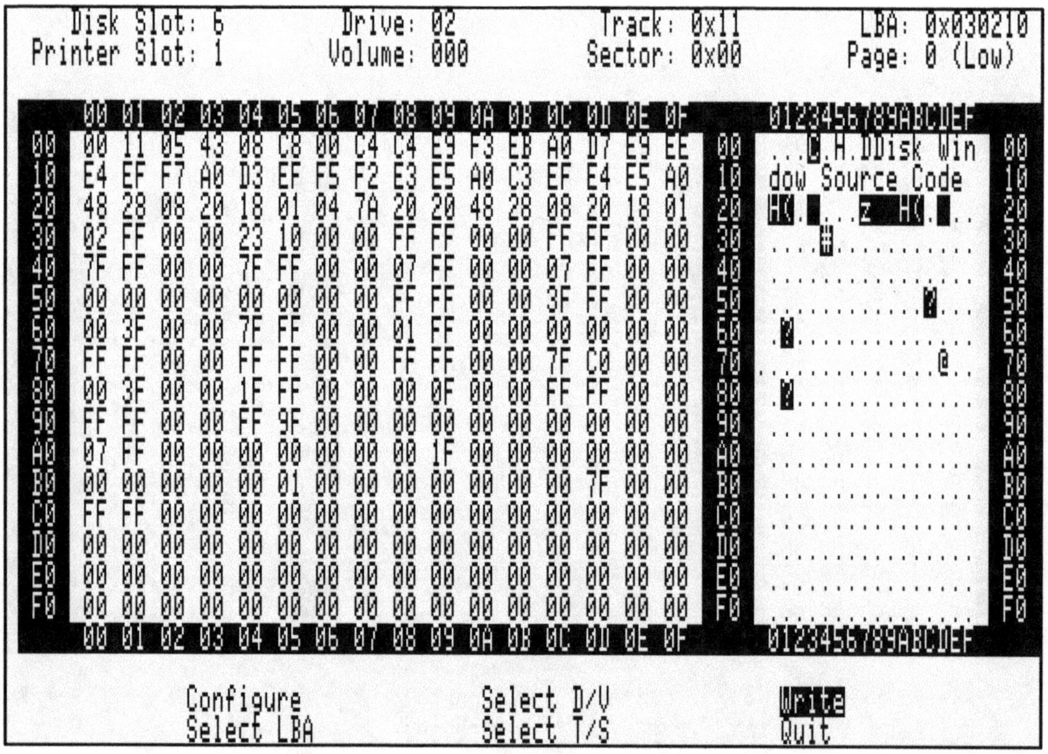

Figure V.1.4. Write Sector Data Screen

180

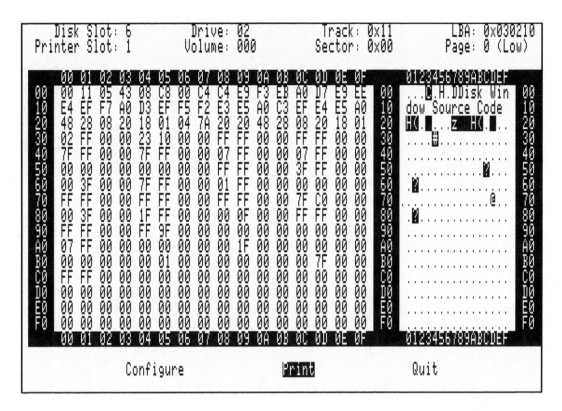

Figure V.1.5. Print Sector Data Screen

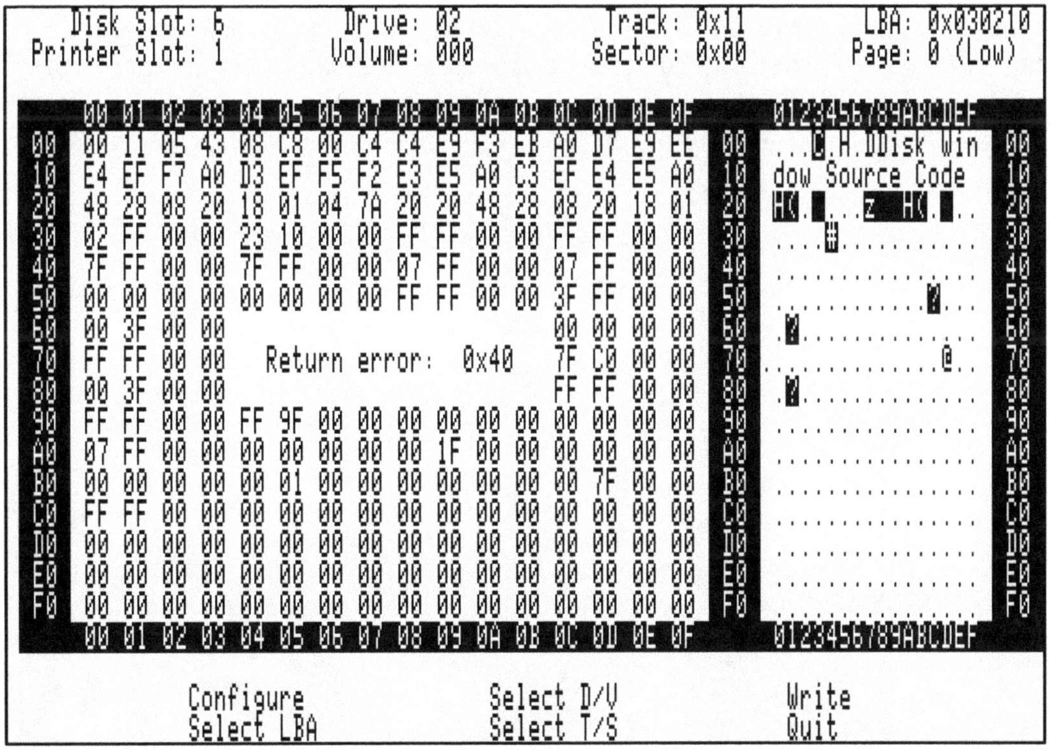

Figure V.1.6. Disk Window Error Message Display

I originally wrote *Disk Window* after I purchased the Videx UltraTerm video display card for my Apple][+. This card had a number of beautiful character sets with inverse display for both upper and lower case characters. The cursor could be placed anywhere on the screen using a GOTO routine I developed since the normal CH and CV locations could not be used when the values were outside the normal Apple 40-column screen locations. I believe this display card was well worth every penny and the firmware was very well thought out. Unfortunately, when I began working on an Apple //e all my 80-column screen handling code in *Disk Window* did not work. The task of modifying *Disk Window* to support the 80-column display in the Apple //e gave me a first-hand view of how dumbed-down this display is as compared to the Videx UltraTerm. As a result, I have very mixed opinions as to Apple's solution in doubling the column characters by doubling the computer memory in using Auxiliary memory. I also question Apple's logic in retaining its wide selection of upper case display options and very limited selection of lower case display options. Would Wozniak have designed the Apple //e display differently? I wonder.

Disk Window is certainly a giant leap from Worth's and Lechner's utility Zap, but they are the giants whose shoulders I stood on in utilizing their insight and their enthusiasm for everything Apple][. I know my efforts in creating *Disk Window* serve to genuinely compliment Worth and Lechner and to return my thanks for their efforts early in the history making of the Apple][computer.

To assemble the *Disk Window* source code, place the DOS 4.3 Tools volume DOS.4.3.Tools in disk drive 1, boot, and start *Lisa80*. Enter the SE command-line command to select the *SETUP80* utility in order to verify or set the Start of Source Code to 0x4000 and the Start of Symbol List to 0x7800. Place the Disk Window Source volume DISKWINDOW.Source in disk drive 2, load the DW.L file into memory, and start the assembler by entering either the A or the Z command-line command. If a printed version of the screen output is desired simply preface the A or the Z command with the P1 command-line command. Five object code files will be created on the Disk Window Source volume named SEG01 to SEG05. The five object code files can be combined in memory sequentially starting at 0x0900 using the ctrl-P command. The complete binary image can be saved to the Disk Window Source volume or to any other volume as DW.

2. EPROM Operating System (EOS) for quikLoader

Southern California Research Group's (SCRG) quikLoader as well as their PROmGRAMER were must-have peripheral slot cards when they first appeared in the early 1980's. Without question data can be read many, many times faster from the Disk][than data read from cassette tape. But data can be read many, many times faster from a quikLoader EPROM than data read from the Disk][. Literally in a fraction of a second DOS can be read into memory from a quikLoader EPROM and begin its command-line processing.

I attended a Los Angeles computer convention where I bought the quikLoader after seeing several demonstrations in what it could do. Essentially, it is a very simple, though elegant peripheral slot card that can hold up to eight 2716 to 27512 EPROMs. The card has some hardware logic that maps the selected quikLoader EPROM to the 0xC100 to 0xFFFF address space.

The software SCRG provided with the quikLoader resides in the first EPROM, or EPROM 0, and this EPROM has room for a few additional programs as well. The SCRG documentation explained how to organize the contents of other programs and utilities in an EPROM and how to build a catalog for those contents. Once an EPROM was programmed with its catalog and its program contents, and seated in the quikLoader, a selected Primary program would be read into memory after pressing its EPROM number followed by the RESET key. The EPROM Catalog was displayed when the letter Q followed by RESET was pressed. I built several quikLoader EPROMs using the SCRG software interface, but I found the process to be tedious and cumbersome, and I thought I might be able to design a better interface. Once I sourced the SCRG EPROM control code, I realized their software interface could have been perhaps better thought out. And I saw there was absolutely no way to programmatically access any of the quikLoader EPROM contents using the current SCRG hardware unless I included a substantial amount of their EPROM control routines within my software. The EPROM control routines were not actually published, so that made accessing quikLoader contents even more tenuous.

Peripheral slot cards for the Apple][typically incorporate and utilize firmware code in its peripheral-card ROM memory, that is, 0xCs00 to 0xCsFF where s is the slot number of the peripheral slot card. Also, a peripheral slot card can use its peripheral-card expansion ROM memory, 0xC800 to 0xCFFF, for additional firmware code when the slot card is enabled. As an aside, putting 0xCFFF (i.e. CLRROM) onto the address bus should turn off all peripheral-card expansion ROMs. Doing so will allow another peripheral slot card, enabled by accessing its peripheral-card ROM memory, to utilize its peripheral-card expansion ROM. This protocol will prevent memory contention with other peripheral slot cards. The quikLoader hardware did not have the ability to utilize its peripheral-card ROM memory and, therefore, could not utilize any peripheral-card expansion ROM memory for any of its interface software. This inability is simply a hardware design choice, but I viewed it as a hardware design deficiency.

I did find one unused 74LS08 AND gate on the quikLoader. That single AND gate allowed me to modify the quikLoader hardware logic such that it was now possible to access its peripheral-card ROM memory that was mapped to a single page of quikLoader EPROM data. Now I had something physical I could work with, and this led me to develop the EPROM Operating System, or *EOS*. In addition to this very minor hardware logic modification, I added an LED to glow when the quikLoader was enabled and an SPDT switch to logically disable the quikLoader without having to physically remove it from its slot in the computer. The complete circuit diagram of the quikLoader with my modifications is shown in Figure V.2.1.

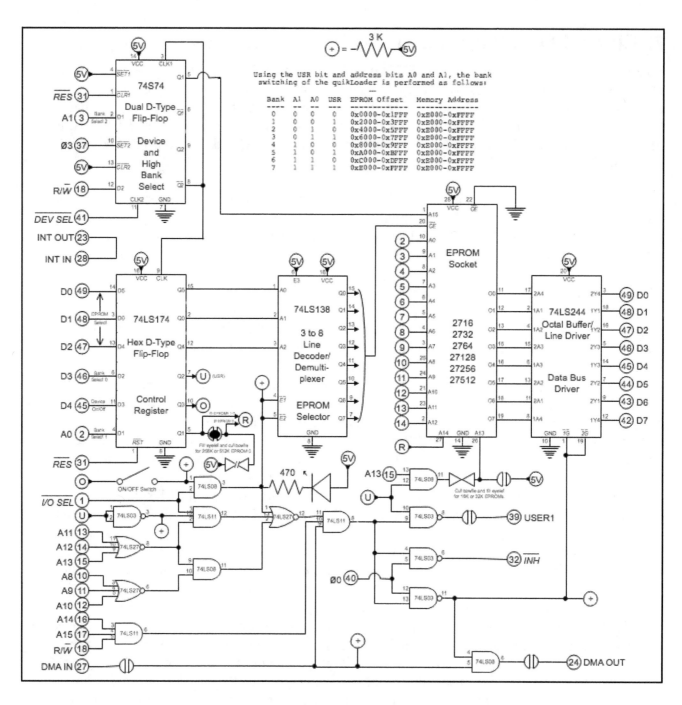

Figure V.2.1 quikLoader Schematic with Circuit Modifications

Fortunately, I had acquired the "improved" quikLoader, the model capable of addressing a 27512 EPROM. A 74LS74 dual D flip-flop was added to capture the state of the 6502 A1 address line when writing to the quikLoader's 74LS174 control register, and to ever so slightly delay the 6502 clock edge for latching quikLoader EPROM data. The control register data byte can be written to any of the sixteen I/O memory locations dedicated to the quikLoader's slot: 0xC0n0 through 0xC0nF, where n is equal to the slot number of the quikLoader plus eight. However, only the first four address locations (or their relatives) do anything different since the control register only latches the state of address line A0 while the added 74LS74 latches the state of address line A1. The state of address lines A2 and A3 are not latched, so their values are not utilized. Data lines D0, D1, and D2 are latched by the control register and they select one of eight quikLoader EPROMs. Data line D3 is latched for the USR bit and data line D4 is latched to turn the quikLoader ON or OFF. If data line D4 is zero the quikLoader is turned ON. The state of data lines D5, D6, and D7 are not utilized.

The SCRG documentation describes how an area of quikLoader EPROM memory at a given offset is mapped to the Apple][['s 0xC100 to 0xFFFF address space, but I found using the first half of this address space strange and confusing, and not very amenable to programmatic utilization. Rather, I found that I could access an entire 27512 EPROM by using eight 8-KByte banks, where each bank uses the upper 0xE000 to 0xFFFF address space. The described function of the USR bit was also strange and confusing, as well as the role it was to perform according to the SCRG documentation. The USR bit was intended to be used as a master/slave flag when multiple quikLoaders are used in the same computer. For the moment I have quite a few programs that I routinely use, and those programs and *EOS* fit comfortably into three 27512 EPROMs. I cannot imagine needing more than one quikLoader in my computer, so my vision of *EOS* became even more tailored when I limited *EOS* to manage a single quikLoader and use the USR bit for bank selection. Table V.2.1 lists the six EPROM sizes the quikLoader can address, their associated memory banks, and the latched control register data values necessary for USR (D3), A0, and A1 to access those banks.

Bank	EPROM	EPROM Access	Memory Access	A1	A0	USR
0	2716	0x0000-0x07FF	0xF800-0xFFFF	0	0	0
0	2732	0x0000-0x0FFF	0xF000-0xFFFF	0	0	0
0	2764	0x0000-0x1FFF	0xE000-0xFFFF	0	0	0
0	27128	0x0000-0x1FFF	0xE000-0xFFFF	0	0	0
1		0x2000-0x3FFF	0xE000-0xFFFF	0	0	1
0	27256	0x0000-0x1FFF	0xE000-0xFFFF	0	0	0
1		0x2000-0x3FFF	0xE000-0xFFFF	0	0	1
2		0x4000-0x5FFF	0xE000-0xFFFF	0	1	0
3		0x6000-0x7FFF	0xE000-0xFFFF	0	1	1
0	27512	0x0000-0x1FFF	0xE000-0xFFFF	0	0	0
1		0x2000-0x3FFF	0xE000-0xFFFF	0	0	1
2		0x4000-0x5FFF	0xE000-0xFFFF	0	1	0
3		0x6000-0x7FFF	0xE000-0xFFFF	0	1	1
4		0x8000-0x9FFF	0xE000-0xFFFF	1	0	0
5		0xA000-0xBFFF	0xE000-0xFFFF	1	0	1
6		0xC000-0xDFFF	0xE000-0xFFFF	1	1	0
7		0xE000-0xFFFF	0xE000-0xFFFF	1	1	1

Table V.2.1. quikLoader Bank Switching

Offset	Name	Description
0x00	QLASEOS	Applesoft interface entry, parses command variables
0x62	QLEXIT10	Return Unknown Command error, 0x10
0x65	QLEXIT20	Return Wrong Number of Parameters error, 0x20
0x68	QLEXIT30	Return Search Range Invalid error, 0x30
0x6B	QLEXIT40	Return File Not Found error, 0x40
0x6E	QLEXIT00	Return no error, 0x00
0xA0	QLEXIT1	If ZipChip present flush cache and enable it, fall into QLEXIT2
0xC6	QLEXIT2	Turn quikLoader OFF, jump to QBMEXIT at 0x0118
0xCE	QLUSER	Return from DOS CMDUSER
0xE0	QLBINEOS	Turn quikLoader ON, load QBMCODE, jump to BINEOS
0xF0	QLEOS	Turn quikLoader ON, jump to *EOS* at 0xE800
0xF8	QLBINTXT	ASCII QLBINEOS used to find the slot number for a quikLoader

Table V.2.2. quikLoader Firmware Entry Points

When RESET is pressed the 74LS174 and 74LS74 data control registers are cleared in order to select quikLoader EPROM 0, force EPROM Bank 0 to be mapped into memory from 0xE000 to 0xFFFF, and turn the quikLoader ON. The 6502-microprocessor automatically loads the RESET vector at 0xFFFC/0xFFFD into the program counter and continues to fetch instructions from there. As an aside, the NMI vector is at 0xFFFA/0xFFFB and the IRQ/BRK vector is at 0xFFFE/0xFFFF. These three vectors all point to the start of *EOS* which begins at 0xE800 in Bank 0 of EPROM 0. *EOS* must reside within the remaining 0x17FA bytes in Bank 0 memory for a 2764 EPROM, at a minimum. Otherwise, some sort of bank switching would need to be utilized in order to extend *EOS* processing into another EPROM bank, an option I did not wish to employ. Table V.2.2 shows the firmware entry points of one of seven copies of the firmware that is mapped to the peripheral-card ROM memory of the quikLoader by incorporating that single, unused 74LS08 AND gate as shown in Figure V.2.1. I am sure a "knock-off" quikLoader design would be a bit silly if it did not incorporate the same modifications, including an LED and switch, I made to my original quikLoader.

Fortunately, there is enough room in *EOS* to process the 26 commands shown in Figure V.2.2. There is even room for the EPROM Catalog function, the Applesoft interface (ASEOS), the assembly language interface (BINEOS), the ZipChip configuration software to support a ZipChip if one is present, and the software to manage Primary files. Unlike the SCRG interface, *EOS* does not capture the state of the keyboard at the moment the RESET key is pressed. Instead, *EOS* displays an "EOS Main Menu", and any of the displayed options may be selected. I simply chose those programs and utilities I liked best to display in the "EOS Main Menu". Someone else may display a different set of favorite utilities. The way I have organized EPROM 0 is so simple that all one needs to do is to model their EPROM 0 after mine. The remaining seven banks in EPROM 0, a 27512, contain DOS 4.3H, *Lisa80*, *SETUP80*, and *LOADLISA80*, RAM Disk Installation, *FID*, *ADT*2, *Set Clock*, *Volume Copy*, *BURNER*, *ASLIST*, and *ROM Copy*. Table V.2.3 shows the contents of EPROM 0 that contains *EOS*. Both *Disk Window* and *VOLMGR* reside on other quikLoader EPROMs. *EOS* uses the power and flexibility of BINEOS to load and run those utilities without regard to a specific quikLoader EPROM number. An example *EOS* Catalog screen is shown in Figures V.2.3 and V.2.4.

Bank	Offset	Memory	Size	Contents
0	0x0000	0xE000	0x0004	Sync bytes
	0x0004	0xE004	0x00FC	Catalog
	0x0100	0xE100	0x0100	Slot 1 ASEOS/BINEOS interface
	0x0200	0xE200	0x0100	Slot 2 ASEOS/BINEOS interface
	0x0300	0xE300	0x0100	Slot 3 ASEOS/BINEOS interface
	0x0400	0xE400	0x0100	Slot 4 ASEOS/BINEOS interface
	0x0500	0xE500	0x0100	Slot 5 ASEOS/BINEOS interface
	0x0600	0xE600	0x0100	Slot 6 ASEOS/BINEOS interface
	0x0700	0xE700	0x0100	Slot 7 ASEOS/BINEOS interface
	0x0800	0xE800	0x17FA	*EOS* software
	0x1FFA	0xFFFA	0x0002	NMI vector, address of *EOS*
	0x1FFC	0xFFFC	0x0002	RESET vector, address of *EOS*
	0x1FFE	0xFFFE	0x0002	IRQ/BRK vector, address of *EOS*
1	0x2000	0xE000	0x2A00	DOS4.3H
2	0x4A00	0xEA00	0x2800	LISA80.1 code segment
3	0x7200	0xF200	0x1000	LISA80.2 code segment
4	0x8200	0xE200	0x0630	LISA80.3 code segment
4	0x8830	0xE830	0x1977	*SETUP80*
5	0xA1A7	0xE1A7	0x0195	*LOADLISA80*
5	0xA33C	0xE33C	0x1B00	RAM Disk
5	0xBE3C	0xFE3C	0x12CE	*FID*
6	0xD10A	0xF10A	0x0DAD	*ADT2*
6	0xDEB7	0xFEB7	0x064A	*Set Clock*
7	0xE501	0xE501	0x0418	*Volume Copy*
7	0xE919	0xE919	0x07F6	*BURNER*
7	0xF10F	0xF10F	0x06D9	*ASLIST*
7	0xF7E8	0xF7E8	0x0818	unused

Table V.2.3. quikLoader EPROM 0 Containing EOS and Programs

Value	Catalog	Description
0x01	T	Text file, NULL terminated, like an EXEC file
0x02	A	Applesoft file
0x04	B	Binary file, Main memory
0x08	B	Binary file, Language Card Bank 1 memory
0x10	B	Binary file, Language Card Bank 2 memory
0x20	R	Reserved file
0x40	S	System file
0x80	P	Primary file

Table V.2.4. EOS File Types

```
                EOS Main Menu
A DOS4.3H Boot        N Copy ROM->RAM
B Warmstart DOS       O -> RAM Monitor
C Coldstart DOS       P -> RAM Reset
D Disk Window         Q -> ROM Monitor
E EOS Catalog         R -> ROM Reset
F Select SDV          S Run HELLO (SDV)
G   Boot  Slot S      T   CATALOG  (SDV)
H   Hook  Slot S      U   VTOC  Manager
I Unhook Slot S       V Volume Manager
J FID                 W Volume Copy
K ADT                 X EPROM Burner
L Lisa80              Y   Clock   Config
M RamDisk Init        Z ZipChip Config

                      SDV S=7 D=01 V=000
   ZipChip State
    -> Out <-         RTN Toggle ZipChip


Enter Selection:    ■
```

Figure V.2.2. EOS Commands after RESET

```
          quikLoader EOS Catalog
           Slot 4       EPROM 0


    B 0x04 >RamDisk Install

    B 0x04  FID

    B 0x04  Applesoft Formatter

    B 0x04  ADT2

    B 0x04  Set Clock

    B 0x04  Volume Copy

    B 0x04  BURNER

    P 0x84  LOADLISA80


    RTN - File Info          (L)oad
    SPC - Next EPROM         (R)un
    0-7 - Select EPROM       (Q)uit
```

Figure V.2.3. EOS Catalog for quikLoader EPROM 0, Part 1

```
            quikLoader EOS Catalog
               Slot 4        EPROM 0


        P  0x84    LOADLISA80

        B  0x04    SETUP80

        S  0x5C    DOS4.3.08H

        S  0x48    LISA80.1

        S  0x50    LISA80.2

        S  0x44    LISA80.3

        R  0x20    ROM Copy

        R  0x20   >Catalog Sync


        RTN - File Info           (L)oad
        SPC - Next EPROM          (R)un
        0-7 - Select EPROM        (Q)uit
```

Figure V.2.4. EOS Catalog for quikLoader EPROM 0, Part 2

Table V.2.4 shows the definition of the file types used in *EOS*, how each file type is displayed in the *EOS* Catalog screen, and the hexadecimal value of each file type. Notice in Figure V.2.4 that DOS.4.3.08H is file type S with a value of 0x5C. This value is derived from the logical OR of System file, Binary file Main memory, Binary file Bank 1, and Binary file Bank 2 because parts of DOS.4.3.08H reside in all those memory locations. Mathematically, the file type for the DOS.4.3.08H file is:

$$\text{FILETYPE} = 0x40 \lor 0x04 \lor 0x08 \lor 0x10 = \underline{0x5C}$$

EOS provides Applesoft users with three commands when using the Applesoft, or ASEOS interface: LOAD file, RUN file, and CATALOG. In order to access ASEOS, the quikLoader control register must be initially configured to quikLoader EPROM 0, Bank 0, and turned OFF. For example, if the quikLoader resides in slot 4, the program must "POKE 49344, 16" (i.e. POKE 0xC0C0,0x10) to initially configure the quikLoader hardware before making the CALL to ASEOS. That will bring *EOS* into focus. In this example "CALL 50176" (i.e. CALL 0xC400) will begin ASEOS processing. The CALL command must be followed by some required arguments, and there are some optional arguments as well. These arguments **must be** integer variables, integer arrays, ASCII strings, or ASCII string arrays where indicated. Real variables and real arrays must **never** be used in an ASEOS CALL statement because these numbers are floating point values and they are not supported by the ASEOS routines.

1) LOAD file. This command loads a file into memory from a quikLoader EPROM using ASEOS:

```
        QL    = quikLoader slot number
        OFF   = 16                                ; 0x10
        DEV   = QL * 16 + 49280                   ; QL * 0x10 + 0xC080
        EOS   = QL * 256 + 49152                  ; QL * 0x100 + 0xC000
        C%    = 1                                 ; LOAD file command
        S%    = -1                                ; set Status to ERROR
        E%    = EPROM search range
        F$    = Filename (1 to 24 upper ASCII characters)
        A%    = Alternate load address (optional)

        POKE DEV, OFF
        CALL EOS, C%, S%, E%, F$ [, A%]
```

2) RUN file. This command loads a file into memory from a quikLoader EPROM and runs that file using ASEOS:

```
        QL    = quikLoader slot number
        OFF   = 16                                ; 0x10
        DEV   = QL * 16 + 49280                   ; QL * 0x10 + 0xC080
        EOS   = QL * 256 + 49152                  ; QL * 0x100 + 0xC000
        C%    = 2                                 ; RUN file command
        S%    = -1                                ; set Status to error
        E%    = EPROM search range
        F$    = Filename (1 to 24 upper ASCII characters)
        [A%] = Alternate load address (optional)

        POKE DEV, OFF
        CALL EOS, C%, S%, E%, F$ [, A%]
```

3) CATALOG files. This command catalogs the quikLoader EPROMs using ASEOS:

```
        QL          = quikLoader slot number
        OFF         = 16                          ; 0x10
        M%          = Maximum number of anticipated entries
        DEV         = QL * 16 + 49280             ; QL * 0x10 + 0xC080
        EOS         = QL * 256 + 49152            ; QL * 0x100 + 0xC000
        C%          = 3                           ; CATALOG command
        S%          = -1                          ; set Status to error
        E%          = EPROM search range
        N%          = Last index used returned (set to start index)
        F$(N%)      = Filename array (1 to 24 upper ASCII characters)
        [P%(0,N%)]= Parameter Array returned (optional)

        DIM F$(M%), P%(4,M%) : N% = 0
        POKE DEV, OFF
        CALL EOS, C%, S%, E%, N%, F$(N%) [, P%(0,N%)]
```

Returned Status values for all commands:

```
S% = 0      no error
S% = -1     Number of Parameters Exceeded      ; 0xFF
S% = 16     Unknown Command                    ; 0x10
S% = 32     Number of Parameters Invalid       ; 0x20
S% = 48     Search Range Invalid               ; 0x30
S% = 64     File Not Found                     ; 0x40
```

EPROM search range for all commands:

```
E% = 0-7 for a single, specific quikLoader EPROM
E% = 0-7:0-7, or ( last EPROM ) * 16 + ( start EPROM )
```

Optional Parameter Array returned for command #3:

```
P%(0,N%) = quikLoader EPROM number
P%(1,N%) = file type
P%(2,N%) = EPROM offset
P%(3,N%) = file size in bytes
P%(4,N%) = destination memory address
```

EOS file types were shown previously in Table V.2.4 with their value and their display designation in the *EOS* Catalog function. *EOS* currently uses two Reserved type files: the ROM code from 0xD000 to 0xFFFF and the four Catalog sync bytes. Primary files are Binary files that can use the BINEOS interface and they may be activated directly by the quikLoader *EOS* Catalog function in order to load or to run System files. The quikLoader *EOS* Catalog function **cannot** directly load or run System files. System files may be Text, Applesoft, or other Binary files. System files may be attached to a Primary file, or loaded or run by activating its associated Primary file either using the quikLoader *EOS* Catalog function, ASEOS, or BINEOS. *EOS* is not designed to support Integer BASIC type files because DOS 4.3 does not support Integer BASIC type files. A DOS image and the software tool *Sourceror* are examples of System type files. The program that loads *Sourceror* into memory for execution is an example of a Primary file. System and Primary files used in *EOS* are different in function and concept than those files that are used in the SCRG interface.

A quikLoader EPROM Catalog for the files contained in that EPROM is prefaced with four sync bytes, 0xC4, 0xB8, 0x90, and 0xED. The actual catalog begins at offset 0x0004 and it may contain any number of entries, where each entry is a variable size depending on the length in bytes for its filename. An EPROM Catalog filename is a character string that uses lower ASCII for all of its bytes except for the last byte in the string which is in upper ASCII. The *Lisa* assembler calls this use of lower and upper ASCII for strings the DCI format. The catalog is terminated with a NULL (i.e. 0x00) character. An example catalog file entry structure is shown in Table V.2.5.

Offset	Length	Variable	Description
0	1	FILETYPE	File type as defined in Table V.2.4
1	2	SRCVAL	EPROM source address (EPROM offset)
3	2	LENVAL	File length or size in bytes
5	2	DSTVAL	Destination memory address (Apple][memory)
7	1–24	FILENAME	Filename, 1 to 24 ASCII bytes (DCI format)

Table V.2.5. EOS Catalog File Entry Structure

```
0800                    1                ttl "QLBINEOS Utilization, QLBINEOS.L"
0800                    2    ;
0800                    3    ;
0800                    4    ; QLBINEOS.L
0800                    5    ;
002A                    6    SRCPTR    epz $2A
002E                    7    DSTPTR    epz $2E
0800                    8    ;
0000                    9    ZERO      equ $00
00FF                   10    NEGONE    equ $FF
0800                   11    ;
0000                   12    QLON      equ $00
0010                   13    QLOFF     equ $10
0800                   14    ;
C080                   15    QLSELC    equ $C080
0800                   16    ;
C0E0                   17    QLBINEOS  equ $C0E0
C0F8                   18    QLBINTXT  equ $C0F8
0800                   19    ;
C700                   20    PAGEC7    equ $C700
E700                   21    PAGEE7    equ $E700
0800                   22    ;
CFFF                   23    CLRROM    equ $CFFF
0800                   24    ;
0800                   25    ;
0800                   26              org $800
0800                   27              obj $800
0800                   28              usr
0800                   29    ;
0800 20 0C 08          30              jsr FINDQL          ; find quikLoader
0803 B0 07             31              bcs FINDERR
0805                   32    ;
0805 A0 6A             33              ldy #EOSDCBL        ; address of
0807 A9 08             34              lda /EOSDCBL        ;   LOAD DCB
0809                   35    ;
0809 20 5C 08          36              jsr QLBINJMP        ; LOAD the file
080C                   37    ;
080C                   38    ;         :::
080C                   39    ;
080C                   40    FINDERR:
080C                   41    ;         :::
080C                   42    ;
080C A0 00             43    FINDQL    ldy #PAGEC7         ; get 0xC700 slot
080E A9 C7             44              lda /PAGEC7         ;   address
```

```
0810                    45   ;
0810 84 2A              46            sty SRCPTR              ; store address at
0812 85 2B              47            sta SRCPTR+1            ;  source pointer
0814                    48   ;
0814 A9 E7              49            lda /PAGEE7             ; get EPROM Bank 0 address
0816                    50   ;
0816 84 2E              51            sty DSTPTR              ; store address at
0818 85 2F              52            sta DSTPTR+1            ;  destination pointer
081A                    53   ;
081A A9 07              54            lda #7                  ; initialize
081C 8D 5F 08           55            sta QLSLOT              ;  for slot 7
081F                    56   ;
081F AD 5F 08           57   ^1       lda QLSLOT              ; get slot number
0822                    58   ;
0822 0A                 59            asl                     ; multiply by 16
0823 0A                 60            asl
0824 0A                 61            asl
0825 0A                 62            asl
0826                    63   ;
0826 AA                 64            tax                     ; use as index
0827                    65   ;
0827 A9 00              66            lda #QLON               ; turn quikLoader ON
0829 9D 80 C0           67            sta QLSELC,X
082C                    68   ;
082C 2C FF CF           69            bit CLRROM              ; detach shared slot memory
082F                    70   ;
082F A0 F8              71            ldy #QLBINTXT           ; point to QLBIN text
0831                    72   ;
0831 B9 6A 07           73   ^2       lda QLTEXT-QLBINTXT&NEGONE,Y ; get QLBIN text
0834                    74   ;
0834 D1 2A              75            cmp (SRCPTR),Y          ; compare slot memory
0836 D0 16              76            bne >3
0838                    77   ;
0838 D1 2E              78            cmp (DSTPTR),Y          ; compare EPROM memory
083A D0 12              79            bne >3
083C                    80   ;
083C C8                 81            iny
083D D0 F2              82            bne <2
083F                    83   ;
083F A9 10              84            lda #QLOFF              ; turn quikLoader OFF
0841 9D 80 C0           85            sta QLSELC,X
0844                    86   ;
0844 A5 2B              87            lda SRCPTR+1            ; get slot memory address
0846 8D 61 08           88            sta QLBINADR+1          ; save to vector
0849                    89   ;
0849 2C FF CF           90            bit CLRROM              ; detach shared slot memory
084C                    91   ;
084C 18                 92            clc                     ; quikLoader found
084D                    93   ;
084D 60                 94            rts
084E                    95   ;
084E C6 2B              96   ^3       dec SRCPTR+1            ; next slot memory
0850 C6 2F              97            dec DSTPTR+1            ; next quikLoader slot
0852                    98   ;
0852 CE 5F 08           99            dec QLSLOT              ; next slot number
0855 D0 C8              100           bne <1
0857                    101  ;
0857 2C FF CF           102           bit CLRROM             ; detach shared slot memory
```

```
085A                  103    ;
085A 38               104            sec                    ; no quikLoader found
085B                  105    ;
085B 60               106            rts
085C                  107    ;
085C                  108    ;
085C 6C 60 08         109    QLBINJMP  jmp (QLBINADR)
085F                  110    ;
085F                  111    QLSLOT    dfs 1,ZERO           ; quikLoader slot
0860                  112    ;
0860 E0 C0            113    QLBINADR  adr QLBINEOS         ; QLBINEOS vector
0862                  114    ;
0862 D1 CC C2         115    QLTEXT    asc "QLBINEOS"       ; QLBIN text
0865 C9 CE C5
0868 CF D3
086A                  116    ;
086A                  117    ;
086A                  118    EOSDCBL:
086A                  119    ;
086A 01               120    DCBLCMD   hex 01               ; LOAD command
086B 70               121    DCBLEP    hex 70               ; search all EPROMs
086C 00 00            122    DCBLOAD   hex 0000             ; no alternate LOAD address
086E FF               123    DCBLSTAT  hex FF               ; return status
086F 0F               124    DCBLFLEN  byt FILENDL-FILNAML  ; filename length
0870 72 08            125    DCBLFADR  adr FILNAML          ; filename address
0872                  126    ;
0872 C1 F0 F0         127    FILNAML   asc "Apple File List"
0875 EC E5 A0
0878 C6 E9 EC
087B E5 A0 CC
087E E9 F3 F4
0881                  128    FILENDL:
0881                  129    ;
0881                  130    ;

BSAVE QLBINEOS,A$0800,L$0081
0881                  131            usr QLBINEOS
0881                  132    ;
0881                  133    ;
0881                  134            end 000

*** End of Assembly
```

Figure V.2.5. Example Code for QLBINEOS Utilization

EOS provides assembly language users with three commands when using the assembly language, or
BINEOS interface: LOAD file, RUN file, and CATALOG. An eight-byte Data Context Block, or DCB is
used for the input variables and returned status. The structure of the DCB is command specific. Any
assembly language program like Primary files can use QLBINEOS to load and run System files.
QLBINEOS is located at the 0xE0th byte in the peripheral-card ROM memory of the quikLoader as
shown in Table V.2.2. For example, if the quikLoader resides in slot 4, QLBINEOS is at memory
address 0xC4E0. The code shown in Figure V.2.5 shows how to utilize the QLBINEOS interface.

LOAD file. This DCB loads a file into memory from a quikLoader EPROM using BINEOS:

```
EOSDCBL    equ *                    ; LOAD file DCB
DCBCMDL    hex 01                   ; LOAD command
DCBEPNL    hex 70                   ; search all EPROMs
DCBFALTL   hex 0000                 ; no alternate address
DCBSTATL   hex FF                   ; return status
DCBFLENL   byt FILENDL-FILNAML      ; filename length
DCBFADRL   adr FILNAML              ; filename address

FILNAML    asc "Applesoft File List"
FILENDL    equ *
```

RUN file. This DCB loads a file into memory from a quikLoader EPROM and runs that file using BINEOS:

```
EOSDCBR    equ *                    ; RUN file DCB
DCBCMDR    hex 02                   ; RUN command
DCBEPNR    hex 70                   ; search all EPROMs
DCBFALTR   hex 0000                 ; no alternate address
DCBSTATR   hex FF                   ; return status
DCBFLENR   byt FILENDR-FILNAMR      ; filename length
DCBFADRR   adr FILNAMR              ; filename address

FILNAMR    asc "Volume Copy"
FILENDR    equ *
```

CATALOG files. This DCB catalogs the quikLoader EPROMs using BINEOS:

```
EOSDCBC    equ *                    ; CATALOG EPROMs DCB
DCBCMDC    hex 03                   ; CATALOG command
DCBEPNC    hex 70                   ; CATALOG all EPROMs
DCBCALT    hex 0000                 ; not used
DCBSTATC   hex FF                   ; return status
DCBCNUM    hex 00                   ; CATALOG entries number
DCBCADR    adr CATBUFR              ; CATALOG buffer address

CATBUFR    dfs 32*n,ZERO            ; n 32-byte entries
```

The call to BINEOS will return one of the following Status values:

```
0x00 = no error
0x10 = Unknown Command
0x20 = Filename Length Invalid
0x30 = Search Range Invalid
0x40 = Buffer/Filename Address error
```

Offset	Length	Variable	Description
0	1	FILEPNUM	EPROM number containing this file
1	1	FILETYPE	File type
2	2	SRCVAL	EPROM source address (EPROM offset)
4	2	LENVAL	File length or size in bytes
6	2	DSTVAL	Destination memory address (Apple][memory)
8	24	FILENAME	Filename, space padded, upper ASCII

Table V.2.6. BINEOS Catalog File Entry

The quikLoader EPROM search range and file types are the same in BINEOS as they are in ASEOS. The Catalog buffer will contain the number of entries given by DCBCNUM. Each Catalog entry will be thirty-two bytes in size regardless of the length of the filename in bytes. The filename will be converted to upper ASCII and padded with the upper ASCII SPACE (i.e. 0xA0) character to be exactly twenty-four characters in length. A BINEOS Catalog file entry is structured as shown in Table V.2.6.

EOS makes extensive use of the 6502-microprocessor stack page from 0x0110 to 0x018D for the QBMCODE consisting of the routines QLCONFIG, QLMOVE, QLJMP, QLJSR, QLRTN, and QLEXEC. When *EOS* is activated it initializes the stack pointer to 0xFF to ensure that these temporary stack page routines are safe while *EOS* is active. And, it is extremely unlikely that the ASEOS interface will load these stack routines over a stack pointer in this memory region because Applesoft tightly controls this pointer. The same argument can be made for software using the BINEOS interface as long as that software is mindful of its stack pointer location and where the QBMCODE routines reside. *EOS* also makes extensive use of the text input page from 0x0280 to 0x02EF. It is extremely unlikely that a lengthy Applesoft or DOS command will ever be issued during ASEOS or BINEOS processing. However, an Applesoft user should be aware that *EOS* does use the upper half of the INPUT page. *EOS* uses the stack and input pages so that the memory page from 0x0300 to 0x03CF is still left available for program loaders. The loader for *Sourceror* (a Primary file) is one example of a very short binary program that uses 0x300 to 0x32C to load *Sourceror* (a System File) from a quikLoader EPROM to memory address 0x8900 using a LOAD DCB. The original code segment to set MAXFILES to 0x01 is unnecessary for DOS 4.3. The possibilities are virtually endless in how *EOS* can be utilized to obtain information and data from an EPROM or from all EPROMs residing in a quikLoader.

To assemble the *EOS* source code, place the DOS 4.3 Tools volume DOS4.3.Tools from the *EOS* directory in disk drive 1 and boot. *Lisa80* is automatically started. Enter the SE command-line command to select the *SETUP80* utility in order to verify or set the Start of Source Code to 0x4000 and the Start of Symbol List to 0x7800. Remove the DOS 4.3 Tools volume and place the EOS Binaries volume EOS.512.Binaries in disk drive 1. Place the EOS Source volume EOS.512.Source in disk drive 2, load the EOS.L file into memory, and start the assembler by entering either the A or the Z command-line command. If a printed version of the screen output is desired simply preface the A or the Z command with the P1 command-line command. Eight object code files will be created on the EOS Binaries volume named SEG01 to SEG08. Load the MOVE.L file into memory from the EOS Source volume, remove the EOS Source volume and place the EOS Image volume EOS.512.Image in disk drive 2, and start the assembler using the Z command-line command. The eight object code files will be copied from the EOS Binaries volume to the EOS Image volume. The first four object code files on the EOS Image volume can be combined in memory sequentially starting at `0x1000` using the `ctrl-P` command. The complete binary image can be saved to the EOS Image volume as `EOS1` as shown in Figure V.2.6. The last four object code files on the EOS Image volume can be combined in memory sequentially starting at `0x1000` using the `ctrl-P` command. The complete binary image can be saved to the EOS Image volume as `EOS2` as shown in Figure V.2.7. The EOS Image volume also contains a copy of the utility *BURNER*. When the EOS Image volume is transferred to an Apple //e using A2V2 on the Macintosh (including all the other varieties of Mac computers like a MacBook Pro) and *ADT* on the Apple //e, the utility *BURNER* can easily program a 27512 EPROM using the `EOS1` and `EOS2` binary images as binary input files. `EOS1` must be programmed to the first half of the quikLoader EPROM and `EOS2` must be programmed to the second half of the quikLoader EPROM.

To assemble the *PGM1* source code with *Lisa* already running, place the PGM1 Binaries volume `PGM1.512.Binaries` in disk drive 1. Place the PGM1 Source volume `PGM1.512.Source` in disk drive 2, load the `PGM.L` file into memory, and start the assembler using either the `A` or the `Z` command-line command. If a printed version of the screen output is desired simply preface the `A` or the `Z` command with the `P1` command-line command. Eight object code files will be created on the PGM1 Source volume named `SEG01` to `SEG08`. Remove the PGM1 Binaries volume and place the PGM1 Image volume `PGM1.512.Image` in disk drive 1, load the `MOVE.L` file into memory from the PGM1 Source volume, and start the assembler using the `Z` command-line command. The eight object code files will be copied from the PGM1 Source volume to the PGM1 Image volume. The first four object code files on the PGM1 Image volume can be combined in memory sequentially starting at `0x1000` using the `ctrl-P` command. The complete binary image can be saved to the PGM1 Image volume as `PGM1`. The last four object code files on the PGM1 Image volume can be combined in memory sequentially starting at `0x1000` using the `ctrl-P` command. The complete binary image can be saved to the PGM1 Image volume as `PGM2`. The PGM1 Image volume also contains a copy of the utility *BURNER*. When the PGM1 Image volume is transferred to an Apple //e using A2V2 on the Macintosh and *ADT* on the Apple //e, the utility *BURNER* can easily program a 27512 EPROM using the `PGM1` and `PGM2` binary images as binary input files. `PGM1` must be programmed to the first half of a 27512 EPROM and `PGM2` must be programmed to the second half of the 27512 EPROM.

To assemble the *PGM2* source code with *Lisa* already running, place the PGM2 Binaries volume `PGM2.512.Binaries` in disk drive 1. Place the PGM2 Source volume `PGM2.256.Source` in disk drive 2, load the `PGM.L` file in memory, and start the assembler using either the `A` or the `Z` command-line command. If a printed version of the screen output is desired simply preface the `A` or the `Z` command with the `P1` command-line command. Remove the PGM2 Binaries volume and place the PGM2 Image volume `PGM2.512.Image` in disk drive 1, load the `MOVE.L` file into memory from the PGM2 Source volume, and start the assembler using the `Z` command-line command. The eight object code files will be copied from the PGM2 Source volume to the PGM2 Image volume. Create `PGM1` and `PGM2` on the PGM2 Image volume as above and program a 27512 EPROM with these two files.

Seat all three 27512 EPROMs in a quikLoader being mindful that the EPROM containing *EOS* must be seated in Socket 0. Plug the quikLoader into an available slot and power the Apple //e ON. The EOS `Main Menu` as shown in Figure V.2.2 will be displayed.

```
 Segments = #4
First Seg = #1
  Address = $1000
BLOAD SEG01,A$1000
BLOAD SEG02,A$3000
BLOAD SEG03,A$5A00
BLOAD SEG04,A$8A00

Load end = $9000
Save file = EOS1
BSAVE EOS1,A$1000,L$8000

!■
```

Figure V.2.6. EOS1 Image File Creation

```
 Segments = #4
First Seg = #5
  Address = $1000
BLOAD SEG05,A$1000
BLOAD SEG06,A$39B5
BLOAD SEG07,A$68F6
BLOAD SEG08,A$8105

Load end = $9000
Save file = EOS2
BSAVE EOS2,A$1000,L$8000

!■
```

Figure V.2.7. EOS2 Image File Creation

3. VTOC Manager (VMGR)

The Volume Table of Contents (VTOC) Manager, or *VMGR*, is a utility I developed while I was designing the enhancements to the DOS 4.1 VTOC and volume Catalog. *VMGR* provides the user the ability to display and change the contents of a volume's VTOC for any given slot, drive, and volume number. Figure V.3.1 displays the Option Menu for *VMGR*. When the program first starts, it displays the slot, drive, and volume number values currently in focus. The user can change those values using Option 1. Option 2 reads the VTOC for the selected volume and displays the VTOC contents as shown in Figure V.3.2. Option 3 displays the same VTOC contents shown in Figure V.3.2 except that the user can edit, or change the information. Great harm can easily be done to a volume, even making the volume unusable, if the VTOC information is changed inappropriately. It is critical that the user understands the effects of any changes to the VTOC and to accept all consequences. Options 4 and 5 display and edit the sector bitmap, respectively. Figure V.3.3 displays the sector bitmap contents of the same volume shown in Figure V.3.2.

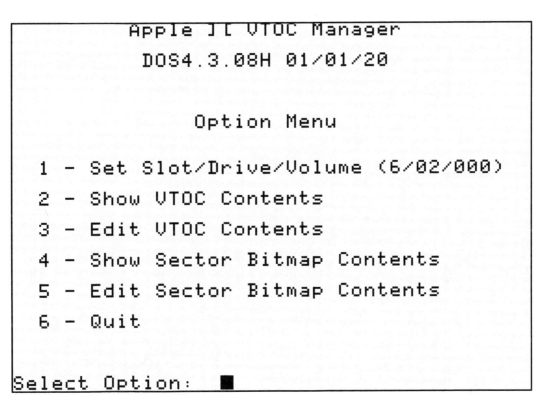

```
        Apple ][ VTOC Manager
         DOS4.3.08H 01/01/20


              Option Menu

   1 - Set Slot/Drive/Volume (6/02/000)

   2 - Show VTOC Contents

   3 - Edit VTOC Contents

   4 - Show Sector Bitmap Contents

   5 - Edit Sector Bitmap Contents

   6 - Quit


Select Option:  ■
```

Figure V.3.1. VMGR Option Menu

```
            VTOC Contents
1st Cat T/S    - 0x11/0x05
DOS Version    - 4.3
DOS Build      - 08
DOS RAM        - H (High RAM)

Volm Number    - 0x00 (000)
Volm Type      - D (Data Disk)
Volm Subject   - 0x50A0 (20640)
Volm DiskName  - VTOC Manager Source Code
Volm DateTime  - 01/01/20 08:28:48
VTOC DateTime  - 01/01/20 08:28:48

T/S Pairs      - 0x7A (122)
Next Track     - 0x21 (33)
Tk Allocation  - 0x01 (positive)
Volume Lock    - 0x00 (unlocked)
Volume Tracks  - 0x23 (35)
Track Sectors  - 0x10 (16)
Track Phases   - 0x04 (04)
Sector Bytes   - 0x100 (256)

            Press Any Key
```

Figure V.3.2. VTOC Contents for Option 2 and 3

```
         Sector Bitmap Contents

              35 Tracks


Trk | 00001111  00001111  00001111  00001111
Num | C840C840  C840C840  C840C840  C840C840
Rng | FB73FB73  FB73FB73  FB73FB73  FB73FB73
-----------------------------------------------
 00 | 00000000  00000000  00000000  00000000
 04 | 3FFF0000  FFFF0000  FFFF0000  FFFF0000
 08 | FFFF0000  FFFF0000  FFFF0000  FFFF0000
 0C | FFFF0000  FFFF0000  FFFF0000  FFFF0000
 10 | FFFF0000  FFC00000  001F0000  00000000
 14 | 00000000  00000000  003F0000  07FF0000
 18 | 001F0000  07FF0000  1FFF0000  00000000
 1C | 3FFF0000  3FFF0000  7FFF0000  7FFF0000
 20 | 7FFF0000  7FFF0000  FFFF0000

            Press Any Key
```

Figure V.3.3. VTOC Sector Bitmap Contents for Option 4 and 5

200

Each track of a DOS 4.3 volume may contain either 16 or 32 sectors depending on the hardware media. The VTOC can support up to 50 tracks. Figure I.5.1 shows the complete sector bitmap that begins at byte 0x38 in the VTOC. The sector bitmap allocates four bytes, or 32 bits, for every track to determine if a sector in that track is available or not. If a sector is available its respective bit is set to one. If a sector is not available its respective bit is set to zero. Table I.5.2 shows the sector order from left to right: sectors 0x0F to 0x00 for the left two bytes followed by sectors 0x1F to 0x10 for the right two bytes. DOS 4.3 indirectly interacts with the VTOC bitmap by means of the variable NEXTSECR exclusively OR'd with the value of 0x10. Therefore, if a volume only supports 16 sectors per track, the right two bytes will be set to 0x00. In Figure V.3.3 track 24 (0x18) contains five free sectors and track 28 (0x1C) contains fourteen free sectors.

To assemble the *VMGR* source code place the DOS 4.3 Tools volume DOS4.3.Tools in disk drive 1, boot, and start *Lisa80*. Enter the SE command-line command to select the *SETUP80* utility in order to verify or set the Start of Source Code to 0x4000 and the Start of Symbol List to 0x7800. Place the VMGR Source volume VMGR.Source in disk drive 2, load the VMGR.L file into memory, and start the assembler by entering either the A or the Z command-line command. If a printed version of the screen output is desired simply preface the A or the Z command with the P1 command-line command. Four object code files will be created on the VMGR Source volume named SEG01 to SEG04. The four object code files can be combined in memory sequentially starting at 0x0900 using the ctrl-P command. The complete binary image can be saved to the VMGR Source volume or to any other volume as VMGR.

4. Big Mac

I first started using *Big Mac* by Glen E. Bredon on my Apple][+ as soon as I took an interest in writing assembly language programs. Also, *Sourceror* was designed as a subsidiary tool to *Big Mac* that created *Big Mac* source code files from assembly language object code files. *Big Mac* and *Sourceror* are also capable of assembling and sourcing *SWEET16* instructions, respectively. The main menu for *Big Mac* is shown in Figure V.4.1. This is another example where I have used lowercase characters to assist in making the Apple][screen text easier for me and other users to read. When I started working at Sierra On-Line the programmers there only used *Lisa*, not *Big Mac*. However, whenever I use *Sourceror* I am still dependent on *Big Mac* to perform some edits on the output source files that are generated by *Sourceror*. I use the ED/ASM mode in *Big Mac* to make the edits and then save the files as TEXT files which happen to be compatible with *Lisa*. *Lisa* is able to EXEC the *Big Mac* TEXT files into its assembler quickly. And this is precisely the procedure I still use today.

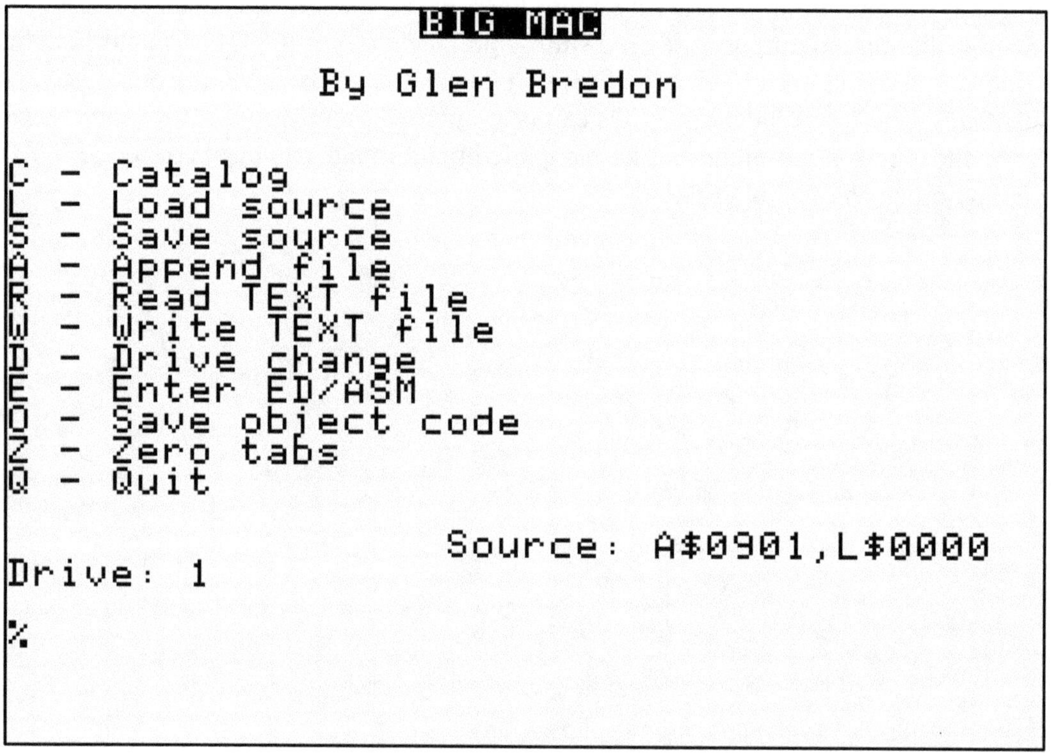

```
                      BIG MAC
                   By Glen Bredon

C  -  Catalog
L  -  Load source
S  -  Save source
A  -  Append file
R  -  Read TEXT file
W  -  Write TEXT file
D  -  Drive change
E  -  Enter ED/ASM
O  -  Save object code
Z  -  Zero tabs
Q  -  Quit

                    Source: A$0901,L$0000

Drive: 1

:
```

Figure V.4.1. Big Mac Main Menu

Big Mac made frequent use of DOS 3.3 internal routines so it was not at all compatible with DOS 4.1 and, therefore, DOS 4.3. I needed to know every instance where *Big Mac* utilized DOS 3.3 internals, and then modify those dependencies to make use of the DOS 4.3 interfaces. *Big Mac* was certainly a challenge because it packaged a huge wallop of a program into the limited space of the Language Card. Creating source code for *Big Mac* that could be modified required a huge effort. It is one thing to have source code that assembles to object code which compares perfectly to the original object code. It is quite another thing to turn that source code into routines whose addresseses may change as some code is modified, deleted, and added, and still assemble into a working, viable program. I did remove the

202

`ASSEM` re-entry command because DOS 4.3 provides no visibility into its command tables, the command handler addresses, and the companion keyword tables for a reason. (A seasoned *Lisa* user may wish to add the `ASSEM` command to DOS 4.3 in addition to any other DOS commands, assemble this unique version of DOS 4.3, and create a bootable *Big Mac* volume having that version of DOS 4.3.) However, DOS 4.3 does provide access to structures for drive number, file start address, and file length. I am satisfied that my sourced and modified version of *Big Mac* is fully DOS 4.3 compliant and, as a utility, is still providing me with a terrific interface between *Sourceror* and *Lisa*.

In order to make *Big Mac* fully DOS 4.3 compliant required me to relocate *Big Mac* to Auxiliary memory. Why? Because DOS 4.3 is resident in Language Card memory and *Big Mac* is resident in Language Card memory as well. Both cannot reside concurrently in the same Language Card memory. But Auxiliary memory also contains its own Language Card memory. It seemed natural to relocate *Big Mac* to Auxiliary memory. It was definitely a challenge to understand how to master Auxiliary memory in terms of its operation and what it could provide and what it could not provide in resources. Certainly, to assist in its operation would be to decide which side of memory would handle input data (keyboard and disk) and which side of memory would handle output data (screen and disk). Once I established the operating rules it became very clear how to build the interface between Main memory and Auxiliary memory specifically for *Big Mac*. Fortunately, I was able to leverage on lessons learned from relocating *Lisa* to Auxiliary memory. Since DOS 4.3 occupied Language Card memory in Main memory it was quite logical to utilize Main memory for the input and the output of all disk data. It was totally unnecessary to maintain two page-zeros particularly for the variables `CH`, `CV`, `BASL`, `BASH`, and the text window variables. So, all keyboard and screen display are handled within Auxiliary page-zero memory.

Big Mac contains its own version of the Monitor. This Monitor mostly resembles the monitor found in the Apple][+. In order for *Big Mac* to utilize any of the various iterations of the Apple //e Monitor, *Big Mac* simply copies the ROM Monitor for its RAM Monitor. The interface between Main memory and Auxiliary memory is injected primarily at the `COUT` (i.e. `0xFDED`) routine. A small handler is needed for the `GETFMCB`, `CALLFM`, `HOOKDOS`, `PRTERROR`, `GOTODOS`, `GOTOMON`, `GOTOCOLD`, and `GOTOWARM` vectors. DOS errors had to be handled uniquely by the interface in order to re-enter *Big Mac* appropriately. The state of the Language Card bank currently in focus had to be captured in order to reconfigure Auxiliary memory for all subroutines returning to *Big Mac*. Because *Big Mac* utilizes Language Card Bank 1 for its symbol list and Bank 2 for its software routines, there is no way to know which bank is in focus at any given time during *Big Mac* processing. The greater challenge was to align *Big Mac* and *Sourceror*, particularly in terms of assembling and sourcing *SWEET16* instructions.

Initially, *Big Mac* could process only some of the *SWEET16* opcodes. And, as it turned out, *Big Mac* could not even process its own unique `EVAL` opcode because there is no entry in any of the *Big Mac* hash tables for that opcode. To this end, I chose to update *Sourceror* and *Big Mac* so that they could both process my version of the *SWEET16* opcodes. *Sourceror* was already able to recognize 65C02 opcodes because my Apple //e Monitor could display 65C02 instructions (you must tear apart *Sourceror* to understand what I mean by this). *Big Mac*, however, could not recognize nor process any of the 65C02 instructions. It was fairly easy to update *Big Mac*'s Monitor support logic so it could at least parse and display those instructions. It was not so easy to give *Big Mac* the ability to assemble 65C02 instructions. The tables and logic in *Big Mac* that give it its ability to parse 6502 instructions and handle all the addressing mode rules is exceedingly dense. The original tables were found at `0xF339` to `0xF4DD`. Now, the tables are found at `0xF339` to `0xF4FF`. To make this possible, a number of routines and ASCII tables had to be moved elsewhere.

```
   :              :           :
E740 AD 34 02    640    HE740    lda  H0234        ; get first character
E743             641    ;
E743 0A          642             asl               ; shift left
E744 0A          643             asl               ; shift left
E745 0A          644             asl               ; shift left
E746             645    ;
E746 85 EA       646             sta  H00EA        ; save to hashA
E748             647    ;
E748 AD 35 02    648             lda  H0235        ; get second character
E74B             649    ;
E74B 6A          650             ror               ; shift right
E74C 66 EB       651             ror  H00EB        ; save bit to hashB
E74E             652    ;
E74E 6A          653             ror               ; shift right
E75F 66 EB       654             ror  H00EB        ; save bit to hashB
E751             655    ;
E751 29 07       656             and  #7           ; keep lower 3 bits
E753 05 EA       657             ora  H00EA        ; add to hashA
E755 85 EA       658             sta  H00EA        ; save to hashA
E757             659    ;
E757 AD 37 02    660             lda  H0237        ; get fourth character
E75A 29 5F       661             and  #$5F         ; looking for SOUT
E75C             662    ;
E75C C9 44       663             cmp  #$44         ; set carry if T
E75E F0 07       664             beq  HE767        ; bypass if SOUT
E760             665    ;
E760 AD 36 02    666             lda  H0236        ; get third character
E763 49 BF       667             eor  #$BF         ; looking for @
E765 C9 FF       668             cmp  #NEGONE      ; set carry if 0x40
E767             669    ;
E767 AD 36 02    670    HE767    lda  H0236        ; get third character
E76A 29 1F       671             and  #$1F         ; keep lower 5 bits
E76C 2A          672             rol               ; shift in carry
E76D             673    ;
E76D 05 EB       674             ora  H00EB        ; add to hashB
E76F 85 EB       675             sta  H00EB        ; save to hashB
   :              :           :
```

Figure V.4.2. Big Mac Mnemonic Hashing Algorithm

In order to add the STZ, TRB, and TSB hash entries, for example, to the end of the table data starting at 0xF4EC, I had to move two ASCII tables. One table was at 0xF4E8 and the other was at 0xF4EF. Combined, they were fifteen bytes and I needed twelve bytes for those three new instructions. I did have an 18-byte gap in the code at 0xE408 and this is where I moved those two ASCII tables. The 10-byte table at 0xF4DE simply moved down to 0xF501. To the best of my ability I have verified that *Big Mac* can assemble all 65C02 instructions and increment its program counter correctly for all addressing modes. Furthermore, the *Big Mac* Monitor support code can display all 65C02 instructions correctly with opcode, value, address, and displacement.

Mnemonic	Table Address	Hash Value		Handler Address
		0xEA	0xEB	
]@	0xF339	0xE8	0x00	0xEFE0
EQU	0xF33D	0x2C	0x6A	0xEFE0
^^^	0xF341	0xF7	0xBC	0xF118
PMC	0xF345	0x83	0x46	0xF118
HEX	0xF349	0x41	0x70	0xEE80
DFB	0xF34D	0x21	0x84	0xEE68
DA	0xF351	0x20	0x40	0xEE42
DDB	0xF355	0x21	0x04	0xEE41
DS	0xF359	0x24	0xC0	0xF08C
LST	0xF35D	0x64	0xE8	0xEEB1
AST	0xF361	0x0C	0xE8	0xF04B
ORG	0xF365	0x7C	0x8E	0xF243
OBJ	0xF369	0xF2	0x42	0xF22A
SET	0xF36D	0x99	0x68	0xE892
SKP	0xF371	0x9A	0xE0	0xF048
PAG	0xF375	0x80	0x4E	0xF041
PAU	0xF379	0x80	0x6A	0xEB57
EXP	0xF37D	0x2E	0x20	0xEEB5
PUT	0xF381	0x85	0x68	0xF1DC
TR	0xF385	0xA4	0x80	0xEEA3
CHK	0xF389	0x1A	0x16	0xF20B
VAR	0xF38D	0xB0	0x64	0xEE35
SAV	0xF391	0x98	0x6C	0xF27B
KBD	0xF395	0x58	0x88	0xEF9E
END	0xF399	0x2B	0x88	0xF5B2

Table V.4.1. Hash Table 1 – Assembly Directives

Mnemonic	Table Address	Hash Value		Handler Address
		0xEA	0xEB	
ASC	0xF39D	0x0C	0xC6	0xEF60
DCI	0xF3A1	0x20	0xD2	0xEF5F
PLS	0xF3A5	0x33	0x26	0xEF53
INV	0xF3A9	0x4B	0x55	0xEF55

Table V.4.2. Hash Table 2 – Text Directives

Mnemonic	Table Address	Hash Value		Handler Address
		0xEA	0xEB	
\\\	0xF3AE	0xE7	0x38	0xF18F
DO	0xF3B2	0x23	0xC0	0xF101
ELS	0xF3B6	0x2B	0x26	0xF0F8
MAC	0xF3BE	0x68	0x46	0xF0B1
EOM	0xF3C2	0x2B	0xDA	0xF18F

Table V.4.3. Hash Table 3 – Macro Directives

Mr. Bredon utilized a hashing algorithm to calculate a hash value for each assembly instruction he encountered as his *Big Mac* program assembled source code. The hash value is used to identify a table entry that provides additional data and/or format used to process that particular instruction. The GETHASH routine in *Big Mac* is found at 0xE740 and is shown in Figure V.4.2. The lower ASCII value of the assembly instruction text is always placed starting at 0x0234, and the 2-byte hash value created from the assembly instruction text is placed in page-zero at 0xEA and 0xEB. The hash value is unique to each assembly instruction including assembly directives, macro instructions and *SWEET16* instructions.

The first hash table in *Big Mac* is found at 0xF339, and this table processes assembly directives. This table is shown in Table V.4.1 and each entry begins with a 2-byte hash value followed by the address of the software handler for this instruction. The next hash table is found at 0xF39D, and is shown in Table V.4.2. This second table is similar in structure to Table V.4.1 and it is terminated with a NULL (i.e. 0x00) character so *Big Mac* can reconfigure its indexing and pointers. The address bytes for each instruction handler in both these tables are decremented and reversed so they can be pushed onto the stack in that order. The third table shown is Table V.4.3 and it contains the macro instructions that can be used in *Big Mac*. It is structured like Table V.4.2 and it is also terminated with a NULL character.

Table V.4.4 contains all the single byte 65C02 and *SWEET16* instructions. This table is found at 0xF3C7 and each entry begins with the 2-byte hash value followed by the opcode for that instruction. These instructions are the easiest to process and very little supporting code is required. It is to this table I added the *SWEET16* RSNS instruction. All the branch instructions for both the 65C02 Instruction Set and the *SWEET16* opcodes are contained in Table V.4.5 which is found at 0xF428. As in Table V.4.4 each entry begins with the 2-byte hash value followed by the opcode for that instruction. However, a branch offset, or displacement needs to be calculated for these instructions as well. *Big Mac* must refer to its symbol list and subtract the current program counter from the address of the symbol the branch statement references. This calculation provides a signed two's complement value from -128 to +127, and is a byte displacement relative to the address of the following instruction. It is to this table I added the *SWEET16* BSNS instruction. Both Tables, V.4.4 and V.4.5 are terminated with a NULL character.

Mnemonic	Table Address	Hash Value 0xEA	Hash Value 0xEB	Opcode
CLC	0xF3C7	0x1B	0x06	0x18
DEX	0xF3CA	0x21	0x70	0xCA
DEY	0xF3CD	0x21	0x72	0x88
INX	0xF3D0	0x4B	0xB0	0xE8
INY	0xF3D3	0x4B	0xB2	0xC8
RTS	0xF3D6	0x95	0x26	0x60
SEC	0xF3D9	0x99	0x46	0x38
TAX	0xF3DC	0xA0	0x70	0xAA
TAY	0xF3DF	0xA0	0x72	0xA8
TXA	0xF3E2	0xA6	0x02	0x8A
TYA	0xF3E5	0xA6	0x42	0x98
PHA	0xF3E8	0x82	0x02	0x48
PHP	0xF3EB	0x82	0x20	0x08
PLA	0xF3EE	0x83	0x02	0x68
PLP	0xF3F1	0x83	0x20	0x28
TSX	0xF3F4	0xA4	0xF0	0xBA
TXS	0xF3F7	0xA6	0x26	0x9A
CLD	0xF3FA	0x1B	0x08	0xD8
SED	0xF3FD	0x99	0x48	0xF8
SEI	0xF400	0x99	0x52	0x78
RTI	0xF403	0x95	0x12	0x40
CLI	0xF406	0x1B	0x12	0x58
CLV	0xF409	0x1B	0x2C	0xB8
NOP	0xF40C	0x73	0xE0	0xEA
BRK	0xF40F	0x14	0x96	0x00
PHX	0xF412	0x82	0x30	0xDA
PHY	0xF415	0x82	0x32	0x5A
PLX	0xF418	0x83	0x30	0xFA
PLY	0xF41B	0x83	0x32	0x7A
RTN	0xF41E	0x95	0x1C	0x00
RS	0xF421	0x94	0xC0	0x0B
RSNS	0xF424	0x94	0xDC	0x0D

Table V.4.4. Hash Table 4 – Single Byte Instructions

Table V.4.6 contains the hash values and opcode/code for the single byte *SWEET16* instructions that utilize a *SWEET16* register. Several of the entries may appear puzzling. The first entry is actually nibblized for the LD and the LD@ instructions. The second entry is nibblized for the ST and the ST@ instructions. It does not matter whether the actual opcode is in the upper or lower nibble of the opcode/code byte for these instructions. Whenever *Big Mac* finds an instruction in Table V.4.6, it knows how to formulate the upper nibble of the *SWEET16* opcode and logically OR this nibble with a register number to complete the opcode. Table V.4.6 is terminated with a NULL character.

Mnemonic	Table Address	Hash Value 0xEA	0xEB	Opcode
BCC	0xF428	0x10	0xC6	0x90
BCS	0xF42B	0x10	0xE6	0xB0
BEQ	0xF42E	0x11	0x62	0xF0
BMI	0xF431	0x13	0x52	0x30
BNE	0xF434	0x13	0x8A	0xD0
BCC	0xF437	0x13	0x28	0x90
BCS	0xF43A	0x11	0xCA	0xB0
BPL	0xF43D	0x14	0x18	0x10
BVC	0xF440	0x15	0x86	0x50
BVS	0xF443	0x15	0xA6	0x70
BRA	0xF446	0x14	0x82	0x80
BR	0xF449	0x14	0x80	0x01
BNC	0xF44C	0x13	0x86	0x02
BC	0xF44F	0x10	0xC0	0x03
BP	0xF452	0x14	0x00	0x04
BM	0xF455	0x13	0x40	0x05
BZ	0xF458	0x16	0x80	0x06
BNZ	0xF45B	0x13	0xB4	0x07
BM1	0xF45E	0x13	0x62	0x08
BNM1	0xF461	0x13	0x9A	0x09
BS	0xF464	0x14	0xC0	0x0C
BSNS	0xF467	0x14	0xDC	0x0E

Table V.4.5. Hash Table 5 – Branch Instructions

Mnemonic	Table Address	Hash Value 0xEA	0xEB	Opcode/ Code
LD & LD@	0xF46B	0x61	0x00	0x24
ST & LD@	0xF46E	0x9D	0x00	0x35
LDD@	0xF471	0x61	0x08	0x06
STD@	0xF474	0x9D	0x08	0x07
POP@	0xF477	0x83	0xE0	0x08
STP@	0xF47A	0x9D	0x20	0x09
ADD	0xF47D	0x09	0x08	0xA0
SUB	0xF480	0x9D	0x44	0xB0
POPD	0xF483	0x83	0xE1	0x0C
CPR	0xF486	0x1C	0x24	0xD0
INR	0xF489	0x4B	0xA4	0xE0
DCR	0xF48C	0x20	0xE4	0xF0

Table V.4.6. Hash Table 6 – Single Byte SWEET16 Register Instructions

The last table of hash values in *Big Mac* is Table V.4.7 and it begins at 0xF490; it is terminated with a NULL character. It is the most complex table because it contains entries for those 65C02 instructions that can be used in multiple addressing modes. This table also contains two *SWEET16* instructions because they require special processing. Each entry begins with the 2-byte hash value followed by a format byte and an opcode base value. Depending on the format, the opcode base value is adjusted by one of ten mode values, with eight of them found at 0xF501 (formally 0xF4DE). Those eight mode values are shown in Table V.4.8. It only takes a cursory look at the 65C02 Instruction Set to understand how Mr. Bredon was able to reconstruct the opcodes for the instructions in Table V.4.7: he used the opcode base value and one of those eight mode values based on how the instruction is used in context. The format byte stipulates all of the legal addressing modes for that instruction. Each bit in the format byte is mapped to a particular addressing mode. When a bit is ON, that addressing mode is valid for that instruction. Table V.4.8 shows the definition for each bit in the format byte.

Mnemonic	Table Address	Hash Value		Valid Formats	Base Value for Opcode
		0xEA	0xEB		
STA	0xF490	0x9D	0x02	0x3E	0x81
STX	0xF494	0x9D	0x30	0x01	0x82
STY	0xF498	0x9D	0x32	0x04	0x80
LDA	0xF49C	0x61	0x02	0xBE	0xA1
LDX	0xF4A0	0x61	0x30	0x83	0xA2
LDY	0xF4A4	0x61	0x32	0x8C	0xA0
ADC	0xF4A8	0x09	0x06	0xBE	0x61
AND	0xF4AC	0x0B	0x88	0xBE	0x21
ASL	0xF4B0	0x0C	0xD8	0x4C	0x02
CMP	0xF4B4	0x1B	0x60	0xBE	0xC1
CPX	0xF4B8	0x1C	0x30	0x80	0xE0
CPY	0xF4BC	0x1C	0x32	0x80	0xC0
DEC	0xF4C0	0x21	0x46	0x4C	0xC2
EOR	0xF4C4	0x2B	0xE4	0xBE	0x41
INC	0xF4C8	0x4B	0x86	0x4C	0xE2
JMP	0xF4CC	0x53	0x60	0x20	0x4C
JSR	0xF4D0	0x54	0xE4	0x00	0x20
SBC	0xF4D4	0x98	0x86	0xBE	0xE1
ORA	0xF4D8	0x7C	0x82	0xBE	0x01
LSR	0xF4DC	0x64	0xE4	0x4C	0x42
BIT	0xF4E0	0x12	0x68	0x8C	0x20
ROL	0xF4E4	0x93	0xD8	0x4C	0x22
ROR	0xF4E8	0x93	0xE4	0x4C	0x62
STZ	0xF4EC	0x9D	0x34	0x0C	0x64
TRB	0xF4F0	0xA4	0x84	0x00	0x10
TSB	0xF4F4	0xA4	0xC4	0x00	0x04
SOUT	0xF4F8	0x9B	0xEA	0x80	0x0A
SJMP	0xF4FC	0x9A	0x9A	0x00	0x0F

Table V.4.7. Hash Table 7 – Multiple Addressing Mode Instructions

Bit	7	6	5	4	3	2	1	0
Mode	IMM	ACC	(IND,X)	(IND),Y	ABS,X	ZP,X	ABS,Y	ZP,Y

Table V.4.8. Format Byte Definition

The addressing modes shown in Table V.4.8 are Immediate (IMM), Accumulator (ACC), Indirect (IND) using the X-register, Indirect using the Y-register, Absolute (ABS) using the X-register, page-zero (ZP) using the X-register, Absolute using the Y-register, and page-zero using the Y-register. The remaining two modes, Absolute and page-zero, are determined at the time of processing since a register is not associated with those two modes. Also, the standalone (IND) mode, new to the 65C02 Instruction Set except for the JMP instruction, must be determined by the context of the source code.

The source code that I have generated for *Big Mac* is not perfect. I have verified that two *SWEET16* branch displacements in the source code have the same value as what exists in the original object code. I think Mr. Bredon somehow allowed two coding errors through his design reviews. More likely, Mr. Bredon hand-coded the two routines (they are close in proximity), and for one reason or another these two displacements were simply not verified or checked. The first displacement error occurs at 0xD2C0 for a BP instruction having a 0xD3 displacement. That displacement would put 0xD295 into the program counter register. There is a BZ instruction at 0xD294 and an ST instruction at 0xD296. I would choose the ST instruction as the more logical branch. The second displacement error occurs at 0xD2DE for a BNZ instruction having a 0x08 displacement. That displacement would put 0xD2E8 into the program counter register. There is a BZ instruction at 0xD2E7 and a SET instruction at 0xD2E9. I would choose the SET instruction as the more logical branch. I have not yet had an opportunity to do more than document these errors, so I have not yet changed these displacement values. If I cannot ascertain a strategy to exercise this section of code, then I will not have any more information than I already have (which is no information) to make an educated decision as to what Mr. Bredon intended.

Another interesting anomaly in *Big Mac* occurs in the routine that begins at 0xDC60. For all intents and purposes the code looks unremarkable until 0xDC91. At that point there is a JSR instruction to 0xC9AA. Bizarre! I am aware of only one possible reason for this call. In the Apple //e CX ROM code there does exist a purposefully placed Pascal 1.0 output entry point at 0xC9AA called PXWRITE. The nearby routines in this area of code must either branch around or leave room for the PXWRITE entry point. PXWRITE loads the A-register from the variable CHAR located at 0x067B, and then it jumps to 0xC356, an address in the Slot 3 peripheral-card ROM memory, presumably to write that data to a Pascal object. Why would Mr. Bredon make such a call in *Big Mac* when *Big Mac* was originally written for the Apple][+? This Pascal interface did not even exist for the Apple][+. If Mr. Bredon did update *Big Mac* for the Apple //e, why didn't he also update his *Big Mac* Monitor to display the full 65C02 Instruction Set? So far this call to 0xC9AA is just an interesting anomaly in *Big Mac*. Perhaps Mr. Bredon modified the address for the JSR at 0xDC91 "on the fly." I see no evidence of a label in that area of code to make such an address modification. The code could also be hogwash. I have yet to investigate this subject any further.

In order to display the 65C02 specific instructions in the Monitor, two format bytes need to be included in the FMT2 table. These format bytes are for the (ZP) format and the (ABS,X) format. For one reason or another every monitor or MiniAsm monitor I have studied set the (ZP) format to 0x4B and the (ABS,X) format to 0x5A. I have no problem with the value for the (ABS,X) format. However, I strongly believe the value for the (ZP) format must be 0x49. This value becomes even more critical for the proper operation of the ROM based mini-assembler. Even though *Big Mac* does not have enough room nor any reason to support the code for a mini-assembler, the FMT2 table is still necessary to properly display the 65C02 Instruction Set.

To assemble the *Big Mac* source code, place the DOS 4.3 Tools volume DOS4.3.Tools in disk drive 1, boot, and start *Lisa80*. Enter the SE command-line command to select the *SETUP80* utility in order to verify or set the Start of Source Code to 0x4000 and the Start of Symbol List to 0x7800. Place the Big Mac Source volume BIGMAC.Source in disk drive 2, load the BIGMAC.L file into memory, and start the assembler by entering either the A or the Z command-line command. If a printed version of the screen output is desired simply preface the A or the Z command with the P1 command-line command. Seven object code files will be created on the Big Mac Source volume named SEG01 to SEG07. The seven object code files can be combined in memory sequentially starting at 0x010B0 using the ctrl-P command. The complete binary image can be saved to the Big Mac Source volume or to any other volume as BIGMAC.

5. CFFA Card

The CompactFlash For Apple, or CFFA card is an Apple II peripheral slot card that is able to read from and write to a CompactFlash memory card seated in its on-board CF card socket or to an external hard drive by means of a 40-pin IDE header socket. Later enhancements of the CFFA replaced the 40-pin IDE header socket with a USB socket. This peripheral card is able to present the onboard flash storage as either a hard drive or a stack of floppy disks when using Disk][emulation firmware. Richard Dreher of R&D Automation created the CFFA card, and the first production run was released in 2002. I purchased my card in 2006, CFFA Version 2.0, revision B. It is my understanding that the CFFA card was most likely designed to be more compatible with ProDOS. Unfortunately, I never participated in the ProDOS movement. When ProDOS was introduced my software interests became redirected to UNIX based high-end professional workstations manufactured by SGI (running IRIX) and SUN (running SunOS). In view of my recent development of DOS 4.1, and now DOS 4.3, I began working on my own Disk][emulation firmware specifically for the CFFA card. I simply want a means to digitally archive my hundreds (yes, many hundreds) of 5.25-inch diskettes, and the CFFA card is the ideal reservoir.

I understand, however, that Mr. Dreher has enhanced the CFFA card in many ways since my purchase in 2006. I have no idea if the hardware interface of the current version of the CFFA card resembles that of the past interface and whether or not my firmware will even function on the current version of hardware. I strongly suspect my CFFA card firmware will function perfectly on the current hardware design if it still interfaces a CF memory card. Table V.5.1 shows the entry points of the firmware interface I developed that is mapped to the peripheral-card ROM memory for the CFFA card.

The CFFA firmware interface allows access to each of the 512-byte blocks on a CompactFlash memory card up to eight GBs in size. Each block has a Logical Block Address (LBA) that is 24-bits in size, divided into three bytes, and saved to three of the sixteen peripheral-card I/O memory locations. Even the Master Boot Record (MBR) can be read and saved. Only three processing commands are necessary to utilize the CFFA: READ, WRITE, and ID. If the peripheral-card I/O locations have been changed to accept a 32-bit LBA, my CFFA firmware interface will not function on that CFFA card.

Offset	Name	Description
0x00	CFBOOT	Entry point for DOS PR# command to boot selected DOS
0x10	ROMHOOK	Entry point to attach the CFFA to the DOS in memory
0x18	ROMUHOOK	Entry point to detach the CFFA from the DOS in memory
0x20	USRBOOT	Boot selected DOS image
0x30	VOLBOOT	Boot selected volume DOS image
0x3B	DISKRWTS	DOS 3.3 RWTS entry if DOS 3.3 is in memory
0x4B	CFRWTS	DOS 4.1 and DOS 4.3 RWTS entry if DOS 4.1 or if DOS 4.3 is in memory
0x5C	VOLBOOT2	Disk][firmware entry point for Boot Stage 1 code at 0x0801
0x64	CFRWTS2	Convert DVTS to LBA to seek, read, write, and format CF volumes
0xF3	MODOS3	Entry point to modify DOS 3.3 during Boot Stage 2 for CFFA use
0xFE/FF	VERSION	Version number for CF firmware (0x38): Version 3, Build 8

Table V.5.1. CFFA Card Firmware Entry Points

The complete firmware interface fits comfortably in the peripheral-card ROM memory and expansion ROM memory of the CFFA card. The peripheral-card ROM memory has the normal slot boot entry signature bytes with a CFFA unique byte at offset 0x00, my standard DOS connection ON/OFF at offsets 0x10 and 0x18, respectively, a user boot entry at offset 0x20, and a volume boot entry at offset 0x30. The user can boot one of six versions of DOS and 32 LBA blocks are provided for each DOS image. The first four DOS images include DOS 3.3, DOS 4.1L, DOS 4.1H, and DOS 4.3H. Thus, there is room for two User Defined DOS images that may be installed. Additionally, the CFFA firmware can boot any bootable volume on any drive within the CF whether the boot tracks contain DOS 3.3, DOS 4.1, or DOS 4.3.

Card Size	Cylinders	Heads	Sectors	Total Blocks
256 MB	0x03D4	0x10	0x20	0x07A800
512 MB	0x03E1	0x10	0x3F	0x0F45F0
1.0 GB	0x07C2	0x10	0x3F	0x1E8BE0
2.0 GB	0x0F82	0x10	0x3F	0x3D0FE0
4.0 GB	0x1F1C	0x10	0x3F	0x7A7E40
8.0 GB	0x3E08	0x10	0x3F	0xF43F80

Table V.5.2. CompactFlash Card CHS Parameters

Address	Name	I/O	Description
0xC0n0	ATADATAH	R/W	Used with register #8. Write this byte first
0xC0n1	SETCSMSK	R/W	Disable 6502 pre-fetch when writing to CF
0xC0n2	CLRCSMSK	R/W	Enable 6502 pre-fetch when reading CF
0xC0n6	ATASTAT2	R	Secondary CF status register; does not clear IRQ
0xC0n6	ATADEVCT	W	Device control register to disable IRQ
0xC0n8	ATADATAL	R/W	Used with register #0. Read this byte first
0xC0n9	ATAERROR	R	Processing error source when register #15 not zero
0xC0nA	ATASECCT	R/W	Number of blocks to read or write; always set to 1
0xC0nB	ATASECTR	R/W	Bits 07:00 of LBA
0xC0nC	ATACYLNL	R/W	Bits 15:08 of LBA
0xC0nD	ATACYLNH	R/W	Bits 23:16 of LBA
0xC0nE	ATAHEAD	R/W	Select LBA or CHS mode; bits 27:24 of LBA
0xC0nF	ATASTAT	R	Primary CF status register; does not clear IRQ
0xC0nF	ATACMD	W	Command register

Table V.5.3. CFFA Firmware Interface Control Registers

Table V.5.2 shows the sizes of available CompactFlash cards in total blocks based on their Cylinder, Head, and Sector (CHS) geometry according to CompactFlash datasheets. Knowing a particular card's geometry allows one to convert CHS to LBA. However, it is not necessary to know or even to utilize this conversion to LBA in order to address the CFFA in LBA mode. Also, the CFFA card I own was designed and manufactured to address a CompactFlash card up to 8.0 GB in size and smaller.

As stated above the LBA value is 24-bits in size, divided into three bytes. The READ and WRITE processing commands are the only commands necessary to read or to write any data block in the CF card. The ID command can be used to read the IDENTIFY DEVICE block in the CF card. That block provides the card's serial number, model number, and its capacity in LBA addressable blocks as well as other useful information. Table V.5.3 shows the peripheral-card I/O memory locations that are used to initiate a CF processing command. The value of **n** in 0xC0n0, for example, equals the slot number of the CFFA card plus eight.

I approached my design of the CFFA firmware interface as a way to communicate with a massive data storage device. To that end, I devised an equation to convert Drive/Volume/Track/Sector (DVTS) to LBA and an algorithm to perform the reverse conversion. There is only one unique solution for either conversion routine. The ranges allowed in my CFFA firmware for the variables Drive, Volume, Track, and Sector are shown in Table V.5.4.

Parameter	Range	Description
Drive	1 - 81	in order to support an 8 GB CF card
Volume	0 - 255	supported by the DOS 4.3 VTOC
Track	0 — 47	supported by the DOS 4.3 VTOC
Sector	0 - 31	supported by the DOS 4.3 VTOC

Table V.5.4. CFFA Firmware DVTS Variable Range

The equations to convert DVTS to LBA are given by:

```
    block = Sector & 0x0F
     page = Sector & 0x10
  offset1 = 0x100

    LBA = ( ( Drive-1 ) * 0x30000 ) +
            ( Volume * 0x300 ) +
            ( Track * 0x10 ) + block + offset1
```

These equations imply that each Drive contains 0x30000 LBA blocks and each Volume contains 0x300 LBA blocks. A Volume can consist of up to a maximum of 48 Tracks and each Track has 16 LBA blocks. Since an LBA block contains 512 bytes, the block is partitioned by the page variable such that disk sectors 0x00 to 0x0F reside on page 0 (the lower half of the LBA block) and disk sectors 0x10 to 0x1F reside on page 1 (the upper half of the LBA block). I agree that forcing a Volume to be 768 LBA blocks (i.e. 1536 disk sectors) in size rather than 576 disk sectors in size is wasting a lot of space on the CompactFlash card. DOS 4.3 has the potential to utilize a volume having

214

up to 50 tracks in size, but I considered 48 to be the better upper limit for mathematical reasons and for ease in calculating LBA from DVTS. Because the VTOC can support 32 sectors per track and an LBA block is 512 bytes in size, it makes sense to split an LBA block into a lower 256-byte disk sector and an upper 256-byte disk sector. The algorithm to calculate an LBA for a given DVTS using the above equation is very fast because all the multiplication is done by using the addition of values obtained from three lookup tables. These lookup tables are simply indexed by Drive, Volume, and Track.

From the total blocks in CompactFlash cards shown in Table V.5.2, the total number of drives and extra volumes are shown in Table V.5.5. The conversion equation for DVTS to LBA stipulates that 0x30000 LBA blocks comprise one Drive and 0x300 LBA blocks comprise one Volume. For example, a 1.0 GB CompactFlash card contains ten full drives and the last, or eleventh drive has room for only forty-six volumes. There is 0x0E0 unused LBA blocks after accounting for offset1 which is 0x100 LBA blocks. Table V.5.6 shows the block utilization for a 1.0 GB CompactFlash card.

Card Size	Sectors	Drives	Extra Volumes	Residue
256 MB	0x07A800	2	141	0x000
512 MB	0x0F45F0	5	22	0x2F0
1.0 GB	0x1E8BE0	10	46	0x0E0
2.0 GB	0x3D0FE0	20	90	0x0E0
4.0 GB	0x7A7E40	40	212	0x140
8.0 GB	0xF43F80	81	106	0x080

Table V.5.5. CompactFlash Card Drive/Volume Parameters

Block Start	Block End	Description
0x000000	0x00000F	Not used
0x000010	0x00003F	Drive descriptions
0x000040	0x0000FF	DOS Images (room for 6 images)
0x000100	0x1E00FF	10 Drives each having 256 volumes
0x1E0100	0x1E8AFF	1 Drive having 46 volumes
0x1E8B00	0x1E8BDF	Not used

Table V.5.6. Block Utilization for a 1.0 GB CompactFlash Card

As shown in Table V.5.6 the 0x30 blocks allocated for drive descriptions provide enough room for 96 descriptions, each 256 bytes in size. The drive description contains the drive name in the first twenty-four bytes, the date and time the drive description was created in the next six bytes, and the actual NULL-terminated drive description verbiage in the remaining 226 bytes. The LBA and page value for a particular drive description is calculated as follows:

```
offset = 0x10

LBA = | ( ( Drive-1 ) / 2 ) | + offset
page = ( Drive-1 ) − ( ( LBA − offset ) * 2 )
```

There is sufficient room for six complete DOS images following the drive descriptions. The first four images are reserved for DOS 3.3, DOS 4.1L, DOS 4.1H, and for DOS 4.3H. The remaining two DOS images are left for User Defined DOS images. Each DOS image contains a 256-byte image mapper that contains the name of the DOS image, its date and time stamp, how the DOS image is partitioned, where each partition is mapped to memory, and a description. Table V.5.7 shows the image mapper and values for DOS 4.3. Each DOS image has room for a 16128-byte image (i.e. 63 256-byte pages). DOS 4.3 is a 10752-byte image because it uses 42 disk sectors. Memory type for a partition is defined as: 0=Main memory, 1=Bank 1 Language Card memory, and 2=Bank 2 Language Card memory.

Address	Variable	Size	Description
0x0800	DOSNAME	24	Name of DOS image (DOS4.3H IMAGE)
0x0818	DOSDATE	6	Date/Time stamp of DOS image (0x482808200101)
0x081E	DOSSIZE	1	Size of DOS image in 256-byte pages (0x2A, up to 0x3F)
0x081F	DOSPRTS	1	Number of image partitions (0x03, up to 0x08)
0x0820	DOSRCMD	1	Value of CMDVAL command in DOS image (0x10)
0x0821	DOSINFO	1	Byte offset to DOS image description (0x48)
0x0822	DOSRADR	2	Address of CMDVAL command in DOS (0xBEEC)
0x0824	DOSSADR	2	Address of SNUM16 value in RWTS IOCB (0xBFE0)
0x0826	DOSINIT	2	Address of DOS initialization entry point (0xBF5E)
0x0828	PARTADR	2	Start address for partition #1 (0xD000)
0x082A	PARTYPE	1	Memory type for partition #1 (0x02)
0x082B	PARTPGS	1	Size of partition #1 in 256-byte pages (0x1A)
0x082C	DOSPRT2	4	Partition #2 parameters (0xD000, 0x01, 0x0E)
0x0830	DOSPRT3	4	Partition #3 parameters (0xBE00, 0x00, 0x02)
0x0834	DOSPRT4	4	Partition #4 parameters
0x0838	DOSPRT5	4	Partition #5 parameters
0x083C	DOSPRT6	4	Partition #6 parameters
0x0840	DOSPRT7	4	Partition #7 parameters
0x0844	DOSPRT8	4	Partition #8 parameters
0x0848	DOSDESC	184	DOS image description (upper ASCII, NULL terminated)

Table V.5.7. CFFA Image Mapper for DOS 4.3

Connecting the CFFA to DOS 4.3 is trivial because DOS 4.3 contains a reserved address location for each slot that contains a peripheral slot card that is a Disk][-like I/O device that has an RWTS interface address. When the CFFA is booted with an installed default DOS, DOS 4.3H for example, Boot Stage 1 is monitored for ROMSECTR to become 0x00 and BOOTPGS to become negative. Unlike DOS 3.3,

Boot Stage 1 in DOS 4.3 reads sectors 0x0F to 0x00 on track 0x00 in descending order into memory from 0xD000 to 0xDD00 and 0xBE00 to 0xBF00 in ascending order. After sector 0x00 is read into memory at 0xBF00, all of DOS 4.3 RWTS is now available to read into memory the remaining pages (i.e. sectors) of DOS 4.3. Normally, a Disk][-like I/O device only boots from drive one of two possible drives (or four in the case of the Rana Interface card) regardless of the diskette's volume number. However, the CFFA must be able to boot from any of its drives and from any of its volumes, so this puts a special burden on monitoring the Boot Stage 1 process.

In addition to the boot variables BOOTADR and BOOTPGS common to all varieties of DOS, and the DOS 4.3 Disk Address table, there is a variable called BCFGNDX that is actually an index to a structure on page 0xBF00. This index points to the BOOTCFG table of variables that is used to initialize the RWTS IOCB by the RWPAGES routine during Boot Stage 2. It is at this crucial time when Boot Stage 1 completes, but before Boot Stage 2 begins, that the BOOTCFG table must be updated with the current CF Drive and Volume that is currently booting. The values for DNUM and VOLEXPT will be utilized by Boot Stage 2 and pushed onto the CFRWTS interface using the RWTS IOCB so that the correct LBA will be calculated from the booting DVTS. Unfortunately, the situation for a booting DOS 3.3 volume is a horrible nightmare for any firmware, and the CFFA firmware is no exception, but certainly not impossible to monitor and to manage correctly.

Boot Stage 1 for DOS 3.3 reads sectors 0x09 to 0x00 on track 0x00 in descending order into memory from 0xBF00 to 0xB600, also in descending order. After sector 0x00 is read into memory at 0xB600, all of DOS 3.3 RWTS is now available to read into memory the remaining pages of DOS 3.3. During Boot Stage 2 DOS 3.3 initializes the RWTS IOCB with DNUM set to 0x01 and VOLEXPT set to 0x00, which allows any volume to boot in disk drive 1. These values must be patched, or overwritten in order for the CF firmware to calculate the correct LBA from the booting DVTS. Once the routine RWPAGES has read in the remaining pages of DOS using the correct Drive and Volume values, the DOS 3.3 code must be patched yet again in order for it to function properly within the CF environment. The prime issue with DOS 3.3 is how DOS 3.3 manages (or mismanages in my opinion) Volume number. In the CF environment Volume number cannot be ascertained from a sector's address field because there are no address fields to read. Therefore, a DOS 3.3 routine such as CATHNDLR that handles the DOS CATALOG command must not presuppose any value for the booting Volume number. Similarly, the SETDFLTS routine must not initialize or change the current value for Volume number so that other DOS 3.3 commands will work properly when the V keyword is not included with a DOS 3.3 command. Furthermore, in order for DOS 3.3 to read into memory any DOS 4.3 file, the filename length must be adjusted down to twenty-four bytes in length. Before any CF volume is initialized with DOS 3.3 all patches like the ones just described probably should be removed. A simple tool can do this, of course, but in order for DOS 3.3 to communicate with the CF firmware and perform volume initialization, its CALLRWTS routine must remain patched. Thus, I believe the better solution is to leave DOS 3.3 patched and totally useable in the CF environment, initialize a CF volume as desired, and overwrite the DOS image on tracks 0x00, 0x01, and 0x02 with whatever "pure" DOS 3.3 image you wish knowing full well that it may not boot or function properly in the CF environment. There may be other equally viable solutions. Table V.5.8 documents all the patches that are applied to DOS 3.3 before and after Boot Stage 2 by the CF firmware.

Referring to Table V.5.8, all variables listed that are in lowercase reside in CF firmware. The uppercase variables reside in DOS 3.3 source code. The first four substitutions are made just after Boot Stage 1 completes. The address for the firmware entry point MODOS3 as shown in Table V.5.1 is used to replace the address for DOSSTRT, or 0x9D84, at 0xB748/0xB749. Once Boot Stage 2 completes, DOS 3.3 will re-enter the CF firmware to install its remaining patches and code replacements. After the patches have been made, the CF firmware simply jumps to the intended DOSSTRT address at this time. I fondly recall meeting many software engineers, particularly those at Sierra Online, who I refer to as "DOS 3.3 Purists." "Thou shalt not modify DOS 3.3!" Only when we were able to demonstrate to Ken Williams that we were able to make DOS 3.3 smarter, faster, and safer did Ken remove the DOS 3.3 Purity Shield. Now, from my current vantage point, I see that DOS 3.3 contained a lot of crappy code based on some very silly ideas, like how volume number was handled, and mishandled, and complimented, and substituted. So, I see nothing wrong with "adjusting" DOS 3.3 to function decently in the CF environment. Hopefully, DOS 4.3 will demonstrate how simple and powerful using volume number can be in the CF environment; that is, using volume number like any other parameter including slot number, drive number, track number, and sector number.

Address	Old	New	Boot Stage 2	Description
0xB707	0x01	drive	before	update for DNUM
0xB7EB	0x00	volume	before	update of VOLEXPT
0xB748	0x84	#modos3	before	replace address of DOSSTRT with
0xB749	0x9D	cfpage	before	MODOS3 at 0xB748/0xB749
0xAA66	VOLVAL	volume	after	update for VOLVAL
0xB7EB	VOLEXPT	volume	after	update of VOLEXPT
0xA0DA	0x66	0x65	after	bypass initialization of VOLVAL
0xA95B	0x02	cfmaxdrv	after	update KWRANGE for DRIVE
0xAD9E	0xF9	0xFE	after	bypass setting VOLNUMBR to 0xFF in CATHNDLR
0xB203	0x1E	0x18	after	compare 24 character filenames
0xB707	drive	0x01	after	restore original value
0xB748	#modos3	0x84	after	restore address of DOSSTRT at
0xB749	cfpage	0x9D	after	0xB748/0xB749

Table V.5.8. DOS 3.3 Patches for CFFA

There are times when desperation leads to utilizing very creative and sneaky programming techniques. To be sure I was desperate in finding enough memory space to include the DOS 4.3 interface into the CFFA. I did not want to exclude the DOS 3.3 or DOS 4.1 interfaces, and I did not want to remove any of the informational text messages when a DOS volume is connected to or detached from the CFFA. I had already faced a similar dilemma for the DOS 4.3 HELP command where I desperately needed a little more memory space. There, I used every scheme in the arsenal and still it was not enough. What saved the day was recursive programming. Recursive programming depends upon solutions to smaller instances of the same problem. In C-language recursive programming is very simple to implement and it is very much like winding up a spring. The spring continues to be "wound" until a solution end-point is reached, and then the spring is allowed to unwind transferring each "next" solution to the "previous" iteration. It was the final weapon to win the battle for more memory in the DOS 4.3 HELP command. For the CFFA firmware, it was the utilization of phrases. Each error message contains three phrases, so the error message data can be highly compacted. Not only was I able to include the DOS 4.3 interface and retain all informational and error message texts (including the new DOS 4.3 text messages), but I succeeded in obtaining an additional twenty-seven bytes that I used for managing a new DOS image mapper. Using phrases and recursive programming in this instance proved to be the right solution.

To assemble the CFFA Firmware source code, place the DOS 4.3 Tools volume DOS4.3.Tools in disk drive 1, boot, and start *Lisa80*. Enter the SE command-line command to select the *SETUP80* utility in order to verify or set the Start of Source Code to 0x4000 and the Start of Symbol List to 0x7800. Place the CFFA Firmware volume CFFA.Firmware in disk drive 2, load the CFFA.L file into memory, and start the assembler by entering either the A or the Z command-line command. If a printed version of the screen output is desired simply preface the A or the Z command with the P1 command-line command. Both binary images will be saved to the CFFA Firmware volume as CFFA_SLOT_BUILD38 and CFFA_ROM_BUILD38. The utility *COPY_CFFA* can be used to copy these two binary files to the CFFA Programs volume CFFA.Programs. Simply follow the directions on the screen and press any key to begin the copy.

The CFFA Tools volume CFFA.Tools contains the utility *DOS_TOOLS* to copy and process the DOS binary file DOS3.3 on the DOS.3.3.Source volume, copy and process the DOS binary file DOS4.1.46L on the DOS.4.1.Image volume, copy and process the DOS binary file DOS4.1.46H on the DOS.4.1.Image volume, and copy and process the DOS binary file DOS4.3H on the DOS.4.3.Image volume. From the DOS3.3 binary file, *DOS_TOOLS* creates the binary file DOS3.3 IMAGE. From the DOS4.1L binary file, *DOS_TOOLS* creates the binary file DOS4.1L IMAGE. From the DOS4.1H binary file, *DOS_TOOLS* creates the binary file DOS4.1H IMAGE. From the DOS4.3H binary file, *DOS_TOOLS* creates the binary file DOS4.3H IMAGE. The utility *INSTALL33* can install DOS3.3 or DOS3.3 IMAGE. The utility *INSTALL41L* can install DOS4.1L or DOS4.1L IMAGE. The utility *INSTALL41H* can install DOS4.1H or DOS4.1H IMAGE. The utility *INSTALL43* can install DOS4.3H or DOS4.3H IMAGE.

To assemble the CFFA Tools source code with *Lisa* already running, place the CFFA Tools volume CFFA.Tools in disk drive 2. Load each *Lisa* file into memory, and start the assembler using either the A or the Z command-line command. If a printed version of the screen output is desired simply preface the A or the Z command with the P1 command-line command. The complete binary image for each *Lisa* file will be saved to the CFFA Tools volume. The utility *COPY_TOOLS* can be used to copy all the utilities and DOS images from the CFFA Tools volume CFFA.Tools to the CFFA Programs volume CFFA.Programs. Simply follow the directions on the screen and press any key to begin the copy.

Along with the CFFA Firmware object code files and the CFFA Tools utilities and DOS images, the CFFA Programs volume CFFA.Programs contains the executable object code for *VOLMGR*, *BOOTVOL*, and *BOOTDOS*. The next section discusses these programs in great detail. It is the CFFA.Programs volume that I transfer from my Macintosh to a diskette in an Apple //e Disk][drive using A2V2 on the Macintosh and *ADT2* on the Apple //e. The CFFA card is only resident in the Apple //e, not in the Macintosh. Now, *VOLMGR* can easily install the new CFFA firmware image and any or all of the four DOS images. There is sufficient disk space remaining on the CFFA.Programs volume for two additional DOS images. Is there anyone interested in adding another DOS image to the CFFA? I sure hope so. You have no idea how exciting it is to see "your baby" run!

6. Volume Manager (VOLMGR)

The Volume Manager (*VOLMGR*) is a utility I developed in order to manage the CFFA firmware interface, manage the CFFA CompactFlash card utilization and identity, manage the CF Drives, manage the CF Volumes of a CF Drive, and manage the CF User DOS Images. The following eight figures, Figures V.6.1 to V.6.8, show a few of the primary menu screens from *VOLMGR* as well as an example display of the Device Identity contents of a CompactFlash card. Additionally, the utility *BOOTDOS* can be used to boot any of the six (only four are currently defined) DOS images on the CF card and the utility *BOOTVOL* can be used to boot any bootable volume on any of the CF volumes and drives. *VOLMGR* will detect a previously unmodified CFFA card by inspecting the first eight firmware bytes known as the signature bytes, and continue processing. This will allow the user to save the current CFFA firmware to a file and install the new CFFA firmware to the CFFA card. After *VOLMGR* installs the new CFFA firmware these signature bytes will be changed to those listed for the CFFA card in Table II.7.2.

Boot Stage 1 and Boot Stage 2 cannot be monitored when loading any of the six selectable DOS images. Therefore, the DOS image must be modified in two locations before exiting the CFFA by means of the DOS initialization address. The CFFA Image Mapper shown in Table V.5.7 contains the value of the CMDVAL command, its address, and the address to modify the SNUM16 value in the RWTS IOCB. The slot*16 value of the CFFA is simply copied to this address. This is a significant modification to the DOS 4.1 CFFA Image Mapper in order to eliminate much of the *DOS_TOOLS* processing. Any valid DOS command can be used for the CMDVAL command value, though I have found the DOS CLOSE command (i.e. 0x10) value to be quite suitable.

```
        CFFA Volume Manager

        DOS 4.3, Build 08

     Copyright (c) 2020 January 1

                by

     Walland Philip Vrbancic Jr


    Use this CompactFlash For Apple
      installer and the accompanying
    software programs at your own risk.

   You are responsible for any damage or
   loss of productivity this installer or
     the accompanying software may cause.

        If you agree to these terms
       press any key to continue, or
     press ESC to exit this program now.
```

Figure V.6.1. VOLMGR Product Warning Screen

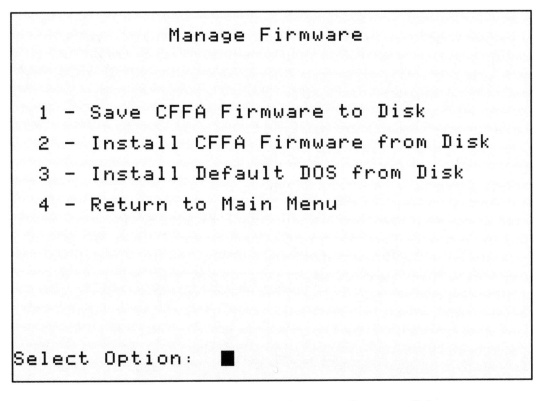

```
        CFFA Volume Manager Main Menu


   1 - Manage Firmware

   2 - Manage CompactFlash

   3 - Manage Drives

   4 - Manage Volumes

   5 - Manage User DOS Images

   6 - Exit Volume Manager



Select Option:  ■
```

Figure V.6.2. VOLMGR Main Menu

```
             Manage Firmware



   1 - Save CFFA Firmware to Disk

   2 - Install CFFA Firmware from Disk

   3 - Install Default DOS from Disk

   4 - Return to Main Menu






Select Option:  ■
```

Figure V.6.3. VOLMGR Manage Firmware Menu

```
              Manage CompactFlash


    1 - Display CF Memory Utilization
    2 - Display Device Identity Contents
    3 - Save Device Identity to Disk
    4 - Save Selected LBA to Disk
    5 - Restore Selected LBA from Disk
    6 - Clear Selected LBA Range
    7 - Return to Main Menu


Select Option:   ■
```

Figure V.6.4. VOLMGR Manage CompactFlash Menu

```
         Display Device Identity Contents


        Cylinders - 0007C2
            Heads - 000010
   Sectors/Track - 00003F
     Maximum LBA - 1E8BE0
   Serial Number - 020805J2806R5550
         Firmware - HDX 4.03
            Model - SanDisk SDCFB-1024



Status:  Okay, press any key
```

Figure V.6.5. VOLMGR Device Identity Contents

```
                        Manage Drives



        1 - List All Drives
        2 - Display Drive Information
        3 - Change Drive Information
        4 - Return to Main Menu






Select Option:   ■
```

Figure V.6.6. VOLMGR Manage Drives Menu

```
                        Manage Volumes



        1 - Display Initialized Volumes on a
            Drive
        2 - Display Volume VTOC Information
        3 - Display Sector Bitmap Information
        4 - Initialize a CF Volume
        5 - Boot a CF Volume
        6 - Return to Main Menu



Select Option:   ■
```

Figure V.6.7. VOLMGR Manage Volumes Menu

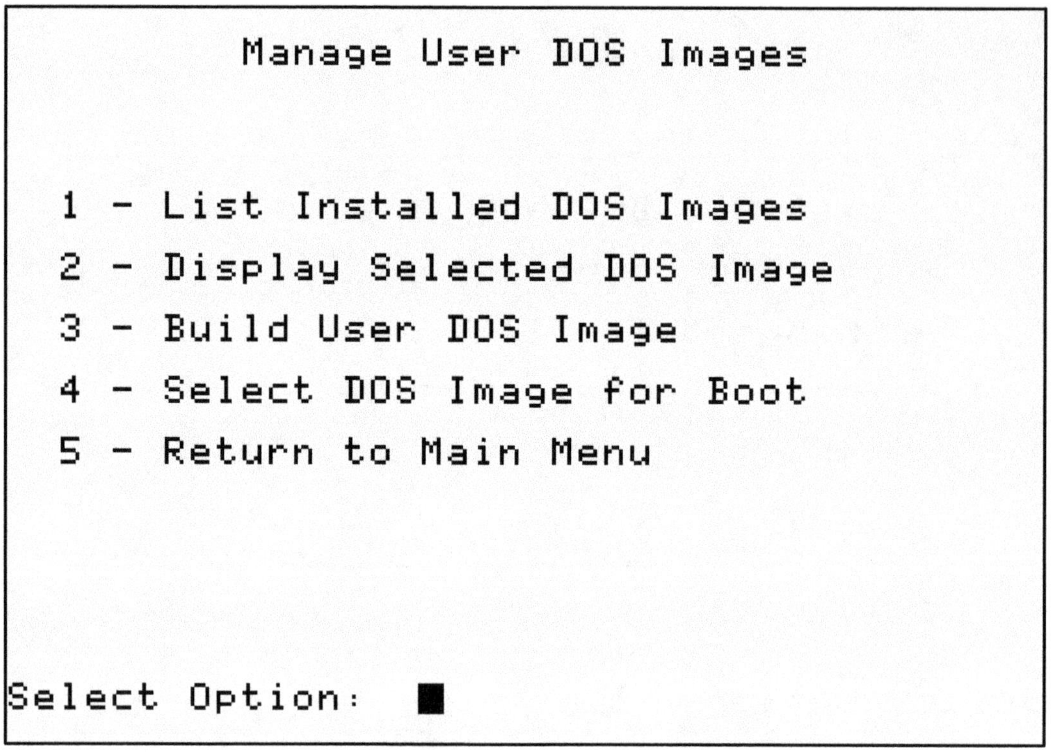

```
        Manage User DOS Images


    1 - List Installed DOS Images
    2 - Display Selected DOS Image
    3 - Build User DOS Image
    4 - Select DOS Image for Boot
    5 - Return to Main Menu




Select Option:  ■
```

Figure V.6.8. VOLMGR Manage User DOS Images Menu

To assemble the *VOLMGR* source code, place the DOS 4.3 Tools volume `DOS4.3.Tools` in disk drive 1, boot, and start *Lisa80*. Enter the `SE` command-line command to select the *SETUP80* utility in order to verify or set the `Start of Source Code` to `0x4000` and the `Start of Symbol List` to `0x7800`. Place the VOLMGR Source volume `VOLMGR.Source` in disk drive 2, load the `VOLMGR.L` file into memory, and start the assembler by entering either the `A` or the `Z` command-line command. If a printed version of the screen output is desired simply preface the `A` or the `Z` command with the `P1` command-line command. Five object code files will be created on the VOLMGR Source volume named `SEG01` to `SEG05`. The five object code files can be combined in memory sequentially starting at `0x0900` using the `ctrl-P` command. The complete binary image can be saved to the VOLMGR Source volume or to any other volume as `VOLMGR`.

To assemble the *BOOTVOL* and the *BOOTDOS* source code with *Lisa* already running, load each *Lisa* file into memory, and start the assembler using either the `A` or the `Z` command-line command. If a printed version of the screen output is desired simply preface the `A` or the `Z` command with the `P1` command-line command. The complete binary image for each *Lisa* file will be saved to the VOLMGR Source volume. The utility *COPY_VOLMGR* can be used to copy *VOLMGR*, *BOOTVOL*, and *BOOTDOS* from the VOLMGR Source volume to the CFFA Programs volume `CFFA.Programs`. Simply follow the directions on the screen and press any key to begin the copy.

7. File Developer (FID)

File Developer (*FID*) was an original Apple][assembly language utility found on the DOS 3.3 System Master diskette I received with my Apple][+. I suspect it was the most widely used DOS utility of all time. Instead of writing my own file management utility for DOS 4.3 having Volume number and Phase Number included as input parameters, I decided to source *FID* and add what I needed to that software. Anytime I start tearing into someone else's software I find it to be a real, sometimes rare educational experience. *FID* utilizes the RWTS and the File Manager interfaces as noted elsewhere in this book, which gave me a good insight in how the "Apple Experts" made use of those interfaces. I received the most grief from *FID*'s hardcoded insistence that track 0x00 could never be used for data storage, and that it was a track used only for booting DOS. There were only a few locations in the *FID* software where I had to insert the parameter TRKZERO (i.e. 0x40) so that *FID* would accommodate track 0x00 properly, as a data track, as it is accommodated properly in DOS 4.3.

```
************************************************
*            Apple ][ File Developer          *
*       Version N with DOS 4.3, Build 08      *
*                                             *
*    Copyright 1979 Apple Computer Inc.       *
************************************************



    Choose One of the Following Options

        <1>    Copy Files
        <2>    Catalog
        <3>    Space on Disk
        <4>    Unlock Files
        <5>    Lock Files
        <6>    Delete Files
        <7>    Reset Slot, Drive, Volume
        <8>    Verify Files
        <9>    Undelete Files
        <Q>    Quit

Which Option would you like:    ※
```

Figure V.7.1. FID Main Menu

I found that the most essential task was to implant the use of Volume number because I wanted *FID* to work with the CFFA hardware. This CFFA, using my Disk][emulation firmware, can access up to 81 Drives (for an 8 GB CompactFlash card), where each drive can support 256 Volumes. Actually, I derived this dependency on Volume number from the Sider firmware that utilized Volume number in order to calculate the sector number for the start of each DOS 3.3 volume on its 10 MB hard drive. And, of course, I wanted *FID* to include my new DOS URM command in order to undelete files because that capability exists in DOS 4.3 by means of the File Manager. *FID* also makes use of the Catalog command's SUBCODE to display the current list of files on a volume with or without listing the deleted files as well. *FID* had to use the free sector bitmap in the VTOC properly, as it is used properly in DOS 4.3, and not how it is used improperly in DOS 3.3. Finally, *FID* had to include the Phase number for the Source and Target volumes in order to share files between those two volume structural formats. Phase number is like all the other parameters used in either the RWTS IOCB or in the File Manager Context Block. The main menu for *FID* that is modified for DOS 4.3 is shown in Figure V.7.1.

Because *FID* uses the File Manager to copy files from one volume to another, there are certain limitations that one needs to be aware of. Whatever sectors that are associated with a file that are specified in a file's TSL are copied from the source volume to the destination volume. The File Manager has no idea whether all or some of those sectors are actually being used by that file. For example, if a Binary file is created with the DOS "BSAVE TEST1,A$1000,L$6000" command, a file having ninety-eight sectors will be created: there will be one sector for the TSL sector and ninety-seven track-secctor entries specified in the TSL sector for the data sectors. Then, if the DOS "BSAVE TEST1,A$1000,L$1000" command is issued next, the DOS Catalog will still show ninety-eight sectors used for TEST1. *FID* will blindly copy all ninety-seven data sectors even though only the first seventeen data sectors now contain valid data. This same situation can occur with Applesoft files as well. If the original Applesoft file utilizes forty-one sectors, then edited to nearly half its size and saved, the Applesoft file will continue to utilize forty-one sectors and not, say, twenty-five sectors unless the file is saved under a new name. There is no way for *FID* to know whether a file uses all or some of the sectors specified in its TSL. If disk space is a premium then *FID* should not be used to copy files; the files should be copied manually or by another utility.

Why does DOS (any DOS for that matter) potentially waste valuable disk space when one is saving less data to a file that already exists in the volume Catalog? There are probably many reasons, some of which are valid and some are merely cosmetic. I believe the most valid reason is safety. In order to guarantee that a file only uses the disk space it truly requires when that file already exists in the volume Catalog would be to first delete the existing file, create a new file with the same name, and finally save the requested data to that new file. But would this procedure be entirely safe? What if something causes an error after the file was deleted but before the new file was created, or before the requested data could be saved? Is having a DOS URM command enough insurance if such a situation like this should ever occur? Perhaps the requested data should be saved to a XXTEMPXX file first, then the original file could be safely deleted before the XXTEMPXX file is renamed? There may not be enough disk space to have two copies of the file, or there may not be enough room in the volume Catalog for an additional file entry. This procedure would also rearrange the order of files in the volume Catalog which may not be appealing to some. I believe the best alternative is to save the requested data to an existing file using that file's TSL resources, and if there are more entries in the TSL than needed, those entries should be marked as unused (zeroed out), and the sectors returned to the volume's VTOC bitmap. Of course, I would only use this algorithm for the DOS SAVE, BSAVE, LSAVE, and TSAVE commands. It would be a moderately interesting exercise to implement this algorithm, and certainly be the cause for the release of yet another DOS 4.3 build. At this moment there is not enough code space left in DOS 4.3 to even consider implementing such an algorithm.

DOS 4.3 does provide the use of the B keyword to implement the "File Delete/File Save" strategy for the DOS SAVE, BSAVE, LSAVE, and TSAVE commands if desired. I have found this strategy to be quite useful and it has not caused me any concerns for the safety of my files: I tend to back up my work regularly, regardless. However, I believe I would be more inclined to suggest the creation of a simple utility devoted to the sole task of expunging unused TSL entries from a TSL sector, and then return those sectors to the volume's VTOC bitmap. Applesoft and Binary files would be the easiest to process since the size (in bytes) of those files is found at the head of its data on disk. Text files would be problematic to process, particularly if they are random-access Data files. Sequential Text files would have to be read completely in order to locate its terminating NULL character before any extra TSL entries could be safely expunged. There is no way to identify whether a Text file is a random-access Data file or a sequential Text file, though one could compile a list of possible filters. I have already stated that bytes 0x08/0x09 or 0x09/0x0A as shown in Figure I.7.2 could have been utilized for the value of the L keyword instead of requiring the L keyword to OPEN a random-access Data file. That would have definitely distinguished a random-access Data file from a sequential Text file.

For the time being *FID* is perhaps the easiest utility to use in order to copy a set of files from one volume to another volume. *FID* is certainly not perfect in that it cannot differentiate between valid data sectors and bogus data sectors. Because *FID* can cross Volume and Phase barriers makes it exceedingly powerful in the DOS 4.3 environment. It would indeed be an interesting challenge to add additional logic to *FID*, selectable of course, that would verify TSL utilization for Applesoft and Binary files at a minimum.

To assemble the *FID* source code, place the DOS 4.3 Tools volume DOS.4.3.Tools in disk drive 1, boot, and start *Lisa80*. Enter the SE command-line command to select the *SETUP80* utility in order to verify or set the Start of Source Code to 0x4000 and the Start of Symbol List to 0x7800. Place the FID Source volume FID.Source in disk drive 2, load the FID.L file into memory, and start the assembler by entering either the A or the Z command-line command. If a printed version of the screen output is desired simply preface the A or the Z command with the P1 command-line command. The complete binary image will be saved to the FID Source volume as FID.

8. Lazer's Interactive Symbolic Assembler (Lisa)

I have to say that I have spent a considerable amount of time and energy adjusting and fine tuning Lazer's Interactive Symbolic Assembler (*Lisa*) to my every whim and need. It truly has been a joy! First and foremost, my task was to modify *Lisa* to use the DOS 4.3 interfaces in order for *Lisa* to obtain the various parameters it requires for some of its special functions. Next, I wanted to eliminate the need for *Lisa* to save the first file of a multiple-file program as `.TEMP` before it completes its Pass 1 processing. That task required adding a new directive. I wanted the sort algorithm that is used to sort the Symbol List to be part of *Lisa*, and an option to print a selected Symbol List(s). I wanted to add an additional new directive to define the text for the Symbol List title. I wanted `LED` (Lisa EDitor) to be an integral part of *Lisa* and always be included whenever *Lisa* was activated. I wanted an easier way to enter a DOS `PR#` and a `ctrl-D` command. I wanted an additional command-line command besides `A` to assemble source code that forces the `PRNTFLAG` to be `OFF` as if the `NLS` directive was the first directive in the source code. I wanted *Lisa* to obtain the date and time from DOS 4.3. I wanted to move *Lisa* to Auxiliary memory. I wanted to fix some of the quirkiness *Lisa* sometimes displays. And, I wanted *Lisa* to display and edit source code in 80-column mode. I also found and fixed a few more coding errors in *Lisa*. Ah, have I made *Lisa* absolutely perfect? Maybe. I think so!

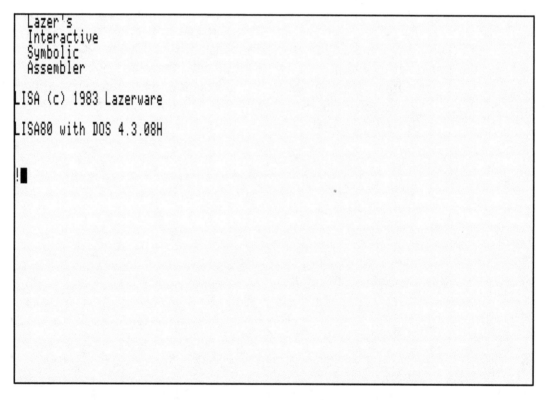

Figure V.8.1. Lisa80 Startup Screen

Unlike *Big Mac*, *Lisa* resides in both banks of the Language Card memory, and `LED`, written by Bob Rosen of RSQ Software Products © 1983, now occupies the address space from `0xB934` to `0xBCD7`. *Lisa* only requires one DOS buffer but it no longer changes the number of DOS buffers in DOS 4.3.

The momentous task of sourcing *Lisa* took many, many hours, not just for the conversion of the assembly language object code to source code, but the laborious task of understanding the idiosyncrasies of how Randall Hyde designs and writes software. The optimal desire is to understand the newly generated source code so that 1) it assembles and perfectly matches the original, and 2) it can be modified and all structures and tables and their lengths and sizes will remain unaffected. Quite frequently an author may pass the address of a structure or a data table in a register or two, or as an index into a table of other addresses or values, and initially the source code appears like that structure or those values are hardcoded. What needs to be done is to assign a variable name to the structure or data table so that if the structure or table shifts up or down in memory, the registers will always contain the variable's correct address location. It is necessary to find all such occurrences in order to reach that optimal state of perfectly sourced code. *Sourceror* can only do so much magic! Figure V.8.1 shows the *Lisa* startup screen showing that *Lisa80* is running under DOS 4.3 in 80-column display mode. Figure V.8.2 shows the first screen of the *Lisa80* source code in 80-column display mode.

```
 1          ttl "LISA80 Source Code, LISA.L"
 2          src "LISA.L"
 3  ;
 4  ;
 5  ; LISA.L
 6  ;
 7  ;
 8  ; LISA80 Source Code
 9  ;
10  ; 2020 January 1
11  ;
12  ;
13  ; DOS 4.3, Build 08
14  ;
15  ; 2020 January 1
16  ;
17  ;
18  ; Start of Source Code:   0x4000
19  ; Start of Symbol List:   0x7800
20  ;
21  ;
22  ; Copyright (c) 2020 January 1 by
```

Figure V.8.2. Lisa80 Source Code List Screen

In order to make *Lisa* fully DOS 4.3 compliant required me to relocate *Lisa* to Auxiliary memory. Why? Because DOS 4.3 is resident in Language Card memory and *Lisa* is resident in Language Card memory as well. Both cannot reside in the same Language Card Memory concurrently. However, Auxiliary memory also contains its own Language Card memory. It seemed natural to relocate *Lisa* to Auxiliary memory. It was definitely a challenge to understand how to master Auxiliary memory in terms of its operation and what it could provide and what it could not provide in resources. Certainly, to assist in its operation would be to decide which side of memory would handle input data (i.e.

229

keyboard and disk) and which side of memory would handle output data (i.e. screen and disk). Once I established the operating rules it became very clear how to build the interface between Main memory and Auxiliary memory specifically for *Lisa*. Since DOS 4.3 occupied Language Card memory in Main memory it was quite logical to utilize Main memory for the input and the output of all disk data. It was totally unnecessary to maintain two page-zeros particularly for the variables CH, CV, BASL, BASH, and the other text window variables. Furthermore, DOS 4.3 had to be in complete control of all input and output data for a volume. Thus, all keyboard and screen data are handled within Auxiliary memory.

Lisa contains its own version of the Monitor. Previously, this Monitor mostly resembled the monitor found in the Apple][+. In order to prepare *Lisa* to make use of the Apple //e 80-column display, the Apple //e Monitor needed to be utilized, whatever version that Monitor was. Unfortunately, Mr. Hyde embedded a few routines within his Monitor that has no place in the Apple //e Monitor. And, so, back to the drawing board in order to squeeze out even more code space within *Lisa* to provide a place for those displaced routines. In order for *Lisa* to utilize any of the various iterations of the Apple //e Monitor, *Lisa* simply copies the ROM Monitor for its RAM Monitor. The interface between Main memory and Auxiliary memory is injected primarily at the COUT (i.e. 0xFDED) and RDKEY2 (i.e. 0xFD18) routines in *Lisa's* RAM Monitor. A small handler is needed for the HOOKDOS, DOSWARM, WRMSTRT, PRTERROR, and READCLK vectors. DOS errors have to be handled uniquely by the interface in order to re-enter *Lisa* appropriately. Finally, the state of the Language Card bank currently in focus has to be captured in order to reconfigure Auxiliary memory for all subroutines returning from Main memory. Because *Lisa* utilizes both Language Card banks, it is difficult to know which bank is in focus at any given moment during *Lisa* processing. However, the greater challenge was to modify *Lisa's* source code editing capabilities while displaying source code in the Apple //e 80-column mode.

```
SETSCRN    sta STR80ON        ; enable PAGE Soft Switches
           sta PAGE1ON        ; assume Main memory
           lda OURCH          ; get character index (ROM)
           sta CH             ; save index to CH
           lsr                ; shift LSB into carry flag
           tay                ; copy |OURCH/2| to Y-reg
           bcs >1             ; branch if odd (Main memory)
           sta PAGE2ON        ; enable Auxiliary memory
^1         rts                ; return to caller
```

Figure V.8.3. Lisa80 SETSCRN Routine

The page-zero variable CV for screen line number is used to calculate the BASL/BASH pointer. The page-zero variable CH for line character index is used to address an ASCII character on the screen. As easy as it is to write to the screen, reading from the screen is just as easy. Mr. Hyde utilized these variables in his source code line editing routines. The Apple //e requires twice the size for the text buffer in order to display 80-column text. The additional buffer comes from Auxiliary memory such that every other odd screen character comes from Main memory and every other even screen character comes from Auxiliary memory. The variables OURCH (0x057B) and OURCV (0x05FB) are used instead for character index and line number, respectively. In order to provide the same line editing capabilities for the 80-column display mode it is necessary to read and write screen characters using a different algorithm. The `SETSCRN` routine shown in Figure V.8.3 demonstrates one component of this complicated algorithm. The `PAGE` Soft Switches only function in 80-column mode when 80-Column Store, or `STR80ON` (`0xC001`) is enabled as shown in that figure. The `READSCRN` routine shown in Figure V.8.4 utilizes `SETSCRN`. The final routine `SAVESCRN` shown in Figure V.8.5 also utilizes `SETSCRN` to save the character of interest to the screen.

```
READSRN1    sty OURCH          ; save character index
READSCRN    jsr SETSCRN        ; select screen PAGE
            lda (BASL),Y       ; read the screen character
            ldy CH             ; get original index from CH
            rts                ; return to caller
```

Figure V.8.4. Lisa80 READSCRN Routine

```
SAVESRN1    sty OURCH          ; save character index
SAVESCRN    pha                ; save character on stack
            jsr SETSCRN        ; select screen PAGE
            pla                ; retrieve character
            sta (BASL),Y       ; write the screen character
            ldy CH             ; get index from CH
            rts                ; return to caller
```

Figure V.8.5. Lisa80 SAVESCRN Routine

There are certainly other routines needed to handle all of the `ctrl`-key functions that *Lisa* provides, but the above code samples are the most basic routines. Because the 80-column ROM routines already support the left and right arrow keys, I chose to replace the Cursor Left (`ctrl-J`) and the Cursor Right (`ctrl-K`) options with the `Go To Start of Line` (`ctrl-C`) and `Go To End of Line` (`ctrl-D`) options. (I liked these two cursor movement routines so much that I added them to the 40-column version of Auxiliary memory *Lisa*.) The other configuration parameters in *Lisa* may be modified using the *SETUP80* utility. *SETUP80* may be invoked simply by typing the `SE` command on the *Lisa80* command line. The *SETUP80* utility is activated from the Lisa Image volume `LISA80.Image` in disk drive 1. Figure V.8.6 shows the main `L.I.S.A. SETUP80 Utility` screen and Figure V.8.7 shows the `Screen Editing Definitions` screen.

```
       L.I.S.A. SETUP80 Utility


Current values are:

1) Start of Source Code    - 0x4000
2) Start of Symbol List    - 0x7800
3) Start of Page 2 Source  - 0x7800
4) Start of Page 2 Symbols - 0x9800
5) End of Symbol List      - 0xB7C0

6) Number of Lines/Page    - 68
7) Print Title on Page     - YES
8) Lower Case Mnemonics    - YES

9) Screen Editing Definitions

Q) Quit

Enter option:  █
```

Figure V.8.6. Lisa80 SETUP80 Utility

```
        Screen Editing Definitions

A) Cursor up             ^O, 0x0F
B) Cursor down           ^L, 0x0C
C) Go to end of line     ^D, 0x04
D) Go to start of line   ^C, 0x03
E) Insert character      ^I, 0x09
F) Delect character      ^R, 0x12
G) Home and Clear        ^Q, 0x11
H) Clear to end of line  ^E, 0x05
I) Clear to end of screen ^F, 0x06
J) Delete current line   ^N, 0x0E
K) Insert a line         ^V, 0x16
L) Skip blanks character ^S, 0x13
M) Quit insert mode      ^A, 0x01

Enter Q to leave.

Enter option:  █
```

Figure V.8.7. Lisa Screen Editing Definitions

Having DOS in Language Card memory provides substantially more memory for object code, source code, and the symbol list. The judicious selection of memory locations and sizes for object code, source code, and the symbol list will ensure a successful assembly no matter how large or how complex a program or a set of program modules are. The values shown in Figure V.8.6 provide 56 pages for object code (`0x0800` to `0x3FFF`), 56 pages for source code for a single program or one module of a complex program (`0x4000` to `0x77FF`), and nearly 64 pages for the symbol list (`0x7800` to `0xB7CF`). Each symbol requires ten bytes, eight for the symbol name and two for the value of the symbol. This symbol list allocation will provide room for about 1600 symbols. *Lisa80* uses `0x1EF0` bytes for its symbol list of 792 symbols. On the other hand, DOS 4.3 uses `0x33F4` bytes for its symbol list of 1330 symbols. This information is found just before the symbol list is printed when the A command is used on the *Lisa* command line. These setup values are my recommended settings and they should be appropriate for nearly every program instance. But, of course, there are situations where a program or a program module may exceed 56 pages, in other words, a file that is 57 sectors in size having one `TSL`.

I give full credit to Robert Heitman who I met at Sierra On-Line for the `USR` directive routines and the `ctrl-P` routine contained in *Lisa* and *Lisa80*. Heitman's original source code modules were called `LOADER.S` and `LINKER.S`, respectively. I may have adjusted them slightly for my own particular needs, but essentially the `USR` functionalities are Heitman's. The `USR` directive has a number of important uses depending on how it is utilized in the source code and which arguments are used with the directive. Its syntax is shown in Table V.8.1. The combination of

$$\text{ORG } \$\$/\text{OBJ } \$\$/\text{USR}/\text{<some code>}/\text{USR <filename>}$$

is a very powerful set of directives.

Command	Context	Description
USR	after OBJ $$	uses OBJ address to save start address for BSAVE
USR FN	at end of code	will BSAVE current code to filename; follow with another USR
USR .FN	to BLOAD file	will BLOAD the filename to the current object code pointer

Table V.8.1. Lisa USR Command

The first use of the USR directive alone, at the top of a program after the ORG and OBJ directives, saves the current value of the object code pointer set by the "OBJ $$" directive, where $$ is some hexadecimal address. After some source code has been assembled, the generated object code can be saved to a file using the "USR FN" directive, where FN is some filename. USR FN uses the address value saved by the first USR, calculates the length of the code segment knowing the current memory location in the object code pointer, and constructs a DOS BSAVE command. The "USR .FN" (that is, 'period' + FN) directive is useful in order to read a Binary file into memory at the current memory location in the object code pointer. Once the Binary file is in memory, the object code pointer needs to be incremented using the DFS directive knowing the size of the included file. I use the USR .FN directive in order to BLOAD into memory every object file that is to be contained in an EPROM image.

Source code for programs such as *Big Mac* or *Lisa* or DOS 4.3 cannot possibly fit in the Apple][memory along with its generated object code, its symbol list, DOS, and the assembler. Large or complex software programs need to be segmented into manageable sizes and their assembled outputs saved to separate object files that will be ultimately linked to form the complete executable program. *Lisa*, DOS, and some program source code must reside concurrently in memory and still have room for its generated object code and its complete symbol list at a minimum. It is amazing what can be accomplished in such a small amount of memory as that found in the Apple computer when judicious values are chosen for *Lisa's* memory configuration.

The source code files that comprise DOS 3.3 are shown in Figure V.8.8. Several source files are processed before their collective object code is saved to a binary file. The convention used to name these object code files is to begin the filename with a `SEG` prefix and end the filename with a two digit number suffix generally beginning with `01`. The reason will become apparent shortly. It makes no difference how many `SEG` files are created; remembering, of course, that each file created also requires an additional disk sector for its `TSL`. In the case of DOS 3.3 there are only seven volume sectors remaining, so there is little volume space left to make any significant changes to this source code. When all `SEG` files are sequentially read into memory the entire image for DOS 3.3 will be created. I have the convention, if not the habit, to begin the load of an object code file at address `0x1000`. Loading the first `SEG` file is easy, as in "BLOAD SEG01,A$1000". To what address is `SEG02` next loaded? If the R keyword is used with the `BLOAD` command, the length of `SEG01` will be given, and one can simply calculate the load address for `SEG02`: "BLOAD SEG02" at "0x1000 + length of SEG01" and so forth. There is an easier method built into *Lisa*: a `ctrl-P` user function that will load a range of sequentially numbered `SEG` files. Thank you, Bob Heitman! *Lisa* provides software hooks to the two `0xDF00` pages where a user can add any routine(s) of their choosing. The `USR` directive mentioned earlier is found at `0xDF00` when Bank 2 is selected using "BIT 0xC080". The `ctrl-P` user function is also found at `0xDF00` when Bank 1 is selected using "BIT 0xC088".

The `ctrl-P` function allows the user to enter the number of segments to be loaded into memory, the segment start number, the object code start address, and optionally the filename to save the composite image comprised of all the object code segments. If the filename is not entered, the length of the image and its final memory address are displayed. Figure V.8.9 shows all the `SEG` files that are created when the *EOS* source code is assembled. Those `SEG` files need to be linked into two `0x8000` byte files that will be used to program a 27512 EPROM. In order to do that most efficiently, `SEG` files 1 to 4 are linked into one file and `SEG` files 5 to 8 are linked into the second file. The `ctrl-P` user function is the perfect tool to perform this linking task.

Figure V.8.10 shows how `SEG` files 1 to 4 are linked into the first *EOS* image, `EOS1`, and Figure V.8.11 shows how `SEG` files 5 to 8 are linked into the second *EOS* image, `EOS2`. Now, the two binary image files `EOS1` and `EOS2` are ready to be programmed into an erased 27512 EPROM where `EOS1` is programmed in the first half and `EOS2` is programmed in the second half of the EPROM. In fact, the utility *BURNER* is conveniently located on the same volume as these two image files. This makes the process of preparing and programming an EPROM very simple, very reliable, and very accurate.

```
CATALOG

S=6 D=01 V=000 F=0007 11/13/18 11:53:40

  L 005 DOS3.3.L        11/13/18 11:51:21
  L 037 INCL.L          11/13/18 11:51:21
  L 017 DISK.L          11/13/18 11:51:22
  L 008 BUFR.L          11/13/18 11:51:22
  L 054 CMD1.L          11/13/18 11:51:22
  L 045 CMD2.L          11/13/18 11:51:22
  L 040 CMD3.L          11/13/18 11:51:22
  L 040 CMD4.L          11/13/18 11:51:23
  L 068 MNGR1.L         11/13/18 11:51:23
  L 072 MNGR2.L         11/13/18 11:51:23
  L 069 RWTS.L          11/13/18 11:51:23
  B 015 SEG01           11/13/18 11:52:33
  B 015 SEG02           11/13/18 11:52:33
  B 010 SEG03           11/13/18 11:52:33
  B 037 DOS3.3          11/13/18 11:52:52
  L 010 COPY3.3.L       12/17/18 17:00:40
  B 003 COPY3.3         12/17/18 17:00:42

!█
```

Figure V.8.8. DOS 3.3 Source Code Volume

```
!/LSR

LSR

M=4308H P=04 T=EOS 512 Image Files

B=4308H data L=0x3032 01/01/20 08:28:48

S=6 D=02 V=000 F=0012 01/01/20 08:28:48

  001 0x12,0x0F BURNER
  002 0x13,0x0F EOS1
  003 0x1C,0x0F EOS2
  004 0x00,0x0F SEG01
  005 0x10,0x06 SEG02
  006 0x0C,0x0F SEG03
  007 0x08,0x0F SEG04
  008 0x07,0x0F SEG05
  009 0x04,0x0F SEG06
  010 0x1B,0x01 SEG07
  011 0x08,0x07 SEG08

!█
```

Figure V.8.9. EOS Image Segment Files

```
!
 Segments = #4
First Seg = #1
  Address = $1000
BLOAD SEG01,A$1000
BLOAD SEG02,A$3000
BLOAD SEG03,A$5A00
BLOAD SEG04,A$8A00

Load end = $9000
Save file = EOS1
BSAVE EOS1,A$1000,L$8000
!
```

Figure V.8.10. EOS1 Image Creation

```
!
 Segments = #4
First Seg = #5
  Address = $1000
BLOAD SEG05,A$1000
BLOAD SEG06,A$39B5
BLOAD SEG07,A$68F6
BLOAD SEG08,A$8105

Load end = $9000
Save file = EOS2
BSAVE EOS2,A$1000,L$8000
!
```

Figure V.8.11. EOS2 Image Creation

Lisa makes three passes through all source code files as its data input in order to create object code as its data output. The first pass can be terminated using the `ENZ` directive, or "ENd of page-Zero" parameter definitions. Pass 2 and Pass 3 must process all source code files. In order to return to the first, or initial source code file when an `ICL`, or "InCLude filename", directive is encountered, *Lisa* has always saved the initial source code file as an additional file named `.TEMP`. In this way processing can begin with a known first file for the next pass. Certainly, this method is the easiest to implement but comes with an unfortunate price: it wastes some valuable disk space by duplicating the initial file. In the example above for the volume containing the DOS 3.3 source code, Figure V.8.8, there is little disk space available for a sizeable `.TEMP` file having the same contents as the initial source code file, or `DOS3.3.L` in this example.

Lisa had a few unused opcodes available, so I added the `SRC` directive that requires a filename in parenthesis as shown in Figure V.8.2. The complete syntax is `SRC "<filename>"`. I gave `LED` some additional memory at its end, where I moved the `.TEMP` filename, and that is where the `SRC` directive copies its filename. Naturally, if the `SRC` directive is not used and there is at least one use of the `ICL` directive, *Lisa* will create a `.TEMP` file as usual. The filename specified in the `SRC` directive should be the filename of the file where the directive is found, but this does not necessarily have to be the case. Referring to Figure V.8.8, if the `SRC` directive in the `DOS3.3.L` file was `SRC "INCL.L"`, the file `DOS3.3.L` would not be processed during Pass 2 and Pass 3, thus saving some processing time, but at the expense of not including the `DOS3.3.L` file as part of the complete print listing, if an incomplete print listing is acceptable. Personally, I like to place the `SRC` directive on line 2, right after the `TTL` directive, in the very first file when there are several source code files comprising a program. Even if all the source code resides in a single file, using the `SRC` directive will do no harm.

I challenged myself to make room in *Lisa* to include the sort algorithm and the code found in the external program called `SYMBOLS`. If `SYMBOLS` is activated immediately after *Lisa* processes some source code, it would print out the complete symbol list alphabetized, and then print it again with the symbols ordered by value. I liked what `SYMBOLS` did but not well enough to fumble around locating a copy of it, even if I did have it in EPROM, especially after processing a huge project like `DOS3.3`. (I never considered adding another command-line command like `SY` to `BRUN SYMBOLS` similar to how I added the `SE` command-line command to `BRUN SETUP`.) Fortunately, `SYMBOLS` is a little program and it did not take much effort to source its code. Now I had some idea how much room I required for `SYMBOLS` within *Lisa*. Of course, I could always make `LED` larger, thus rob memory from the symbol list, source code, and object code memory areas.

I know Randall Hyde used good sense when he developed his routines for each opcode for the Pass 2 implementation and separately for the Pass 3 implementation. Regardless of good sense, I studied those routines and found a number of ways to compact a rather large amount of this code giving me more than enough code space for `SYMBOLS`. Now that *Lisa* was headed down this path, I thought it would be exemplary to provide a means to give the symbol list a name on the page title line. I replaced the `CSP` directive (it mixes a `JSR` instruction with a `.DA` directive) with the `STT` directive whose syntax is `STT "<title>"`. This directive copies the string `title` to the buffer currently used by the `TTL` directive during Pass 3. If the symbol list is printed its pages will contain the new `TTL` title. If this directive is not used the symbol list pages are printed with the same title from the initial `TTL` directive. Now, if the `TTL` directive is used at the end of the source code to title the symbol list pages instead, the last printed page of the assembled code will contain the symbol list title and not its source code title. I did not care for that solution.

To complete this challenge required one further modification, and that was to the END directive. This directive provided the perfect location to control which of three symbol lists to print after the assembled code listing: no symbol lists, unsorted symbols (new), alphabetically sorted symbols, and numerically sorted symbols. Regardless which if any listings are desired, if at least one is selected the symbol list includes the memory address where the symbol list begins and where the symbol list ends. From Figure V.8.6 the absolute physical end of the symbol list is set at 0xB7C0. If there is substantial memory not used from the Symbol List start/end as reported in the assembled code listing and 0xB7C0, the End of Symbol List in Figure V.8.6 could be adjusted to allow for larger source code files. It is always good to have visibility in how effectively *Lisa* is configured particularly when problems due to source code file size begin to generate errors during assembly. Therefore, to complete this discussion, the END directive now allows a three-digit binary parameter to control which of the three symbol lists to print in the order stated above. The syntax for the directive is END nnn where **n** can be a 0 or a 1 for OFF and ON, respectively.

I prefer to keep the default setting of the PRNTFLAG variable ON during Pass 3 in order to obtain a printed listing of the assembly, particularly when I am using Virtual][. Rarely do I use the LST and NLS directives anymore. However, when I am debugging software using real Apple][hardware and the RAM Disk 320, leaving the PRNTFLAG variable ON greatly impacts assembly throughput, even with the ZipChip and the Parallel Printer Buffer enabled. And, it is a nuisance having to insert and then delete the NLS directive in the source code during the debugging development phase. So, I added the Z command-line command to *Lisa* that functions like the A command-line command to start the assembly process. Now, the Z command-line command sets the PRNTFLAG variable to OFF instead of to ON as if the NLS directive is the first directive in the source code.

Many times it is necessary to enter a DOS command directly on the *Lisa* command line. In order to do so a ctrl-D must precede the command so that *Lisa* will know to send the command to DOS rather than parsing the command for itself. I found it cumbersome for me to enter a ctrl-D before each and every DOS command when I needed some information from DOS. So, I added another *Lisa* command-line command, "/", which is so much easier for me to enter before a DOS command. For example, to display the contents of the VTOC sector, the following can be entered on the *Lisa* command line:

        !/TS A17

The *Lisa80 SETUP80* utility shown in Figure V.8.6 no longer has the options to select the clock slot number and its 0xCs05 and 0xCs07 values, respectively, where **s** is the clock slot number. *Lisa* used to obtain the date and time information similarly in how DOS 4.3 obtains that information, so *Lisa* also required a value for the current year because the Thunderclock lacks a year register. Instead of having a duplicate date and time algorithm and a duplicate YEARVAL variable to manage in *Lisa*, I removed the date and time algorithm and YEARVAL variable from *Lisa* and utilized the DOS 4.3 RDCLKVSN vector at 0x3E1. I placed the CLKBUFF buffer conveniently at 0x3C8. Now, whenever *Lisa* requires the current date and time it requests that information from DOS 4.3. The *SETUP* or *SETUP80* utilities no longer configures the clock slot, its 0xCs05 and 0xCs07 values since *Lisa* no longer requires that information.

It is always an unspoken goal whenever sourcing someone else's software to never introduce new and unwanted problems. On the other hand, there is always a very good opportunity in finding and repairing someone else's mistakes because of the intensity in concentration that is required to understand every single line of code. I suspect there might be some mistakes still in *Lisa* that I have yet to uncover, but for the moment *Lisa* is rock solid stable and it is providing me with object code output files that are true to their source code input files. Whether the source code input files are necessarily perfect is quite another story.

Relocating *Lisa* to Auxiliary memory was an exhilarating experience. Much of the action of an assembler is to display the assembled code to the screen and, quite often, to the printer. The assembler code can function virtually in any memory space; the screen and printer display code cannot. Main memory and Auxiliary memory in the Apple //e can be partitioned in a variety of ways. I chose to keep the fundamental *Lisa* code in Language Card memory in Auxiliary memory. Doing so drove the relocation design in using only two Soft Switches to control memory management: `AUXZPOFF` (i.e. `0xC008`) and `AUXZPON` (i.e. `0xC009`). The default Apple //e memory configuration is with `AUXZPOFF` such that Main memory is enabled with its own page-zero, stack, and Language Card memory. With `AUXZPON` Auxiliary memory page-zero, stack, and Language Card memory are enabled leaving the bulk of memory from Main memory enabled (i.e. memory from `0x0800` to `0xBDFF`). In other words, whether `AUXZPOFF` or `AUXZPON` are used, the object code, the source code, and the symbol list are all visible to both *Lisa* and to DOS because these code areas occupy memory from `0x0800` to `0xBDFF`. That area of memory is not toggled using these two Soft Switches.

The *Lisa* loader *LOADLISA* cannot load *Lisa* from disk directly into Auxiliary memory. Either Language Card Main memory or Language Card Auxiliary memory is in focus, not both, and one cannot be set for read and the other set for write. So, the *LOADLISA* loader calls on DOS to load each of the first two *Lisa* files into Main memory at `0x1000` sequentially, and copies each of the file's content to Auxiliary Language Card memory after setting `AUXZPON`. The third *Lisa* file containing the Main/Auxiliary control and interface routines and LED is loaded directly to `0xB7D0`. Hence, the End of Symbol List is set at `0xB7C0`, or sixteen bytes before `0xB7D0` for safety. The DOS command `MON C,I,O` is issued, `AUXZPON` is set, Bank 2 of the Language Card is enabled, and a jump is made to the *Lisa* `COLDSTRT` entry point at `0xE000`.

The functional relocation of *Lisa* to Auxiliary memory is only made possible by the Main/Auxiliary control and interface routines I have developed. It is this code, from `0xB7D0` to `0xB934` that makes this relocation functional. Some of the routines have familiar names because they are the necessary counterpart routines that toggle between `AUXZPOFF` and `AUXZPON`. The routines include `XCONSOLE`, `CONSOLE`, `HOOKDOS`, `XDOSWARM`, `XWRMSTRT`, `XCSWL`, `XKSWL`, `GETVALS`, `PUTVALS`, `READCLK`, `PUTZP`, `GETZP`, `ROMON`, and `AUXRTN`. Both DOS and *Lisa* share the Text Page from `0x400` to `0x7FF` in both Main and Auxiliary memory, but they do not share the same page-zero or stack. Screen coordinates are calculated by their respective Monitor routines so keeping track of whose turn it is to update the Text Page is paramount. Similarly, it is necessary to keep track when a DOS command is issued by *Lisa* and when that command is completed by DOS. It is necessary to handle additional `CSWL` traffic when the printer is enabled. `KSWL` traffic is not as complex, but it still has to be managed. Because *Lisa* operates in both Language Card banks, the current bank status has to be read (`0xC011`), saved, and restored (`0xC080` or `0xC088`) for external routines to reenter *Lisa* properly. As I stated above, relocating *Lisa* to Auxiliary memory was an exhilarating experience.

The *Lisa80* installer *INSTALL80* can be used to copy the *Lisa80* object code, *LOADLISA80* utility, and *SETUP80* utility to another volume. Like the *SETUP80* utility, *Lisa80* has a built-in command to invoke its action. When the command "U" is entered on the *Lisa80* command line the *INSTALL80* utility is activated from the Lisa Image volume `LISA80.Image` in disk drive 1. The target volume receiving the *Lisa80* object code, *LOADLISA80* utility, and *SETUP80* utility must be in disk drive 2. Table V.8.2 lists all *Lisa* command-line commands as well as all `LED` commands.

Command	Usage	Description
BR	BR	Break, enter Monitor with beep
LO	LO filename	Load *Lisa* file into memory
LE	LE	Print length of source code in memory in HEX
SA	SA filename	Save source code in memory to a *Lisa* file
SE	SE	`BRUN SETUP` utility
AP	AP filename	Append source code in memory with another *Lisa* file
U	U	`BRUN INSTALL` utility
I	I \<line number\>	Insert more source code at optional \<line number\>
D	D start,end	Delete range of source code using line number start,end
L	L \<start,end\>	List range of source code at optional start,end
A	A	Assemble the source code currently in memory
Z	Z	Assemble the source code in memory, `PRNTFLAG=OFF`
N	N	Clear all source code from memory and begin new code
M	M start,end	Modify range of source code using line number start,end
W	W \<start,end\>	Write range of source code to `TEXT` file at optional start,end
F	F string	Find all occurrences of string in source code
FC	FC \<n\>	`CATALOG` volume or disk drive \<n\>
FT	FT token	Find all occurrences of *Lisa* token in source code
FM	FM srt,end\>new	Move lines of source code to new location
FR	FR srt,end\>new	Replicate lines of source code to new location
FP	FP \<n\>	Show source code Page number; select source code Page
FX	FX \<#\>	Check for damaged source code; # enables print flag
R	R \<n,\> filename	Read `TEXT` file into memory as source code; at line number
P	P \<#\>	Issue a `PR#` command to DOS to change `CSW` address
^P	^P	`ctrl-P` command to sequentially load `SEG` files into memory
/	/ command	Call `HOOKDOS`, issue `ctrl-D`, send command to DOS

Table V.8.2. Lisa Command-Line Commands

How does a software design engineer accomplish a task of this magnitude, of moving a software program having the complexity and size of *Lisa* from Main memory to Auxiliary memory? I believe the first paragraph in Section I.3 helps to answer this question: "In order to design reliable software for a particular machine or platform, one must understand the machine's complete architecture." Start any task with a list of requirements. From those requirements decide how hardware can be or should be utilized. It is not necessary to know how to accomplish hardware utilization for the moment, but you should be able to decide how the hardware can be or could be or should be configured. As you develop the scope of your software design, that will drive the list of "knowns" and "unknowns" for each segment of the design. A list of "unknowns" can be very frustrating to the software engineer when that list contains unknown hardware functionality. Breaking an unknown down into smaller segments and pairing them with sufficient testing will usually yield the necessary knowledge to move forward. The task becomes an incredible mosaic of many hundreds if not thousands of bits of knowledge woven together to allow only a precise stream of consciousness to occur, or flow as I like to imagine a software design. Now the interface is under control. The primary key to be gained here is derived solely from "sufficient testing."

Continual testing of each design segment is incredibly important. After a design segment has been thoroughly tested and verified to provide the results as per its design, another design segment can be developed. The completed project will only require a simple system verification test when all design segments have been developed in this manner. I have been developing tasks using this methodology for so long that it has become ingrained in how I approach every software design. This methodology assures me that the final product will conform to all established requirements.

To assemble the *Lisa80* source code, place the Lisa Image volume `LISA80.Image` in disk drive 1 and boot. *Lisa80* will start automatically into the 80-column display mode. Enter the `SE` command-line command to select the *SETUP80* utility in order to verify or set the `Start of Source Code` to `0x4000` and the `Start of Symbol List` to `0x7800`. Place the Lisa Source volume `LISA80.Source` in disk drive 2, load the `LISA.L` file into memory, and start the assembler by entering either the `A` or the `Z` command-line command. If a printed version of the screen output is desired simply preface the `A` or the `Z` command with the `P1` command-line command. Three object code files will be created on the Lisa Image volume named `LISA.1`, `LISA.2`, and `LISA.3`.

The *SETUP80* utility can be assembled by loading the `SETUP80.L` file into memory from the Lisa Image volume. The assembler can be started by entering either the `A` or the `Z` command-line command. If a printed version of the screen output is desired simply preface the `A` or the `Z` command with the `P1` command-line command. The *LOADLISA80* and *INSTALL80* utilities from the Lisa Image volume can be assembled in the same way.

The 40-column version of *Lisa* resides on the `LISA.Image` and `LISA.Source` disks. All routines are assembled in exactly the same way.

9. Program Global Editor (PGE)

When I received my Apple][+ in the early 1980's, I spent my first few months writing Applesoft programs. I was fortunate to obtain a copy of the Program Global Editor (*PGE*) written by C. A. Greathouse and Garry Reinhardt. *PGE* certainly made programming Applesoft much easier especially when one has excellent tools at hand. I have to say that there is one particular difficulty when writing Applesoft programs, and that is dealing with program line numbers. So many functions depend upon program line numbers making the line numbers a highly critical part of any Applesoft program. There are not many ways to partition an Applesoft program into functions and subroutines except by using program line numbers that may use large line increments from function to function, and smaller line increments within a function. Or, many "REM ***" statements can be used to partition an Applesoft program, but those statements consume program line numbers as well as memory, which also impacts program execution. Here is where *PGE*'s forte provided me the most assistance, its program line renumbering capability.

PGE functionality requires the ability to modify the WARMADR and RESETADR vectors, and to obtain the values found at ADRVAL and LOADLEN within DOS. *PGE* simply modified those vectors and read the ADRVAL and LOADLEN parameters directly from within DOS 3.3 knowing the location of these vectors and parameters. DOS 4.3 has these vectors and parameters, of course, and a set procedure to read and write them. As shown in Table I.8.1 the address of INITVAL is 0xBFFA. The address at 0xBFFA points to the table of address vectors shown in Table I.8.5. This is where the vectors WARMADR at offset 0x00 and RESETADR at offset 0x06 can be found. The address of the vector MNGVALS is at 0xBFF4 as shown in Table I.8.1. Section IV.23 shows how to access or change the value of any CMDVALS variable. According to Table I.12.1 the offset for ADRVAL is 0x2E and the offset for LOADLEN is 0x36. The representative code in Figure I.12.1 to access and change CMDVALS variables can be used as a model to access and change the value for the variables ADRVAL and LOADLEN. As long as a program like *PGE* does not utilize the Language Card for any purpose it may safely employ these procedures under DOS 4.3. After I adjusted the *PGE* software to locate the vectors and parameters it needs from DOS 4.3 using the procedures just outlined, *PGE* executes its commands flawlessly.

One of the worst Applesoft functions is the LIST function because of the 40-column width of the display: program lines are truncated, multiple space characters are used between tokens and data, and there are only 24 lines making up the display. The LIST function in *PGE* parses the Applesoft tokens and displays them as well as the remaining ASCII program data without any spaces whatsoever. Perhaps the screen is more difficult to read, but considering the "day and age" when *PGE* was utilized for program editing, screen clutter was a small sacrifice, even respected. Printer paper and ink were expensive at that time, and it was not practical to print programs a multitude number of times during their development. In those days most software engineers initially wrote out their code using paper and pencil, and typed in their programs after reviewing their code for logic structure and for the most obvious errors. I found that the activity of typing in a program from my written notes served as another major logic review process as well. So, *PGE* was very useful in displaying more lines of code per screen for their review. However, the 80-column card changed all that. Figure V.9.1 shows the Applesoft LIST function and Figure V.9.2 shows the *PGE* LIST function for the beginning lines of the HELLO file on the DOS.4.3.Tools disk. I believe all will agree that Figure V.9.1 is far more readable in displaying program code. Although, if the two displays were compared in 40-column mode the *PGE* LIST function would be for more practical in displaying the most program code.

```
JLIST 1,999

10 D$ =  CHR$ (13) +  CHR$ (4)
15  DIM NAM$(20),CMD$(20),PGM$(20),ADR(20)
20  HOME : HTAB 16: PRINT "Tools Menu"
30  READ N: FOR I = 0 TO N - 1: READ NAM$(I),CMD$(I),PGM$(I),ADR(I): GOSUB
    200: NEXT :I = 0
40  INVERSE : GOSUB 200: GOSUB 300: NORMAL : GOSUB 200: IF A% = 27 THEN
     HOME : PRINT D$;"CATALOG": PRINT : NEW
50  IF A% = 21 THEN I = (I + 1) * (I < N - 1): GOTO 40
55  IF A% = 10 THEN I = (I + 1) * (I < N - 1): GOTO 40
60  IF A% = 8 THEN I = I - 1 + N * (I = 0): GOTO 40
65  IF A% = 11 THEN I = I - 1 + N * (I = 0): GOTO 40
70  IF A% < > 13 THEN 40
80  PRINT D$;CMD$(I);PGM$(I);: IF ADR(I) THEN  PRINT ",A";ADR(I);
90  PRINT : END
200 I% = I / 2: VTAB 4 + 2 * I%: HTAB 2: IF I% * 2 < > I THEN  HTAB 21
210 A$ =  LEFT$ (NAM$(I),18): PRINT A$;: RETURN
300  POKE 49168,0
310 A% =  PEEK (49152): IF A% < 128 THEN  GOTO 310
320  POKE 49168,0:A% = A% - 128: RETURN
```

Figure V.9.1. Applesoft LIST Function

```
READY
[L1,999
10 D$=CHR$(13)+CHR$(4)
15 DIMNAM$(20),CMD$(20),PGM$(20),ADR(20)
20 HOME:HTAB16:PRINT"Tools Menu"
30 READN:FORI=0TON-1:READNAM$(I),CMD$(I),PGM$(I),ADR(I):GOSUB200:NEXT:I=0
40 INVERSE:GOSUB200:GOSUB300:NORMAL:GOSUB200:IFA%=27THENHOME:PRINTD$;"CATALOG":P
RINT:NEW
50 IFA%=21THENI=(I+1)*(I<N-1):GOTO40
55 IFA%=10THENI=(I+1)*(I<N-1):GOTO40
60 IFA%=8THENI=I-1+N*(I=0):GOTO40
65 IFA%=11THENI=I-1+N*(I=0):GOTO40
70 IFA%<>13THEN40
80 PRINTD$;CMD$(I);PGM$(I);:IFADR(I)THENPRINT",A";ADR(I);
90 PRINT:END
200 I%=I/2:VTAB4+2*I%:HTAB2:IFI%*2<>ITHENHTAB21
210 A$=LEFT$(NAM$(I),18):PRINTA$;:RETURN
300 POKE49168,0
310 A%=PEEK(49152):IFA%<128THENGOTO310
320 POKE49168,0:A%=A%-128:RETURN

READY
[
```

Figure V.9.2. PGE LIST Function

```
]&

READY
[R1,99,4,8

READY
[L1,99
8 D$=CHR$(13)+CHR$(4)
12 DIMNAM$(20),CMD$(20),PGM$(20),ADR(20)
16 HOME:HTAB16:PRINT"Tools Menu"
20 READN:FORI=0TON-1:READNAM$(I),CMD$(I),PGM$(I),ADR(I):GOSUB200:NEXT:I=0
24 INVERSE:GOSUB200:GOSUB300:NORMAL:GOSUB200:IFA%=27THENHOME:PRINTD$;"CATALOG":P
RINT:NEW
28 IFA%=21THENI=(I+1)*(I<N-1):GOTO24
32 IFA%=10THENI=(I+1)*(I<N-1):GOTO24
36 IFA%=8THENI=I-1+N*(I=0):GOTO24
40 IFA%=11THENI=I-1+N*(I=0):GOTO24
44 IFA%<>13THEN24
48 PRINTD$;CMD$(I);PGM$(I);:IFADR(I)THENPRINT",A";ADR(I);
52 PRINT:END

READY
[
```

Figure V.9.3. PGE RENUMBER Function

PGE excelled in renumbering small portions, larger portions, and even entire portions of programs. Upon initialization *PGE* remaps the ampersand vector to its "READY [" prompt. The renumber command R requires four parameters for start number, end number, increment, and new start number. *PGE* scours the entire Applesoft program and changes every occurrence of a program line number within the specified range to the new program line number based on the new start number and some program line number increment, say 5 or 10 or 100. To say the results were marvelous would be an understatement. As one's Applesoft programming capabilities mature, better choices for line numbers are usually made, and it becomes easier to create sections of code that resemble a function or a subroutine. In these instances, being able to renumber a small section of code is quite powerful. Figure V.9.3 demonstrates how simple it is to renumber the beginning lines of the HELLO program shown in Figure V.9.1. This program now begins with line number "8" and the line increment is set to "4" for all lines up to "52". The line numbers following line "90" in Figure V.9.1 are not affected except when those earlier line numbers are referenced within the later line numbers. An astute observer will notice that *PGE* only accepts uppercase ASCII commands. I have no doubt that it would be easy to modify *PGE* to accept lowercase ASCII commands as well.

The downside to using *PGE* occurs when *PGE* is used to renumber Applesoft programs that have attached binary programs. When the renumber function finds the triple-zero termination marker for an Applesoft program, it sets the end of program at ASPEND (0xAF/B0) to that memory address. In other words, *PGE* processing will lose the address of the true end of program and change it to the address where the triple-zero termination marker is found regardless whether the Applesoft program has attached binary programs or not. This situation is not unsurmountable because the binary programs may be easily re-attached using Binary File Installation (*BFI*) described in Section V.16. It is a little inconvenient having to re-install binary programs after *PGE* processing, but certainly nothing is compared to the overwhelming convenience of *PGE* line number renumbering.

PGE requires a short program to load the *PGE* program into memory and to set FRETOP (0x6F/70), HIMEM (0x74/75), and the ampersand vector at 0x3F5. The *PGE* program used the upper part of the INPUT buffer from 0x2D0 to 0x2FF. Two 256-byte buffers are used at the end of the *PGE* program as well as a number of variables at the end of a third 256-byte buffer from 0xnnE0 to 0xnnFF, where **nn** is the page number for that third buffer. I had already completely sourced the *PGE* code so it would function at any memory address. I decided to combine the *PGE* loader, the page-two variables, and the variables at the end of the third buffer into a page preceding the *PGE* code. Now, the *PGE* system has been drastically simplified and only one file needs to be launched. *PGE* still depends upon reading and writing directly to the TEXT pages using CH and BASL. There are some *PGE* problematic functions that will not work properly if the 80-column card in enabled. The renumber function is not one of those problematic functions. I have placed *PGE* at 0x8E00 and HIMEM is set at 0x8DF0. The two 256-byte *PGE* buffers are now located at 0xAB00 and 0xAC00. Now, *GPLE* can be placed at 0xAD00 and not overwrite the DOS 4.3 Language Card interface at 0xBE00.

To assemble the *PGE* source code, place the DOS 4.3 Tools volume DOS.4.3.Tools in disk drive 1, boot, and start *Lisa80*. Enter the SE command-line command to select the *SETUP80* utility in order to verify or set the Start of Source Code to 0x4000 and the Start of Symbol List to 0x7800. Place the PGE Source volume PGE.Source in disk drive 2, load the PGE.L file into memory, and start the assembler by entering either the A or the Z command-line command. If a printed version of the screen output is desired simply preface the A or the Z command with the P1 command-line command. Two object code files will be created on the PGE Source volume named SEG01 and SEG02. The two object code files can be combined in memory sequentially starting at 0x8E00 using the ctrl-P command. The complete binary image can be saved to the PGE Source volume or to any other volume as PGE.

10. Global Program Line Editor (GPLE)

Another invaluable Applesoft program editing tool that I was fortunate enough to obtain was Global Program Line Editor (*GPLE*). Neil Konzen published *GPLE* in 1982, and I obtained version V3.4. *GPLE* uses the entire Bank 1 of the Language Card beginning at 0xD000, so it is obviously not compatible with DOS 4.3 in its original format. *GPLE* did not utilize any vectors or parameters within DOS 3.3 so I did not have to adjust any of my sourced code of *GPLE* whatsoever in order for it to execute at another memory location. What I like about *GPLE* is that it works very much like a word processor for Applesoft programming. It has the ability to globally search and replace any variable, word, or character with any other variable, word, or character within an Applesoft program. And *GPLE* does its work extremely fast.

The original *GPLE* loader first verifies that the Apple][computer contains at least 48 KB of memory and that a Language Card is available. Then the loader write-enables Bank 1 of the Language Card and issues a DOS BLOAD command to load *GPLE* to memory address 0xD000. Finally, the *GPLE* loader copies a set of routines comprised of the ctrl-Y entry location, the ampersand entry location, the CSWL entry location, and the KSWL entry location to 0xB6B3 to 0xB6F9, a small, unused area within DOS 3.3. These routines also control the bank switching of the Language Card as well as providing the entry location for a modifiable JSR instruction used in *GPLE* processing. Of course, DOS 4.3 does not have seventy bytes free at 0xB6B3, or seventy bytes free at any other address, for these routines.

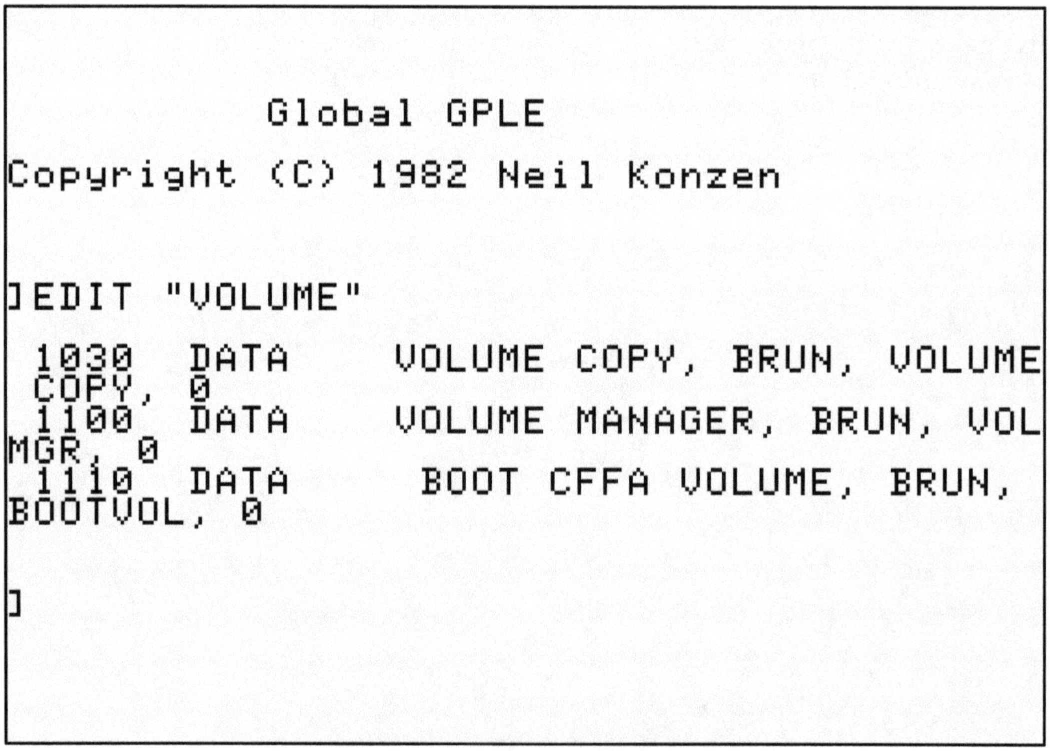

```
              Global GPLE
Copyright (C) 1982 Neil Konzen


]EDIT "VOLUME"

  1030   DATA      VOLUME COPY, BRUN, VOLUME
  COPY, 0
  1100   DATA      VOLUME MANAGER, BRUN, VOL
MGR, 0
  1110   DATA      BOOT CFFA VOLUME, BRUN,
BOOTVOL, 0


]
```

Figure V.10.1. GPLE FIND Function

I decided to combine the *GPLE* loader, the `ctrl-Y`, `CSWL`, and `KSWL` routines, and *GPLE* into one, drastically simplified program. Thus, only one file needs to be launched. *GPLE* still depends on reading and writing directly to the `TEXT` pages using `CH` and `BASL`. Therefore, some *GPLE* functions will not work properly if the 80-column card in enabled. I disabled the ampersand entry location since its only function is to initialize `GPLE`. The ampersand function is reserved for `PGE`. *GPLE* provides a host of `ctrl` short cuts that, for example, are intended to issue certain DOS commands, calculate the size of an Applesoft program in memory, or calculate the number of free sectors in a volume. Because I only use *GPLE* to find and replace text in Applesoft programs I have ignored these other, special features of `GPLE`. These features are primarily intended for the DOS 3.3 architecture and I have not had the interest to modify or update this area of `GPLE`. Figure V.10.1 shows *GPLE* after it has initialized. The `ctrl-E` function, or `EDIT`, provides access to all of the editing capabilities found in `GPLE`. It is this function that I use exclusively.

I made a gallant attempt to modify *GPLE* so that it would do its work with the 80-column card enabled. I even used some of the routines I had developed for *Lisa* so that I could use *Lisa* with the 80-column card enabled. Even after several bouts of frustration I finally had to shelve that effort. I did, however, manage to update the *GPLE* `CSWL`/`KSWL` routines and capture the state of the Language Card bank setting. These two vectors must restore not only the state of the Language Card, but also which bank was enabled at the moment when either vector was entered since DOS 4.3 utilizes both banks of the Language Card for its processing.

Once *GPLE* has been launched, my generic `HELLO` program on my `DOS.4.3.Tools` volume will not function properly in order to launch another program, say *PGE*. All keystrokes are filtered through *GPLE*, and any control character such as the arrow keys are trapped. The `HELLO` program needs the arrow key information in order to function properly. When the user requires the services of both *GPLE* and *PGE*, the global editor *PGE* should be launched first. Once *PGE* is operational, `HELLO` can be used to launch *GPLE* and work can begin.

To assemble the *GPLE* source code, place the DOS 4.3 Tools volume `DOS.4.3.Tools` in disk drive 1, boot, and start *Lisa80*. Enter the `SE` command-line command to select the *SETUP80* utility in order to verify or set the `Start of Source Code` to `0x4000` and the `Start of Symbol List` to `0x7800`. Place the GPLE Source volume `GPLE.Source` in disk drive 2, load the `GPLE.L` file into memory, and start the assembler by entering either the `A` or the `Z` command-line command. If a printed version of the screen output is desired simply preface the `A` or the `Z` command with the `P1` command-line command. Two object code files will be created on the GPLE Source volume named `SEG01` and `SEG02`. The two object code files can be combined in memory sequentially starting at `0xAD00` using the `ctrl-P` command. The complete binary image can be saved to the GPLE Source volume or to any other volume as `GPLE`.

11. Axlon RAM Disk 320

I first became aware of the Axlon RAM Disk 320 when I was self-employed and working under contract for Sierra On-Line around 1985. Living in Oakhurst, California, was really awesome, and being able to work at home was even better. Except when the thunderstorms came and electrical power was temporarily interrupted, otherwise it was heavenly to live and work in Oakhurst. Uninterrupted Power Supplies, or UPS battery backups were not easy to obtain and were not very affordable at that time. But when I was in the middle of a massive software development session and the power went out, and I lost hours of work, the cost of a UPS seemed trivial. That was the time when I decided to purchase an Axlon RAM Disk. Actually, I purchased two because a friend of mine wanted a RAM Disk, too. The RAM Disk emulates two 40-track disk drives using DRAM memory, and it has its own built-in power supply and backup lead-acid battery. As long as the power outage did not last more than four hours, all my files were safe in the RAM Disk. My software development pace vastly accelerated as well because files were assembled from RAM, not diskette. And when the RAM Disk was mated with the ZipChip, large projects could be assembled and linked in seconds rather than in many minutes.

Axlon provided excellent software utilities with the RAM Disk. Their RAM Disk initialization software could transfer an entire diskette to one of the RAM drives in the time it took the Disk][(revolving at 300 revolutions per minute) to make 35 revolutions, 1 revolution per track, in 35 * (60 / 300) = 7 seconds. That is impressive. From their software and from the design of their peripheral slot card I truly learned the importance of reading the CLRROM (i.e. 0xCFFF) address in order to detach peripheral-card expansion ROM memory.

Whenever the 6502-microprocessor fetches an instruction in the peripheral-card ROM memory, 0xCs00 to 0xCsFF, where s is the slot number of the peripheral slot card, the peripheral slot card typically enables its peripheral-card expansion ROM memory, 0xC800 to 0xCFFF. And that is true for the RAM Disk peripheral slot card only in the address range of 0xCs00 to 0xCs7F. Interesting. Software residing in the upper half of its peripheral-card ROM memory can read the CLRROM address to detach the expansion ROM memory without re-enabling it. That was indeed a very, very clever design. I made good use of that hardware design in all my versions of RAM Disk firmware. Another interesting design of the RAM Disk peripheral slot card was its use of a static RAM chip, a 6116, for their firmware. The static RAM chip needs to be programmed only once when power is first turned on, and regardless how many times the Apple][is powered off and back on again, the static RAM chip retains its data because its operating power comes from the RAM Disk and not from the Apple][.

The first static RAM chip page is mapped to the peripheral-card ROM memory (i.e. 0xCs00 to 0xCsFF) and the 0xC8 page is mapped to the selected page of RAM Disk DRAM. The remaining static RAM chip pages are mapped to the peripheral-card expansion ROM memory, 0xC900 to 0xCFFF. I made use of the idea of utilizing a static RAM chip instead of an EPROM when I was testing my new firmware for the Sider peripheral slot card. It was amazing how much easier it was to test different software algorithms for the Sider without having to program yet another, and another EPROM. However, I have recently replaced the RAM Disk static RAM chip with a 28C16A EEPROM. I connected Pin 18, its chip enable, to an SPDT switch in order to write-protect the EEPROM. This EEPROM needs to be programmed only once, and it retains its data until it is programmed another time. It has the convenience of both a static RAM chip and an EPROM. This EEPROM cannot be programmed quickly like a static RAM chip so care must be taken in developing any EEPROM programming software.

I no longer remember when and where I became an owner of a 128K RAM peripheral slot card, or RAM Card. It may have been left inside a used Apple //e I purchased at a garage sale. Regardless, I have no idea who manufactured this RAM Card. This RAM Card is designed to operate like a Language Card in any peripheral slot in an Apple][+ or in an Apple //e, and it can be easily configured as one of eight Language Card blocks. Since Address Bit A02 is ignored when configuring the Language Card using its dedicated Soft Switches, this RAM Card utilizes Address Bit A02 to select a Language Card block. Table V.11.1 shows the memory management Soft Switches used by the RAM Card. Simply reading address 0xC084 selects RAM Card block 0, or reading address 0xC08D selects RAM Card block 5.

Address	Access	Name	Description
0xC080	R	RAM2WP	Select Bank 2; write protect RAM
0xC081	R ‖ RR	ROM2WE	Deselect Bank 2; enable ROM ‖ write enable RAM
0xC082	R	ROM2WP	Deselect Bank 2; enable ROM; write protect RAM
0xC083	R ‖ RR	RAM2WE	Select Bank 2 ‖ write enable RAM
0xC084	R	RCBLK0	Select RAM Card block 0
0xC085	R	RCBLK1	Select RAM Card block 1
0xC086	R	RCBLK2	Select RAM Card block 2
0xC087	R	RCBLK3	Select RAM Card block 3
0xC088	R	RAM1WP	Select Bank 1; write protect RAM
0xC089	R ‖ RR	ROM1WE	Deselect Bank 1; enable ROM ‖ write enable RAM
0xC08A	R	ROM1WP	Deselect Bank 1; enable ROM; write protect RAM
0xC08B	R ‖ RR	RAM1WE	Select Bank 1 ‖ write enable RAM
0xC08C	R	RCBLK4	Select RAM Card block 4
0xC08D	R	RCBLK5	Select RAM Card block 5
0xC08E	R	RCBLK6	Select RAM Card block 6
0xC08F	R	RCBLK7	Select RAM Card block 7

Table V.11.1. RAM Card Memory Configuration Soft Switches

The hardware circuit of the RAM Card is shown in Figure V.11.1. The circuit utilizes an Intel 3242 address multiplexer and refresh counter in order to periodically refresh the sixteen dynamic RAM chips on board. This address multiplexer is designed to refresh 16K dynamic RAMs, not 64K dynamic RAMs like those found on this RAM card. Therefore, the RAM Card circuit derives Row Address 7 from the selected RAM Card block number. Data that is read from or written to the RAM Card is latched in the 0xD000 to 0xFFFF memory address range. Therefore, the RAM Card must pull the INH line low in order to disable the Apple][ROMs appropriately and enable the respective Language Card block according to which configuration Soft Switch shown in Table V.11.1 was last read. In order to utilize the RAM Card for anything useful software must be specifically designed to access the RAM Card as eight individual Language Cards, or an interface driver must reside somewhere else in memory to provide RAM Card memory access. Neither of these ideas appealed to me, and I wanted to use the 128K memory of the RAM Card in a more generic fashion.

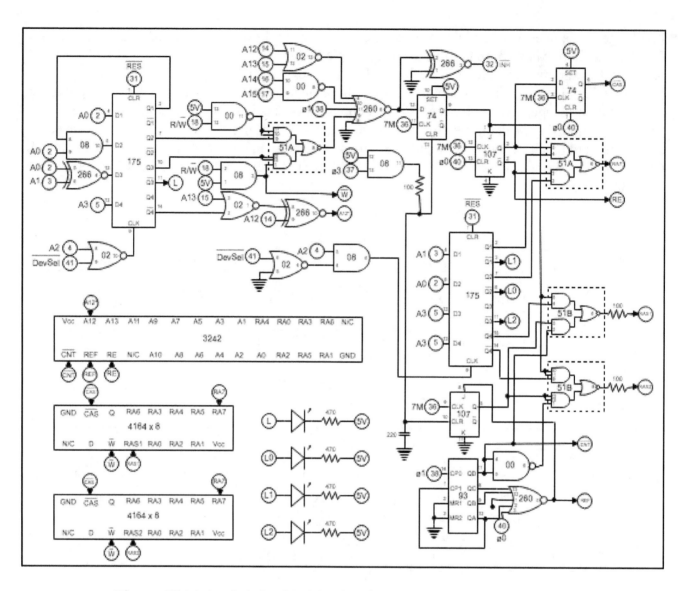

Figure V.11.1. Original RAM Card Hardware Circuit Diagram

The hardware of the RAM Disk responds only to the first two of the sixteen peripheral-card I/O memory locations dedicated to the RAM Disk in order to select sector and track, so Address Bit A02 will always be low. The RAM Card is designed to latch Address Bits A00, A01, and A03 when Address Bit A02 of its sixteen peripheral-card I/O memory locations is high. Thus, the active peripheral-card I/O memory locations for the RAM Disk and the RAM Card are mutually exclusive in selecting RAM Disk sector and track versus RAM Card Language Card block number. For example, if the RAM Disk resides in slot 7, sector number is saved to 0xC0F0 and track number is saved to 0xC0F1. If the RAM Card resides in slot 7, block number is selected by reading 0xC0F4 to 0xC0F7 or 0xC0FC to 0xC0FF. Once I understood the hardware circuit of the RAM Card vis-á-vis its software utilization, I thought perhaps the circuit could be easily re-engineered. I also had plenty of room for additional software within the RAM Disk peripheral-card expansion ROM memory and some room left within the RAM Disk peripheral-card ROM memory. From within the RAM Disk peripheral-card ROM memory, I knew I could turn off the RAM Disk peripheral-card expansion ROM memory and use that address space to possibly access eight continuous pages of the RAM Card.

Therefore, instead of accessing RAM Card data in the `0xD000` to `0xFFFF` memory address range, RAM Card data would be accessed in the peripheral-card expansion ROM memory from `0xC800` to `0xCFFF`.

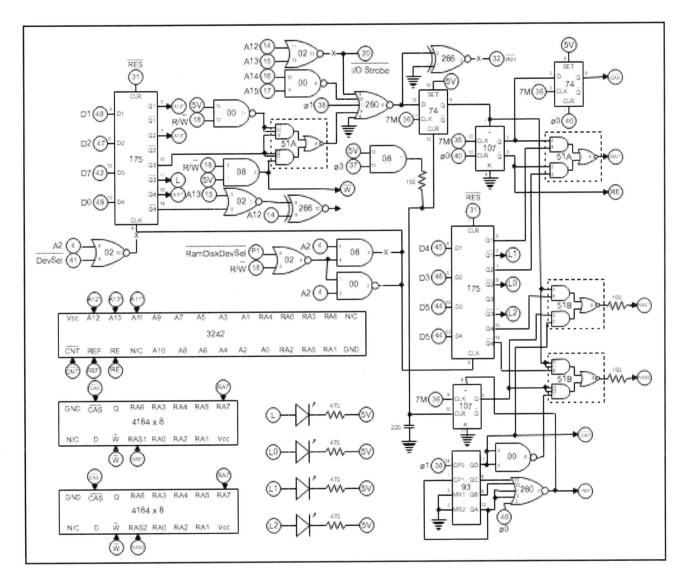

Figure V.11.2. Modified RAM Card Hardware Circuit Diagram

It was around 1992 when I worked out a way to physically modify the RAM Card in order to allow the firmware of the RAM Disk to control it, and to access it as if it was a RAM disk drive having 32 tracks. This modification required me to connect the RAM Card to the RAM Disk using a single wire, however. I found that Slot 3 was the perfect slot for the RAM Card because the RAM Card no longer needed to respond to its own *DEVICE SELECT* signal, but rather responded to the simulated *DEVICE SELECT* signal generated by the RAM Disk hardware. When the RAM Disk connects to DOS 4.3 it puts the address of its disk handlers in the disk address table `DISKADRS`, one for the RAM Disk and one for the RAM Card. To be sure, the RAM Disk firmware is handling all of the `RWTS IOCB` traffic for the RAM Disk as well as the traffic for the RAM Card. Regardless which slot the RAM Card occupies, the RAM Disk firmware saves the track and sector from the RWTS IOCB to the 0xC0n4 (where **n** is equal the slot number of the RAM Disk plus eight) peripheral-card I/O memory location on behalf of the RAM Card. Formatting either the RAM Disk drives for 40 tracks or the RAM Card for 32 tracks is easy in DOS 4.3 because the DOS INIT command can set the ENDTRK variable to those specific values using the A keyword.

Figure V.11.2 shows the modified RAM Card hardware circuit diagram. The 74LS175 quad D flip-flops latch the data bus bits except for Data Bit D6. Data Bits D0 to D5 hold the desired sector/track number and Data Bit D7 is used to enable the RAM Card. The desired 6-bit sector/track number is calculated as follows:

```
N = ( track number * 2 ) + ( sector number / 8 )
P = sector number ^ 7
```

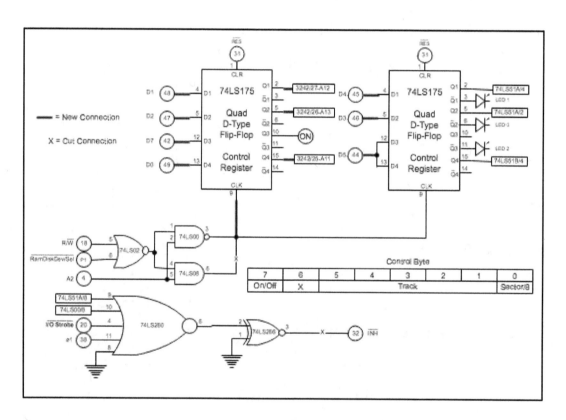

Figure V.11.3. RAM Card Hardware Modifications

The selected page P within the RAM Card peripheral-card expansion ROM memory is determined from the first three bits of the sector number. The modified RAM Card circuit does not bring the INH line low anymore because it is now unnecessary to disable the Apple][ROMs. Figure V.11.3 shows the actual modifications made to Figure V.11.1 to obtain Figure V.11.2. One 74LS00 gate was available in order to clock the 74LS175 control registers.

In Figure V.11.3 the Control Byte is latched into the two control registers on the RAM Card only when Address Bit `A02` is high as in "`STA 0xC084,X`" where the X-register contains the slot number of the RAM Disk times sixteen. The RAM Disk hardware does not respond to any value written to its peripheral-card I/O memory location when Address Bit `A02` is high, but it generates a suitable *DEVICE SELECT* signal for the RAM Card. Before the RAM Card is enabled the `CLRROM` address is read in order to disable the peripheral-card expansion ROM memory `0xC800` to `0xCFFF`. The moment the RAM Card is enabled the peripheral-card expansion ROM memory is instantly mapped to eight selected pages of RAM Card memory. Bit `0` of the Control Byte contains bit `3` of the desired sector number. Therefore, the peripheral-card expansion ROM memory will display sectors `0x00` to `0x07` when Control Byte bit `0` is zero and sectors `0x08` to `0x0F` when Control Byte bit `0` is one. Bits `1` to `5` of the Control Byte contain the desired track number. Bit `6` of the Control Byte is not used and bit `7` is used to enable or disable the RAM Card. The RAM Card can no longer function as a Language Card after having had these hardware modifications.

Table V.11.2 shows the firmware entry points for the RAM Disk and for the RAM Card for the firmware that is mapped to the peripheral-card ROM memory of the RAM Disk.

Offset	Name	Description
0x00	RDBOOT	Entry point for DOS PR# command to boot DOS in drive 1
0x10	ROMHOOK	Entry point to attach the RAM Disk/RAM Card to DOS in memory
0x18	ROMUHOOK	Entry point to detach the RAM Disk/RAM Card from DOS in memory
0x20	RDENTRY	Entry for DOS 4.1/4.3 RAM Disk RWTS processing
0x30	RDRWTS3	Entry for DOS 3.3 RAM Disk RWTS processing
0x50	RCENTRY	Entry for RAM Card RWTS processing
0x5C	ROMBOOT	Disk][firmware-like entry point for Boot Stage 1 code at 0x0801
0x70	MODOS3	Patch DOS 3.3 after Boot Stage 2
0x80	BOOTEXIT	Issue CLRROM, jump to 0x0801
0x88	RCEXIT	Turn RAM Card off, fall into RDEXIT
0x91	RDEXIT	Update RWTS error code, issue CLRROM, return to caller
0x98	HOOKEXIT	Exit for ROMHOOK and ROMUHOOK
0xA4	EXIT3	Exit for MODOS3
0xAB	RCRDWRT	Turn on RAM Card, read/write RAM Card, branch to RCEXIT
0xD3	RCFORMT	Issue CLRROM, turn on RAM Card, clear sectors, branch to RCEXIT
0xFE/FF	VERSION	Version number for RAM Disk firmware (0x38): Version 3, Build 8

Table V.11.2. RAM Disk 320 Firmware Entry Points

According to manufacturing documentation the 28C16A is a fast, low power, 5V-only CMOS Parallel EEPROM organized as 2K x 8-bits. It requires a simple interface for in-system programming. On-chip address and data latches, self-timed write cycle with auto-clear, and Vcc power up/down write protection eliminate additional timing and protection hardware. This chip is designed to endure 10,000 program/erase cycles and has a data retention of ten years. Fast read access time is 200 nsecs and fast write cycle time is a maximum of 10 msecs. The programming algorithm I developed writes a byte of data to the EEPROM, reads the EEPROM, and then compares that byte read to the byte that was written until they are the same. The EEPROM is read in a 300 μsec loop for a maximum of 48 retries. This algorithm provides a generous 14.4 msecs for the write cycle time for each byte written, though data is typically written much faster than that. If, for some reason, a data byte cannot be written within 14.4 msecs, programming is terminated and an error routine is called. Once the EEPROM is fully programmed a verification routine is called to confirm the entire EEPROM image. The complete programming procedure does take a couple of minutes to fully program an EEPROM of this size, but it only needs to be done once rather than having to program a static RAM chip every time the RAM Disk is powered on. Figure V.11.4 shows the Connect Program main screen that will copy a 35-track diskette to the RAM Disk in seven seconds.

```
RamDisk 320/RamCard 128 Connect Program


    Drive Slot:      4        5        6        7

RamDisk Slot:        4        5        6        7

RamCard Slot:        2        3        4        5


       Drives:                1        2


       RamDisk:    Init   Connect   Load Disk

       RamCard:    Init   Connect    Ignore


    Insert Disk into Drive 1, Slot 6


           Press Any Key to Load
```

Figure V.11.4. RAM Disk/RAM Card Connect Program

To assemble the RAM Disk source code, place the DOS 4.3 Tools volume `DOS.4.3.Tools` in disk drive 1, boot, and start *Lisa80*. Enter the `SE` command-line command to select the *SETUP80* utility in order to verify or set the `Start of Source Code` to `0x4000` and the `Start of Symbol List` to `0x7800`. Place the RAM Disk Source volume `RAMDISK.Source` in disk drive 2, load the `RD.L` file into memory, and start the assembler by entering either the `A` or the `Z` command-line command. If a printed version of the screen output is desired simply preface the `A` or the `Z` command with the `P1` command-line command. Six object code files will be created on the RAM Disk Source volume named `SEG01` to `SEG06`. The six object code files can be combined in memory sequentially starting at `0x4000` using the `ctrl-P` command. The complete binary image can be saved to the RAM Disk Source volume or to any other volume as `RD`.

12. RanaSystems EliteThree

I met a very knowledgeable engineer at Hughes Aircraft Company a year or so after I was hired into the Digital Simulation and Integration Laboratory in 1986. Kathryn provided consulting services to small companies and designed proprietary databases for her customers. In order to document and track her services, she used a database system of her own design hosted on an Apple][computer connected to a single Disk][drive and a RanaSystems EliteThree drive as her massive database data storage container. She preferred the large storage capacity of the Rana and she thought the access time was a bit faster than the Disk][. When she sold her consulting business, she offered to sell me the Rana drive for $100.00 on November 14, 1988: I had put her dated invoice in a folder along with the Rana manual she gave me. Obviously, the Rana was used, but certainly not dead, and I jumped at the offer. My first investigations into the Rana and its installation software revealed to me how tightly coupled it was to DOS 3.3. I didn't much care for all the modifications the installation software had to make to DOS 3.3 in order to provide the various configurations the hardware was capable of supporting. These modifications were provided by Rana Enhancement Utilities and were specifically designed to modify DOS and *FID* on a Master DOS diskette. The Rana can read and write either side of a diskette, it can create tracks half the size of Disk][tracks, that is, it can create eighty tracks on each side of a diskette, and the Rana peripheral slot card is capable of controlling up to four disk drives of any manufacture. I basically left it at that, and put the Rana away for another time to explore its capabilities.

Well, that time has arrived to have another look at the RanaSystems EliteThree vis-à-vis DOS 4.3. Any configuration utilizing the hardware capabilities of the Rana needs to address the current VTOC structure, and how it can possibly be expanded to provide for more than fifty tracks for a disk volume. The Rana can seek up to eighty tracks on a double-sided, double-density diskette. The Rana can also access both sides of a diskette without having to flip the diskette over to access the backside, thereby providing direct access to one hundred sixty tracks.

I recall fondly the time in 1968 when I sat in the Audio Music Library in Schoenberg Hall at UCLA listening to magnetic tape recordings for my class on Johann Sebastian Bach. The library used an array of four Viking 80 magnetic tape recorders to playback audio assignments for music students. I happened to own a Viking 880 (which used vacuum tubes for its circuits). The only difference is that the 880 came installed in a suitcase with two 2x6 inch speakers and a small stereo, solid state audio amplifier. This recorder had the ability to physically adjust the position of the erase, record, and playback heads in order to record or playback magnetic tapes recorded in half-track mode as well as magnetic tapes recorded in quarter-track mode. The signal-to-noise ratio for half-track recordings was obviously far superior to quarter-track recordings because twice as much magnetic material was used for the recorded signal. Even though the Viking was using a quarter-track playback head to read a half-track recording, the increased signal-to-noise ratio was still apparent. Why I mention half-track versus quarter-track magnetic audio recording is that the concepts are quite similar when applied to magnetic disk recording using a Disk][recorder versus a Rana EliteThree recorder. The recording head gap length, or track size in the Rana is half the recording head gap length in the Disk][, so recordings made by the Rana would have a smaller signal-to-noise ratio than those recordings made by the Disk][: half as much magnetic material is used for the recorded signal in the Rana. Pure havoc would occur if the Disk][tried to read a Rana disk recorded in 80 track mode.

Information is recorded in a magnetic material when that material is brought over an electromagnet that contains a small gap where magnetic flux can easily flow across that gap. The width of that physical gap, its spacing, is critical and it is an important design component of the recording and playback circuitry. The required magnetic flux to impose changes in the magnetic material is determined by the current flowing in, the voltage across, the impedance of, and the width of the gap of the magnetic coil within the R/W head. I simply point this out so that there is no confusion between the gap width and the gap length of a R/W head because width and length are easily confused and thought to be synonymous when referring to the R/W head gap.

It would be possible to differentiate between diskettes recorded using the standard prologue bytes in the Address Field and the Data Field headers, and those diskettes using other prologue header bytes. This simply makes this diskette readable by one RWTS and not another. The Rana could certainly use such a protocol but I believe there is simply not enough code space in the peripheral-card expansion ROM memory to make this work for more than one or two configurations regarding the number of tracks in the volume, the number of sectors per track, and the expansion of any of its VTOC bitmap data. Whatever configuration that uses the full capabilities of the Rana is most likely not going to be compatible with the Disk][. The DOS 4.3 VTOC structure is the only place where any compatibility argument can be derived for the Rana and the Disk][. I believe that whatever can fit in the Disk][VTOC is what should be used to decide how best to utilize the Rana.

Considering the lessons learned from half-track and quarter-track magnetic audio recording, and in view of the rather limited availability of double-sided, double-density magnetic media, I chose to implement full-track recording for the Rana, thus providing forty tracks on each side of the diskette knowing full well that the physical length of the recording head gap in the Rana is half that of the recording head gap in the Disk][. I also chose to implement recording all track sectors 0x00 to 0x0F on the notched side of the diskette and recording all track sectors 0x10 to 0x1F on the un-notched side of the diskette. The VTOC can fully accommodate this configuration. The Rana EPROM can also accommodate this configuration within its available code space and implement all of the RWTS commands for DOS 4.3. This configuration will provide forty tracks, each track having thirty-two sectors, for a volume having a total of 1280 sectors. If the VTOC and Catalog use six of those sectors, a Data disk would potentially have 1274 sectors for storage, a rather massive amount of disk space accessible on a single diskette. This is precisely the configuration I chose to implement. Table V.12.1 shows the firmware entry points for the firmware that is mapped to the peripheral-card ROM memory in the Rana EliteThree peripheral slot card.

Offset	Name	Description
0x00	RANABOOT	Entry point for PR# DOS command to boot DOS in drive 1
0x10	ROMHOOK	Entry point to attach the Rana to the DOS in memory
0x18	ROMUHOOK	Entry point to detach the Rana from the DOS in memory
0x20	RANARWTS	Issue CLRROM; enter RWTS processing
0x5C	BOOTFW	Disk][firmware-like entry point for Boot Stage 1 code at 0x0801
0x83	FNDADR	Read address field header for volume, track, and sector
0xA6	FNDDATA	Read 342 disk nibbles, post-nibblize to memory, jump to 0x0801
0xFE/FF	VERSION	Version number for Rana firmware (0x38): Version 3, Build 8

Table V.12.1. Rana Disk Firmware Entry Points

The signal-to-noise ratio for the Rana drive is still very much a concern because the Rana RWTS FORMAT algorithm rejects many of the double-sided/double-density diskettes I recently purchased, and marks them as not safely recordable, but they are perfectly recordable using the Disk][hardware. Diskettes having been previously recorded by a Disk][will still contain residual and problematic magnetic information even after the Rana overwrites such a diskette using FORMAT due to its smaller head gap length. It was after the successful formatting of several virgin diskettes that allowed me to finally test the Rana firmware I designed. Designing this firmware gave me the opportunity to learn more about how the volume format was originally conceived to use a free sector bitmap that supports up to fifty tracks, each track having 32 sectors. These bitmap findings are thoroughly discussed in Sections I.5 and I.6. Needless to say, a CFFA volume having forty-eight tracks where each track can have thirty-two sectors is just a minor extension to what I designed and implemented for a Rana volume. Truth be said, the education I received from exploring the Rana and its capabilities proved to be absolutely invaluable in the design of DOS 4.3. Perhaps a future enhancement to DOS 4.3 would be an extension to the VTOC bitmap area.

VTOC bytes 0xF8 through 0xFF are normally used for the track 0x30 and track 0x31 (i.e. 48 and 49) bitmaps, but they are currently unused even by the CFFA. I believe these eight bytes could easily serve as some sort of VTOC bridge to another available or designated sector in order to extend the free sector Bitmap of a Rana volume. Perhaps the Rana firmware could carry the burden of expanding the free sector Bitmap rather than DOS 4.3 as it is the Rana that is able to read and write far more tracks than other disk hardware. I believe it is possible to modify the Rana peripheral slot card to access a larger EPROM that could possibly bank switch the peripheral-card expansion ROM memory area. Having substantially more expansion ROM memory could easily support the additional software necessary to extend the free sector Bitmap of the Rana VTOC. The calculation of Free Space on a volume would have to ignore these last eight bytes and include those bytes on the expanded Bitmap.

DOS 4.3 uses a new, and unique algorithm to move the read/write head from one track to an adjacent track. Section I.10 describes the DOS 4.3 RWTS interface and the spacing of adjacent tracks in terms of half-phases. I have considered replacing the Rana firmware I designed that supports DOS 4.1L and DOS 4.1H. This firmware uses two independent sets of WRITSCTR and READSCTR routines because NBUF1 and NBUF2 are located in different memory locations for DOS 4.1L and DOS 4.1H. If the Rana firmware simply targeted DOS 4.3H there would be sufficient room in the peripheral-card expansion ROM memory for stepping the R/W head in half-phase increments as it is done in DOS 4.3. Alternatively, if the Rana interface firmware does not attach to the DOS 4.3 DISKADRS table and is simply treated as a Disk][-like drive, then all of the DOS 4.3 RWTS half-phase tracking will be utilized. This seems to be the better solution as long as this interface card is used only for two drives and not for four drives as it was designed to handle. Because the Rana can access forty four-half-phase spaced tracks, it would be reasonable to expect the Rans to access forty-eight three-half-phase spaced tracks. Not only is this expectation reasonable, it is absolutely possible and factual.

To assemble the Rana source code, place the DOS 4.3 Tools volume DOS4.3.Tools in disk drive 1, boot, and start *Lisa80*. Enter the SE command-line command to select the *SETUP80* utility in order to verify or set the Start of Source Code to 0x4000 and the Start of Symbol List to 0x7800. Place the Rana Source volume RANA.Source in disk drive 2, load the RANA.L file into memory, and start the assembler by entering either the A or the Z command-line command. If a printed version of the screen output is desired simply preface the A or the Z command with the P1 command-line command. The complete binary image will be saved to the Rana Source volume as RANA.

13. First Class Peripherals Sider

Around the year of 1985 my mother asked me to build her a computer system to store her genealogy records and data. She was becoming overwhelmed with ancestry information, and she knew and understood how invaluable a computer would be to store and link all of her information. I knew of a product called *Family Roots* by Stephen C. Vorenberg and marketed by Quinsept, Inc., that would give my mother the power and the flexibility she needed to contain and organize her ancestry information. Her *Family Roots* database initially filled four data diskettes besides the three program diskettes when she asked me if there was a better alternative than swapping diskettes in order to generate a family report. In its documentation *Family Roots* suggested using the Sider from First Class Peripherals, a fixed disk drive subsystem featuring 10 MB of hard disk drive data storage partitioned mostly as DOS 3.3 volumes. And, to tell the truth, I had been very interested in the Sider when I first heard about the drive but I just didn't have the reason or the bankroll to afford such a luxury. Mom had both. When I inherited my mother's Apple //e computer system she had filled more than 16 DOS 3.3 volumes with genealogy data on her Sider. The Sider proved to be the perfect data storage system for that era.

The Sider consists of a peripheral slot card connected to an external housing by means of an IDE cable. The housing contains a Xebec 1410A controller board and a 10 MB Winchester hard drive. The peripheral slot card contains a 2716 EPROM and it uses only two of its sixteen peripheral-card I/O memory locations to communicate with the Xebec controller. Essentially, the firmware transfers the first six bytes an eight-byte Data Context Block, or DCB to the controller. The DCB contains the command, a 24-bit Logical Block Address (LBA), a block count, a step option, and a buffer address to write 256 bytes of data to the Sider or read 256 bytes of data from the Sider. Thus, the LBA buffer address specifies one 256-byte page of data. A DOS 3.3 volume contains 560 pages, or Sider blocks of data. Even though a Sider may be configured not to use CP/M or ProDOS or Pascal formatted volumes, some Sider blocks are still set aside for those partitions. The Sider is partitioned only once to establish the sizes of the DOS 3.3, CP/M, ProDOS, or Pascal partitions. In the case of my mother's Sider, we partitioned it for the maximum number of DOS 3.3 volumes and the minimum number of CP/M, ProDOS, and Pascal volumes. Her 10 MB Sider contained 69 DOS 3.3 volumes beginning with Volume 0. *Family Roots* utilizes volume number in order to locate all system programs and all genealogy data. Of course, I was fascinated to learn how the Sider modified DOS 3.3 to "tame" volume number such that a program like *Family Roots* could utilize this valuable parameter.

Table V.13.1 shows the logical block structure of the Sider based on LBA number. The Xebec controller determines how this LBA number, or Sider block number is mapped to the hard drive. It is important to note that a volume is a contiguous group of blocks and each volume follows the previous volume, or group of blocks. Table V.13.2 shows the modifications I made to the Sider Logical Block Structure to support DOS 4.1 and DOS 4.3. The new Sider peripheral-card ROM firmware I designed boots the DOS 4.3H image starting at block 338. Alternately, the DOS 4.1L image can be booted by calling 0xCs20, where s is the slot number of the Sider peripheral slot card, typically slot 7. The DOS 4.1H image can be booted by calling 0xCs28. When a DOS image boots it will insert the Sider's RWTS handler address, 0xCs70, into its Disk Address Table. Table V.13.3 shows all the Sider firmware entry points for the firmware that is mapped to the peripheral-card ROM memory.

There is a mathematical relationship between LBA and volume, track, and sector found in the RWTS IOCB. The first volume is Volume 0 and it begins at LBA address 464, or 0x01D0. There are 35 tracks in a Sider volume and 16 blocks in a track. Each volume is 560 (i.e. 0x0230) blocks.

$$LBA = (volume * 0x230) + (track * 0x10) + sector + 0x01D0$$

LBA Range		Description
Start	**End**	
0	0	Sider boot block
1	1	Sider parameter block
2	36	DOS 3.3 boot image (35 blocks)
37	84	RAM card image (DOS) (48 blocks)
85	135	CP/M boot image point #1 (51 blocks)
136	255	Reserved for future use (120 blocks)
256	258	CP/M boot image point #2 (3 blocks)
259	463	Free area for any application (205 blocks)
464	1023	DOS 3.3 volume 0xFD (BU volume)
1024	????	User data area
????	????	12 alternate tracks

Table V.13.1. Sider Logical Block Structure

LBA Range		Description
Start	**End**	
0	0	Sider boot block
1	1	Sider parameter block
2	36	DOS 3.3 boot image (35 blocks)
37	84	RAM card image (DOS) (48 blocks)
85	135	CP/M boot image point #1 (51 blocks)
136	255	Reserved for future use (120 blocks)
256	258	CP/M boot image point #2 (3 blocks)
259	263	Free blocks (5 blocks)
264	295	DOS 4.1L boot image (32 blocks)
296	337	DOS 4.1H boot image (42 blocks)
338	379	DOS 4.3H boot image (42 blocks)
380	463	Remaining free blocks (84 blocks)
464	1023	Volume 0
1024	39103	Volumes 1 to 68
39136	39136	Park heads block

Table V.13.2. Modified Sider Logical Block Structure

In order to calculate the LBA efficiently and with great speed, lookup tables are used that essentially do all the multiplication by using simple addition. There is sufficient room in the 2716 EPROM for these four tables. The RWTS IOCB volume, track, and sector values are range-checked before the track and volume are used as indices into the pair of tables each for track and volume, and the extracted values are added to the sector value. The offset 0x01D0 is already incorporated within the data of the volume tables. I added the address of the DOS 4.1L image at index 69, the address of the DOS 4.1H image at index 70, and the address of the DOS 4.3H image at index 71 to the volume tables. Any of these DOS images or a selected Sider volume having a DOS image can be booted using the BOOTVOL entry point from Table V.13.3 at 0xCs40. The track and sector values are set to 0x00 and the regular boot sequence is initiated. If the boot image is a DOS 3.3 image, the SDRWTS3 address is used to replace the RWTS address found at 0xB7B8 and 0xB7B9. Otherwise, if the boot image is a DOS 4.1 or a DOS 4.3 image, the SDRWTS address is copied into their respective DOS Disk Address Table.

Offset	Name	Description
0x00	BOOTHR	Entry point for PR# DOS command to boot DOS 4.3H
0x10	ROMHOOK	Entry point to attach the Sider to the DOS in memory
0x18	ROMUHOOK	Entry point to detach the Sider from the DOS in memory
0x20	SDOS4.1L	Entry point to boot DOS 4.1L
0x28	SDOS4.1H	Entry point to boot DOS 4.1H
0x40	BOOTVOL	Entry point to boot any bootable volume on the Sider
0x50	PARK	Entry point to call ROMUHOOK and park the disk heads
0x5C	ROMBOOT	Simulate Disk][entry point for Boot Stage 1 code at 0x0801
0x70	SDRWTS	RWTS handler in DOS 4.1 or DOS 4.3 Disk Address Table
0x80	SDRWTS3	RWTS handler for DOS 3.3
0xA0	SDRIVER	Read/write a Sider LBA using an eight-byte DCB in regs Y/A
0xC0	GETSTAT	Get Sider status in Carry flag
0xD0	READSTAT	Read Sider status into a four-byte user buffer
0xF0	MODOS3	Patch DOS 3.3 after Boot Stage 2
0xFE/FF	VERSION	Version number for Sider firmware (0x38): Version 3, Build 8

Table V.13.3. Sider Firmware Entry Points

Family Roots utilizes Diversi-DOS in order to speed up the loading of its humungous Applesoft programs, and it also utilizes Diversi-DOS's DDMOVER to relocate most of DOS 3.3 to the Language Card. Still, *Family Roots* requires four file buffers, and in Diversi-DOS's implementation these buffers remain in lower memory. *Family Roots* chains from program to program keeping all of its global values in memory. This technique certainly makes *Family Roots* appear to seamlessly transfer control from one program to the next program particularly with the disk speedup routines in Diversi-DOS. I have to say that I derived my inspiration from Diversi-DOS to incorporate speedup routines native to DOS 4.1 initially, and to move an early version of DOS 4.1, perhaps Build 32 or Build 33, to the Language Card. DOS 4.3 is based on that Language Card version of DOS 4.1. Diversi-DOS moves pieces and parts of DOS 3.3 to the Language Card and it has to modify the addresses of all JMP and JSR instructions. Diversi-DOS createe a software interface between the routines it leaves in lower memory and the routines it moves to Language Card memory in order to perform all necessary Language Card protocol and bank switching. Designing DDMOVER must have been a momentous effort to be sure, and having most of DOS 3.3 in the Language Card certainly gives *Family Roots* the "breathing room" it needs in view of the size of its Applesoft programs and the size of its variable and ASCII data arrays. And yet the Language Card is actually less than fully utilized.

I certainly understood how Diversi-DOS by Bill Basham at Diversified Soft Research was able to speed up the File Manager's I/O routines, as well as understanding how SPEEDOS from Applied Engineering worked for its RamWorks products. I also looked at David DOS by David Weston and TurboDOS used for *Lisa*. I'm sure there were others who had forsaken the DOS INIT command and utilized that code space for their particular ingenious speedup algorithm. Even Don Worth and Pieter Lechner went so far as to suggest modifying the sector interleave table to speed up the reading of large Applesoft and Binary program. None of these algorithms seemed to be the very best solution for managing disk I/O in DOS 3.3. At Sierra On-Line a software engineer colleague of mine (a gentleman from the United Kingdom, actually) did provide an additional BLOAD keyword that provided a Page parameter. This keyword parameter provided an additional and new "read pages" subcode for the File Manager. His BLOAD was certainly fast and, if I recall correctly, it was used on the first version of King's Quest.

I decided that my goal to speed up DOS I/O was not to rewrite the File Manager, but to add some additional logic to the File Manager. This logic would read pages of a file when it was appropriate. For example, the first two bytes of an Applesoft file must be read in order to calculate the end of its program address before the rest of the file is read into memory. The remaining 0xFE bytes in its file buffer are copied to memory, one byte at a time. However, the remaining sectors of the file, except for the last sector most likely, can be read directly into memory one page at a time. If there is a last sector that contains some bytes, the sector can be read into its file buffer and the remaining bytes copied to memory, again one byte at a time. Binary files are handled in the same way except the first four bytes are copied into the DOS parameter area from its file buffer; that is, the file's target memory address and the file's size in bytes. The remaining 0xFC bytes in its file buffer are copied to memory one byte at a time. The remaining sectors of the file can be read directly to memory one page at a time.

I am quite sure that if DSR, Inc., had access to Apple's source code for DOS 3.3, it could have generated a native Language Card version for DOS 3.3 that did not require software like DDMOVER. My vision of having DOS 4.3 in the Language Card required that it must boot directly into the Language Card, therefore be wholly resident in the Language Card for the most part. It is one thing to cobble together a system from pieces of a previous system, but quite another thing when a complete system is fully designed from the ground up specifically for the Language Card. From DOS 4.1L I designed DOS 4.1H to occupy the Language Card natively. It has all of the functionality found in DOS 4.1L and more. All file buffers, up to five, are fully contained in the Language Card as well. There is even enough code space to provide a DOS HELP command that provides the basic syntax for all DOS commands. It is this version of DOS that initially became DOS 4.3. Therefore, regardless of the number of file buffers in use, HIMEM is always set to 0xBE00, the highest possible address in order to provide an Applesoft environment that can support monster programs like those found in *Family Roots*.

Furthermore, DOS 4.3 contains the same CHAIN algorithm found in DOS 4.1. Preliminary tests have shown that DOS 4.3 and CHAIN function beautifully with *Family Roots*. There are empty volumes on the Sider that can be used to conduct further tests with DOS 4.3 and *Family Roots*. Or, the *Family Roots* programs and data volumes can be moved to a drive on the CFFA and tested there. Either location would certainly verify the migration of *Family Roots* to DOS 4.3. I believe my mother would have certainly been very impressed, and she would have certainly provided me with hours of hands-on testing.

```
                Sider Connect Program




Sider Slot:          4        5        6        ▞



          Sider:    Reconnect    Init    Abort
```

Figure V.13.1. Sider Connect Program

```
                Useful Entry Points

                          Type From  Type From
                          Applesoft   Monitor
DOS 4.3H Boot:       CALL -14592     C700G
DOS Connect:         CALL -14576     C710G
DOS Disconnect:      CALL -14568     C718G
DOS 4.1L Boot:       CALL -14560     C720G
DOS 4.1H Boot:       CALL -14552     C728G
DOS Volume Boot:     CALL -14528     C740G

Park Heads:          CALL -14512     C750G

DOS 4.3 RWTS:        CALL -14480     C770G
DOS 4.1 RWTS:        CALL -14480     C770G
DOS 3.3 RWTS:        CALL -14464     C780G

Sider DCB Driver:    CALL -14432     C7A0G
Request Status:      CALL -14400     C7C0G
Receive Status:      CALL -14384     C7D0G
           Press Any Key to Continue
```

Figure V.13.2. Sider Entry Points

262

I replaced the Xebec 2716 EPROM with a 6116 static RAM chip and connected its R/W pin to finger 18 of the peripheral slot card. This allows me to experiment with my own firmware for the Sider in order to support the ability to boot different DOS images. Early versions of this firmware utilized some memory in the static RAM to save variables such as slot number, slot number times sixteen, and DOS version currently in memory. Using the static RAM for certain variables was the easiest way to implement communication with the Xebec controller. I simply ported over the RAM Disk Connect Program since the RAM Disk peripheral slot card also uses a 6116 static RAM. Figures V.13.1 and V.13.2 show the Sider Connect Program I use to load the static RAM with each iteration of the Sider firmware. Now that I have established a strong confidence level in the operation of that firmware, I have re-engineered the firmware to utilize the public and private memory bytes on the TEXT screen reserved for peripheral slot cards. This allows me to once again utilize a 2716 EPROM for the Sider firmware. Or, I suppose I could use the 28C16A EEPROM in this application as I did for the RAM Disk peripheral slot card. The Init function shown in Figure V.13.1 would require the same software timing procedure I developed for the RAM Disk Init function for its connect program.

It is interesting to note that the hardware logic on the Sider peripheral slot card maps the first seven pages of its EPROM data to the peripheral-card expansion ROM address range 0xC800 to 0xCEFF. The last page of its EPROM data is mapped to its peripheral-card ROM address range 0xCs00 to 0xCsFF, where s is the slot number of the Sider peripheral slot card. With the Sider peripheral-card expansion ROM enabled, the 0xCF00 to 0xCFFF data is the same as the 0xCs00 to 0xCsFF data. The hardware engineers at RanaSystems designed their peripheral slot card for the EliteThree disk drive using the very same EPROM to memory mapping. There really isn't a better EPROM to memory mapping scheme when a 2716 EPROM is selected. I believe a 2732 EPROM would be a far better choice. The first eight pages of the 2732 would be mapped to the peripheral-card ROM memory, one page for each slot. The bytes in the first page would be programmed to 0xFF and left unused. Absolute addressing instructions could be used for the software routines used by each slot like I designed for *EOS*: the software is identical for each slot except for their absolute addressing instructions that enable or disable the quikLoader. The last eight pages of the 2732 would be mapped to the peripheral-card expansion ROM memory. This memory would contain the generic routines used by each slot no matter which slot the Sider peripheral slot card resides in. More importantly, the hardware logic design of the peripheral slot card would be greatly simplified. I wonder if the availability of 2716 verses 2732 EPROMs drove the design of the Sider and the RanaSystems peripheral slot cards. Perhaps cost was chosen over simplicity. Another page of peripheral-card expansion ROM memory would have been rather nice. Perhaps this would be an interesting hardware upgrade project for these two peripheral slot cards?

To assemble the Sider source code, place the DOS 4.3 Tools volume DOS.4.3.Tools in disk drive 1, boot, and start *Lisa80*. Enter the SE command-line command to select the *SETUP80* utility in order to verify or set the Start of Source Code to 0x4000 and the Start of Symbol List to 0x7800. Place the Sider Source volume SIDER.Source in disk drive 2, load the SIDER.L file into memory, and start the assembler by entering either the A or the Z command-line command. If a printed version of the screen output is desired simply preface the A or the Z command with the P1 command-line command. Seven object code files will be created on the Sider Source volume named SEG01 to SEG07. The seven object code files can be combined in memory sequentially starting at 0x4000 using the ctrl-P command. The complete binary image can be saved to the Sider Source volume or to any other volume as SIDER.

14. Sourceror

I first "sourced" *Sourceror* so I could modify its source code in order to create a more pleasing display of its available commands using uppercase and lowercase ASCII before processing other object code files. *Sourceror*, like *Big Mac*, was written by Glen Bredon. *Sourceror* is a Binary program that originally executed at `0x8900` after `MAXFILES` was set to 1. This placed *Sourceror* just below the first file buffer for DOS 3.3 and DOS 4.1L. I found only one error in *Sourceror*, a missing `CLC` instruction where the software handles 65C02 instructions. Occasionally, not always, the program counter was incremented one byte too much because a *Sourceror* routine assumed that the `Carry` flag would always be clear upon the return from a call to `GETNUM` at `0xFFA7`. Obviously, the `Carry` flag was not always clear. After I developed DOS 4.1H, I was able to relocate *Sourceror* to 0xAC00 thus allowing the sourcing of far larger object code files. A few more changes to the source code allowed *Sourceror* to function beautifully in concert with DOS 4.3.

Sourceror already contained the text of a number of symbols in order for it to generate a symbol listing at the end of the source code as per the convention that *Big Mac* uses for its source files. I added a number of additional symbols to its list that includes `CLRROM`, `RAM2WE`, `ROM2WE`, `ROM2WP`, `RAM2WE`, `RAM1WP`, `ROM1WE`, `ROM1WP`, `RAM1WE`, `STROBE`, `LATCH`, `DATAIN`, and `DATAOUT`.

Figure V.14.1 shows the initialization screen after `LOADSRCRR` has launched `SOURCEROR`. Figure V.14.2 shows the startup, or Help screen *Sourceror* displays with its command-line prompt "$". Figure V.14.3 shows the Monitor source listing of *Sourceror* after the first `L` instruction is issued.

```
Press RETURN to accept default Source
Code address 0x4000, or enter 0x


If the present location of the code
to be disassembled is at its original
location, press RETURN.  If not,
enter PRESENT location 0x900


In disassembling, use the ORIGINAL
location 0xAC00※
```

Figure V.14.1. Sourceror Initialization

```
SOURCEROR - 65C02 - UDS4.3

              by Glen Bredon

A HEX byte nn after commands T or H
limits the output to nn bytes.

Commands (alone or after HEX address):

L - Disassemble (current mode)
N - Normal (next mode)
S - Sweet 16 (next mode)
T - Text (TT defeats DCI)
W - Address (W-: Address-1, WW: DDB)
H - HEX data (1 byte default)

R - Read (does not create source)
/ - Retrieve last default address
I - Instructions
Q - Quit

$▓
```

Figure V.14.2. Sourceror Startup/Help Screen

```
$AC00L
                        ORG     $AC00
AC00-   78              SEI
AC01-   20 58 FF        JSR     $FF58
AC04-   BA              TSX
AC05-   BD 00 01        LDA     $0100,X
AC08-   58              CLI
AC09-   C9 AC           CMP     #$AC
AC0B-   F0 03           BEQ     $AC10
AC0D-   4C D3 03        JMP     $03D3
AC10-   4C 06 B0        JMP     $B006
AC13-   8D 8D 3C        STA     $3C8D
AC16-   09 0E           ORA     #$0E
AC18-   16 05           ASL     $05,X
AC1A-   12 13           ORA     ($13)
AC1C-   05 3D           ORA     $3D
AC1E-   03              ???
AC1F-   0E 14 12        ASL     $1214
AC22-   2E 20 03        ROL     $0320
AC25-   08              PHP
AC26-   2E 3E 20        ROL     $203E
AC29-   7C 46 4C        JMP     ($4C46,X)
$▓
```

Figure V.14.3. Sourceror Monitor Source Listing

Many years ago I used *Sourceror* to provide visibility and complete insight into DOS 3.3, and recently, insight into the CFFA firmware, and everything that came in between, before, and after those two major projects in the last 35 years. Because of *Sourceror* I understand a fair amount of what there is to know about Apple][hardware architecture and about the design of Apple][software that is used to manage and exploit that hardware architecture. I have a tremendous debt of gratitude for Glen Bredon, his software utilities, and his brilliant insight into Apple][hardware and software architecture.

To assemble the *Sourceror* source code, place the DOS 4.3 Tools volume `DOS.4.3.Tools` in disk drive 1, boot, and start *Lisa80*. Enter the `SE` command-line command to select the *SETUP80* utility in order to verify or set the `Start of Source Code` to `0x4000` and the `Start of Symbol List` to `0x7800`. Place the Sourceror Source volume `SOURCEROR.Source` in disk drive 2, load the `SOURCEROR.L` file into memory, and start the assembler by entering either the `A` or the `Z` command-line command. If a printed version of the screen output is desired simply preface the `A` or the `Z` command with the `P1` command-line command. The complete binary image will be saved to the Sourceror Source volume as `SOURCEROR`. Also, the `LOADSRCRR` source code can be assembled using the same procedure.

15. Applesoft Formatter

After about six months of writing test and demonstration Applesoft programs on my new Apple][+, I began thinking about writing a serious Applesoft program. Binary File Installation was that program, but it became a hybrid program because it included attached assembly language routines as described in section V.16. I also thought I was now capable of writing a standalone assembly language program. How an Applesoft program appeared on the screen when listed or printed by my printer appalled me, and I was determined to use assembly language to design and write an *Applesoft Formatter* program. I wanted *Applesoft Formatter* to align program line numbers and consistently space all parentheses the way I liked them spaced. (This spacing of parentheses carried over into how I formatted all my C language software.) Two inherent features of this program were to optionally split multiple BASIC commands on one line so that they would appear on separate lines, and to optionally indent BASIC commands within a FOR/NEXT loop no matter how nested the loops became. Since I owned an Epson MX100 printer I could easily print up to 120 characters on each line if I used wide paper. Basically, this program became an exercise in parsing Applesoft tokens, keeping track of FOR/NEXT loops, and counting quotes. As an interesting aside, I wrote this software so that it could execute at any memory address. It was certainly an intriguing exercise in order to develop relocatable object code.

```
]LOAD TEST

]LIST

 10 MN = 1:MX = 10: PRINT
 20 I = 0: FOR I = MN TO MX: IF I
     = 5 THEN  GOSUB 100
 30 S$ = "Entry #" +  STR$ (I):J =
     I + 7
 40 T$ = S$ +  STR$ (J): NEXT
 50  END
 100  PRINT "I = ";I;", J = ";J;"
     , S$ = ";S$: RETURN

]

]RUN

I = 5, J = 11, S$ = Entry #4

]
```

Figure V.15.1. Applesoft Program Listing

A very simple, unimaginative Applesoft test program is shown in Figure V.15.1 along with some results when it is RUN. I have purposefully put several Applesoft commands on the same line and embedded a FOR/NEXT loop within those lines. Even when this program is listed to a printer it

267

appears just as awkward and difficult to read. Needless to say, a program many times this size would be exceedingly difficult to read, debug, and analyze. I am sure there must have been at least one utility if not more available in the early 1980's like Roger Wagner's Apple-Doc, that could format Applesoft programs with multiple formatting options. And, I am sure those programs did their task work magnificently, too. But that was not my intention, to purchase someone else's labor and product.

I wanted to understand how to parse an Applesoft program in assembly language, and I wanted to understand how to separate Applesoft command tokens from variable names and embedded ASCII text. So, this exercise would require me to do some research, analysis, and a little hard work. Figure V.15.2 shows the output of *Applesoft Formatter* when the Split Line and Indent line options are enabled. Seriously, this generated listing is totally easy to read, debug, and analyze now that the Applesoft test program has been formatted in an appealing and precise composition. I also gained an exceptional understanding of assembly language programming for the 6502-microprocessor, how best to use an assembler, and how to create relocatable object code. Obviously, the lessons learned in writing *Applesoft Formatter* were forever invaluable to me, and the effort paid off handsomely.

To assemble the *ASLIST* source code, place the DOS 4.3 Tools volume `DOS.4.3.Tools` in disk drive 1, boot, and start *Lisa80*. Enter the `SE` command-line command to select the *SETUP80* utility in order to verify or set the `Start of Source Code` to `0x4000` and the `Start of Symbol List` to `0x7800`. Place the ASLIST Source volume `ASLIST.Source` in disk drive 2, load the `ASLIST.L` file into memory, and start the assembler by entering either the `A` or the `Z` command-line command. If a printed version of the screen output is desired simply preface the `A` or the `Z` command with the `P1` command-line command. The binary image will be saved to the ASLIST Source volume as `ASLIST`.

```
Maximum Characters/Line (<161):   31

Split Line (Y,N):   Y

Indent (Y,N):   Y

Echo to Screen (Y,N):   Y

    10    MN = 1
          MX = 10
          PRINT
    20    I = 0
          FOR I = MN TO MX
             IF I = 5 THEN GOSUB 100
    30       S$ = "Entry #" + STR$( I )
             J = I + 7
    40       T$ = S$ + STR$( J )
          NEXT
    50    END
   100    PRINT "I = "; I; ", J = "; J;
          "  S$ = "; S$
          RETURN

] ※
```

Figure V.15.2. Applesoft Program Programmatically Formatted

16. Binary File Installation (BFI)

Binary File Installation (*BFI*) was the first totally useful Applesoft program I wrote for my Apple][+.
I began writing Applesoft programs initially, but soon I explored assembly language for various data
sort algorithms and disk I/O routines that fascinated me. If I wrote the data sort algorithms and disk
I/O routines such that they could execute at any memory address, then I could attach their binary code
to the end of an Applesoft program, modify some page-zero pointers, and save the composite, albeit
hybrid program. Whenever I ran the Applesoft program, the program logic was designed to obtain its
program size from certain page-zero locations and then calculate the addresses where the data sort
algorithm and/or the disk I/O routines resided in memory knowing their lengths in bytes, or that many
bytes before the end of the program. A CALL could then be made directly to the address of the data
sort algorithm or the disk I/O routine from any location within the Applesoft program. This capability
of CALLing my own relocatable assembly language routines within an Applesoft program was
exhilarating to me, and I talked about this capability to all my co-workers who would listen, or to those
who were patient with my "Apple computer" programming excitement.

I learned I could even pass parameters to an assembly language routine and also have values returned
to the Applesoft program. Any number of relocatable routines could be attached to the end of an
Applesoft program and CALLed as long as their location in memory could be precisely determined. I
thought a utility could more easily handle this attachment process, so I created Binary File Installation
to do just that. The user tells *BFI* which Applesoft program to target that is to receive the binary file
attachment(s), and a selection of all the relocatable binary files that could be attached. Then, *BFI*
modifies the size of the Applesoft program on disk (i.e. its first two bytes in the file) and calls the File
Manager to append the binary files directly to the end of the program on disk just after its last three
NULL bytes: simple, clean, and efficient. Once the attachment is done, *BFI* prints the order and the
size of all the binary files it attached. The Applesoft program can still be edited at any time using the
Apple command line and cursor move routines. However, if a tool such as *GPLE* or *PGE* is used to
edit the Applesoft program, any attached binary files will be stripped from the program when the
edited file is saved to disk. I have yet to explore how to disable this feature in both *GPLE* and PGE.

I have modified *BFI* a number of times as I increased my knowledge of the VTOC and RWTS, as well
as the HIRES screen and the HIRES drawing routines. Sierra On-Line's ScreenWriter product used a
HIRES screen font that I adapted for *BFI*, and *BFI* uses an adaptation of the HIRES icon drawing
routine I developed for Sierra's HomeWord Speller product. I even wrote the icon development and
editing tool that I use to create and generate the "shape table" data for all screen icons used in *BFI*.
After the initial splash screen, the Main Menu screen is displayed as shown in Figure V.16.1. The
Peripheral Selection screen allows one to easily select the Hardware icons displayed as shown in
Figure V.16.2.

BFI displays the results of the binary file installation after it completes its processing, and the user can
selectively print this report as well. Figure V.16.3 shows the report that is generated after *BFI* attaches
all the binary files required by the *BFI* Applesoft code. I probably learned more about the design of
my Apple][hardware and firmware from this single program: I was then at a very early stage in my
computer programming self-education after having been recently graduated with a bachelor's degree in
Electrical Engineering.

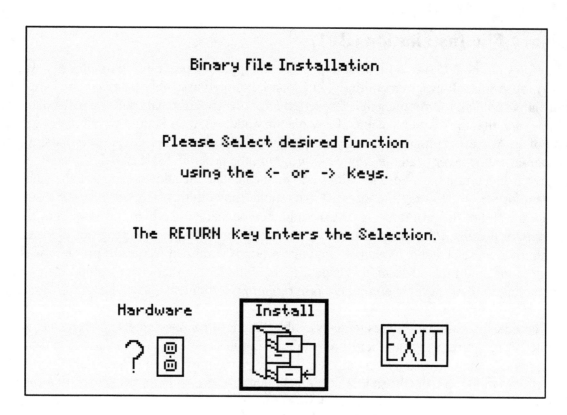

Figure V.16.1. BFI Main Menu

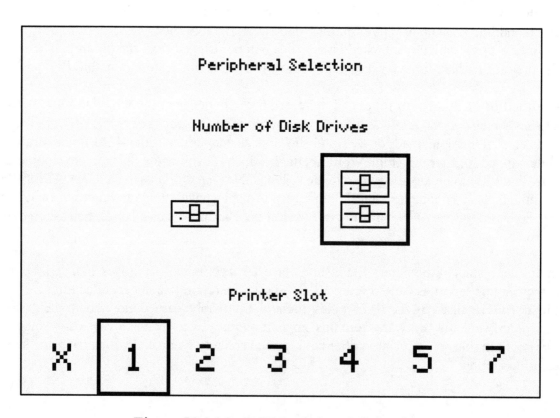

Figure V.16.2. BFI Peripheral Selection

```
                Binary File Installation Report

*** Applesoft File ***                    Length in Bytes
BFI                                              6337

*** Binary Files ***
CR                                                453
SS                                                336
RW                                                178
FA                                                129
MM                                                 93
FS                                                 78
IC                                                 33
DI                                               1486
SD                                               1115

                               Total:          10238
```

Figure V.16.3. BFI Installation Report on BFI

To assemble the relocatable *BFI* assembly language source code routines, place the DOS 4.3 Tools volume `DOS.4.3.Tools` in disk drive 1, boot, and start *Lisa80*. Enter the `SE` command-line command to select the *SETUP80* utility in order to verify or set the `Start of Source Code` to `0x4000` and the `Start of Symbol List` to `0x7800`. Place the BFI Source volume `BFI.Source` in disk drive 2, load a *Lisa* assembly language source code file into memory, and start the assembler by entering either the `A` or the `Z` command-line command. If a printed version of the screen output is desired simply preface the `A` or the `Z` command with the `P1` command-line command. The complete binary image of that source code routine will be saved to the BFI Source volume. Continue to assemble all of the *BFI* assembly language source code routines until all of the routines have been assembled. *BFI* determines its end address from the value found in `0xAF/0xB0`, and calculates the addresses of its attached binary file routines in the opposite order of their attachment.

Reboot with the DOS 4.3 Tools volume, remove the BFI Source volume `BFI.Source` from disk drive 2, place that volume in disk drive 1, and run `BFI`. Select a single drive installation and whatever slot the printer interface slot card resides in. Select `BFI.RAW` for the target Applesoft program and successively select the binary files shown in Figure V.16.3. Binary files from other volumes may be selected as well. Perform the installation and print the Binary File Installation Report if desired.

Alternatively, place the BFI Source volume `BFI.Source` in disk drive 1 and run `BFI`. Select a two-drive installation and whatever slot the printer interface slot card resides in. Remove the BFI Source volume and place the volume containing a target Applesoft program in disk drive 1 and the volume containing the relocatable binary files to install in disk drive 2. Select the target Applesoft program in disk drive 1 and the necessary binary files to install in disk drive 2, perform the installation, and print the Binary File Installation Report if desired.

17. SCRG PROmGRAMER

The quikLoader marketed by the Southern California Research Group is of little value without a means to easily write (i.e. program) EPROMs. So, SCRG also marketed the PROmGRAMER, designed by Bob Brice, which could program EPROMs for the quikLoader, the Apple //e character generator ROM, and the Apple //e firmware ROM(s). The PROmGRAMER is designed to be configurable using DIP switches in order to access 2716, 2716A, 2732, 2732A, 2764, 27128, 27128A, 27256, and 27512 type EPROMs. The PROmGRAMER software by Bob Sander-Cederlof resides in memory beginning at 0x0803, and the program cannot extend beyond 0x0FFF because the desirable EPROM image start address is set at 0x1000. This is necessary particularly in order to program a 27256 or a 27512 EPROM. For a 27256 EPROM its entire 0x8000 byte image must reside in memory for convenience, and if 0x1000 is its start address, then 0x8FFF will be its end address, and that was very close to the beginning of the third DOS 3.3 file buffer. When MAXFILES is 3 in DOS 3.3, HIMEM is set to 0x9625. To program a 27512 EPROM a 0x10000 byte image must be divided into two or more parts, so the EPROM must be programed in two or more sessions. It is for this reason that I highly recommend finding the midpoint for the contents of a 27512 EPROM so that it can be programmed in only two sessions where each session programs 0x8000 bytes. As a reminder, DOS 4.3 provides a useable memory workarea from 0x0800 to 0xBDFF.

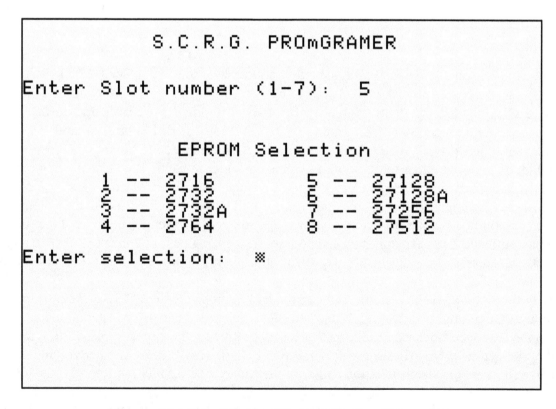

Figure V.17.1. PROmGRAMER Configuration

As shown in Figures V.2.6 and V.2.7, the 27512 EPROM image needs to be split at the 0x8000 byte halfway point. The source code is designed to have the *Lisa* assembler do all the work of splitting the image at the correct place. Therefore, only two EPROM programming sessions will be required. The software Mr. Sander-Cederlof provided for the PROmGRAMER allowed the user to enter a command, such as F (for Fast program), and the default parameters would be entered and used to program a 27256 or the first half of a 27512 EPROM image. There was no command with default parameters to program the second half of a 27512 EPROM, so the parameters had to be entered on the command line manually. I found this to be unfortunate after I ruined one too many 27512 EPROM programming sessions: I mistakenly entered the wrong parameters while attempting to program the upper, or second half of the EPROM. So, I sourced the PROmGRAMER object code software and I added all the additional commands that I thought would be necessary to support the programming of a 27512 EPROM. Figure V.17.1 shows the configuration screen for PROmGRAMER and Figure V.17.2 shows all the commands now available to the user. The commands I added that support the 27512 EPROM are S, T, G, and A. I had to heavily modify the original code in order for that code and the additional code that supports these new commands to fit within the limited space from 0x0803 to 0x0FFF. It works. I'm happy.

To assemble the *BURNER* source code, place the DOS 4.3 Tools volume DOS.4.3.Tools in disk drive 1, boot, and start *Lisa80*. Enter the SE command-line command to select the *SETUP80* utility in order to verify or set the Start of Source Code to 0x4000 and the Start of Symbol List to 0x7800. Place the BURNER Source volume BURNER.Source in disk drive 2, load the BURNER.L file into memory, and start the assembler by entering either the A or the Z command-line command. If a printed version of the screen output is desired simply preface the A or the Z command with the P1 command-line command. The complete binary image will be saved to the BURNER Source volume as BURNER.

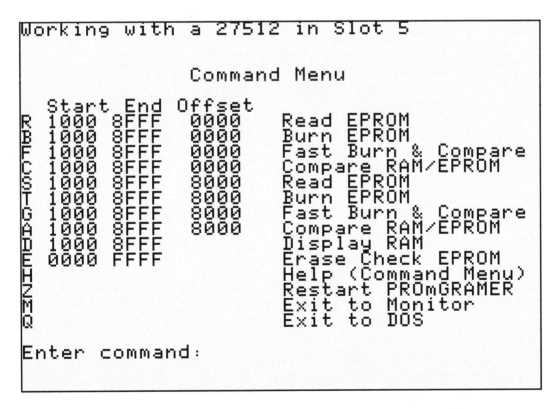

Figure V.17.2. PROmGRAMER Expanded Command Menu

18. Real Time Clock

The experience I gained in building the memory upgrade for my Apple][+ described in Section V.22 led me to design and build my own *Real Time Clock* peripheral slot card. I had to learn some new skills in order to build a peripheral slot card that would fit within the dimensions allowed for a slot card in the Apple][+ computer. I had never etched a double-sided copper clad board that large nor had I thought about how to place TTL components in terms of organization, data and control signal flow, wire length, and clean power. I also had to include and manage additional circuitry to charge the onboard rechargeable batteries. All these ideas mattered one way or another I am sure, but honestly, I didn't have much of a clue. In hindsight I should have taken a class in TTL circuit board design and layout before I was graduated with my degree in Electrical Engineering. My garage was my ultimate laboratory and workshop! But most importantly I wanted the hardware design to provide a simple, elegant, and thoroughly elementary firmware interface for software.

Pin	Name	Function
1	CS2	chip select #2, active high, low to disable
2	WRITE	write port, active high to write data, 2.0 μsec minimum
3	READ	read port, active high to read data, 1.0 μsec minimum
4	D3	read and write data bit 3
5	D2	read and write data bit 2
6	D1	read and write data bit 1
7	D0	read and write data bit 0
8	Vss	ground connection
9	ADRWRT	address write port, active high to latch address, hold time 0.1 μsec, pulse time 0.5 μsec
10	*BUSY*	active low, wait until high to continue
11	STOP	stop enable port, active high, low to run
12	TEST	test enable port, active high, low to test
13	CS1	chip select #1, active high, low to disable
14	NC	no connection
15	NC	no connection
16	Vdd	+5 volt connection

Table V.18.1. SaRonix RTC58321 Real Time Clock Pinout

I wanted to design my *Real Time Clock* card around the SaRonix RTC58321 Real Time Clock module, which I probably obtained from Jameco Electronics in the mid 1980's. The pinout of the RTC58321 is shown in Table V.18.1 and it incorporated an internal quartz crystal in a single 16-pin DIP package thereby eliminating the need for an external crystal and timing circuit. This clock module provided me with everything I needed: read and write for date and time values and an external *BUSY* signal. I wanted the firmware interface to be as simple as possible so I put a lot of effort into the design of the slot card hardware logic so that the hardware would negotiate with the RTC58321's data and address setup time requirements. Unfortunately, the 6502-clock read/write period happens to be far too short for the required data and address setup time needed for the RTC58321.

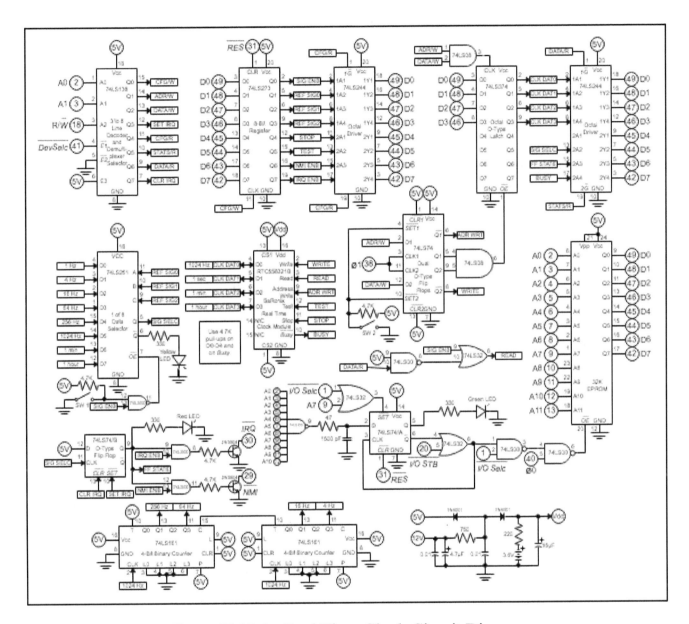

Figure V.18.1. Real Time Clock Circuit Diagram

I used a breadboard for the TTL logic components in order to figure out how to best negotiate with the RTC58321 using a full 6502-clock period and utilizing a flip-flop to increase the clock period. Then I wrote the slot interface firmware for the onboard 2732 EPROM. I modeled my general user Applesoft interface after the Applied Engineering TimeMaster II Applesoft interface. Whatever commands the TimeMaster could handle, I made sure my clock card could handle in addition to all the other commands and capabilities I could devise and had room for in the EPROM. And I figured out how to make use of the standard signals generated by the RTC58321 to pull the IRQ and/or NMI line low in

275

order to initiate a hardware interrupt. Once I had the schematic drawn and the components organized, I drilled all the necessary holes for chip sockets and components, and etched the copper for the power, ground, and some logic lines. I hand-wired and soldered the remaining connections for the interface board slot finger, chip sockets, transistors, batteries, LEDs, configuration block, resistors, and capacitors. My *Real Time Clock* card is fully operational even today as it was over thirty-two years ago. I've only had to replace the rechargeable batteries a couple of times! Figure V.18.1 shows the complete circuit diagram for my *Real Time Clock* card that I had originally drawn on March 20, 1988.

Address	Operation	Description
0xC0s0	read	Read configuration register
0xC0s0	write	Write configuration register
0xC0s1	read	Read status register
0xC0s1	write	Write clock register number
0xC0s2	read	Read clock data register
0xC0s2	write	Write clock data register
0xC0s3	read	Clear interrupt flip-flop
0xC0s3	write	Arm interrupt flip-flop

Table V.18.2. Real Time Clock Peripheral Slot Card I/O Addresses

Bit	Description
0	Interrupt enable, 0 = OFF
1	Interrupt rate select A
2	Interrupt rate select B
3	Interrupt rate select C
4	STOP enable, 0 = RUN
5	TEST enable, 0 = normal operation
6	NMI enable, 0 = OFF
7	IRQ enable, 0 = OFF

Table V.18.3. Real Time Clock Configuration Register

Only four of the sixteen peripheral-card I/O memory locations are used for clock configuration, clock address, clock status, clock register, clock data, and interrupt clear and set. Table V.18.2 shows the description of those memory locations where **s** is equals to the slot number of the *Real Time Clock* card plus eight. Only memory address bits A0 and A1 are captured so it does not matter what is used for memory address bits A2 and A3. Addresses 0xC0s4, 0xC0s8, and 0xC0sC are all valid for 0xC0s0 in order to read and write the *Real Time Clock* configuration register. Table V.18.3 shows the description of the configuration register bits. This register retains its configuration until it is changed by another write to 0xC0s0 or when RESET is pressed. When RESET is pressed this register is cleared to `0x00`. Before loading the clock data registers it is important to stop the clock by setting the `STOP` Enable bit to one. Once the clock is loaded, the configuration register can be restored with its previous configuration data. Table V.18.4 shows the description of the eight interrupt rates that are available for the generation of `IRQ` and/or `NMI` interrupts. The selected interrupt rate is made active by setting the Interrupt Enable bit to one as shown in Table V.18.3. In order for interrupts to be generated either the `NMI` Enable bit and/or the `IRQ` Enable bit must be set to one. The configuration register also provides control of the `TEST` enable port of the RTC58321. I no longer can locate any documentation that describes how to test the RTC58321 using the `TEST` enable port.

C	B	A	Description
0	0	0	1 Hz interrupt rate
0	0	1	4 Hz interrupt rate
0	1	0	16 Hz interrupt rate
0	1	1	64 Hz interrupt rate
1	0	0	256 Hz interrupt rate
1	0	1	1024 Hz interrupt rate
1	1	0	1 minute interrupt rate
1	1	1	1 hour interrupt rate

Table V.18.4. Interrupt Rate Selection

Reg	D3	D2	D1	D0	Name	D3	D2	D1	D0	Count	Notes
00	0	0	0	0	S1	s8	s4	s2	s1	0 to 9	1-second digit
01	0	0	0	1	S10	-	s40	s20	s10	0 to 5	10-second digit
02	0	0	1	0	MI1	mi8	mi4	mi2	mi1	0 to 9	1-minute digit
03	0	0	1	1	MI10	-	mi40	mi20	mi10	0 to 5	10-minute digit
04	0	1	0	0	H1	h8	h4	h2	h1	0 to 9	1-hour digit
05	0	1	0	1	H10	24/ 12	PM/ AM	h20	h10	0 to 2 0 to 1	10-hour digit
06	0	1	1	0	W	-	w4	w2	w1	0 to 6	week digit
07	0	1	1	1	D1	d8	d4	d2	d1	0 to 9	1-day digit
08	1	0	0	0	D10	leap year		d20	d10	0 to 3	10-day digit
09	1	0	0	1	MO1	mo8	mo4	mo2	mo1	0 to 9	1-month digit
0A	1	0	1	0	MO10	-	-	-	mo10	0 to 1	10-month digit
0B	1	0	1	1	Y1	y8	y4	y2	y1	0 to 9	1-year digit
0C	1	1	0	0	Y10	y80	y40	y20	y10	0 to 9	10-year digit
0D	1	1	0	1	reset	-	-	-	-		reset register
0E	1	1	1	0	idle	1	1	1	1024		standard signal
0F	1	1	1	1	idle	hour	min.	sec.	Hz		register

Table V.18.5. Real Time Clock Registers

Table V.18.5 lists the sixteen registers available in the RTC58321. Any time when an 0x0E or 0x0F register number is latched the clock module is put into its idle state and the standard signals are available at its data ports when the READ port of the RTC58321 is set to one. Setting the READ port of the RTC58321 to one is accomplished by setting the Interrupt Enable bit in the configuration register to one as shown in Table V.18.3. The 1024 Hz signal is divided by two 74LS161 binary counters to obtain the remaining interrupt rates that can be selected by the configuration register. Even though the *Real Time Clock* card can also generate NMI interrupts, the EPROM firmware only has provisions to generate and handle IRQ interrupts. Nevertheless, software can easily be written to utilize an NMI interrupt if there is an occasion for such an interrupt to be generated.

Setting data bit 3 in register 0x05 of the RTC58321 will select 24-hour mode. Doing this will clear data bit 2 of the same register. If 12-hour mode is selected then data bit 2 will select PM if that bit is set to one. The RTC58321 divides the 10-year digit in register 0x0C by 4 in order to determine leap year. The remainder of this division is saved to data bits 2 and 3 of register 0x08. If the remainder is zero then leap year is selected. The RTC58321 may be reset by latching register 0x0D and writing any data to that register. This sets the WRITE port of the RTC58321 to one as shown in Table V.18.1. The EPROM firmware does not RESET the RTC58321.

The *Real Time Clock* card utilizes two switches to control its function. Closing Switch 1 disables the frequency data selector module and blocks the output of the selected interrupt rate. Therefore, the clock card cannot generate an interrupt even if the NMI enable bit or the IRQ enable bit is set to one in the configuration register. Closing Switch 2 will disable the Address Write and Data Write flip-flops. Therefore, the data in the clock module cannot be changed rendering the RTC58321 write protected. The clock card utilizes three LEDs to indicate what function the clock card is performing. The Green LED lights whenever the 2732 EPROM is accessed. The Yellow LED lights at the same frequency as the selected interrupt rate if the frequency data selector module is enabled by the Interrupt Enable bit of the configuration register and if Switch 1 is open. The Red LED lights whenever the output of the Interrupt Flip-Flop is set to one (i.e. armed) regardless whether the NMI enable bit or the IRQ enable bit is set to one in the configuration register. If either bit is set the base of a 2N3904 general purpose transistor is pulled high thereby allowing its collector-emitter junction to conduct and pull the respective interrupt line safely to ground. I placed an R/C network between the output of the 74LS133 and the data input to the EPROM enable flip-flop in order to slightly extend the derived CLRROM signal because of the slight delay inherent in the clock pulse to that flip-flop.

The first half of the 2732 EPROM is used for eight copies of the same interface firmware for the peripheral-card ROM memory, one copy for each possible slot in which the Clock card could reside. The second half of the EPROM maps into the peripheral-card expansion ROM memory. Whenever the 6502-microprocessor fetches an instruction only in the first half of the peripheral-card ROM memory, 0xCs00 to 0xCs7F, where s is the slot number of the Clock card, the peripheral-card expansion ROM memory, 0xC800 to 0xCFFF, is enabled. The peripheral-card expansion ROM memory is not re-enabled when CLRROM is used in the second half of the peripheral-card ROM memory, a hardware design trick I learned from the hardware design of the RAM Disk 320 peripheral slot card. Table V.18.6 shows all the entry points in the EPROM slot firmware for the *Real Time Clock* card. This firmware conforms to the clock card protocol where the first two instructions are PHP and SEI, and the last byte, the clock ID, is 0x03. Clock ID 0x07 can also be used. DOS 4.3 accepts either value as valid.

Offset	Name	Description
0x00	MAINSELC	PHP instruction, DOS PR# and IN# command handler
0x01		SEI instruction
0x02		Issues CLRROM, branches to INITCLK
0x08	WRITSELC	Issues CLRROM, branches to LOADCLK
0x10	READSELC	Issues CLRROM, branches to READCLK
0x18	MODESELC	Issues CLRROM, branches to SETMODE
0x20	IRQSELC	Issues CLRROM, branches to SETIRQ
0x28	STRTSELC	Issues CLRROM, branches to STRTCLK
0x30	STOPSECL	Issues CLRROM, branches to STOPCLK
0x38	INITCLK	Saves registers, branches to HNDLINIT
0x3F	LOADCLK	Saves registers, branches to HNDLLOAD
0x46	READCLK	Saves registers, branches to HNDLREAD
0x4D	SETMODE	Saves registers, branches to HNDLMODE
0x54	SETIRQ	Saves registers, branches to HNDLIRQ
0x5B	STRTCLK	Saves registers, branches to HNDLSTRT
0x62	STOPCLK	Saves registers, branches to HNDLSTOP
0x69	WRITCLK	Issues CLRROM, branches to HNDLWRIT
0x71	SETRTN	Issues CLRROM, branches to HNDLRTN
0x79	IRQHNDLR	Issues CLRROM, branches to EXECIRQ
0x80	EXIT	Restores registers, issues CLRROM, returns to caller
0x8A	HNDLINIT	Gets slot, processes input command
0x93	HNDLLOAD	Gets slot, writes clock buffer at 0x2F0-0x2FC to clock
0x9C	HNDLREAD	Gets slot, reads clock to clock buffer at 0x2F0-0x2FC
0xA5	HNDLMODE	Gets slot, stores mode value 0x21-0x3E to MODE, 0x478
0xAE	HNDLIRQ	Gets slot, sets IRQ 0-7, clears IRQBUF, 0x2FD-0x2FF
0xB7	HNDLSTRT	Gets slot, updates clock config, puts SETRTN address in KSWL
0xC0	HNDLSTOP	Gets slot, stops clock, puts SETRTN address in KSWL
0xC9	HNDLWRIT	Saves registers, gets slot, stop CLK, write CLK register, start CLK
0xD7	HNDLRTN	Saves registers, gets slot, puts "RTN" at 0x200-0x201
0xE5	EXECIRQ	Saves registers, gets slot, updates IRQBUF, restores registers, issues CLRROM, returns with RTI instruction
0xFA	VERSION	upper ASCII "43"
0xFC	CLKNAME	upper ASCII "RTC"
0xFF	CLKID	0x03

Table V.18.6. Clock Firmware Entry Points

The program *Set Clock* utilizes some of the special features I designed into the *Real Time Clock* card. Its primary purpose is to set the clock card with the current date and time, of course. The program also displays the current date and time that is stored in its registers, and those values may be automatically selected or new values may be entered for each of the registers. The surprising feature of this program is that it utilizes an interrupt handler. The clock card is configured to generate an IRQ interrupt every second. Every time the IRQ interrupt occurs, its interrupt handler reads the clock card and displays its date and time data. Once the correct date and time data is displayed, that data can be written to the clock card. The interrupt handler will continue to display the current date and time data of the clock card while the *Real Time Clock* continues to update its internal registers. Before the *Set Clock* program exits it restores the data originally found at MASKIRQ (i.e. 0x3FE) as shown in Table I.9.1. and sets the clock card configuration register as shown in Table V.18.3. to 0x00.

The *Set Clock* program first issues the SEI instruction to the 6502 microprocessor to inhibit all interrupts. During initialization it copies the address found at MASKIRQ to a safe location and sets MASKIRQ to the address of the interrupt handler in *Set Clock*. *Set Clock* then sets the clock card configuration register to #%10000001 in order to enable interrupts and to enable the IRQ interrupt specifically. Once the initialization routine issues the CLI instruction to the 6502 microprocessor, the *Set Clock* interrupt handler will be able to field all IRQ interrupts while the user is setting the various values for the date and time. When the interrupt handler is invoked, it first issues the CLD instruction to the 6502 microprocessor, pushes the X- and Y-registers onto the stack, clears the IRQ interrupt on the *Real Time Clock* card, reads the *Real Time Clock* card, displays its current date and time data, restores the X- and Y-registers from the stack, restores the A-register from the page-zero location 0x45, and issues the RTI instruction to the 6502 microprocessor. It is amazing to me how simple it is to use interrupts in this program. Of course, the well-thought-out hardware design of the *Real Time Clock* card makes utilizing interrupts on the Apple][computer so easy and so much fun!

To assemble the *Real Time Clock* EPROM firmware source code, place the DOS 4.3 Tools volume DOS.4.3.Tools in disk drive 1, boot, and start *Lisa80*. Enter the SE command-line command to select the *SETUP80* utility in order to verify or set the Start of Source Code to 0x4000 and the Start of Symbol List to 0x7800. Place the Real Time Clock Source volume CLOCK.Source in disk drive 2, load the CLOCK.L file into memory, and start the assembler by entering either the A or the Z command-line command. If a printed version of the screen output is desired simply preface the A or the Z command with the P1 command-line command. The complete binary image will be saved to the Real Time Clock Source volume as CLOCK.

To assemble the *Set Clock* source code follow the same procedure as above, load the SETCLOCK.L file into memory and start the assembler. The complete binary image will be saved to the Real Time Clock Source volume as SETCLOCK.

19. JFD Parallel Printer Buffer

When I saw the advertisement in one of my 1985 Apple magazines for the JFD Parallel Printer Buffer, I just had to have one. As I recall there were two, perhaps more Buffer configurations one could choose: one set of parallel input/outputs or two sets of parallel input/outputs or perhaps a combination of these two configurations. Always budget minded I chose the Buffer with one set of parallel input/outputs. If I had more than one computer or more than one printer I may have chosen differently.

I had spent so much time waiting for my computer and printer to print hundreds of pages of code that I was more than ready to put this Buffer to work: I could work on the computer while the Buffer was supplying data to the printer, especially data from large graphic files. The Buffer came with 256 KB of dynamic RAM, and once an ASCII listing or a page of graphics had printed, the Buffer had a Copy pushbutton to select the number of additional copies (up to 255) to print if they were desired.

The Buffer connected to the Grappler+ Printer Interface slot card that was in the computer and to my Epson MX100 printer by means of parallel interface flat-ribbon cables. A large wall transformer powered the Buffer supplying it with nine volts DC. Besides the Copy pushbutton there was a Reset pushbutton. The Reset pushbutton caused the Buffer software to initialize. This initialization forced the input of the next print job to start at the beginning of Buffer memory particularly if I needed multiple copies of only that listing. Otherwise, if I used the Copy pushbutton after printing multiple items, the Buffer would print everything in its memory again.

The manual that came with the Buffer did not discuss what happened when input data overflowed memory. I had already seen some bizarre behavior like not printing some paragraphs when I used the Buffer to print many listings, especially when I forgot to press the Reset pushbutton prior to printing the next print job. Momentarily pressing the Copy pushbutton put the Buffer into Pause Mode such that the Buffer could still accept input data; it just did not send any further data to the printer. Momentarily pressing the Copy pushbutton a second time took the Buffer out of Pause Mode and data was again output to the printer. I took advantage of Pause Mode and sent a known, and very large amount of data to the Buffer. Then I took the Buffer out of Pause Mode and sent another known, and very large amount of data to the Buffer. When Buffer memory was filled it appeared to me the Buffer was accepting 256-byte chunks of data after it printed approximately 256 bytes of data for a certain period of time. Then the Buffer started to drop chunks of data, perhaps 256 bytes in size, but I wasn't absolutely sure. I could force this bizarre behavior every time I forced the Buffer memory to overflow. It appeared to me the firmware had some sort of software bug. I saw a challenge waiting to happen.

I opened the Buffer and found a voltage regulator, an 8035-microprocessor, a 2716 EPROM, eight 1257-15 NMOS dynamic RAM chips, and an assortment of eight-bit latches and logic chips. There were PCB locations for an additional input parallel connector and for an additional output parallel connector. The Ready LED was inconveniently located on the rear apron of the Buffer. I moved this LED to the front apron since there was only one input parallel connector and plenty of space next to it. Ideally, I would have liked to have moved that input parallel connector to the rear apron alongside the output parallel connector. I worked at Hughes Aircraft at that time, I had access to virtually any data book available, and I was able to obtain data sheets on the microprocessor and the RAM chips.

Being able to source and compile the MCS-8048 Instruction Set was certainly going to be a challenge, but I had already had some experience doing something similar for an external keyboard that used a 6802 microprocessor on its interface board. My technique was to set up a series of equates within *Lisa*, one equate for each MCS-8048 instruction. I had to keep in mind which instructions required additional parameters. Actual coding within *Lisa* simply required the `BYT` directive followed by an MCS-8048 instruction equate, and then followed by any required parameter. I put a comment on each line documenting what the `BYT` directive and the instruction equate were actually doing. The next step was to reverse engineer the code contained in the Buffer's EPROM.

Dumping the data contained in the 2716 Buffer EPROM was easy using the PROmGRAMER. Sourcing that data was also easy because I wrote an Applesoft program that translated the MCS-8048 instructions into a Text file using the `BYT` directive *Lisa* could easily `EXEC` into its memory. Analyzing that sourced code took the most time and effort because I had to fully understand the architecture of the 8035-microprocessor, the operation of the 1257-15 dynamic RAM for data access and refresh requirements, and the hardware function of the eight-bit latches and supporting logic chips. The Grappler+ and the Epson printer also had handshake and data acknowledgement requirements as well. Slowly, I plowed my way through the code finding all the necessary logic to perform RAM refresh, access RAM data, read Input data, and write Output data as well as perform data initialization, print diagnostic status information, read the Reset and Copy pushbuttons, and control the LED.

Unfortunately, I could not locate an error in the software logic that would cause the bizarre behavior that I could manufacture. I did locate the general logic where the Buffer would wait for a free page (256 bytes) of memory should the write pointer address approach the read pointer address. Dropping or skipping a page of memory was occurring somewhere in this area of logic when the data pointers were near the end of memory, but I could not find the wrong logic or instructions. I'm sure it was some silly addition error, probably involving the `Carry` flag, when transitioning from the `0x3FFxx` page to the `0x000xx` page for accessing the continuum of data in the 256 KB buffer.

I decided to scrape the original code and write my own version of this firmware. Of course, I had to borrow the original logic to access and refresh RAM, but I thought I could do a better job at controlling the data pointers and handling the memory overflow situation. I set up hardware to emulate a 2716 EPROM so I could compile and test my software without having to program an actual EPROM. This hardware setup made it extremely easy to develop MCS-8048 software for the 8035-microprocessor. In May, 1989, I was successful in developing new firmware for the Buffer that did not fail any of my previous Buffer overflow tests. This firmware also behaved exactly like the original firmware for Pause Mode and for the Copy function. The Reset function also behaved exactly like the original firmware. I programmed a 2716 EPROM, installed it, and used the Buffer with this firmware thereafter.

I performed timing tests and documented the results for the original firmware and for my new Buffer firmware. I had calculated the time it should take the firmware to test all 256 KB of RAM with a minimum of a write followed by a read and a compare. The initialization routine for the original firmware did not take the required amount of time that it should have. My initialization routine took precisely the amount of time to complete in the time I had predicted. I also timed how long each firmware version took to fill memory with Pause Mode enabled and disabled. With Pause Mode enabled the original firmware took about 2.5 times longer to fill memory: 2.91 KB/sec versus 7.28 KB/sec for my firmware. With Pause Mode disabled the results were 2.91 KB/sec versus 6.90 KB/sec for my firmware. I sent a letter to JFD explaining what I had observed when memory overflow occurred, my timing test predictions and results, and a printed copy of my firmware. I did not receive even an acknowledgement to my letter from JFD. I was terribly disappointed. Whatever.

Recently, I took some time to look over and review the Buffer firmware I wrote back in 1989. I've had a lot of time to increase my knowledge and to mature my programming skills vis-à-vis hardware architecture. I noticed that I used the built-in 8035-microprocessor Interval Timer for timing events such as pushbutton debounce like it was done in the original Buffer firmware. I thought, what a waste of a perfectly good Interval Timer! What became especially clear to me was how to use the Interval Timer to provide the basic timing for dynamic RAM refresh without having to guess and to hope that the RAM refresh routine was called often enough. In my version of the firmware, like that in the original JFD firmware, the MAIN loop called the REFRESH routine, the CHECKT0 routine, and, if the printer was ready to accept another data character, the SENDMEM routine in that order in an infinite loop. The CHECKT0 routine checked if the Copy pushbutton was pressed, and if so, would flash the LED on and off at a 0.5 Hz rate in order to set the number of desired copies. CHECKT0 could take huge amounts of time away from the REFRESH routine leaving me pondering why memory never became corrupted. I wondered if this was the actual cause of the bizarre behavior I had observed so many years ago? Or, did this Buffer RAM have built-in refresh capabilities? I didn't think so.

If I followed the 1257-15 dynamic RAM data sheet requirement to perform a RAS-only refresh every 4.0 milliseconds or less, I could use the Interval Timer to schedule a dynamic RAM refresh at that rate. The Interval Timer could also serve as the base for all other timing requirements like pushbutton debounce and LED flash rate. Central to the 8035-microprocessor are the RESET interrupt, the EXTIRQ interrupt, and the TIMRIRQ interrupt. The Reset pushbutton is connected to the RESET Interrupt pin, the Input connector from the computer is connected to the External Interrupt pin, and the Interval Timer is connected to the Timer Interrupt pin of the 8035-microprocessor. Each of these events is handled by a unique vector to an interrupt handler routine that is at a hard-wired address in page-zero of EPROM memory: 0x00, 0x03, and 0x07. There are also thirty-two bytes of indexed User RAM in internal microprocessor memory that is only slightly clumsy to access, but nevertheless available for use to store program variables, vectors, pointers, and data.

The 8035-microprocessor is clocked using a 6.0 MHz external crystal. This frequency is divided by fifteen internal to the microprocessor, so the cycle time (i.e. Tcy for instructions) is 2.5 µsecs. Most instructions require one cycle, and all other instructions require only two cycles. The Interval Timer prescaler divides Tcy by thirty-two making it 80 µsecs in duration. Thus, loading the timer counter with a value of 0xFF will cause a TIMRIRQ interrupt in 80 µsecs when the timer counter overflows to 0x00 after one count. Loading the timer with a value of 0xCF will cause a TIMRIRQ interrupt in 3.920 msecs. However, the instructions to reset the Interval Timer require eight cycles, so the total timer interval is 3.940 msecs. This time is certainly within the specifications to refresh the 1257-15 dynamic RAM chips.

Part of the Interval Timer handler routine is to increment a 2-byte counter. Whatever value is pre-loaded into this counter is incremented every 3.94 msecs. Naturally, a number representing the negative of a number would be ideal to use in this application such that when the most significant byte becomes zero, the desired time will have been reached. For example, if a 63-millisecond debounce time is desired, then -16 must be pre-loaded into the 2-byte counter, or 0xFFF0. Also, an approximate 1.0 second wait time period can be achieved by loading 0xFF00 into the 2-byte counter; that is, 3.940 msec. * 256 = 1.00864 seconds.

Using the Interval Timer as the primary method to refresh the Buffer's dynamic RAM changed the code only for the MAIN routine. Now, MAIN simply calls the CHECKT0 routine and the SENDMEM routine if the printer is ready to accept another data character, in an infinite loop. The CHECKT0 can take all the time it needs in order to count the number of LED flashes representing the desired number of copies. I added another bit-flag to the System Flag byte called the Overflow State Flag. If the write memory pointer should ever reach 0x00000 and overflow memory, the Overflow State Flag will be turned ON. If that flag is ON the Buffer software will bypass the copy counting logic in the CHECKTO routine and, as a protection, not allow whatever there is in memory to be sent to the printer as another copy. Of course, pressing the Reset pushbutton will reset all of the State Flag bits including the Overflow State Flag, and re-enable the ability to make copies of whatever there will be again in memory. If copies are selected using the Copy pushbutton immediately after pressing the Reset pushbutton, nothing should be printed as expected. I programmed a 2716 EPROM with this version of the firmware, installed it, and this is the firmware I have been using in the Buffer. Again, I have seen no further bizarre behavior even when the Buffer memory has reached memory overflow.

Byte Offset	Size	Name	Description
0x00	8 bytes	SELRB0	Primary registers, Bank 0
0x08	16 bytes	PSW	12-bit program counter & 4-bit status bits (PSW) in an 8 level stack
0x18	8 bytes	SELRB1	Secondary register, Bank 1
0x20	32 bytes	USERRAM	User RAM for indexed word locations

Table V.19.1. 8035 Microprocessor Memory Map

Bit	Name	Description
0	S0	Bit 0 of stack pointer
1	S1	Bit 1 of stack pointer
2	S2	Bit 2 of stack pointer
3	–	not used, set to 1
4	BS	Register bank select
5	F0	User flag 0
6	AC	Auxiliary carry flag
7	CY	Carry flag

Table V.19.2. User Flag 1

I have heavily documented the Printer Buffer source code as I developed the routines that utilize the Interval Timer for all timing functions. The MCS-48 8035-microprocessor utilizes sixty-four bytes of internal memory for its operation. The configuration of this memory is shown in Table V.19.1. There are two banks of eight 8-bit registers, an eight level stack for subroutine return addresses and status bits, and thirty-two bytes of indexed User RAM. It is this User RAM that is only slightly clumsy to access. Only four bytes are used in the indexed user RAM. The User Flag 1, or F1, is shown in Table V.19.2. F1 is not part of the Program Status Word. Table V.19.3 shows Port 1 and Port 2 utilization, that is, how each of the bits are used for both ports. The utilization of SELRB0 is shown in Figure

V.19.4 and the utilization of SELRB1 is shown in Figure V.19.5. The R/W Block Number Bits in Primary Register R3 is shown in Figure V.19.6 and the System Flag Bits in Secondary Register R3 are shown in Figure V.19.7.

Port:Bit	Name	Description
1:0	n/a	not used, set to 1
1:1	PDATENBL	Processor data enable, 1=disable
1:2	OLATENBL	Outport latch enable, 1=disable
1:3	n/a	not used, set to 1
1:4	ODATRDY	Outport data ready, 1=ready
1:5	n/a	not used, set to 1
1:6	n/a	not used, set to 1
1:7	PMEMENBL	PPB memory enable, 1=disable
2:0	ADR08ON	Address bit ADR08, 1=ON
2:1	LED1TGL	Test LED 1, 1=ON
2:2	LED2TGL	Test LED 2, 1=ON
2:3	RDLEDON	Ready LED, 1=ON
2:4	IDATENBL	Inport data strobe, 1=disable
2:5	n/a	not used, set to 1
2:6	n/a	not used, set to 1
2:7	OCTLENBL	Octal latch enable, 1=disable

Table V.19.3. Port Utilization

Register	Description
R0	Input/output working
R1	EXTIRQ reg-A save
R2	Temporary data byte
R3	R/W block number for address bits 0x08 & 0x11
R4	Address bits 0x00-0x07, read data RAS
R5	Address bits 0x09-0x10, read data CAS
R6	Address bits 0x00-0x07, write data RAS
R7	Address bits 0x09-0x10, write data CAS

Table V.19.4. SELRB0 Utilization

To assemble the Printer Buffer source code, place the DOS 4.3 Tools volume DOS.4.3.Tools in disk drive 1, boot, and start *Lisa80*. Enter the SE command-line command to select the *SETUP80* utility in order to verify or set the Start of Source Code to 0x4000 and the Start of Symbol List to 0x7800. Place the Printer Buffer Source volume PRINTBUFFER.Source in disk drive 2, load the `PPB.L` file into memory, and start the assembler by entering either the `A` or the `Z` command-line command. If a printed version of the screen output is desired simply preface the `A` or the `Z` command with the `P1` command-line command. The complete binary image will be saved to the Printer Buffer Source volume as `PPB`. A 2716 EPROM can be programmed with the `PPB` file.

Register	Description
R0	Input/output working
R1	REFRESH reg-A save
R2	Temporary data byte
R3	System flags
R4	Copy number
R5	Refresh counter, LSB
R6	Timer counter, LSB
R7	Timer Counter, MSB

Table V.19.5. SELRB1 Utilization

Bit	Description
0	Read block number LSB
1	Read block number MSB
2	zero
3	zero
4	Write block number LSB
5	Write block number MSB
6	zero
7	zero

Table V.19.6. Primary R3 R/W Block Number Bits

Bit	Description
0	Refresh counter, ADR08
1	zero
2	zero
3	Overflow state flag, 0=OFF
4	Message state flag, 0=OFF
5	Copy state flag, 0=OFF
6	Pause state flag, 0=OFF
7	EXTIRQ state flag, 0=OFF

Table V.19.7. Secondary R3 System Flag Bits

20. Asynchronous Data Transfer (ADT)

I have done a serious amount of software development for the Apple][using a MacBook Pro running the Virtual][emulation program by Gerard Putter. Virtual][can launch a utility called A2V2 that can transfer a 140 KB volume image to and from an Apple][that is concurrently running a program called Asynchronous Data Transfer, or *ADT* by Paul Guertin and enhanced by Gerard Putter. My Apple //e uses a Super Serial slot card connected to a Keyspan serial to USB adapter using a serial cable. The Keyspan is connected to the MacBook Pro using a USB cable. Only 140 KB volume images are currently allowed to be transferred. Because the RAM Disk 320 supports up to forty tracks and I typically use it to receive disk images, I would like to see the 140 KB restriction removed from A2V2 and *ADT*. I would even like to have Virtual][support forty-eight track diskettes, too, but Mr. Putter rejected that request. Regardless, I did source *ADT* so I could add an Update command to its command repertoire as shown in Figure V.20.1. After configuring *ADT*, Update will save *ADT* with its new configuration set as its new default. The *ADT* Configuration screen is shown in Figure V.20.2, which uses lowercase characters to assist in making the Apple screen text, in my opinion, easier for me to read. If and when 160 KB and 200 KB disk images are supported, I will be ready. But let's not stop there! My RanaSystems EliteThree drive can support forty tracks with each track having thirty-two sectors, so 320 KB disk images are possible, too. In order to process 320 KB disk images *ADT* may need to utilize the 80-column display. Finally, a CFFA volume having forty-eight 32-sector tracks would require a 400 KB disk image. Now, that would be a seriously fun project: using an 80-colum display to show the transfer of volumes having up to forty-eight 32-sector tracks.

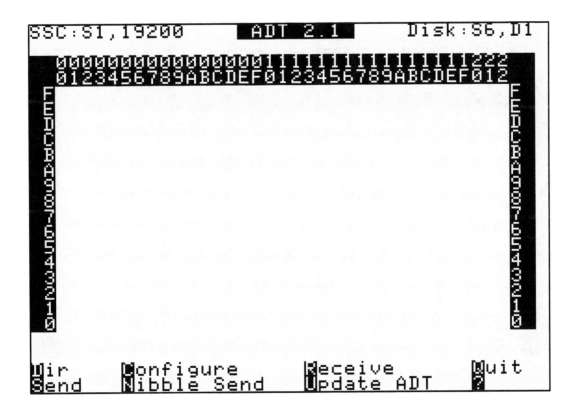

Figure V.20.1. ADT Window

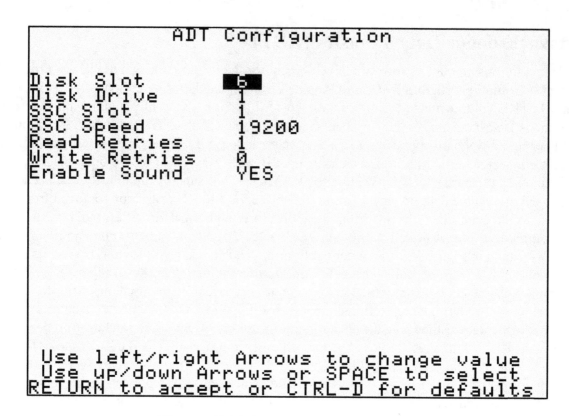

Figure V.20.2. ADT Configuration

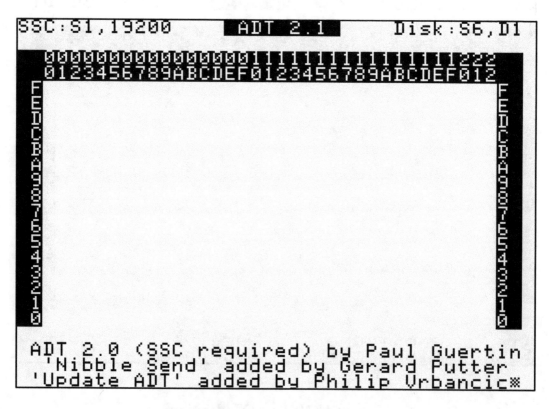

Figure V.20.3. ADT Software Credits

The "?" command displays credits to Paul Guertin, Gerard Putter, and myself for adding enhancements to *ADT* as shown in Figure V.20.3.

To assemble the *ADT* source code, place the DOS 4.3 Tools volume `DOS.4.3.Tools` in disk drive 1, boot, and start *Lisa80*. Enter the `SE` command-line command to select the *SETUP80* utility in order to verify or set the `Start of Source Code` to `0x4000` and the `Start of Symbol List` to `0x7800`. Place the ADT Source volume `ADT.Source` in disk drive 2, load the `ADT.L` file into memory, and start the assembler by entering either the `A` or the `Z` command-line command. If a printed version of the screen output is desired simply preface the `A` or the `Z` command with the `P1` command-line command. The complete binary image will be saved to the ADT Source volume as `ADT2`.

21. TrackScan

I found the process of developing an algorithm to control the movement of the R/W head of a Disk][down to a half-phase to be extremely exciting, if not down-right challenging. There are so many physical parameters to consider while designing such an algorithm. In order to verify whether an algorithm is even working or coming close to providing the desired results, good tools are absolutely essential. Visual inspection that the Cam Table is being turned appropriately is also invaluable information. As shown in Figures I.10.2 and I.10.3 I used a very fine liquid-ink pen to mark where the Cam Rider stopped along the Cam Channel as I positioned the R/W head over tracks 0x00, 0x01, 0x02, and 0x03 before I started testing various half-phase-stepping algorithms. I already knew there were four half-phases between each track, so I could indicate where those half-phase steps would occur along the Cam Channel with more ink marks. I also noticed that track 0x00 was not actually at the Cam Stop, but very, very close to the Cam Stop. That told me that Electromagnet 0 must be held in the ON state to ensure that Phase 0 coincides precisely with track 0x00. No matter how many half-phases the Cam Table has to be turned in order to return the R/W head back to track 0x00, Electromagnet 0 is the last electromagnet to be de-energized and track 0x00 always coincides with Phase 0.

During the development of DOS 4.1, I spent a considerable amount of time and energy mapping the processing steps of RWTS. I needed to include additional processing at the entry point of RWTS in order to calculate the correct entry offset for the disk peripheral slot card based on its slot number that is used to index into the Disk Address Table. If a non-Disk][disk peripheral slot card handler is connected to the Disk Address Table I had to include provisions to make sure its peripheral-card expansion ROM memory is fully detached after its RWTS processing. After determining a better set of processing steps for RWTS in DOS 4.3, I attacked the formatting routine with gusto. I was already well acquainted with the read and write address field routines as well as the read and write data field routines. I also knew the lead-in and lead-out requirements for those fields so that the disk peripheral slot card firmware could always synchronize to the data about to be read. It is critical that the write address field and write data field routines incorporate these requirements in their processing.

A minimum of **five** 40-μsec auto-sync bytes are necessary for the Disk][peripheral slot card firmware to synchronize to the address field data or to the data field data about to be read. At least one 32-μsec sync byte must follow the final three epilogue bytes of an address field or a data field in order to correctly read at least the first two epilogue bytes. Sync bytes are always 0xFF (or 32 μsec in length) and auto-sync bytes are 0x3FC (or 40 μsec in length). Timing is absolutely critical in these routines in order to write all 11 32-μsec address field data bytes and all 350 32-μsec data field data bytes: Disk][peripheral slot card firmware does not have the capability nor the capacity to read any other data except for data bytes that are 32 μsec in length and auto-sync bytes that are 40 μsec in length. Thus, the write address field routine and the write data field routine must not write data bytes that are anything other than 32 μsec in length or auto-sync bytes that are anything other than 40 μsec in length.

When I was analyzing the volume formatting routines of RWTS, I started to develop software tools that could read and store the raw disk data into memory for an entire track. I knew that a sector required 361 (11 + 350) 32-μsec bytes for the address field, data field, and the prologue and epilogue bytes for those fields, and a bare minimum of 10 40-μsec auto-sync bytes. However, the routine WRITADR writes SYNCNT auto-sync bytes before an address field and the routine WRITSCTR writes **six** auto-sync bytes before a data field. A track comprised of sixteen sectors would require 5776 32-μsec bytes and 96 40-μsec auto-sync bytes. The Disk][peripheral slot card firmware would take a minimum of 188,672 (5776*32 + 96*40) μsec to read all those disk bytes. A diskette spinning at 300 revolutions per minute would make five revolutions per second, or take 200,000 μsec to make one revolution. This would leave 11,328 μsec available for all auto-sync bytes before the address field of all sectors on a track assuming perfect speed control of the disk][hardware.

The DISKFMT routine initializes SYNCNT, the number of auto-sync bytes written before an address field, to thirty-two. Before the TRACKFMT routine begins writing the address field for sector 0x00 on track 0x00, it writes 128 auto-sync bytes. Before each address field for the sectors following sector 0x00, the TRACKFMT routine writes SYNCNT auto-sync bytes. The TRACKFMT routine then analyzes the track it just wrote to determine if it can read the address field for sector 0x00. Obviously, an initial 608 (128 + 32*15) auto-sync bytes are about 325 auto-sync bytes too many, but this exercise provides a good start to determine the optimal value for SYNCNT. TRACKFMT then reduces SYNCNT and tries to format track 0x00 again. As soon as TRACKFMT can discover the address field for sector 0x00, TRACKFMT reduces SYNCNT a final time and uses that stored value for the number of auto-sync bytes it writes before the address field of all sectors other than sector 0x00: TRACKFMT always begins the format of a track with 128 auto-sync bytes before the address field for sector 0x00. Typically, the epilogue bytes of the data field for last sector, or sector 0x0F, are written somewhere within those initial 128 auto-sync bytes. In order to verify that TRACKFMT, as I designed it, performs its function correctly and as intended, I wrote a utility that reads and stores the raw disk data into memory for an entire track, and it analyzes that data so that it can be properly displayed. That utility is *TrackScan*, and its Main Menu is shown in Figure V.21.1. I developed *TrackScan* using *VMGR* as its model. However, instead of specifying VOLUME as in *VMGR*, *TrackScan* uses PHASE in order to format a diskette with that parameter before displaying the raw data of a track. *TrackScan* will format a diskette with 35, 36, 40, or 48 tracks.

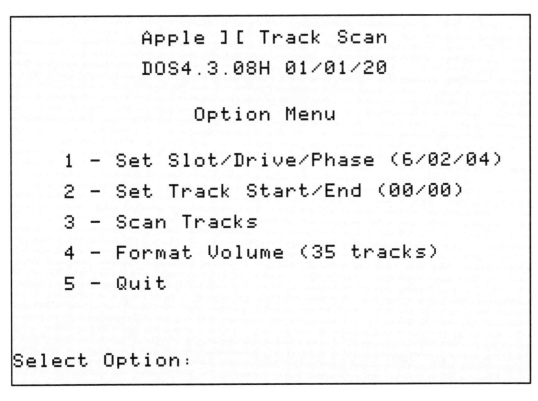

```
        Apple ][ Track  Scan
        DOS4.3.08H  01/01/20


              Option Menu

     1 - Set Slot/Drive/Phase (6/02/04)

     2 - Set Track Start/End (00/00)

     3 - Scan Tracks

     4 - Format Volume (35 tracks)

     5 - Quit



Select Option:
```

Figure V.21.1. TrackScan Main Menu

TrackScan will scan and process any track on any volume; *TrackScan* does not have to format a volume before scanning a track on that volume. After *TrackScan* has scanned a selected track, it analyzes the raw track data after it locates the address field for sector `0x00` and verifies that it can locate the next copy of the address field for sector `0x00`. *TrackScan* uses a total of eight processing steps to analyze the raw track data for each sector. It decodes the address field data and displays that information first along with the number of sync bytes prior to the address field and the number of data bytes within the address field. Recall that a sync byte is `0xFF` in value and is 32 μsec in length. It is not possible to distinguish sync bytes and auto-sync bytes except indirectly. *TrackScan* processing continues by locating the data field that follows the address field, and it analyzes its structure and content. The number of sync bytes prior to the data field, the number of data bytes within the data field, and the error status are next displayed for that sector. The error status shows the number of successful processing steps TrackScan completed for that sector's analysis and a final error value. *TrackScan* continues its processing for each of the sectors contained in the raw track data.

TrackScan will display the final value it determines for `SYNCNT` when *TrackScan* is used to format a volume. `SYNCNT` is used for the number of auto-sync bytes written prior to the address field for a sector after track `0x00` has been successfully formatted. Six auto-sync bytes (i.e. `HDRSYNC`) are always written prior to the data field for a sector. The results shown in Figures V.21.2 and V.21.3 were obtained from a volume that was formatted by *TrackScan* with thirty-five tracks and a `PHASE` of four. *TrackScan* reported obtaining a value of `0x0E` for `SYNCNT`. This information and the data shown in Figures V.21.2 and V.21.3 can be used to determine if the actual number of auto-sync bytes written can be verified indirectly. Once the disk data latch has been loaded with a sync byte, data one's will be clocked out by the peripheral slot card firmware to be recorded onto a volume. When `WRITADR` finishes writing an address field, it exits via `WRITEXIT` and leaves a sync byte stored in the data latch before returning the latch configuration to read-mode. By the time `WRITSCTR` begins its processing and enables the data latch for write-mode again, already 66 μsec has elapsed. After `WRITSCTR` has written six auto-sync bytes, the total time from the end of the address field to the start of the data field is given by 66 + 6*40 = 306 μsec. Figures V.21.2 and V.21.3 show that the second `Gap` column of numbers was observed to be between 9 and 11 32-μsec bytes with an average value of 9.25 bytes. The DOS 4.3 `TRACKFMT` routines predict that 306 / 32 = 9.6 bytes should be observed. Given minor fluctuations in drive speed, the predicted and observed results through raw track data analysis are very much in agreement for the gap size between the address field and the data field.

Previously, it was determined that 11,328 μsec should be available for additional auto-sync bytes before an address field assuming perfect speed control of the diskette. Figure V.21.2 shows from the first `Gap` column of numbers that sector `0x00` and `0x01` are indeed different by two bytes as intended by software design. The total number of sync bytes observed before all address fields for track `0x00` is 322 from Figure V.21.2. The total number of sync bytes observed before all address fields for track `0x11` is 321 from Figure V.21.3. Reducing `SYNCNT` from `0x10` for track `0x00` to `0x0E` for all other tracks ensures that sector `0x00` will be found, even on the very last track of the volume. The summation of all observed sync bytes found through raw track data analysis before an address field for track `0x00` would be (22 + 20*15) * 32 = 10,304 μsec. This is only 1024 μsec less than the predicted value of 11,328 μsec. The summation of all observed sync bytes found through raw track data analysis before an address field of all other tracks would be (51 + 18*15) * 32 = 10,272 μsec. This is only 1056 μsec less than the predicted value of 11,328 μsec.

```
            Apple ][ Track Scan

Vol   Trk   Sec   Gap   Hdr   Gap   Data   Err
---   ---   ---   ---   ---   ---   ----   ---
000   00    00    022    4    09    343    8-0
000   00    01    020    4    09    343    8-0
000   00    02    020    4    09    343    8-0
000   00    03    020    4    09    343    8-0
000   00    04    020    4    09    343    8-0
000   00    05    020    4    09    343    8-0
000   00    06    020    4    09    343    8-0
000   00    07    020    4    09    343    8-0
000   00    08    020    4    09    343    8-0
000   00    09    020    4    09    343    8-0
000   00    10    020    4    09    343    8-0
000   00    11    020    4    09    343    8-0
000   00    12    020    4    09    343    8-0
000   00    13    020    4    09    343    8-0
000   00    14    020    4    08    343    8-0
000   00    15    020    4    09    343    8-0
```

Figure V.21.2. TrackScan for Track 0x00

```
            Apple ][ Track Scan

Vol   Trk   Sec   Gap   Hdr   Gap   Data   Err
---   ---   ---   ---   ---   ---   ----   ---
000   00    00    051    4    11    343    8-0
000   00    01    018    4    09    343    8-0
000   00    02    018    4    09    343    8-0
000   00    03    018    4    09    343    8-0
000   00    04    018    4    09    343    8-0
000   00    05    018    4    09    343    8-0
000   00    06    018    4    10    343    8-0
000   00    07    018    4    09    343    8-0
000   00    08    018    4    10    343    8-0
000   00    09    018    4    09    343    8-0
000   00    10    018    4    09    343    8-0
000   00    11    018    4    09    343    8-0
000   00    12    018    4    09    343    8-0
000   00    13    018    4    09    343    8-0
000   00    14    018    4    09    343    8-0
000   00    15    018    4    09    343    8-0
```

Figure V.21.3. TrackScan for Track 0x11

293

Another way to demonstrate how closely the raw track data analysis results compare with reality is to sum all of the data results shown in Figures V.21.2 and V.21.3.

From raw track data analysis for track 0x00, the sum of values for all sectors would be:

{ (22 + 20*15) + (11 + 9 + 350) * 16 } * 32 = 199744 μsec

This is only 256 μsec less than the time it takes to rotate the diskette once, or 200,000 μsec.

From raw track data analysis for track 0x11, the sum of values for all sectors would be:

{ (51 + 11 + 11 + 350) + (18 + 11 + 9 + 350) * 13 + (18 + 11 + 10 + 350) * 2 } * 32 = 199840 μsec

This is only 160 μsec less than the time it takes to rotate the diskette once, or 200,000 μsec.

It is obvious that *TrackScan* is a very important tool that can be used to verify the efficacy of the DOS 4.3 TRACKFMT routines. Being able to initialize a volume with precision and being able to scan and analyze each track on that volume for correctness provides the necessary insight that confirms the validity of the TRACKFMT routines that comprise this algorithm. Now that a suitable volume formatting algorithm can be certified using *TrackScan*, a new algorithm to control the movement of the R/W head of a Disk][that is any multiple of a single half-phase can be developed. *TrackScan* was instrumental in developing such an algorithm for it absolutely demonstrates the ability to read, analyze, and display every sector on every track after a volume has been initialized utilizing useful values for track PHASE separation.

To assemble the *TrackScan* source code, place the DOS 4.3 Tools volume DOS.4.3.Tools in disk drive 1, boot, and start *Lisa80*. Enter the SE command-line command to select the *SETUP80* utility in order to verify or set the Start of Source Code to 0x4000 and the Start of Symbol List to 0x7800. Place the TrackScan Source volume TRACKSCAN.Source in disk drive 2, load the SCAN.L file into memory, and start the assembler by entering either the A or the Z command-line command. If a printed version of the screen output is desired simply preface the A or the Z command with the P1 command-line command. The complete binary image will be saved to the TrackScan Source volume as SCAN.

22. Apple][+ Memory Upgrade

Now that I was an Electrical Engineering graduate student in the early 1980's, I certainly wanted to use my Apple][+ as an opportunity to make some practical hardware modifications. First and foremost I wanted to incorporate a shift key modification, add in keyboard repeat logic, and provide an "alt" key circuit to the keyboard that would set or clear specific bits in the keyboard data in order to generate all the other ASCII characters the Apple][+ keyboard could not generate. This drove me to program my own character generator EPROM that included lowercase characters, rather similar to what Dan Paymar was selling as his *Lowercase Adaptor Interface PROM*. Then I fixed the glitch I noticed when switching modes from TEXT, LOWRES, and HIRES using a couple of additional logic gates: it was all a matter of timing in order to alter an inherent logic delay when the display mode was switched. I reached a level of competence when I decided to remove all twenty-four 16 Kb DRAM chips from the motherboard and replaced them with eight 64 Kb DRAM chips. This required cutting some foil traces, rerouting power, and building a satellite circuit board that would generate an additional DRAM row/column address line. The satellite circuit even included logic to model the Language Card in order to emulate the action of certain addresses that act as Soft Switches. In theory it all worked perfectly in my head, of course. The satellite circuit I developed is shown in Figure V.22.1. I paused a very, very long moment before applying power to my modified motherboard the first time. I was pleased, if not absolutely delighted to find that my 48 KB Apple][+ was fully 64 KB functional as if a Language Card resided in Slot 0. There was no blue smoke. Wow! Even today I marvel at how gutsy I was to implement this drastic modification to the motherboard of my beloved Apple][+.

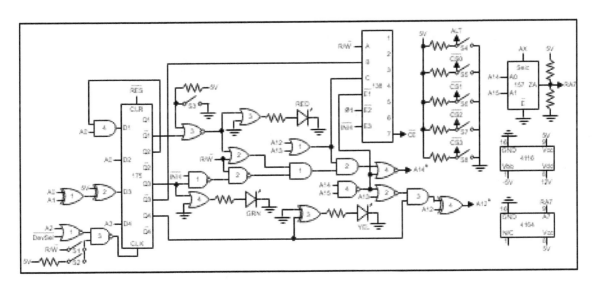

Figure V.22.1. Apple][+ Satellite Circuit Diagram

As shown in Figure V.22.1, the satellite circuit contains eight logic chips, three LED's, eight DIP switches, and a 26-pin connector for the signals shown in Table V.22.1, along with power and ground. Either DIP switch 1 or 2 must be closed, but not both. If DIP switch 1 is closed then the 74LS175 configuration register is clocked only with a read to 0xC08n, where **n** can be 0x0 to 0xF. If DIP switch 2 is closed then the configuration register is clocked with either a read or a write to 0xC08n. Language Card RAM is enabled if 0xC080, 0xC083, 0xC088, or 0xC08B is read, and the green

LED glows. If RAM bank 1 is enabled (i.e. 0xC088 to 0xC08F is read) the yellow LED glows. RAM is write-enabled if 0xC081, 0xC083, 0xC089, or 0xC08B is read twice and DIP switch 3 is closed, then the red LED glows. Opening DIP switch 3 will absolutely write-protect Language Card RAM electrically.

Signal	Location	Signal	Location
ø1	B1,6 (74LS175)	A12	H4,3 (8T97)
AX	C2,14 (74LS195)	A13	H5,3 (8T97)
DevSel	H2,15 (74LS138, Slot 0)	A14	J1,9 (74LS257)
INH	F3,18 (ROM-E8)	A15	J1,12 (74LS257)
RES	A7,3 (keyboard socket)	A12*	to C1,3 (74LS157)
R/W	H5,5 (8T97)	A14*	to F2,14 (74LS139)
A0	H5,11 (8T97)	RA7	to all 4164,9
A1	H4,5 (8T97)	CE	to all EPROM's CE
A2	H5,7 (8T97)	ALT	to all EPROM's A14
A3	H5,9 (8T97)	CS0-CS3	to each EPROM CS

Table V.22.1. Apple][+ Satellite Circuit Board Connections

A 27128 EPROM is the minimum size that will hold the ROM firmware from 0xD000 to 0xFFFF, although the first 32 Kb of this EPROM is not addressed. When a 27256 EPROM is used to contain two ROM firmware images, DIP switch 4 (to pin 27, A14) can be used to select the desired image. If DIP switch 4 is closed, the lower image is selected. DIP switches 5, 6, 7, and 8 select one of four possible EPROMs on the Apple][+ motherboard. I removed all six 24-pin ROM sockets and installed four 28-pin EPROM sockets making sure pins 1, 2, 27, and 28 were electrically isolated from the motherboard. Only one of these four DIP switches should be closed, otherwise multiple EPROMs will be enabled simultaneously. Honestly, I ended up preparing and programming only a single EPROM containing two ROM images. Providing access to three more similar EPROMs never became necessary and was slightly over-kill. Better to have too much than too little EPROM expansion capabilities!

Table V.22.1 lists all the signals I required and the location on the Apple][+ motherboard where I obtained that signal. In order to provide two banks of Language Card RAM for the 0xD000 to 0xDFFF address range, address lines A12* and A14* must be derived from the outputs of the circuit's 74LS175 configuration register, from the A12 and A13 address lines, and from the A14 and A15 address lines. The A14 and A15 address line are from a 74LS257 at motherboard location J1, and they also support memory data access and memory data refresh. These two derived address lines are connected directly to the pins of C1,3 and F2,14. Memory refresh for the 4164 chips is accomplished using the current RA0 through RA6 signals on the motherboard without regard to RA7. The derived RA7 signal simply provides the eighth row and eighth column address in order to access the full 64 Kb of each 4164 DRAM chip. Tables V.22.2 and V.22.3 provide the details of the operation of the Apple][+ Satellite Circuit Board vis-á-vis input address, the state of each LED, whether RAM is read-enabled or write-enabled, whether ROM is read-enabled, and the effective address generated for all other motherboard logic.

Input to 74LS175 Latch	Input Address Bus	Red LED State	Grn LED State	Yel LED State	Final A12* State	RAM Enabled R	RAM Enabled W	ROM Read Enable	Output Address Bus RAM/ROM
0xC080 RAM2 WP %0100	<0xC000	0	1	0	A12	1	1	0	<0xC000
	0xCnnn	0	1	0	0	0	0	0	0xCnnn
	0xDnnn	0	1	0	1	1	0	0	0xDnnn
	0xEnnn	0	1	0	0	1	0	0	0xEnnn
	0xFnnn	0	1	0	1	1	0	0	0xFnnn
0xC081 ROM2 WP %0010	<0xC000	0	0	0	A12	1	1	0	<0xC000
	0xCnnn	0	0	0	0	0	0	0	0xCnnn
	0xDnnn	0	0	0	1	0	0	1	0xDnnn
	0xEnnn	0	0	0	0	0	0	1	0xEnnn
	0xFnnn	0	0	0	1	0	0	1	0xFnnn
0xC081 0xC081 ROM2 WE %0011	<0xC000	1	0	0	A12	1	1	0	<0xC000
	0xCnnn	1	0	0	0	0	0	0	0xCnnn
	0xDnnn	1	0	0	1	0	1	1	0xDnnn
	0xEnnn	1	0	0	0	0	1	1	0xEnnn
	0xFnnn	1	0	0	1	0	1	1	0xFnnn
0xC082 ROM2 WP %0000	<0xC000	0	0	0	A12	1	1	0	<0xC000
	0xCnnn	0	0	0	0	0	0	0	0xCnnn
	0xDnnn	0	0	0	1	0	0	1	0xDnnn
	0xEnnn	0	0	0	0	0	0	1	0xEnnn
	0xFnnn	0	0	0	1	0	0	1	0xFnnn
0xC083 RAM2 WP %0110	<0xC000	0	1	0	A12	1	1	0	<0xC000
	0xCnnn	0	1	0	0	0	0	0	0xCnnn
	0xDnnn	0	1	0	1	1	0	0	0xDnnn
	0xEnnn	0	1	0	0	1	0	0	0xEnnn
	0xFnnn	0	1	0	1	1	0	0	0xFnnn
0xC083 0xC083 RAM2 WE %0111	<0xC000	1	1	0	A12	1	1	0	<0xC000
	0xCnnn	1	1	0	0	0	0	0	0xCnnn
	0xDnnn	1	1	0	1	1	1	0	0xDnnn
	0xEnnn	1	1	0	0	1	1	0	0xEnnn
	0xFnnn	1	1	0	1	1	1	0	0xFnnn
%0001	This configuration is not possible to select, so it is not valid.								
%0101	This configuration is not possible to select, so it is not valid.								

Table V.22.2. Apple][+ Satellite Circuit Board Operation, Part 1

Input to 74LS175 Latch	Input Address Bus	Red LED State	Grn LED State	Yel LED State	Final A12* State	RAM Enabled		ROM Read Enable	Output Address Bus RAM/ROM
						R	W		
0xC088	<0xC000	0	1	1	A12	1	1	0	<0xC000
RAM1	0xCnnn	0	1	1	1	0	0	0	0xDnnn
WP	0xDnnn	0	1	1	0	1	0	0	0xCnnn
	0xEnnn	0	1	1	0	1	0	0	0xEnnn
%1100	0xFnnn	0	1	1	1	1	0	0	0xFnnn
0xC089	<0xC000	0	0	1	A12	1	1	0	<0xC000
ROM1	0xCnnn	0	0	1	1	0	0	0	0xDnnn
WP	0xDnnn	0	0	1	0	0	0	1	0xCnnn
	0xEnnn	0	0	1	0	0	0	1	0xEnnn
%1010	0xFnnn	0	0	1	1	0	0	1	0xFnnn
0xC089	<0xC000	1	0	1	A12	1	1	0	<0xC000
0xC089	0xCnnn	1	0	1	1	0	0	0	0xDnnn
ROM1	0xDnnn	1	0	1	0	0	1	1	0xCnnn
WE	0xEnnn	1	0	1	0	0	1	1	0xEnnn
%1011	0xFnnn	1	0	1	1	0	1	1	0xFnnn
0xC08A	<0xC000	0	0	1	A12	1	1	0	<0xC000
ROM1	0xCnnn	0	0	1	1	0	0	0	0xDnnn
WP	0xDnnn	0	0	1	0	0	0	1	0xCnnn
	0xEnnn	0	0	1	0	0	0	1	0xEnnn
%1000	0xFnnn	0	0	1	1	0	0	1	0xFnnn
0xC08B	<0xC000	0	1	1	A12	1	1	0	<0xC000
RAM1	0xCnnn	0	1	1	1	0	0	0	0xDnnn
WP	0xDnnn	0	1	1	0	1	0	0	0xCnnn
	0xEnnn	0	1	1	0	1	0	0	0xEnnn
%1110	0xFnnn	0	1	1	1	1	0	0	0xFnnn
0xC08B	<0xC000	1	1	1	A12	1	1	0	<0xC000
0xC08B	0xCnnn	1	1	1	1	0	0	0	0xDnnn
RAM1	0xDnnn	1	1	1	0	1	1	0	0xCnnn
WE	0xEnnn	1	1	1	0	1	1	0	0xEnnn
%1111	0xFnnn	1	1	1	1	1	1	0	0xFnnn
%1001	This configuration is not possible to select, so it is not valid.								
%1101	This configuration is not possible to select, so it is not valid.								

Table V.22.3. Apple][+ Satellite Circuit Board Operation, Part 2

23. Apple][+ Keyboard Modification

After I started programming on my new Apple][+ my coworker Randy at Rockwell let me borrow a few of his computer magazines. I wanted to read all about the latest enhancements that were available for my computer. The Dan Paymar *Lowercase Adaptor Interface PROM* fascinated me and that adaptor was instrumental in encouraging me to invest in an EPROM programmer so I could design my own lowercase character set. I was also very interested in adding some digital logic to the piggy-back circuit board of the keyboard in order to provide a CapLock function: I thought that adding a tiny LED to the SHIFT key would be totally awesome to show the shift state. I also wanted to add a pushbutton next to the left SHIFT key. That small pushbutton would set or clear a specific bit in the keyboard data in order to generate all the other ASCII characters the Apple][+ keyboard could not generate.

When I started designing the keyboard modification circuit, I had just accepted employment in the Digital Simulation Laboratory at Hughes Aircraft and I had access to virtually any data book available. I was also not hesitant at all in opening up my Apple][+ and doing some initial testing on the piggy-back circuit board of the keyboard using a few logic chips from my growing toolbox. I had a Heathkit oscilloscope so I could actually view some of the signals on this circuit board. *The Apple][Circuit Description* by Winston D. Gayler helped me to understand the function of S2, a 6-pad connector that contained two electrical bowties that had to be cut in order to modify bits 4 and 5 of the keyboard data byte. If I recall correctly my testing was more trial and error rather than from experience in designing the keyboard modification shown in Figure V.23.1.

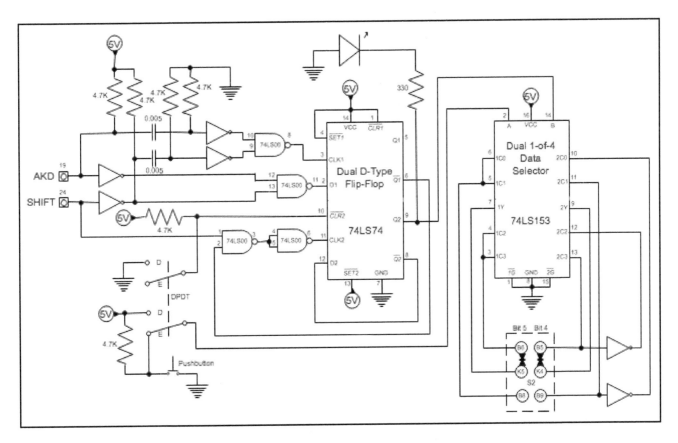

Figure V.23.1. Apple][+ Keyboard Modification

Select Input		Data Inputs				Strobe	Output
B	**A**	**C0**	**C1**	**C2**	**C3**	**G**	**Y**
X	X	X	X	X	X	H	L
L	L	L	X	X	X	L	L
L	L	H	X	X	X	L	H
L	H	X	L	X	X	L	L
L	H	X	H	X	X	L	H
H	L	X	X	L	X	L	L
H	L	X	X	H	X	L	H
H	H	X	X	X	L	L	L
H	H	X	X	X	H	L	H

Table V.23.1. 74LS153 Truth Table

Input Character	Input ASCII	SHIFT Key	Push Button	Output Character	Output ASCII
K	0x4B	ON	ON	[	0x5B
L	0x4C	ON	ON	\	0x5C
K	0x4B	OFF	ON	{	0x7B
L	0x4C	OFF	ON	|	0x7C
M	0x4D	OFF	ON	}	0x7D
N	0x4E	OFF	ON	~	0x7E
O	0x4F	OFF	ON	rub	0x7F

Table V.23.2. Generation of Unavailable Characters

The 74LS153 dual 1-of-4 data selector is the perfect logic chip to generate all of the characters that are unavailable on the Apple][+ keyboard. The truth table for the 74LS153 data selector is shown in Table V.23.1. Select Input A is controlled by the Pushbutton switch I placed next to the left SHIFT key and Select Input B is controlled by the state of the CapLock flip-flop shown in Figure V.23.1. Both of these signals are enabled by a Double-Pole Double-Throw (DPDT) switch I added to my keyboard modification circuit. The data selector chip along with S2 and the 6-pad connector on the piggy-back circuit board of the keyboard, passes bit 5 of the generated keyboard data back into keyboard logic in order to derive the lowercase characters. On the other hand, bit 4 must be inverted in order to derive the ASCII characters that are not available on the keyboard from those characters that are available on the keyboard.

Bit 5 is properly handled by means of S2 connectivity in order to create lowercase and uppercase characters. Of course, this assumes the character generator EPROM contains the bit images (or pixels) for the characters normally in the 0x60 to 0x7F ASCII range and not a repeat of the characters from the 0x40 to 0x5F ASCII range. The inversion of bit 4 is accomplished by using the Pushbutton switch next to the left SHIFT key in combination with an available character much like deriving a control character using the CTRL key. Table V.23.2 shows how to derive the unavailable characters from the available keyboard characters, the SHIFT key, and the Pushbutton. The Pushbutton is a normally open switch so that it does not modify normal keyboard logic when it is not being pressed.

The piggy-back circuit board contains a 555 timer circuit for the REPEAT key that is connected to a signal called Any Key Down (AKD). The REPEAT key in combination with a keyboard key will generate multiple instances of that pressed key. My keyboard modification circuit uses the AKD signal along with an inverted SHIFT key signal to provide automatic toggling of CapLock when the SHIFT key is held a bit longer than normal typing. This is accomplished by generating a digital pulse using a half-monostable circuit made up of a capacitor, a resister, and an inverter for both these signals. When CapLock is ON, an LED mounted in the left SHIFT key glows. The DPDT switch disables CapLock simply by pulling the CLR input of the CapLock flip-flop to ground in order to force its output low. The DPDT switch also disables the Pushbutton by connecting Select Input A to +5 volts.

There is plenty of room to mount the keyboard modification circuit board to the left side of the piggy-back circuit board which is connected to the keyboard using a 40-pin dual incline connector. I used a short length of 10-connector ribbon cable between the keyboard modification circuit board and the piggy-back circuit board. The ten signals are +5 volts, ground, SHIFT, AKD, and the 6-pad connector. The LED and Pushbutton each require two leads to the keyboard modification circuit board. The DPDT slide switch is mounted directly onto the keyboard modification circuit board. I have no idea why anyone would choose to disable the CapLock function or the ability to generate those ASCII characters that are unavailable on the Apple][+ keyboard. Regardless, the keyboard modification can be selectively disabled when desired.

24. Last Concluding Thoughts

There have been many books and articles published telling the story about the history, evolution, and people, some of whom are definitely characters, who have been involved in the Computer Revolution. I must say that I was part of that revolution, though perhaps more realistically on the periphery of that revolution. Ken Williams did attract a host of other entrepreneurs to Oakhurst, California, where Sierra Online was located. Like these other entrepreneurs, he was involved with developing programs and software products targeted for the soon-to-be-released Apple //c. Only on a need to know basis, the Apple //c was very hush hush. It was fascinating to be there in that period of time witnessing those events personally and to know that Wozniak and Jobs were among those who occasionally visited Williams. I know there are many others like me who look back upon those years with a high degree of nostalgia. It was a glorious time to be writing software for the Apple][family of computers!

Even today I must admit that the Apple][computer holds a unique charm for me that continuously draws me into its technical and software environment. People like Gerard Putter and Richard Dreher certainly must also experience this Apple][charm as well. They have created invaluable tools, one software and the other hardware, that keep Apple][enthusiasts like me motivated and excited about creating more and more useful software and hardware products for this computer today. I believe that in creating DOS 4.3 is my way of acknowledging and demonstrating the level of understanding and proficiency I have for the Apple][computer solely in terms of its hardware. It was fortunate that I studied Electrical Engineering at University rather than Computer Science. I certainly absorbed enough Computer Science during my professional career designing and building very, very high speed radar data collection systems.

DOS 4.3 is also the culmination of all the ideas from my previous DOS 4.1 Wish List and from the parameter needs of a large number of commercial software programs. Understanding those commercial software programs was vital in focusing my attention in order to provide an interface between DOS 4.3 internals and DOS 4.3 users. I suppose that studying Control Systems and viewing DOS similarly as a system having inputs, outputs, and feedback loops all contributed in how I wanted to design DOS 4.3 as the proverbial "black box" not to have its internals recklessly poked and prodded. At least for the most part I believe I have succeeded in designing an Apple][disk operating system and file management system that fulfills all of my needs. I certainly think that DOS 4.3 is capable of fulfilling the needs of others, particularly the owners of the CFFA card and the users of commercial programs like *Family Roots* who do not use ProDOS. This has been an incredible journey for me and I have enjoyed solving every problem and issue that has come my way while I was developing, designing, and writing DOS 4.3.

I still believe there is a huge potential use for the 6502-microprocesser `IRQ` and `NMI` interrupts in some sort of hardware/software product. What that product is, is yet another mystery to me. But I still keep thinking about it in view of how much fun I had implementing those interrupts on my clock card. And that is part of the charm the Apple][generates because of its open architecture. It allows people to build their own interface slot cards and plug them into a slot in a real computer! I was so fortunate to have the opportunity to experiment and design and tryout my ideas that significantly increased my knowledge and my understanding of digital hardware and software design. There is no better classroom than an engineer's laboratory, which happened to be my garage. Others may have a basement or a spare room for their laboratory. The point is, book knowledge is essential for understanding theory, but the real learning happens when you apply that theory and build something that is your own design, be it something intellectual or something tangible or something meaningful.

At least that is the case for me especially when I recall that the original Apple I was first designed and built in a garage.

I have yet to explore integrating my love for the Apple][hardware and software and my love for model railroading, specifically S-gauge used by the American Flyer model trains. I have boxes and boxes of those trains and many accessories stored in my garage. Perhaps it is time I introduce Mr. American Flyer to Mr. Apple. The relationship could be rather exciting if not downright explosive. Oh, not in the sense of Addams Family explosive, but in the sense of opening up a whole new world of awesome challenges, struggles, creativity, and a whole lot of downright fun.

Today's generation of young engineers have the opportunity to explore computer-assisted or computer-associated projects particularly with the affordable Raspberry Pi computer. The Raspberry Pi is the size of a credit card having four USB ports, an Ethernet port, HDMI, raw video, and stereo sound outputs, and it only requires an input of five volts at 2.4 amps for full operation and control. The Pi computer uses a micro Secure Digital (SD) memory card that hosts its UNIX-like operating system and its C language compiler and linker. It provides around twenty-six General Purpose Input/Output (i.e. GPIO) pin connections, or ports to the outside world. The GPIOs are software configurable to be an input or an output port that accept or provide a 3.3-volt digital signal, respectively. That is totally genius.

I designed my Sunrise/Sunset computer assisted controller around the Raspberry Pi to control all my outside decorative lightening. My control software considers my location on planet Earth in terms of longitude, latitude, and azimuth in order to calculate precisely when sunrise and sunset occurs each day of the year. The software refers to an input configuration file having selectable offsets in order to adjust program timing so that my decorative lights turn ON thirty minutes after sunset and turn OFF forty-five minutes before sunrise. One GPIO pin is used as a 3.3-volt output port to illuminate the LED of a TRIAC controller. When the TRIAC is turned ON, 120 volts of Alternating Current (AC) is gated to a medium-duty 120 volt AC electromagnetic relay. This relay can control an AC load up to fifteen amps at 240 volts AC. The AC transformer that provides the twelve volts AC to my decorative lights draws no more than eight amps at 120 volts AC through the relay. As the days become longer and the nights shorter my decorative lights turn ON and OFF according to sunset and sunrise, respectively. And, as the days become shorter and the nights longer my decorative lights are appropriately turned ON and OFF.

There is absolutely no need to make any further adjustments to this decorative light controller throughout the year. The Raspberry Pi computer assisted controller is totally maintenance free because it receives its time-of-day from the Internet by means of a USB wireless adapter that communicates with my wireless Internet Router. There must be an interesting project or two that could tie Mr. Apple to Mr. Raspberry Pi. I already use a Keyspan serial to USB adapter with my Apple //e and my Apple MacBook Pro. And I already have the programming tools on the Raspberry Pi to write even more C language programs. The best part is that the Raspberry Pi only costs around $45.00: massive programming power and agility for just pennies in investment cost. The only thing remaining is knowledge.

Would I trade those early years learning how to program on an Apple][for present day years to learn how to program on the Raspberry Pi or other similar computer? I am very fond of all those past memories, and software and hardware in those years did not change very often. It is surprising how many years DOS 3.3 survived. Today, it seems like my iPad or my iPhone receives a new iOS update every other month or so. Software development occurs at a frenzied pace now, and considerations for size of application and available memory are totally unimportant. Of course, I could not last even ten minutes in today's aerospace industry because I do not have the experience of the tools today's young engineers have access to nor do I have their current intellectual growth processes as a foundation. My intellectual foundation was the slide rule where the knowledge of concepts was tested rather than reaching a particular numerical result. So I am satisfied with my memories and the fascinating experiences I had, and the interesting characters I met along the way. It is comforting to know that through my travels in time I may have touched someone else's curiosity.

Curiosity in and of itself is the driving force for all intellectual achievements. Without curiosity nothing would have been created. There would simply be no interest in building today's world without curiosity. Furthermore, curiosity paired with mankind's fundamental and inbred laziness would never have prompt the design and development of the Industrial Revolution. The Industrial Revolution was sparked by the great mathematician, physicist, astronomer, theologian, and author Isaac Newton. It was Isaac Newton's *Philosophiae Naturalis Principia Mathematica* that directly paved the way to our modern world. Laziness, the fundamental human character is what drives mankind to create a world of comfort, pleasure, and safety. Laziness is the star ingredient in the First Postulate that formulates the Theory of Volitional Science.

It was pure laziness that prompt me to create the theoretical design equations for a multiple input operational amplifier summer while I was an Electrical Engineering student. My paper detailing the process in how I arrived at these theoretical design equations was published by IEEE and why my Electrical Engineering professors submitted me for the Alton B. Zerby Outstanding Student Award. Furthermore, it was curiosity that continuously drove all my electrical engineering pursuits. Here is the full story of how laziness, paired with my curiosity, drove me to write my paper on the design of multiple-input operational amplifier summers.

Back in 1981 I registered for Professor Gene H. Hostetter's course in Operational Amplifiers (op amps), which was about seven years before his untimely death in 1988. Dr. Hostetter, still a young man, presented the course materials in syllabus format because this syllabus would eventually become the basis of an electrical engineering textbook. He believed that for learning to be successful it was necessary and important to apply the new theory and concepts he presented in lecture format to real-life design problems. Dr. Hostetter created a huge array of design problems that were generic to the design of multiple input op amp summers. He also wanted his students to filter out those problems that best helped his students to learn the course material: those particular design problems would be included in his forthcoming textbook. I recall Dr. Hostetter assigning fifty design problems on a beautiful Friday afternoon and expecting their solutions by Monday afternoon. The assignment was given in two parts: solve all fifty problems using the techniques he had discussed in class and then solve all fifty problems again to remove all Direct Current (DC) voltage imbalances at the op amp's input connections. A total of one hundred homework problems due Monday would surely prevent any other weekend plans, and I did have plans to party that weekend.

I solved the first two design problems Friday evening. They each took about thirty minutes to complete before and after considering all DC voltage imbalances. I could not believe this weekend was going to spent doing this homework, and only this homework. Being incredibly lazy by nature drove my initial curiosity to apply Kirchhoff's Voltage Law for a closed loop circuit and Ohm's Law for parallel resistance to what Dr. Hostetter presented in class for general op amp theory. It seemed as though the more I manipulated those op amp equations with those fundamental laws, the more I started to see interesting and new relationships develop between the variables on the positive side of the op amp and the variables on the negative side of the op amp along with some feedback from the op amp output. By the end of the evening I had developed a set of equations that I called the "front door equations" and a set of equations that I called the "back door equations." Incredible as it seems these two sets of equations actually reduced to a shared commonality. I now had a tremendously powerful set of theoretical design equations that could be used to solve any multiple input op amp summer design problem. By Saturday afternoon I had solved all one hundred of Dr. Hostetter's homework problems mostly by inspection! That is, little if any calculations were actually required. I spent the rest of the weekend at a well-deserved party totally enjoying myself, to be sure.

Early Monday morning I met with Dr. Hostetter and presented the process I used to develop my op amp design equations. Understand, he had been teaching this subject for nearly twenty years. He was amazed, flabbergasted, excited, and could not wait for class that afternoon. I declined his offer to present my design equations to my classmates because Dr. Hostetter used a brilliant lecture technique that made any topic he discussed easy to follow and easy to understand. In summary all my classmates scored perfectly on their final exam. A year or two later my professor Clement J. Savant Jr. asked if he could publish my design equations in his forthcoming textbook *Electronic Circuit Design An Engineering Approach*. I gave him a resounding YES!

Whatever your particular talents might be or your personal aspirations, your innate curiosity of perhaps building a star ship or growing a garden of flowers will always be realized when you utilize the power of your inbred laziness. It is this wonderful human characteristic from which we all benefit and for which we all strive. Use your curiosity to unlock your full potential and let your desire for more leisure, more down-time, and more pleasure reward you with a better understanding of Mother Nature. She is the ultimate judge on what is good, what works, and what will survive!

VI. Autobiographical Information

Grandfather Vrbančić was born in Trg, Croatia, once a province of Yugoslavia, and he was named Vid. Vid decided to immigrate to the United States around 1907, and he joined his older brother in Rankin, Pennsylvania. There, he and Marko worked in the coal mines. This work did not appeal to him, so he moved to Cleveland, Ohio, to work in the steel mill industry. Vid did not have a profession and he had no desire to learn a trade, so he became one of the many immigrant laborers living in the Cleveland area. There were many other Croatian and Slovenian immigrant laborers living in the same suburbs, and they tended to retain their European style of living and speak their native languages. Vid had lived in America for nearly ten years when he met Veronika Sneperger. Veronika had not been in America as long as Vid, but she became far more fluent in English than he. She was also fluent in six other languages. Vid and Veronika were married on June 25, 1917, in Saint Paul's Church and moved into a lovely, but small apartment on the east side.

Veronika's mother Tvka (Eva) Stefančić had already died in 1910 and the steel mill industry was no longer manufacturing wartime supplies by the 1920's. Vid was finally laid off in 1921 and he could not find any other work in the Cleveland area. He did not want to move his wife, daughter Josephine, and son Andrew to Rankin where his younger brother Franjo was now living and working as a policeman. Veronika's father Jure, a widower for over ten years now, wrote many letters to Vid and Veronika and pleaded with them to return to Croatia. He even promised to give them his home in Maklen and all his farm land if they would agree to care for him in his old age. Vid finally relented and he and his family set sail back to Croatia. Unfortunately, Jure had blatantly lied to both Vid and Veronika as he never intended to give them his home or any of his farm land. He also did not want Vid working his farm land using the methods Vid had learned when he was growing up in Trg. Regardless of their near hopelessness, Mathew was born in February, 1922, in Maklen.

By 1923 the steel mill industry in Cleveland had converted back to manufacturing household and industrial supplies, and they sent pleas to European countries for mill workers. The industry even offered to pay the man's passage and assist him in finding an apartment. Even though Josephine and Andrew were American citizens, Veronika and Mathew were not. When Vid inquired about bringing his family to America, he was told he would need to become an American citizen, have $2000 in a savings account, provide an adequate place for his family to live, and have the required fare for their passage from Maklen to Cleveland. So, if Vid took the job offer, he would have to leave his family behind. After much soul searching and in view of being duped and lied to by Jure, Vid did accept the job offer to return to Cleveland. But, to make financial matters even worse, Vid left Croatia six months before the birth of his fourth child in February, 1924. Grandmother named him Valentin because Father was born on Saint Valentine's Day.

Jure's property would have rightfully gone to his son George (Jure in Croatian) before it would go to Veronika if Jure should die. But George had left for America in 1899 and was never heard from again. Jure never trusted banks or a hiding place at home for his money, so he carried all of his cash with him and made this fact known to all. In 1925 his cousin shot him through the heart and decapitated him while he was taking a shortcut through the woods. To this day there is tree with a four foot cross carved into its bark marking the crime spot. It is believed that teenage boys in the neighborhood keep that cross scrapped clean of bark and retell the killing of Jure. No one was officially charged with the crime, but Jure's cousin admitted to the crime on his deathbed. Even though Veronika inherited her father's home in Maklen and all his farm lands, life was still very hard for Grandmother raising and feeding her four growing children without her husband there.

Josephine and Andrew both attended a one-room school in Brod Moravice; Mathew and Valentin were still too young to attend school. They explored the surrounding villages and farms, but were afraid to venture into the woods where their grandfather had been murdered. They did explore several of the caves in the area only when an older boy accompanied them. Grandmother's farm had many fruit trees they could climb and would feast on the fruit. Vid wrote to his family often and told them he was progressing well with all the requirements needed to bring everyone to Cleveland. He sent Veronika sufficient funds for her to obtain passport photos, visas, clothes, and luggage necessary for the long journey to America. Many government officials had to stamp their passport papers. These included officials in Brod Moravice, officials in the municipality of Delnice, officials in the district of Rijeka, officials in the city of Zagreb (the capital of Croatia), and finally officials in the city of Belgrade (the capital of Yugoslavia). In each case there were fees to be paid to the official for each paper and visa they stamped, and for every outstretched hand (otherwise the papers and visas would be confiscated). In 1930 Veronika and her four children left Maklen, Croatia, forever and boarded the USS Paris in Le Havre, France, for their voyage to the United States of America.

Father says he remembers when the Statue of Liberty first became visible because all the passengers crowded to that side of the ship to get a good look at the Lady who promised so much to newly arriving immigrants. When he gazed upon the statue, he was puzzled why everyone seemed so excited at the sight, but he was only six years old. The ship docked at Ellis Island and everyone had to file through the various designated checkpoints. Father remembers having his hair and body examined, and he was given a mental aptitude test which he thought was some sort of game. Once everyone was examined and tested, Veronika gathered up her children and luggage and boarded a train to Cleveland. When they arrived in Cleveland, Father met his father Vid for the first time. I can only imagine what that stern-faced man had to say, if anything, to his youngest son? Everyone was ushered up to a second floor apartment that had three bedrooms. No one seems to remember when Father's name was changed from Valentin to Walland. Since Father did not speak English, it is believed that a teacher at East Madison Grade School misunderstood the name Valentin when Father pronounced it for her, and she changed it to Walland. Father has been called Wally ever since.

I was named after Father so I was given the Junior suffix. Over the years the name Walland coupled with the last name Vrbančić has given many of my teachers and counselors tremendous pause in how to address me and how to pronounce my name. The diacritic marks over the two "c's" of my last name provided even more confusion except to another Eastern European raised speaking any of the Serbo-Croatian dialects. I have always been called Philip to differentiate me from Father. That part of my journey through life has always been very interesting to me. The fact that I was born with a moderately severe speech impediment, a stutter, has not been so interesting, and only those who also have a stutter know why.

We lived in California and I still have very vivid memories when I was very young, lying on a throw rug in our living room listening to Mother practice her violin. She produced the most wonderful music to my ears and it was then that I became very much attracted to that instrument. Mr. Joe Burger came to my fourth grade classroom looking for potential music students. When he played *The Flight of the Bumblebee* by Nikolai Rimsky-Korsakov, I was forever charmed. I immediately requested a permission slip for my parents to sign so that I could study the violin under Mr. Burger. Mother rented a student-sized violin to see how well I would progress before considering buying a decent instrument. She must have been very happy with my progress because she convinced Father to invest in a "very nice" instrument. Mother took me to meet Mr. Lewis Main in central Long Beach to select my violin. Mr. Main took me alone into his studio at the back of his home where I saw hundreds of instruments, some still wet with varnish, hanging from wires stretched high across the room. He wanted to talk to me privately in order to evaluate what sort of personality I had. He said he could match the violin to the student, much like in the Harry Potter book where Mr. Ollivander matched the wand to the student wizard. I had to wait some months before Mother received a call from Mr. Main. She was so excited and told me Mr. Main had found my violin. Apparently, many appraisers traveled about England to attend estate sales, and the appraiser who worked with Mr. Main only purchased instruments at those particular sort of sales. My violin, a *Gemünder Art* Violin (A266), was handcrafted in 1930 by Oscar A. Gemünder of August Gemünder & Sons, New York, New York. It was purchased new, originally for a young English girl who was beginning her studies on the violin. So, this instrument has traveled across the Atlantic Ocean twice before I became its second owner. Not only did Mr. Main match the instrument to me perfectly, he matched an 1801 French violin to my younger sister a year later. Many years passed when I discovered that the American violinist Camilla Wicks was a close friend to the Main family, and when she and Mr. Main's son were teenagers, they would spar endlessly to see who was the better violinist! When my parents purchased my violin, Mr. Main's son was already a professional violinist and he performed primarily in Las Vegas, Nevada. Camilla Wicks performed as an international soloist. As for my study of the instrument after Mr. Burger, my private violin teachers included Carol Higley (Lakewood, California) in elementary and junior high school, Professor Frank Bellino (Denison University, Granville, Ohio) in high school, Professor Stanley Plummer (University of California, Los Angeles, California) while at University, and Mr. Allan Carter (Long Beach, California) when I wanted to study and perform chamber music in my mid-forties. Plummer and Carter were both students of Vera Barstow (Pasadena, California), though perhaps nearly a generation apart.

I always excelled in mathematics and science classes during high school, so I decided to study Zoology at UCLA as an undergraduate in the mid-sixties after I was graduated from high school. At that time Mother, a registered nurse, was managing the department of surgery at a local hospital and her vision was to send me to medical school after graduation from University. Father, on the other hand, thought my talents were more inclined towards engineering. He was a graduate of the University of Southern California, school of Industrial Engineering, and was a licensed Professional Engineer. My dream or illusion was to become a concert violinist, or at least a professional orchestral musician. Honestly, I was too immature when I attended UCLA, let alone live on campus at Sproul Hall. I was not passionate enough about any of my studies and, unfortunately, I did not have sufficient time nor talent to adequately prepare my lessons for Professor Plummer. It was a dynamic, historical time to attend University during the mid-sixties. The political arena was in an uproar with President Reagan in office. The war in Vietnam was still being waged. Communists like Angela Davis (a student of Herbert Marcuse) were teaching and giving lectures down the hall from my required Political Science (clearly, an oxymoron) class. In hindsight, I should have stepped back, attended a community college for a year or two, so I could mature a bit more emotionally.

One particularly horrifying experience I had at UCLA was when I walked into my second quarter German class and saw the instructor's name written on the blackboard: Frau Milovanović. She pronounced my name perfectly and clearly, rolling the "r" in my last name majestically, when she took attendance, and she asked me to stay after class. I knew she was Serbian, or, at least her husband was Serbian, but that did not matter to me. When the other students left the classroom and were out of earshot, she told me I was a "dirty, filthy Croatian" and she wanted to know if I was going to give her any "trouble" (she used other colorful language as well). Literally shaking in my boots, I told her I was born an American and I did not have any resentment towards any ethnic group of people. I worked my tail off in that class and managed to squeak by with a "C" grade. She found fault in most everything I wrote. After the final exam I thanked her for all the "special" attention she gave me! At least I did not have a "melt down" entirely, but finished my studies, and was graduated with a Bachelor's of Science degree in Zoology.

Father suggested I enroll in a two-year program through USC Medical Center for training as an Orthopedic Physician Assistant. I thoroughly enjoyed every aspect of that program, I completed all the requirements, and I earned my certificate to work as an OPA. I was quickly hired by a local hospital where I worked for over nine years. By the mid-seventies I had already worked as an OPA for about four years when I experienced some sort of intellectual "awakening" and decided Father was right after all: I should have studied engineering, particularly Electrical Engineering. My epiphany to return to another tour of undergraduate studies was perhaps precipitated by the lectures I was attending at that time. The lectures were given by the renowned Astrophysicist Andrew J. Galambos, PhD. Professor Galambos was now an entrepreneur giving lectures on Volitional Science. I had already enrolled in his V-201 course which continued for over a year, one three-hour lecture once a week with a few weekend sessions as well. Previous to the V-201 course, I had enrolled in Professor Galambos's V-50 course which was now being presented by J. S. Snelson. It would not be possible for me to summarize here the knowledge I gained from the V-50 and the V-201 courses, and from several other lectures I attended to celebrate unique and historical events.

Before I enrolled in the OPA program at USC Medical Center, I did work as a phlebotomist in a doctor's office for nearly two years. Both doctors treated obese patients using diet and an array of medications they prescribed and provided onsite. In the early 1970's it was common practice to prescribe either dextroamphetamine sulfate or levoamphetamine sulfate, or any of the combinations of these drugs with other ingredients to help promote weight loss. More importantly, I had a lot of spare time during working hours, and my manager allowed me to read. In fact, she encouraged me to read the works of Ayn Rand. I even attended a few meetings where I was introduced to laissez-faire capitalism. Years later I suppose that when I heard Snelson's presentation of V-50 I was entirely comfortable with the subject of capitalism, and I was amazed at how far the concepts of Galambos had surpassed those of Rand. After attending the V-201 course, it was very difficult for me to manage the "blab forth syndrome", and I was guilty of trying to explain some of the concepts from V-201 to my colleagues for many, many years. Once again, it is something that is difficult to explain in short order.

It was completely normal for me to take apart, dismantle, and study the innards of every toy, train, erector set, chemistry set, or electrical set Santa brought me when I was young, and reconstruct that toy to working order, without inflicting any significant internal damage. Countless times Father would see a radio or tape recorder completely disassembled on the floor of my room and ask me, laughingly, "How long until it works again?" This sense of curiosity even when I was very young should have given me a clue as to what I should have initially studied at University. I have felt some degree of regret that it took me nearly ten years after high school to realize my mistake. Electrical Engineering became my absolute passion: I worked full time on second shift at the hospital and during the morning hours I attended at least three lecture classes and one laboratory class each semester for the next five years. IEEE published my original paper that detailed the theoretical design equations for multiple input operational amplifier summers, and my professors submitted me for the Alton B. Zerby Outstanding Student Award. I won first place in the Region Six IEEE Student Paper contest and placed third nationally that same year during WESCON in 1982. My operational amplifier design equations were also published in a textbook written by one of my professors on that subject. All of these accomplishments coupled with a 4.0 GPA gave me many choices for my next employer. Father worked for Rockwell International, though it was originally known as North American Aviation. I did interview at TRW and I received a very lucrative job offer, but I decided to join the team at Rockwell, in the Space Shuttle Simulation Laboratory. I was hired about five months before the launch of STS-1, thus changing my hospital scrubs for a coat and tie, and a whole lot more money!

About three months after Rockwell hired me, the Simulation Laboratory manager hired a Computer Science Engineer to join the ranks of Initialization Engineers. He and I had the daunting task of learning how to initialize the computers and electronics that comprised the total simulation of a Space Shuttle trajectory from Main Engine Cutoff (MECO) to landing at a few selected sites within the United States. The computers that were initialized with flight and target parameters included a PDP-11 and two Xerox mainframes. The mainframes were initially programmed using front-panel rocker switches: the Sigma 5 had 16 KB of magnetic core memory and the Sigma 9 had 64 KB of magnetic core memory. We used Hollerith cards to insert faults into the General Purpose Computers (GPCs) like those aboard the shuttle. We used a color Eidophor projector to project visual images of our landing site runways into a shuttle cockpit simulator in which the astronauts trained. Finally, we used Nova computers by DEC and DEC word processing software to generate all required customer documentation and, I might add, to play Adventure.

My system initialization colleague was an early Apple][owner when Integer Basic was first available in ROM. The following year Rockwell offered a home computer purchase program and provided us the choice between an IBM PC or the Apple][+ which had the autostart ROM. My colleague strongly encouraged me to request the Apple computer, and he assisted me in selecting the monitor, the disk drive, and the printer accessories. The total cost was a lot of money for me, but Rockwell loaned me the money and paid the total cost. I repaid the interest-free loan through weekly payroll deductions making the purchase relatively painless. Thus, my dream of having my own personal computer began. My ever-constant V-50 and V-201 "blab forth syndrome" did interest another colleague of mine who actually enrolled in the V-50T (i.e. "T" for Tape) course. Later, he enrolled in the V-201 and many other "V" courses after completing V-50T. In fact, he became the personal assistant to Professor Galambos during the last and final trip Galambos made to Budapest, Hungary, his native country. Mrs. Galambos stayed behind to manage the curriculum of their Free Enterprise Institute (FEI). Professor Galambos recognized that he was beginning to display the symptoms of Alzheimer's disease and he entrusted my colleague with handling more and more of the private living affairs for both he and his wife. Andrew J. Galambos and Suzanne J. Galambos established their Natural Estates Trust that was to manage all of their Intellectual Property. From my vantage point it appeared to me that my colleague participated in and contributed to what I considered to be dishonorable activities not in the favorable interests of this Natural Estates Trust. My colleague's activities primarily involved the convoluted publishing of *Sic Itur Ad Astra* by Andrew J. Galambos after the death of Galambos on April 10, 1997.

I became fascinated with all aspects of the Apple][+ computer, and I wanted to incorporate it into my studies for my Master's degree. My assigned advisor was analyzing tomographic reconstructions of the human spinal column, and he thought perhaps I could assist him. He wanted to be able to make measurements between any two points within the computer image of a spinal column, even after rotating or enlarging the image. I was tasked with developing the Fortran programs that could be launched on a Microsoft Z80 peripheral slot card in an Apple][+ that would provide him with these capabilities. I found an ingenious way to reduce the size of the three-dimensional rotational matrix in order to accelerate data image processing and the remapping of the resulting HIRES image to the computer screen. My professor was very pleased with my progress. However, I was becoming increasingly interested in high-speed graphics animation, and the only way I thought I could learn that technology was to work for Ken Williams at Sierra On-Line. I terminated my work on my Master's degree, I gave notice to Rockwell, I packed my bags, and I moved to Oakhurst, California.

At Sierra On-Line I was tasked to assist a colleague in migrating ScreenWriter to the Apple //e which was recently available for purchase. On another project I wrote all the I/O routines and ICON drawing routines for HomeWord Speller. When I started working as a self-employed contractor, I was given the *Goofy's Word Factory* project which was a children's computer game to teach English grammar. Williams had a license to display certain Disney characters on a bit-mapped computer screen per approval by Disney for visual likeness, color, and movement. I would have finished *Goofy's Word Factory* if John (Williams's brother), the assigned designer of the game, could have developed the third game feature (and strategy) in a timely fashion. He apparently could not do so before I secured a position at Hughes Aircraft Company back in Los Angeles. I did utilize Williams's high-speed graphics animation algorithms in *Goofy's Word Factory*, which I had to redesign in order to include collision detection on a dithered background. No other computer game could detect collisions on a dithered background at that time. Williams was impressed, and it was really hard to impress Williams. I stayed all of 18 months at Sierra.

The major observation I made when I was hired by Hughes Aircraft was how different their culture was to the culture I had experienced at Rockwell. At Rockwell I found it exceedingly difficult to have anyone who had written a software tool or program explain to me how that tool or that program worked, and the algorithms the software utilized or exploited. When I was tasked to migrate a software tool from Fortran to C language at Rockwell, I found some incorrect logic that eventually affected the final output data. Given certain input parameters, this tool could calculate a three-dimensional corridor in space and either interpolate points within or extrapolate points outside of that corridor. I presented my findings to its original author showing how I could insert the same incorrect logic into the C code and generate the same wrong output data. He told me to keep the incorrect logic and not disclose my findings to management. I refused. This was totally unthinkable to me, and this would have never happened at Hughes. In fact, CIP awards were given to engineers who found such errors in software and who reported those errors to management. The Hughes culture encouraged the aggressive sharing of knowledge, and it gave rewards to those who made improvements. The Rockwell culture cultivated self-preservation tactics where knowledge was thought to be job security and not to be shared, but to be kept undisclosed. Hughes certainly provided me with a great opportunity in the Digital Simulation Laboratory where I learned about real time executive software that was hosted on Gould SEL mainframe computers (2750, 6750, 8780, and 9780). I also learned about MIL-STD-1553 protocol communication software and real time software interface drivers to a host of various external data processors. Our purpose was to create a digital time frame in order to simulate in real time the environment for a tactical Radar Digital Processor (RDP) flying above the surface of the earth.

Due to the general slowdown in the engineering industry, I returned to Rockwell in 1990. I believed that my knowledge in real time executive software hosted on SEL mainframe computers would be my passport to a nice software engineering career closer to where I wanted to live. How I regret that major blunder in judgment because my employment at Rockwell was terminated just a few years later. I had co-authored a *White Paper* outlining the risks associated with using off-the-shelf RISC processors in certain applications, and the response from my colleagues was very unfavorable. This and my disclosure of software errors I uncovered during a Fortran-to-C language conversion eventually led to my dismissal. Fortunately, my former Hughes management was able to reinstate my position, and I was tasked to gain expertise in real time data collection software for tactical radar systems.

Hughes tactical radar systems are programmed to operate in many different modes depending upon various situations and the immediate needs that are faced by the pilot of a military aircraft. During the

312

development of a radar mode, its processing is heavily instrumented which generates a large amount of output data as the mode progresses through its various processing stages. It is critical to capture all this generated data, primary and incidental in nature, in order to ensure and verify that the mode is behaving as expected and is generating its data according to pre-established boundaries, much like comparing the data to some gold standard. My task was to capture all the In-phase and Quadrature (I/Q) components of radar data in real time, process certain other data components, package the data according to generated source and timestamp, and save the resulting files to some recording device. It is important to understand that there are many independent generating sources of data in a radar system whose timestamps are totally asynchronous. At a later time the data that is packaged in those files would be analyzed to determine if, in fact, the processing modes operated as expected. Physically collecting this I/Q data during real time tactical maneuvers was quite a challenge, and recorders designed to operate in this environment were costly. Preparing for a data collection session involved securing a military aircraft, a flight crew, a ground crew, and people to securely bring the recorded data back to my tempested lab. This certainly added to my responsibilities, and my mantra was to neither add, subtract, nor modify any data word or data bit while that data was in my immediate possession and while my software algorithms extracted and processed that data into prescribed data formats. Those data formats would allow the data analysis tools to function more efficiently for the mode builders.

I was thoroughly vetted and held maximum-security clearances that allowed me to process data from many different and independent classified programs not only in Los Angeles, but also in other locations, and even out of state. The general data collection software engines I began designing in the unclassified world served as my software library for every classified program to which I was assigned. Perhaps I was simply in the right place at the right time that steered my career to become the sole resident expert in Transcription Software Engines. That is, to process, encrypt, and store in real time at least a terabyte of data every second. Or, perhaps I was in the right place at the right time that allowed me to develop a task beyond its envisioned potential. There is a direct ancestral linkage between my unclassified software library of tools, routines, and transcription engines and every single classified program with which I was associated that required my tools, routines, engines, and expertise. I was practicing *code reuse* light-years before it became a topic that some managers thought could reduce software development costs. "How insightful!" I jokingly thought of management, silently and very highly disrespectfully in my private thoughts.

Initially, I was given the opportunity to host my current Transcription Software engine on a newly acquired SGI Origin 300 having four bricks, or 16 CPUs. *Code reuse* made this task fairly straightforward, thus demonstrating the Origin's practicality for this feasibility study. After a fact-finding tour to the SGI facilities at Mountain View, California, I was given the momentous task of designing a Transcription Software engine for an SGI Origin 3000 having eight bricks (i.e. 32 CPUs) running IRIX, and using Big Endian memory management. This turned out to be one of my greatest solo achievements. Even at this time, little did my management understand how effortlessly I could build my Transcription Software engines primarily using *code reuse*. I was extremely fortunate to have had one very intelligent manager who casually asked me to think about the possibility of building a digital playback system. Such a system did not yet exist. Some had tried building an analog playback system a few years earlier with absolutely no success. Instead of analyzing the collected instrumented data, one could observe how the simulated RDP behaved when the recorded high-speed I/Q data and the slow-speed environment data was injected back into its system with a playback system. A few months later I presented my first digital playback recorder and pre-processing system, my last and greatest achievement at Raytheon (former Hughes). I was given the unique privilege to design and build a second digital playback recorder and pre-processing system for another classified program. That program, like the previous program which used my first digital playback recorder and pre-processing system, saved countless hours of analysis time and mission costs before I scheduled my overdue retirement.

A few years after I retired, I was presented with an astonishing diagnosis by my partner that seemed to explain some, if not all of the idiosyncrasies I have displayed my entire life as far back as elementary school: I may have been living with Asperger's. Indeed, how does one know what is truly normal; that which falls under the umbrella of a Gaussian curve? We are all volitional beings and our behavior is internal to each of us. Our brain is composed of carbon-based synapses whose billions of inter-connections and cross-connections compose the very person and personality we have become or have allowed ourselves to become. It is simply miraculous that any of our species reach total fulfillment of their dreams. I would like to believe I have come closer than most in reaching many of my dreams and aspirations.

Now I have the time and the continuing curiosity to delve into the Disk Operating System, that is, the File Management System of the Apple][computer. I now have the opportunity to create my own version of a File Management System that contains the power and the flexibility I always believed an Apple][Disk Operating System ought to and could have.

I called my previous version of Apple][DOS, DOS 4.1. And DOS 4.1 was complete with its 46th build in 2019. What a ride I have been on! Why? To see what I could do for this wonderful machine and its magnificent architecture!

I completed DOS 4.1 around March, 2019, after I agreed to have the Build 45 Manual published by Call-A.P.P.L.E. I requested no fees, no incentives, nor any royalties. But I continued to innovate DOS 4.1 and Build 46 contains the final modifications I wanted to make to this DOS. I felt that I could not take DOS 4.1 any further due to the memory constraints of DOS 4.1L, and I did not want to increase its size nor add additional sectors to its volume image. However, I could continue to develop Apple][DOS if I concentrated only on the Language Card version. I naïvely thought perhaps I could utilize Auxiliary Memory and move DOS there. To that end, I copied my source code for DOS 4.1H into a new directory and gave it a new name. That moment was the birth of DOS 4.3. I continued to develop DOS 4.3 for the remainder of 2019 and into the beginning of 2020. As in the development of DOS 4.1, I have reached a point where I do not want to continue any further development of DOS 4.3. And it is now time to complete the ongoing documentation for DOS 4.3 as well. The End (for now?).

After all that I have seen and done during my life and in my travels through time, I am always comforted when I recall the following expressive thought:

The diversity in the human family should be the cause of love and harmony,
as it is in music where many different notes blend together
in the making of a perfect chord.
~~~ Abdu'l-Bahá ~~~